Sustainable Development Policy

Sustainable Development Policy: A European Perspective uses a variety of multidiscipli-nary perspectives to explore the ways in which sustainable infrastructures can play a more prominent and effective role in international development policy. Building on a solid introduction to sustainability and development policy, this book discusses ways in which viable reform can be promoted through coherent governing, the design of social security systems, education systems and the possibilities of fair trade as an alternative trading concept. *Sustainable Development Policy* generates a platform on which to encourage constructive dialogue on issues surrounding sustainability in the wake of the global scarcity of natural and economic resources.

This edited collection will be of great interest to all students and lecturers of development studies and development policy, as well as researchers from other disciplines looking for an introduction to sustainable development policy and its practical applications.

Michael von Hauff is a Professor of Economics at the University of Kaiserslautern, Germany.

Claudia Kuhnke is a Research Fellow at the University of Kaiserlautern, Germany.

Routledge Studies in Sustainable Development

This series uniquely brings together original and cutting-edge research on sustainable development. The books in this series tackle difficult and important issues in sustainable development including: values and ethics; sustainability in higher education; climate compatible development; resilience; capitalism and de-growth; sustainable urban development; gender and participation; and well-being.

Drawing on a wide range of disciplines, the series promotes interdisciplinary research for an international readership. The series was recommended in the *Guardian*'s suggested reads on development and the environment.

Sustainable Development Policy

A European Perspective

Edited by Michael von Hauff and Claudia Kuhnke

Routledge
Taylor & Francis Group

LONDON AND NEW YORK

earthscan
from Routledge

First published 2017
by Routledge
2 Park Square, Milton Park, Abingdon, Oxon OX14 4RN

605 Third Avenue, New York, NY 10017

Routledge is an imprint of the Taylor & Francis Group, an informa business

British Library Cataloguing-in-Publication Data
A catalogue record for this book is available from the British Library

Library of Congress Cataloging-in-Publication Data
Names: Hauff, Michael von, editor. | Kuhnke, Claudia, editor.
Title: Sustainable development policy : a European perspective / edited by
Michael Von Hauff, Claudia Kuhnke.
Description: Abingdon, Oxon ; New York, NY : Routledge, 2017. |
Series: Routledge studies in sustainble development
Identifiers: LCCN 2016042620| ISBN 978-1-138-28499-9 (hbk) |
ISBN 978-1-138-40043-6 (ebk)
Subjects: LCSH: Sustainable development. | Sustainable development—
International cooperation. | Sustainable development—Government policy.
Classification: LCC HC79.E5 S8669668 2017 | DDC 338.9/27—dc23LC
record available at https://lccn.loc.gov/2016042620

ISBN: 978-1-138-28499-9 (hbk)
ISBN: 978-1-138-40043-6 (ebk)

Typeset in Bembo
by FiSH Books Ltd, Enfield

Contents

Notes on contributors

Prof. Dr. Beate Bergé: Vice-President for Teaching & Quality Management at Constance University of Applied Sciences (HTWG) (Germany).

Dipl.-Ing. Matthias Beyer: Managing Director, mascontour GmbH, Berlin (Germany).

Prof. Raimund Bleischwitz: BHP Billiton Chair of Sustainable Global Resources at University College London, Institute for Sustainable Resources (London), UK.

Heike Dickhut (Graduate biologist, M.A. Sustainable Tourism): Coordinator and research associate at the Centre for Sustainable Tourism (ZENAT), Eberswalde University for Sustainable Development (Germany).

Prof. Dr. Daniel Fischer: Junior Professor for Sustainability Science (Focus on Sustainable Consumption & Sustainability Communication) at Leuphana University of Lüneburg (Germany).

Dr. rer. pol. Klaus Fischer: Deputy Director at Institute for Technology and Work (ITA), Kaiserslautern (Germany).

Florian Flachenecker: Doctoral Researcher at University College London, Institute for Sustainable Resources (London), UK.

Prof. Dr. Oliver Hensel: Head of Department of Agricultural and Biosystems Engineering, University of Kassel (Germany).

Lukas Hermwille (Diploma in Regional Studies of Latin America): Research Fellow for Energy, Transport and Climate Policy at the Wuppertal Institute for Climate, Environment, and Energy (Germany).

Christine Hobelsberger, M.A. International Management: Researcher at the Institute for Ecological Economy Research, Berlin (Germany).

Apl. Prof. Dr. Brigitte A. Kaufmann: Social Ecology of Tropical and Subtropical Land Use Systems at the Faculty of Agricultural Sciences, University of Hohenheim and Director of Research at DITSL (Germany).

Diana Körner: Consultant at mascontour GmbH, Berlin (Germany).

Prof. Dr. Frauke Kraas: Chair of Human Geography, Institute of Geography at the University of Cologne (Germany).

Dr. rer. nat. Mareike Kroll: Research Associate (Postdoc) at Institute of Geography, University of Cologne (Germany).

Claudia Kuhnke (Diploma in Economy): Research Associate at Department of Economic Policy and International Economic Relations at University of Kaiserslautern (Germany).

Associate Professor Dr. Wolfgang Meyer: Deputy Director of Center for Evaluation (CEval), Head of Working Group for Environment and Labor Market, Saarbrücken (Germany).

Prof. Dr. Gerd Michelsen: Senior Professor for Sustainability Science and UNESCO Chair for Sustainable Development in Higher Education at Leuphana University of Lüneburg (Germany).

Prof. em. Dr. F. Nuscheler: Senior Fellow of Johannes Kepler University, Linz (Austria) and Senior Fellow of the Institute of Peace and Development (INEF), University Duisburg-Essen (Germany).

Dr. Imme Scholz: Deputy Director, German Institute for Development Policy/ Deutsches Institut für Entwicklungspolitik (DIE).

Prof. Dr. Reinhard Stockmann: Chair of Sociology at Saarland University and Director of Ceval Saarbrücken (Germany).

Prof. Dr. Wolfgang Strasdas: Director of the Centre for Sustainable Tourism (ZENAT), Eberswalde University for Sustainable Development (Germany).

Dr. rer. pol. Bülent Tarkan: Chancellor, Offenburg University of Applied Sciences (Germany).

Dr. Stefan Thomas: Director of the Research Group for Energy, Transport, and Climate Policy at the Wuppertal Institute for Climate, Environment and Energy (Germany).

Kilian Topp: Project Co-ordinator, Research Group Energy, Transport and Climate Policy at the Wuppertal Institute for Climate, Environment, Energy (Germany).

Prof. Dr. Michael von Hauff: Chair of Economics, Economic Policy and International Economic Relations at University of Kaiserslautern (Germany).

Prof. Dr.-Ing. Dr. h.c. mult. Peter A. Wilderer: Emeritus of Excellence: Former Chair of Water Quality and Waste Technology, Technical University of Munich (Germany).

Associate Professor Dr. Veronika Wittmann: Global Studies, Department of Modern and Contemporary History at Johannes Kepler University Linz (Austria).

Preface

At the Rio de Janeiro Conference in 1992, the international community declared its commitment to the new paradigm of sustainable development which was defined by the Agenda 21. A series of follow-up conferences helped to clarify the paradigm further. In 2015, the Sustainable Development Goals were finally adopted. However, a serious deficiency of the Rio process, which still persists, is that the paradigm of sustainable development has not been effectively introduced into academic disciplines and policy areas. This also applies to development policy.

Therefore, this book aims to demonstrate how the demands of sustainable development can be integrated into the various policy spheres of development policy, and how it is possible to orientate specific policy areas on the basis of sustainable development. Up until now this has not been sufficiently achieved in the literature on the subject, or only very selectively. However, there is a broad international consensus that the three-dimensionality, i.e. the equal status of the three dimensions of ecology, economy and social issues and their amalgamation, together with intra- and intergenerational justice, are the two constituent features of sustainable development. Although at first glance the articles in this book may indicate a certain Eurocentric orientation, all co-authors have proven experience in the international discussion and also maintain close contact with experts in developing countries.

The individual articles in this book are aimed at conveying an introductory overview of the relevant subject areas in development policy, which is the basis for the focus, and the methodological orientation, in the individual contributions. The individual articles are quite deliberately not intended to constitute an analysis of individual countries, case studies or empirically orientated research papers. All the contributions much rather focus on the substantiation of specific development policy topics from the perspective of sustainable development. Although the selection of topics is primarily orientated towards the international focal points of the discussion on development policy, a certain subjectivity is without doubt involved here.

The book is aimed at lecturers and students, as well as experts in the field of development policy, who are looking for an introduction to sustainable development policy. Since both national and international development organizations – and also consultancy firms in the sphere of development policy – increasingly have to meet the requirement to gear their work to a sustainable development policy which considers international agreements, there will be a growing need for experts with specific knowledge of sustainable development policy.

Finally, the editors would like to thank Katrin Falkenthal, Petra Homm, Stefanie Klag and Robin Wagner for their helpful support during all the production stages of this book.

Michael von Hauff
Claudia Kuhnke

Part I

Introduction

1 Sustainable development policy

Michael von Hauff, Claudia Kuhnke and
Christine Hobelsberger

Introduction: from the mainstream to a sustainable development policy

In the past two decades the paradigm of sustainable development has also brought the basis and shaping of development policy to a new level, and thus moulded it to an increasing extent. In general, development policy can be understood as all measures implemented by developing and industrialized countries in order to improve the living conditions of the population in developing countries. This demarcation is so open that it can be the basis for both traditional as well as sustainable development policy. Compared to traditional spheres of economic policy, such as growth policy, foreign trade policy or finance policy for example, development policy as an independent sphere of policy is still a relatively young discipline. However, the basis of underdevelopment and development is not only a question of the economy or a measurement of income, employment or inequality. The essence of development is therefore defined more broadly by Todaro and Smith:

> Development must therefore be conceived of as a multidimensional process involving major changes in social structures, popular attitudes, and national institutions, as well as the accelerations of economic growth, the reduction of inequality, and the eradication of poverty. Development, in its essence, must represent the whole gamut of change by which an entire social system, tuned to the diverse basic needs and evolving aspirations of individuals and social groups within the system, moves away from a condition of life regarded as materially and spiritually better.
>
> (Todaro & Smith 2011, p. 16)

The paradigm of sustainable development is a normative agreement of the world community, which fundamentally has met with broad acceptance. However, articles on the theoretical basis of sustainable development and the formulation of sustainability strategies have up until now often been permeated with varying lines of argumentation. They are therefore not always unequivocal or consistent. This also applies to the development policy of many states, non-governmental organizations and international organizations. Here there is often still a lack of clear and consistent concepts or strategies for sustainable development. It is therefore necessary to proceed from the basis of international agreements and resolutions.

The Brundtland Report, and in particular the United Nations (UN) Conference of 1992 in Rio de Janeiro, were pivotal milestones for the basis and introduction of a sustainable development policy. Agenda 21, presented at the Rio Conference, is the programme for implementing the paradigm of sustainable development for the 21st century. In this programme the objectives, measures and instruments for a sustainable development policy for developing and industrialized countries are likewise very distinct. This introduced a process announced as the Rio Process. In addition to the two follow-up conferences in Johannisburg (2002) and once again in Rio de Janeiro (2012), there were a number of additional conferences since 1992 at which specific topics relating to sustainable development were considered.

The starting point for many articles in the context of sustainable development is the definition of the Brundtland Report. In the Brundtland Commission Report *Our Common Future* sustainable development is defined as follows: "Sustainable Development is development that meets the needs of the present without compromising the ability of future generations to meet their own needs" (WCED 1987, p. 46). An additional constitutive feature of sustainable development, attracting a broad international consensus, is the creation of a balance between the three dimensions of the ecological, economic and social elements (three-dimensionality), although this can never be achieved to a full extent.

Therefore, in the past two and a half decades the paradigm of sustainable development has also brought the basis and shaping of development policy to a new level, and thus moulded it to an increasing extent. Against this background, this chapter investigates the question of how the paradigm of sustainable development formerly made its way into development policy and how it is anchored there. This becomes particularly clear from an initial consideration of the various traditional approaches to development policy, which are presented in section 2 of this chapter.

A development policy geared towards the paradigm of sustainable development only really unfolds fully if it is actually directed towards the intended effects from a long-term perspective. Therefore, in this context the determination of development objectives and indicators, on the basis of which development progress can be measured, is of crucial importance. In this context, the Millennium Develeopment Goals (MDGs) and the UN Sustainable Development Goals (SDGs) are of major significance. However, the discussions and agreements on the effectiveness of development policy also form important framework conditions for the shaping of a sustainable development policy. For this reason sections 3 and 4 concentrate on the negotiation processes in this connection and their major results, before a summary in section 5 of the most important milestones towards a sustainable development policy.

Development decades and their theoretical bases

The development policy framework has been strongly influenced by the substantive orientation of the development decades of the UN. By laying down global and sectoral growth objectives they established guidelines for a development policy process (Nuscheler 1995, p. 43). The various theoretical approaches to development and the recommended actions on the one hand, and the development decades announced by the UN on the other hand, have not always been congruent. Nevertheless, certain theoretical basic positions are discernible during most decades, and these are highlighted briefly below (cf. in this connection in detail Todaro & Smith 2011, pp. 110–131 and Ihne & Wilhelm 2006, pp. 10–18).

The UN announced the **first development decade (1961–1970)** in 1961, and it was marked by development clawback, with the objective of promoting economic growth in the developing countries in order to initiate a modernization process analogous to that in the industrialized countries. Many experts assumed that the growth generated by capital transfer would lead to a "trickle-down effect", which would particularly benefit the poor population.

The prevailing economic development theory in the 1950s and 1960s was the growth and modernization theory. Representatives of the modernization theory, such as Rosenstein-Rodan (1943), saw the cause of the underdevelopment quite essentially in the lack of capital of the national economies concerned. Important determinants of the modernization theory were the role of the state and the need for capital input, which was intended to lead to a Big Push towards industrialization in the developing countries. In terms of realpolitik, one outcome of the objective of a modernization process for the first UN development decade was the set objective of an aggregate minimum growth of 5 per cent of the gross domestic product (GDP) per year (United Nations General Assembly 1961, p. 17).

A further objective of the modernization theory was to promote the process of modernization through technological and organizational improvements geared towards an industrialized and progressive national economy (Akude 2011, p. 74). In this connection there arose the strategies of balanced (Nurkse 1953) and unbalanced growth (Streeten 1959; Hirschman 1969), although these are not to be considered in depth here.

Measured against this target, for many countries in the "Third World" this decade turned out to be economically successful. On average they achieved an annual GDP growth of 6 per cent. However, in the context of the trickle-down effect this macroeconomic success needs to be relativized. For example, per capita growth in South America, Asia and Africa was only between 1.5 and 2.5 per cent. This is simply an average value, which only explains the specific situation to a limited extent. It can therefore be stated that only a small portion of the population profited from the incipient economic growth, and since economic growth was strongly geared towards the industrial sector, the agricultural sector was neglected (Ihne & Wilhelm 2006, p. 10; von Hauff & Werner 1993, p. 21).

The theoretical basis of the modernization theory has also been criticized. This applies above all to the postulate according to which the western development path is the sole means of achieving success. Despite the obvious inadequacies of the theoretical underpinning and the fact that the development process during the first development decade could not be evaluated in unrestrictedly positive terms, in the **second development decade (1971–1980)** the UN adopted the strategy of promoting growth through a modernization process again.

In the second UN decade the demands for the realization of a new world economic order became increasingly clearer. The aim was to enable the less developed countries to participate in the world economy under fairer framework conditions. Furthermore, a reform of the Bretton Woods institutions was designed to take more account of the interests of the developing countries.[1] Finally, following pressure from the Group of 77 – a coalition of developing countries formed in 1964 – several agreements were in fact signed in the mid-1970s, and can be seen as the successful result of the dependency theory approaches (Ihne & Wilhelm 2006, pp. 14–15).

This development theory approach tackled the points of criticism in the modernization theory and is based on the ideas of structuralism permeated by the works of Prebisch (1950, 1959). This rejects the neoclassical foreign trade theories, since the global economic order does not consist of a homogenous economy. By contrast, it is made up of weak peripheries and strong centres. As a result, rather than the postulates in the neoclassical foreign trade theories, international trade and the accompanying division of labour and specialization does not necessarily represent the basis for economic success for all national economies participating in trade (Prebisch 1959, p. 251; Akude 2011, p. 76).

In the view of critics of the dependency theory, the inadequacy of this explanatory approach on the other hand lies in the fact that only external dependency structures are seen as the cause of underdevelopment, whereas historical factors are ignored. Therefore, in statistical terms no "direct correlation between economic and territorial expansion" (Lachmann 2004, pp. 238–239) can be established for the end of the 19th century and beginning of the 20th.

At the same time, criticism of traditional development aid increased, and already by the end of the first development decade industrialized countries raised the question of the rationality of a development policy based exclusively upon growth. The Pearson Report (Pearson 1969) had highlighted what Robert McNamara, the then president of the World Bank, also stressed in his famous speech in 1973: on the one hand, there was clearly continuous economic growth in many developing countries, but on the other hand, the differences in income between rich and poor were becoming greater (McNamara 1973). McNamara therefore presented the view that a successful development policy should not only be geared towards an increase in growth, but also towards distribution. This already establishes a link to the promotion of intra- and intergenerational justice: an additional feature of sustainable development alongside three-dimensionality.

This rethinking was the starting point for the basic needs strategy, or basic needs approach, which is directed towards the availability of a minimum level of essential private goods and access to rudimentary public goods and services. In addition, the possibility of political participation should be made available to the target group of development cooperation. However, the developing countries viewed the criticism of traditional development aid, i.e. the introduction of new social and economic demands, and the resulting political discourse, with a degree of scepticism. Their fear was that this additional challenge could restrict their industrial development and would disregard the new economic order they required (Nuscheler 2005, p. 80). At the end of the decade it was acknowledged that the average growth rate of

5 per cent achieved fell below the annual global growth rate of at least 6 per cent targeted by the UN (United Nations General Assembly 1970). And in this phase, distributive success in terms of a trickle-down effect was scarcely achieved either.

Although many set objectives of the second decade were not achieved, the UN announced a target growth rate of 7 per cent for the following **third development decade (1981–1990)** (United Nations General Assembly 1980, p. 108). In retrospect this target turned out to be over-optimistic and the decade was recorded as "the lost decade" in the history of development policy (Ihne & Wilhelm 2006, p. 15).

As a result of the conservative governments in the United States, Canada, the United Kingdom and Germany, neoliberalism also increasingly found its way into development policy during the course of the 1980s. Todaro and Smith brought together the various theoretical models under the concept "Neoclassical Counterrevolution: Market Fundamentalism" (2011, pp. 126). Contrary to the formerly prevalent economic development theories, which accorded the state an important role in the planning and implementation of development strategies, the basis of the neoliberal theory is that a principal cause of underdevelopment is the intervention of the state in economic affairs. Instead of the state, representatives of neoliberalism therefore saw enterprises as the "motor of a development process" (Akude 2011, pp. 84–86). This concept gave rise to the Structural Adjustment Programmes (SAPs) developed by the international financial institutions. Those had to be implemented by the developing countries which had applied for loans. This formed the basis for entitlement to financial assistance, and – among other steps – included privatization measures, the reduction of subsidies and the limitation or elimination of institutions restricting competition.

However, in many underdeveloped national economies the liberalization process proved to be less useful, or counterproductive, since once again structures specific to individual countries and regions were disregarded. As a consequence, upshots of the SAPs included high inflation rates and mass dismissals of public employees in many countries carrying out these programmes, ending in bloody SAP revolts in some countries (Akude 2011, p. 85).

As a result of the negative developments in the 1980s the formerly valid development strategies have been increasingly called into question. In this connection a closer link was formed between development policy themes and questions of human rights and environmental policy. The concept of development no longer came to be primarily declared to be an economic value, but was extended to the understanding of sustainable development (United Nations General Assembly 1990). As a new action framework for development policy, the UN decade of sustainable development was put into specific terms in the 1990s (**fourth development decade, 1991–2000**). The following chapter focuses on the bases of a sustainable development policy.

Bases of a sustainable development policy

The close connection between a sustainable use of resources and social and economic welfare had already been emphasized in 1980 as an element of the

"World Conservation Strategy" elaborated by the International Union for Conservation of Nature and Natural Resources (IUCN):

> Human beings, in their quest for economic development and enjoyment of the riches of nature, must come to terms with the reality of resource limitation and the carrying capacities of ecosystems, and must take account of the needs of future generations. This is the message of conservation. For if the object of development is to provide for social and economic welfare, the object of conservation is to ensure Earth's capacity to sustain development and to support all life.
>
> (IUCN, UNEP & WWF 1980, p. I)

However, the model of sustainable development only asserted itself as "a paradigm of development theory for the 1990s" in connection with the publication of the Brundtland Report and the conference in Rio de Janeiro. Both in the Brundtland Report as well as in the Declaration of Rio de Janeiro, the protection of the natural environment and the response to questions of development are inseparably linked (WCED 1987, p. 48; UNCED 1992, Principle 4). Furthermore, both documents establish that the fulfilment of the needs of the poor population is to be given the utmost priority in the implementation of the paradigm of sustainable development (WCED 1987, p. 54; UNCED 1992, Principle 6). Through the instabilities of the ecosystems and the accompanying specific threat to natural bases of existence it becomes clear that the production and consumption models of the industrialized nations are not supportable as prototypes for restorative development (Bethge et al. 2011, p. 20; Messner 2011, p. 425). However, in the academic literature the term "development policy" refers almost exclusively to processes of change in developing countries, whereby necessary adaptation measures by the industrialized countries are disregarded (Kuhn 2005, p. 45).

Against this background the paradigm of sustainable development offers a framework in which environmental policy and development strategies can be brought into harmony with each other. In this connection, the concept of "development" applies to both industrialized as well as developing countries. In the Brundtland Report "development" is also understood in the broadest sense:

> The word is often taken to refer to the processes of economic and social change in the Third World. But the integration of environment and development is required in all countries, rich and poor. The pursuit of sustainable development requires changes in the domestic and international policies of every nation.
>
> (WCED 1987, pp. 50–51)

The Seventh Principle of the Declaration of Rio also stresses the necessity of a global partnership to maintain, protect and also restore an intact ecosystem, within whose framework all states bear joint – although varying – responsibility worldwide (UNCED 1992, Principle 7). From a development policy perspective this concept of development consequently implies a departure from the "North-South one-way street" (Messner 2011, p. 429), in that it refers to the needs of all countries for action and development, i.e. not just the developing and emerging countries.

Against this background industrialized countries must also, through exemplary sustainability-orientated action, demonstrate that a departure from the previous economic and lifestyle models need not be accompanied by a deterioration in the quality of life (Jackson 2011, pp. 184–185). Consequently, the challenge for development policy against the background of the sustainability paradigm is to initiate and promote development impulses in developing countries, and at the same time propel a readjustment of the concept of development in the industrialized countries (König 2011, p. 41).

As Ashoff (2010, p. 28) states, in view of the poverty prevailing in many parts of the world, development policy does not lack a basis. There are, however, signs of increasing pressure for justification and thus also a need for legitimation, extending to fundamental criticism proclaiming that development policy has in itself largely failed. This situation leads to an additional concept of sustainability, which is very significant for development policy: the question of "aid effectiveness". This relates not only to rationality and effectiveness, but also to the lasting effectiveness of development policy, beyond the duration of specific projects or programmes (Ashoff 2010, p. 40).

There are numerous possible causes of a lack of effectiveness of development policy in the narrower sense, extending from deficits in the development policy itself, through misdirected development policy measures by the donor and recipient countries and the propagation of problematic strategies through development research, to the counterproductive influence of other political spheres on development policy. Not least, exogenous factors which partner countries and donors have little or no influence upon, such as natural disasters, political crises or external economic shocks, can also negatively affect the effectiveness of development policy (Ashoff 2010, pp. 33–38). Consequently, ensuring and assessing the sustainable effectiveness of development policy is an extremely complex area, requiring efforts on the various levels (of actors), and in some cases extending far beyond development policy.

Against this background, around 150 heads of state and government came together in September 2000 at the UN in New York at the largest meeting of this kind. The objective was "at the dawn of a new millennium, to reaffirm our faith in the Organization and its Charter as indispensable foundations of a more peaceful, prosperous and just world" (United Nations General Assembly 2000, p. 1). The result of these negotiations was the so-called Millennium Declaration of the United Nations, which introduced a new global partnership for development. This led to a new orientation and to a new quality of international development cooperation. According to this document, the opportunities for globalization can only be fully exploited if the principles of human dignity and equal rights are safeguarded equally for all people worldwide.

Against this background, all signatory heads of state and government declare not only a personal responsibility to their respective society, but also a worldwide communal responsibility for mankind, especially the weakest. The declaration concludes that a fulfilment of this responsibility can only be achieved through measures striven for worldwide. Consequently, relationships in the 21st century should be characterized by the basic values of freedom, equality, solidarity, tolerance, respect for nature and jointly borne responsibility (United Nations General Assembly 2000, p. 2). Building onto these principles, the agenda ultimately defines four programmatic fields of action for international policy in the 21st century (United Nations General Assembly 2000, pp. 2–6):

- Freedom, security and disarmament,
- Development and eradication of poverty,
- Protection of our common environment,
- Human rights, democracy and good governance.

Ultimately replacing the development policy decade strategies of the UN, there emerged the international development objectives derived from the Millennium Declaration: the so-called MDGs. Government representatives from 189 countries committed to fulfil, by 2015, on an international level, the 8 goals presented in Table 1.1 and to contribute towards the original 18 set targets (United Nations General Assembly 2002, pp. 21–35), which have since been supplemented by 1.B, 5.B and 6.B.

The MDGs offer the donor countries as well as the recipient countries a joint orientation for the fields of action of development policy, which allocates responsibilities to both sides. Whereas the first six MDGs relate to tasks which are to be performed in situ in the recipient countries with the support of the donors, Millennium Goals 7 and 8 particularly emphasize the role of the industrialized countries: it is incumbent upon them to create the framework conditions which enable the developing countries to fulfil their obligations (Bains & Herfkens 2006, pp. 226–229).

To ensure the measurability of progress in achieving the MDGs, 60 indicators were laid down for the various subject areas and targets. Beyond this, the community of states agreed to regularly examine the implementation of the Millennium Declaration. The overview of the MDGs in Table 1.1 also shows the progress made in achieving the goals. In summary, it can be stated that significant progress has been made over the years, and some of the indicators already demonstrated the result sought prior to 2015. However, not all target values were achieved by the end of 2015, for which reason further efforts are required.

With the agreement on the MDGs a previously unattainable broad consensus on an assessable and chronologically defined reference framework for international development policy was created. Nevertheless, despite this singularly outstanding feature and their significant and trailblazing function, the MDGs were also criticized. Some of these points of criticism are relevant against the background of the implementation of sustainable development and with regard to the post-2015 process.

For example, Loewe points out that individual MDGs could only be achieved at the cost of other development goals. This in turn could lead to not workable development structures beyond 2015. In accordance with the requirements of

Table 1.1 The 8 MDGs and 21 set targets for their realization

Formulation of goals		Progress until 2014
MDG 1	*Eradicate extreme poverty and hunger*	
1.A	Halve, between 1990 and 2015, the proportion of people whose income is less than US$1 a day	The extreme poverty rate has been halved, but major challenges remain
1.B	Achieve full and productive employment and decent work for all, including women and young people	Slow economic growth takes its toll on labour markets
1.C	Halve, between 1990 and 2015, the proportion of people who suffer from hunger	Hunger continues to decline, but major efforts are needed to achieve the hunger target globally by 2015
MDG 2	*Achieve universal primary education*	
2.A	Ensure that, by 2015, children everywhere, boys and girls alike, will be able to complete a full course of primary schooling	Despite impressive strides forward at the start of the decade, progress in reducing the number of children out of school has slackened considerably
MDG 3	*Promote gender equality and empower women*	
3.A	Eliminate gender disparity in primary and secondary education, preferably by 2005, and in all levels of education no later than 2015	Women's status in the labour market is improving, but gender disparity still exists
MDG 4	*Reduce child mortality*	
4.A	Reduce by two thirds, between 1990 and 2015, the under-five mortality rate	The child mortality rate has almost halved since 1990; 6 million fewer children died in 2012 than in 1990
MDG 5	*Improve maternal health*	
5.A	Reduce by three quarters, between 1990 and 2015, the maternal mortality ratio	Much more still needs to be done to reduce maternal mortality
5.B	Achieve, by 2015, universal access to reproductive health	Adolescent childbearing has declined but remains very high in some regions
MDG 6	*Combat HIV/AIDS, malaria and other diseases*	
6.A	Have halted by 2015 and begun to reverse the spread of HIV/AIDS	There are still too many new cases of HIV infection
6.B	Achieve, by 2010, universal access to treatment for HIV/AIDS for all those who need it	Antiretroviral therapy has saved 6.6 million lives since 1995 and expanding coverage can save many more
6.C	Have halted by 2015 and begun to reverse the incidence of malaria and other major diseases	With more than 3 million lives saved in the past decade, the world is on track to achieving the malaria target, but great challenges remain

Table 1.1 continued

Formulation of goals		Progress until 2014
MDG 7	*Ensure environmental sustainability*	
7.A	Integrate the principles of sustainable development into country policies and programmes and reverse the loss of environmental resources	Global greenhouse gas emissions continue their upward trend; Millions of hectares of forest are lost every year, threatening this valuable asset; the world has almost eliminated ozone-depleting substances
7.B	Reduce biodiversity loss, achieving, by 2010, a significant reduction in the rate of loss	Protected areas are increasing, thus helping to safeguard natural resources
7.C	Halve, by 2015, the proportion of the population without sustainable access to safe drinking water and basic sanitation	Access to an improved drinking water source has become a reality for 2.3 billion people since 1990; many people still rely on unsafe water sources
7.D	By 2020, to have achieved a significant improvement in the lives of at least 100 million slum dwellers	Although the MDG target has been met, the number of people living in slum conditions is growing
MDG 8	*Develop a global partnership for development*	
8.A	Develop further an open, rule-based, predictable, non-discriminatory trading and financial system	Trade liberalization has slowed, while least developed countries benefit from truly preferential treatment; average tariffs have declined, but their reduction has moderated
8.B and 8.C	Address the special needs of the least developed countries, landlocked developing countries and small island developing states	Aid is shifting away from the poorest countries
8.D	Deal comprehensively with developing countries' debt	The debt burden of developing countries is much lower than in 2000, but is not declining further
8.E	In cooperation with pharmaceutical companies, provide access to affordable essential drugs in developing countries	No global or regional data are available
8.F	In cooperation with the private sector, make available the benefits of new technologies, especially information and communications	The use of modern information and communications technology continues to grow – with almost 3 billion people online and seven billion mobile-cellular subscriptions

Source: Based on United Nations 2014a, 2014b

sustainable development, such as long-term durability, and the interdependence of ecological, economic as well as social fields of action, there is a risk that these could be disregarded in the achievement of the MDGs (Loewe 2010, p. 113).

An additional point of criticism is the perceived inadequacy of the MDGs to secure ecological sustainability. In the ranking of the MDGs Messner and Scholz (2010, p. 74) see the expression of a "new pragmatism" in development policy, which becomes evident in view of the complexity of the fields of action and the different interests of the industrialized and developing countries. Nuscheler and Roth (2006, p. 31) point out that in the view of many developing countries, environmental protection is a "post-materialistic luxury" which is seen as an obstacle to a country's own development and use of resources. Consequently, in the protection of the environment for example there are noticeable divergences in the priorities set by industrialized and developing countries.

As a result, it is overlooked that the first six MDGs cannot be achieved unless the seventh MDG, to secure ecological sustainability, is fulfilled (WBGU 2005, p. 9). This leads to a loss of the "Rio vision", whereby environmental policy and development policy are inseparably linked. Therefore, the MDGs must not be treated in isolation from the Rio Declaration. Despite these criticisms of the MDGs, it can be stated that through the Millennium Declaration and the resulting MDGs, an important discussion on fundamental improvements to development policy has been prompted: it has led to a further development of the "aid effectiveness" concept.

An initial milestone on this path is the Rome Declaration, which was adopted in 2003 at a high-level forum on the effectiveness of development cooperation. In this document the participants of the forum commit to a stronger harmonization and partnership orientation of their development policy (OECD 2003). Three additional key documents on these efforts towards reform were adopted at the subsequent forums on the effectiveness of development cooperation, in Paris (2005), Accra (2008) and Busan (2011). These will be briefly explained below.

In 2005 in Paris more than 100 representatives of donor and partner countries from international development organizations, business and society jointly agreed for the first time upon partnership obligations with regard to their future development policy. In this connection, the "Paris Declaration on Aid Effectiveness" is based upon the following five fundamental principles:

- In accordance with the principle of ownership, the partner countries commit to exercising leadership in developing and implementing their national development strategies. In return, the donor countries agree to respect partner country leadership and help strengthen their capacity to exercise it.
- Against the background of the principle of alignment the donor countries commit to basing their overall support on the national development strategies, institutions and processes of their partner countries.
- In the interest of collectively higher effectiveness, the principle of harmonization envisages a better mutual coordination of programmes and processes of the donor countries.
- Through Managing for Results the donor countries commit to focus on the results of their development policy action. They should not be guided by the

achievements made in their partner countries, while the partner countries work towards creating results-oriented reporting and orientation framework.

- The principle of mutual accountability ultimately relates to strengthening the accountability of the donor and partner countries, both between each other and with regard to the public and parliaments.

(High Level Forum on Aid Effectiveness 2005, pp. 5–11)

The objective is to create a stimulus as well as a basis for assessing the progress in implementing the principles. For this, the Forum established targets for each of the five principles, which were to be met by 2010 (High Level Forum on Aid Effectiveness 2005, pp. 12–13). In 2008 the Paris Declaration was supplemented by the Accra Action Plan, which was adopted in the Ghanaian capital as the result of the third Forum on Aid Effectiveness.

It is emphasized at the beginning of the action plan that development cooperation can only be a part of development efforts. The document also identifies as the most important driving forces of development the areas of democracy, economic growth, social progress, the careful treatment of the environment, gender equality and the respect for human rights. In this context the Action Plan also raises the question of the effects of other political spheres on the progress of development cooperation. It points out that these subject areas are to be tackled systematically and coherently with all policies (High Level Forum on Aid Effectiveness 2008, p. 2).

In examining the progress which has been made since the Paris Declaration, the Action Plan document comes to the conclusion that it is particularly necessary to overcome the following challenges: on the one hand, the Action Plan once again emphasizes that the principle of own responsibility laid down in the Paris Declaration is a crucial prerequisite for more effective development cooperation. Consequently, the Action Plan envisages an even more intensive adoption of development policy by the governments of developing countries. These are urged to include their parliaments and citizens in shaping this policy. Meanwhile the donors have to commit to respecting the priorities of their partner countries which are specific to these countries. In the implementation of development cooperation, there should be a more concentrated utilization of the resources and systems already existing in the developing countries (High Level Forum on Aid Effectiveness 2008, p. 2).

On the other hand, the Action Plan points to the need to build up more effective and more comprehensive partnerships. In view of the growing number of development policy actors, in particular through the increasing participation of middle-income countries, global funds as well as private and public sector actors, the challenges of managing and coordinating activities should be effectively met in this way (High Level Forum on Aid Effectiveness 2008, p. 3). The Action Plan ultimately reaches the conclusion that the achievement of development results and open reporting on progress made should be accorded the highest priority. It is therefore necessary to fulfil the expectations of citizens of all countries and provide an adequate account of the results of development policy activity (High Level Forum on Aid Effectiveness 2008, p. 6).

At the fourth and final High Level Forum on Aid Effectiveness, which took place in Busan, South Korea, in December 2011, representatives of governments of industrialized and developing countries, multilateral and bilateral organizations, as well as the most diverse private and public sector organizations, joined together in a new partnership: the "Busan Partnership for effective development cooperation". As the report emphasizes (High Level Forum on Aid Effectiveness 2011), this partnership is more broadly and more inclusively structured than before and in this way takes account of the increasingly complex architecture of development cooperation. In this connection, the report particularly highlights the growing influence of so-called "emerging donors" – those states which commit to development co-operation but are not members of the Organization for Economic Co-operation and Development's (OECD) Development Assistance Committee (DAC). At present, 29 states belong to the DAC, the OECD committee which examines questions and fields of action relating to development policy (for a full list see OECD 2015a).

Although the term suggests otherwise, the "emerging donors" or "new donors" are not a new phenomenon in development cooperation. Woods, for example (2008, pp. 1205–1206), refers to the aid projects of Arabic states or projects of the People's Republic of China, which had already begun in the 1950s or 1970s respectively. In view of the greatly increasing investments over the years by countries such as China, India or Brazil, for example, in other developing and emerging countries, a definite power shift among the donor states is discernible. It also entails a scrutinizing or modification of existing structures of development cooperation.

In some cases this development therefore causes dissatisfaction among the "traditional" donor states. Alongside the impending loss of power and influence, this scepticism is also attributable to the tendency of the new donor countries not to interfere in the policies of their partner countries. Unlike in the case of the traditional donor countries, cooperation is not linked to conditions – for example, the efforts of the recipient country towards good governmental leadership or the consideration of ecological and social standards (Woods 2008, pp. 1208–1212). This aspect is particularly relevant against the background of implementing sustainable development or promoting the MDGs, since there is a risk that the efforts of the "traditional" donor states could in this way be undermined.

Against this background the final document of the Conference of Busan stresses the necessity and significance of cooperation, as well as the exchange of experience and knowledge between all donors. At the same time, the document stresses the problem-solution potential of South–South as well as trilateral cooperation.[2] It calls upon all actors to fully exploit this potential through appropriate cooperation. The document likewise points to the special role of the private sector in the context of development cooperation: as actors promoting innovation, income and employment, therefore making important contributions to sustainable growth and combating poverty. Public and private actors should therefore jointly investigate how developmental and entrepreneurial objectives can be promoted to the same extent and in a mutually reinforcing manner (High Level Forum on Aid Effectiveness 2011, p. 10).

Like the previous Accra Action Plan, the final document of the High Level Forum of Busan also tackled the aspect of political coherence. According to this, although development cooperation can play a catalytic and indispensable supporting role in, for example, combating poverty, social security, sustainable development or economic growth, at the same time development cooperation can, however, only be considered to be part of the solution. Consequently, account needs to be taken of the reciprocal interactions of all political fields, not merely development policy, and coordinating these with each other in the interest of development policy targets is a necessity (High Level Forum on Aid Effectiveness 2011, p. 3).

The international community is also endeavouring to make further progress in this direction following the last High Level Forum on Aid Effectiveness. For example, the commitment to effective development cooperation was reinforced at the first High Level Meeting of the Global Partnership for Effective Development Cooperation, which took place in April 2014 in Mexico City. In the Annex to the Communiqué of the High Level Meeting there is an overview of 39 voluntary initiatives intended to serve the realization of the objective of effective development cooperation (Global Partnership for Effective Development Cooperation 2014).

The post–2015 process

Following the introduction of the Millennium Development Goals and the discussion about aid effectiveness, the post-2015 agenda shall now be introduced. Back in 2010 at the UN Summit on the MDGs in New York, after a critical appraisal of MDG progress to date and the call for a stronger promotion of the target agenda, the UN secretary-general was mandated to initiate the forward projection of the MDGs. Ban Ki-moon then initiated a comprehensive process to work out a post-2015 Development Agenda. At its first meetings in September 2013 and July 2014 the High-level Political Forum on Sustainable Development, formed after Rio+20, principally considered the forward projection of the post-2015 agenda. (A detailed presentation of the process is shown in the United Nations General Assembly 2014.)

In accordance with the final document of the Rio+20 Conference, this involves putting into concrete form the post-2015 development agenda by formulating SDGs. This led to the agenda 2030. In this connection the underlying consideration was the need for an effective international sustainability policy and a strong model with a generally recognized normative framework for action, as well as the requirement of a global political consensus on objectives to impel action. This has to be put into concrete form through setting time limits and indicators. Thus at the 68th meeting of the UN General Assembly in 2013 it was resolved to formulate a common agenda, into which sustainability goals are integrated, for the period following the expiration of the Millennium Goals. It was determined as follows:

> Recognizing the intrinsic interlinkage between poverty eradication and the promotion of sustainable development, we underline the need for a coherent

approach that integrates in a balanced manner the three dimensions of sustainable development. This coherent approach involves working towards a single framework and set of goals, universal in nature and applicable to all countries, while taking account of differing national circumstances and respecting national policies and priorities. It should also promote peace and security, democratic governance, the rule of law, gender equality and human rights for all.

(United Nations General Assembly 2013, p. 4)

Various working groups were appointed for preparing a draft of the SDGs. The publications of these working groups were expressed in concrete form in 12 Development Goals at the beginning of March 2014 by national groups from, for example, Germany, France and Switzerland. From these results the open working group prepared up until September 2014 a draft of the specific SDGs, which was presented at the UN General Assembly in 2014 and introduced into the international negotiations. These negotiations ultimately lead in September 2015 to the adoption of the new development agenda at the United Nations Summit in New York (United Nations Department of Economic and Social Affairs 2015). Table 1.2 shows the 17 first provisional and later approved SDGs, whose achievement is to be ensured by reviewing the 169 set targets. It should be positively stressed that the content of the individual goals is given much stronger concrete form than the MDGs. With regard to the timeframe, the goals are to be achieved by 2030.

In summary, it can be stated that the new institutional framework and the comprehensive post-2015 processes initiated by the UN can contribute towards a reinforcement of the international sustainability regime. Therefore, it is to be hoped that by adopting the SDGs sustainable development will become a stronger integral component of the global development agenda compared to the previous MDGs.

However, an important prerequisite for this is that, in accordance with the demands of sustainable development, a real equality between the three dimensions is achieved, i.e. that not too little consideration is taken of the ecological dimension, as was the case with the MDGs. A balance between the three dimensions must continue to be striven for. In this connection, it should be taken into account that a perfect balance can never be achieved, but should at least be aimed at.

In this context criticism was voiced from the outset, and this can only be outlined by way of example here. For instance, in its study *States of Fragility 2015: Meeting post-2015 Ambitions* (in German: *Aspekte der Fragilität – Lassen sich die Ambitionen der Post-2015 Agenda erfüllen?*) the OECD (2015b) states that in the fulfilment of the MDGs fragile states show deficits compared to the less fragile states. Two demands are therefore made: (1) fragility should be judged according to different criteria after 2015; and (2) targeted measures are required to overcome fragility in order to enable the implementation of the post-2015 development goals (OECD 2015b, pp. 13–14).

There are some doubts whether the message that the post-2015 agenda should also be implemented in industrialized countries has been registered by them. It is

Table 1.2 UN sustainable development goals

Goal 1	End poverty in all its forms everywhere
Goal 2	End hunger, achieve food security and improved nutrition and promote sustainable agriculture
Goal 3	Ensure healthy lives and promote well-being for all at all ages
Goal 4	Ensure inclusive and equitable quality education and promote lifelong learning opportunities for all
Goal 5	Achieve gender equality and empower all women and girls
Goal 6	Ensure availability and sustainable management of water and sanitation for all
Goal 7	Ensure access to affordable, reliable, sustainable and modern energy for all
Goal 8	Promote sustained, inclusive and sustainable economic growth, full and productive employment and decent work for all
Goal 9	Build resilient infrastructure, promote inclusive and sustainable industrialization and foster innovation
Goal 10	Reduce inequality within and among countries
Goal 11	Make cities and human settlements inclusive, safe, resilient and sustainable
Goal 12	Ensure sustainable consumption and production patterns
Goal 13	Take urgent action to combat climate change and its impacts★
Goal 14	Conserve and sustainably use the oceans, seas and marine resources for sustainable development
Goal 15	Protect, restore and promote sustainable use of terrestrial ecosystems, sustainably manage forests, combat desertification, and halt and reverse land degradation and halt biodiversity loss
Goal 16	Promote peaceful and inclusive societies for sustainable development, provide access to justice for all and build effective, accountable and inclusive institutions at all levels
Goal 17	Strengthen the means of implementation and revitalize the global partnership for sustainable development

Note: ★Acknowledging that the United Nations Framework Convention on Climate Change is the primary international, intergovernmental forum for negotiating the global response to climate change.

Source: Adapted from United Nation General Assembly 2014, p. 10

therefore demanded that the industrialized countries also consistently adhere to the post-2015 agenda along the lines of the sustainability goals. It is ultimately to be feared that the 17 goals will again be seen and striven for as individual targets. It is therefore doubted that the goals will be treated as an interdisciplinary package, as is demanded in the context of the three-dimensionality of sustainable development.

This is clear from Goal 8 "Promote sustained, inclusive and sustainable economic growth, full and productive employment and decent work for all". Thus inclusive growth, for example, is defined by the OECD as: "Tackling inequalities in incomes, health outcomes, education and well-being, requires breaking down the barriers to inclusive growth and reaching new frontiers in policymaking and implementation. Everyone should be able to realize their potential and to share the benefits of growth and increased prosperity" (OECD Secretary-General n.d.). However, these criteria are not to be found in the additional comments on this goal, and there is no cross-referencing to the other SDGs. To this extent, there should once again be a review of how the content of the SDGs can be better coordinated with each other and interlinked.

Summary

Over several decades international development policy as well as the national development policy of the individual industrialized states have been characterized by successive development decades. The binding link of the development decades has been the demand for more economic growth. However, in most cases it has only been possible to partially fulfil this demand. Whereas theoretical approaches based on own development, which have arisen over the four UN development decades, accorded the state an important role in the development process, with the demand for more economic growth the market has acquired a pivotal significance particularly during the later development decades. As a consequence, particularly during the third development decade the intervention of the state in the economic process was seen as a fundamental cause of underdevelopment.

Nevertheless, during the decade of the 1980s in many developing countries the development processes did not bring about the desired success in terms of comprehensive development either. Therefore, the hitherto popular development strategies were critically analysed to an increasing extent. The concept of development was no longer primarily understood as an economic category, but was expanded through the paradigm of sustainable development. Thus the UN decade of sustainable development emerged in the 1990s, and in 1992 was taken up by the international community at the conference in Rio de Janeiro. This paradigm was given concrete form in the Agenda 21 and in many subsequent conferences.

In September 2000 there was a meeting of 150 heads of state and government at the UN in New York. The result of the negotiations was the Millennium Declaration, which was intended to introduce a new global partnership for development. The strategies as had been laid down for the individual development policy decades were replaced in 2000 by the MDGs, derived from the Millennium Declaration. In this connection, representatives from 189 countries committed to contribute towards fulfilling eight goals by 2015.

In parallel to the endeavours to achieve the MDGs, there was a growing consciousness of the need to realize aid effectiveness. Finally, in 2014 a commitment to implement effective development cooperation was reinforced at a high-level meeting in Mexico City. This undertaking is to be viewed as important, since it had become clear at an early stage that only some of the MDGs would be achieved. For this reason, back in 2010 the foundation was also laid for a post-2015 development agenda. In this respect, against the background of the Rio Conference of 2012, the objective was to shift from the MDGs to a sustainability agenda. It is anticipated that the post-2015 Agenda will make an important contribution towards strengthening the international sustainability regime.

Nevertheless, it has been shown that a sustainability agenda must lead to an equally ranking incorporation of the three dimensions: the ecology, economy and social dimensions. It is therefore a question of a new understanding of balance, which was not sufficiently established with the MDGs. This can, however, only be achieved through the 17 SDGs if a common understanding and a common responsibility is created in the international community.

Notes

1   This involved the World Bank and the International Monetary Fund, which were both formed in 1944 (International Monetary Fund, 2012, p. 1).
2   Meaning cooperation of DAC members, new donor countries and recipient countries.

References

Akude, J. E. (2011): Theorien der Entwicklungspolitik. Ein Überblick, in: König, J.; Thema, J. (eds): *Nachhaltigkeit in der Entwicklungszusammenarbeit. Theoretische Konzepte, strukturelle Herausforderungen und praktische Umsetzung.* Wiesbaden: VS-Verlag, pp. 69–94.

Ashoff, G. (2010): Wirksamkeit als Legitimationsproblem und komplexe Herausforderung der Entwicklungspolitik, in: Faust, J.; Neubert, S. (ed.): *Wirksamere Entwicklungspolitik: Befunde, Reformen, Instrumente.* Baden-Baden: Nomos, pp. 27–68.

Bains, M.; Herfkens, E. (2006): Damit die Millenniums-Entwicklungsziele nicht nur eine Vision bleiben. Herausforderungen für den Norden, in: Nuscheler, F.; Roth, M. (eds): *Die Millennium-Entwicklungsziele. Entwicklungspolitischer Königsweg oder ein Irrweg?*, Bonn: J.H.W. Dietz Nachfolger GmbH, pp. 223–240.

Bethge, J. P.; Steurer, N.; Tscherner, M. (2011): Nachhaltigkeit. Begriff und Bedeutung in der Entwicklungszusammenarbeit, in: König, J.; Thema, J. (eds): *Nachhaltigkeit in der Entwicklungszusammenarbeit. Theoretische Konzepte, strukturelle Herausforderungen und praktische Umsetzung.* Wiesbaden: VS-Verlag, pp. 15–40.

Global Partnership for Effective Development Co-operation (2014): *First High-Level Meeting of the Global Partnership for Effective Development Co-operation: Building Towards an Inclusive Post-2015 Development Agenda,* http://effectivecooperation.org/wordpress/wp-content/uploads/2014/07/ENG_Final-ConsensusMexicoHLMCommunique.pdf, last checked on 26.03.2015.

High Level Forum on Aid Effectiveness (2005): *Paris Declaration on Aid Effectiveness Ownership, Harmonisation, Alignment, Results and Mutual Accountability,* http://www.oecd.org/dac/aideffectiveness/35023537.pdf, last checked on 26.03.2015.

High Level Forum on Aid Effectiveness (2008): *Accra Action Plan,* www.oecd.org/dac/aideffectiveness/42564567.pdf, last checked on 26.03.2015.

High Level Forum on Aid Effectiveness (2011): *Busan Partnership for effective development co-operation,* www.oecd.org/dac/aideffectiveness/49650173.pdf, last checked on 26.03.2015.

Hirschman, A. O. (1969): *The Strategy of Economic Development.* New Haven [inter alia]: Yale University Pres.

Ihne, H.; Wilhelm, J. (2006): *Einführung in die Entwicklungspolitik.* Hamburg: Lit.

International Monetary Fund (2012): *The IMF and the World Bank,* www.imf.org/external/np/exr/facts/pdf/imfwb.pdf, last checked on 26.03.2015.

IUCN; UNEP; WWF (1980): *World Conservation Strategy: Living resource conservation for sustainable development*. Gland, Switzerland: IUCN.

Jackson, T. (2011): *Prosperity Without Growth*, 2nd ed., London: Routledge.

König, J. (2011): Entwicklung und Nachhaltigkeit. Kritische Betrachtung von zwei dehnbaren Konzepten, in: König, J. & Thema, J. (eds): *Nachhaltigkeit in der Entwicklungszusammenarbeit. Theoretische Konzepte, strukturelle Herausforderungen und praktische Umsetzung*. Wiesbaden: VS-Verlag, pp. 41–69.

Kuhn, B. (2005): *Entwicklungspolitik zwischen Markt und Staat. Möglichkeiten und Grenzen zivilgesellschaftlicher Organisationen*. Frankfurt/Main/New York: Campus.

Lachmann, W. (2004): *Entwicklungspolitik*. 2nd ed., Munich, Vienna: Oldenbourg.

Loewe, M. (2010): Entwicklungspolitik, Armutsbekämpfung und Millennium Development Goals, in: Faust, J. & Neubert, S. (eds): *Wirksamere Entwicklungspolitik: Befunde, Reformen, Instrumente (Entwicklungstheorie und Entwicklungspolitik 8)*, Baden-Baden: Nomos Verl.-Ges., pp. 101–135.

McNamara, R. (1973): *Address to the Board of Governors*. World Bank. Nairobi, Kenya, 24.09.1973. http://documents.worldbank.org/curated/en/1980/09/9089951/address-board-governors-robert-s-mcnamara, last checked on 26.03.2015.

Messner, D. (2011): Entwicklungspolitik als globale Strukturpolitik, in: Jäger, T.; Höse, A. & Oppermann, K. (eds): *Deutsche Außenpolitik*. Wiesbaden: VS Verlag für Sozialwissenschaften, pp. 414–442.

Messner, D.; Scholz, I. (2010): Entwicklungspolitik als Beitrag zur globalen Zukunftssicherung, in: Faust, J. & Neubert, S. (eds): *Wirksamere Entwicklungspolitik: Befunde, Reformen, Instrumente*. Baden-Baden: Nomos Verlag., pp. 71–100.

Nurkse, R. (1953): Problems of Capital Formation in Underdeveloped Countries, in: Kattel, R.; Kregel, J. A. & Reinert, E. S. (ed.) (2009): *Ragnar Nurkse Trade and Development*. London; New York: Anthem Press, pp. 99–212.

Nuscheler, F. (1995): *Lern- und Arbeitsbuch Entwicklungspolitik*. 4th ed., Bonn: Bundeszentrale für politische Bildung.

Nuscheler, F. (2005): *Lern- und Arbeitsbuch Entwicklungspolitik. Eine grundlegende Einführung in die zentralen entwicklungspolitischen Themenfelder Globalisierung, Staatsversagen, Hunger, Bevölkerung, Wirtschaft und Umwelt*. 5th completely newly revised ed., Bonn: Dietz.

Nuscheler, F.; Roth, M. (2006): Die Millennium-Entwicklungsziele: ihr Potenzial und ihre Schwachstellen. Eine kritische Zusammenfassung, in: Nuscheler, F. & Roth, M. (eds): *Die Millennium-Entwicklungsziele. Entwicklungspolitischer Königsweg oder ein Irrweg? EINE WELT-Texte der Stiftung Entwicklung und Frieden*, Vol. 20. Bonn: J. H. W. Dietz Verlag, pp. 15–43.

OECD (2003): *Rome Declaration on Harmonisation*, www.oecd.org/development/aideffectiveness/31451637.pdf, last checked on 26.03.2015.

OECD (2015a): *Glossary*, www.oecd.org/dac/dac-glossary.htm#DAC, last checked on 26.03.2015.

OECD (2015b): *Aspekte der Fragilität 2015: Lassen sich die Ambitionen der Post-2015-Agenda erfüllen?*, OECD Publishing, Paris, DOI:10.1787/9789264234345-de, last checked on 11.06.2015.

OECD Secretary-General (n.d.): *Inclusive Growth*, www.oecd.org/fr/sites/inclusivegrowth/, last checked on 11.06.2015.

Pearson, L. B. (1969): *Partners in Development: Report of the Commission on International Development*, Chairman Lester B. Pearson, Pall Mall Press.

Prebisch, R. (1950): *The Economic Development of Latin America and its Principal Problems*. Lake Success: United Nations Dept. of Economic Affairs.

Prebisch, R. (1959): Commercial Policy in the Underdeveloped Countries. *American Economic Review 1959 (2)*, pp. 251–273.

Rosenstein-Rodan, P. N. (1943): Problems of Industrialisation of Eastern and South-Eastern Europe. *The Economic Journal 53 (210/211)*, pp. 202–211.

Streeten, P. (1959): Unbalanced Growth. *Oxford Economic Papers 11 (2)*, pp. 167–190.

Todaro, M.; Smith, S. C. (2011): *Economic Development* (11th edition). Boston: Addison Wesley.

UNCED (1992): *Rio Declaration on Environment and Development*, www.unep.org/Documents.Multilingual/Default.asp?documentid=78&articleid=1163, last checked on 26.03.2015.

United Nations (2011): *World Population Prospects* (The 2010 Revision. Volume 1: Comprehensive Tables). New York: UN.

United Nations (2014a): *The Millennium Development Goals Report 2014*. New York: UN.

United Nations (2014b): *MDG Report Statistical Annex 2014*, http://mdgs.un.org/unsd/mdg/Host.aspx?Content=Products/ProgressReports.htm, last checked on 26.03.2015.

United Nations Department of Economic and Social Affairs (2015): *United Nations Summit to Adopt the Post-2015 Development Agenda*, https://sustainabledevelopment.un.org/post2015/summit, last checked on 07.04.2015.

United Nations General Assembly (1961): *Resolution 1710 (XVI) 19 December 1961. United Nations Development Decade*, www.unpan.org/Portals/0/60yrhistory/documents/GA%20Resolution/GA%20Res%201710%28XVI%29.1961.pdf, last checked on 26.03.2015.

United Nations General Assembly (1970): *Resolution 2626 (XXV) – 24 October 1970. International Development Strategy for the Second United Nations Development Decade*, www.un-documents.net/a25r2626.htm, last checked on 26.103.2015.

United Nations General Assembly (1980): *A/RES/35/56 – 5 December 1980. International Development Strategy for the Third United Nations Development Decade*, www.un.org/documents/ga/res/35/a35r56e.pdf, last checked on 26.03.2015.

United Nations General Assembly (1990): *A/RES/45/199 – 21 December 1990. International Development Strategy for the Fourth United Nations Development Decade*, www.un.org/documents/ga/res/45/a45r199.htm, last checked on 26.03.2015.

United Nations General Assembly (2000): *A/RES/55/2 – 18 September 2000. United Nations Millennium Declaration*, www.un.org/millennium/declaration/ares552e.pdf, last checked on 26.03.2015.

United Nations General Assembly (2002): *Implementation of the United Nations Millennium Declaration – Report of the Secretary-General*, www.un.org/millenniumgoals/sgreport2002.pdf?OpenElement, last checked on 26.03.2015.

United Nations General Assembly (2013): *A/RES/68/6 – 9. October 2013. Outcome Document of the Special Event to Follow up Efforts Made Towards Achieving the Millennium Development Goals*, http://icpdtaskforce.org/resources/N1343981.pdf, last checked on 16.03.2015.

United Nations General Assembly (2014): *A/68/970 – Report of the Open Working Group of the General Assembly of Sustainable Development Goals*, www.un.org/en/ga/search/view_doc.asp?symbol=A/68/970, last checked on 16.03.2015.

von Hauff, M.; Werner, H. (1993): *Entwicklungsstrategien für die Dritte Welt*. Ludwigsburg: Verlag Wissenschaft & Praxis.

WBGU (2005): *Keine Entwicklung ohne Umweltschutz. Empfehlungen zum Millennium+5-Gipfel*, Berlin: WBGU.

WCED (1987): *Our Common Future*, www.unric.org/html/german/entwicklung/rio5/
  brundtland/A_42_427.pdf, last checked on 26.03.2015.
Woods, N. (2008): Whose Aid? Whose Influence? China, Emerging Donors and the Silent
  Revolution in Development Assistance. *International Affairs 84 (6)*, pp. 1205–1221.

2 National strategies for sustainable development between Rio 1992 and New York 2015

Imme Scholz

Origin and state of national sustainable development strategies

Sustainable development strategies go back to the United Nations Conference on Environment and Development (UNCED) in Rio de Janeiro 1992. More than 150 countries participated in this unique summit and, by signing the Rio Declaration, committed themselves to integrating the principles of economic, social and ecological sustainability into their policy strategies and measures. Agenda 21 (chapter 8.7) specified that:

> governments, in cooperation, where appropriate, with international organizations, should adopt a national strategy for sustainable development based on, inter alia, the implementation of decisions taken at the Conference, particularly in respect of Agenda 21. This strategy should build upon and harmonize the various sectoral economic, social and environmental policies and plans that are operating in the country. … It should be developed through the widest possible participation. It should be based on a thorough assessment of the current situation and initiatives.

In 2008, the Commission for Sustainable Development reported that 82 per cent of the United Nations (UN) member states were implementing some sort of national sustainable development strategy (NSDS) (Berger & Gioksi 2009, p. 3). For their compilation, the UN Division for Sustainable Development developed a rather broad definition of NSDSs which included (1) explicit NSDSs generated by new strategy processes, (2) sectoral strategies with a focus on the environment and natural resources and (3) development strategies or poverty reduction strategies which were broadened by including sustainable development principles and policies.

In 2014, a report compiled for Bertelsmann Foundation counted a much smaller number as they referred to strategies at national or subnational level that explicitly aimed to achieve sustainable development in all its dimensions (Jacob et al. 2014, p. 309). Their account reveals only 24 NSDSs (nine of them in developing countries, notably Bhutan, Brazil, China, Costa Rica, Ecuador, Ghana, India, South Africa, Zambia), while they identified 17 strategies at subnational level and 3 strategies in cities (Stockholm, Copenhagen, Vienna).[1] At the same time, the website of the

European Sustainable Development Network lists 27 NSDSs in Europe alone.[2] Currently, there is no easily accessible documentation on the number and implementation state of NSDSs available anymore at UN websites.[3]

Global policy debates concerned with sustainable development today are not focused around NSDSs anymore but around Sustainable Development Goals (SDGs) and related indicators. The SDGs were the most palpable outcome of the Rio+20 summit in Rio de Janeiro 2012: the final outcome document *The Future We Want* dedicates a whole section with seven paragraphs to Sustainable Development Goals, while it mentions NSDS only once (United Nations 2012, p. 46).[4] In early June 2015, the zero draft for the Post-2015 Agenda which will include the SDGs was published (United Nations 2015).

NSDSs may be one instrument for national governments aspiring to implement the SDGs as mentioned in the zero draft. But the international debate has not paid much attention to implementation strategies such as NSDSs in recent years and instead focussed much more on goals and indicators. This is surprising as indicators have been integral elements of many NSDSs for a long time. So, what is the current relevance of NSDSs after two decades of existence? Are NSDSs on the decline, and if so why? Or are the adoption of SDGs and eventual national implementation strategies offering a promising future for reviving this instrument?

In order to answer these questions, the chapter proceeds as follows: in the second section, the concept of NSDSs, as defined by the Organization for Economic Co-operation and Development (OECD) and the UN will be presented. The third section will present some NSDSs from rich and poor countries in order to show the variety of current approaches to sustainable development strategizing. The fourth section will focus on problems of policy coordination and governance of sustainable development, while the fifth section briefly describes the main innovative features of the SDGs and the new light they shed on NSDSs.

The concept of national strategies for sustainable development

Strategies for sustainable development aim at steering processes and measures for economic development so as to generate positive social and environmental outcomes and to avoid or limit possible negative impacts. From the perspective of strategic planning this requires that social and environmental variables and goals are integrated from the start into economic policymaking. Compared to mainstream economic thinking and policymaking, this approach is rather innovative and demanding as it requires the integration of social and environmental concerns into economic policymaking across sectors (i.e. agriculture, energy, land use, infrastructure). In order to support developing countries in this endeavour and to provide guidance for development agencies keen to support NSDS elaboration and implementation, the OECD Development Assistance Committee (DAC) and the UN set up working groups with the task of elaborating concepts and guidelines and analysing existing experience in order to identify best practices.

The definitions and guidance documents elaborated by the OECD and by the UN Department of Economic and Social Affairs (UNDESA) in 2001/2002 are still considered as the main conceptual sources today, more than a decade later. The OECD defines a strategy for sustainable development as comprising a:

> co-ordinated set of participatory and continuously improving processes of analysis, debate, capacity-strengthening, planning and investment, which seeks to integrate the short and long term economic, social and environmental objectives of society – through mutually supportive approaches wherever possible – and manages trade-offs where this is not possible.
>
> (OECD 2001, p. 25)

UNDESA's definition states that:

> a national sustainable development strategy is a coordinated, participatory and iterative process of thoughts and actions to achieve economic, environmental and social objectives in a balanced and integrated manner. The process encompasses situation analysis, formulation of policies and action plans, implementation, monitoring and regular review. It is a cyclical and interactive process of planning, participation and action in which the emphasis is on managing progress towards sustainability goals rather than producing a "plan" as an end product.
>
> (UNDESA 2002, p. 1)

Both definitions and guidelines are very similar in their emphasis on processes which combine action based on knowledge (problem analysis, monitoring and evaluation of the NSDS), on policy (formulation and implementation of policies and action plans) and on participation of multiple stakeholders inside and outside government. Both UNDESA and OECD are much more specific when defining the requirements of planning processes for NSDSs and their coordination than with regards to the goals of NSDSs as they consider the latter as context specific and as the outcome of specific policy processes. Goals are therefore formally defined as a balanced set of objectives which are the result of a coordinated set of processes including participation, communications, analysis, debate, investment and capacity development. Goals need to be regularly revised and adjusted through monitoring and review.

UNDESA (2002) formulated five basic elements for effective NSDSs which build on and include many of the 12 key principles elaborated previously by the OECD DAC:

• promoting country ownership and commitment,
• integrating economic, social and environmental objectives across sectors, territories and generations,
• ensuring broad participation and effective partnerships,
• developing capacity and an enabling environment, and
• focusing on outcomes and means of implementation.

Similarly, the OECD's guidance can be summarized in four basic requirements which need to be fulfilled so that the resulting document can be considered as an NSDS:[5]

- they have to address economic, social and environmental objectives,
- they have to rely on participatory processes of analysis and decision-making in order to balance out trade-offs,
- they have to include specific measures for investment, capacity strengthening and monitoring of results,
- they have to be based on a transparent and robust coordination system that guarantees the above mentioned processes.

At the core of the OECD guidance are 12 key principles which were considered necessary for an effective NSDS. They were derived from an analysis of previous positive and negative experiences with development planning and other sectoral plans in developing countries. UNDESA had followed a similar analytical approach in its own document. They were explicitly listed as each being equally important and detail the meaning of "people-centred approach", "comprehensive and reliable analysis" and "comprehensive and integrative" design of a strategy.

Already five years later, the OECD presented a much leaner and less ambitious view on the role and function of NSDSs. In order to scrutinize the NSDSs elaborated by OECD members, an analytical framework was elaborated that reduced the key elements from 12 to 8 and changed the emphasis in several areas. The analytical framework included (OECD 2006, pp. 7–8):

1   Policy integration – national strategies should give consideration to environmental, economic and social concerns in integrated approaches contained in national plans and reports.
2   Intergenerational timeframe – national strategies should adopt long-term timeframes which enable inclusion of intergenerational principles and indicators.
3   Analysis and assessments – integrated assessment tools should be used in national reports to identify the environmental, economic and social costs and benefits of policy and strategy options.
4   Co-ordination and institutions – a wide range of government departments and agencies should be involved in the formulation and implementation of national strategies, with overall responsibility in the office of the Prime Minister or equivalent.
5   Local and regional governance – local and regional authorities should be fully involved in the development of national strategies, with certain delivery aspects devolved to sub-national levels.
6   Stakeholder participation – stakeholders (e.g., business, unions, nongovernmental organisations) should participate with government representatives in commissions responsible for developing and implementing national strategies.

7   Indicators and targets – strategies should be based on structured indicator systems (enumerated in national plans and reports) to assist in monitoring progress and to serve as quantitative targets.
8   Monitoring and evaluation – independent bodies or processes should be established to act as watchdogs monitoring implementation of national strategies and providing recommendations for their improvement.

These eight key elements are not further elaborated nor is their meaning explained more in detail. A table which compares these eight key elements with the guidance published in 2002 by the UN makes an implicit reference to the OECD guidance of 2001. No explicit comparison is made, though, and an opportunity of evaluating the practical policy experiences with NSDSs in the OECD member states against the original concept of 2001 was thus missed.

A comparison of the eight key elements of 2006 with the detailed description of the 12 key elements of 2001 reveals three main areas of differences. First, with regard to the subjects of sustainable development strategies: in 2001, there had been a clear reference to the poor. The OECD had clearly stated that the people-centred approach should ensure "long-term beneficial impacts on disadvantaged and marginalized groups" and consider "the entitlements and possible needs of future generations" (OECD 2001, p. 27). This explicit reference is missing in the key elements of 2006. Moreover, the OECD analysis clearly shows that "most national strategies have a greater focus on environmental issues with some attempts to incorporate economic aspects. The social pillar has been the most neglected. As a result, few national strategies develop abilities for considering and making trade-offs among the three areas in overall policy-making" (OECD 2006, p. 15).

Second, changes in the institutional constituency behind sustainable development strategies: the analysis of 2006 shows that in "most OECD countries, overall responsibility for strategy implementation is housed in the Ministry of Environment either directly or indirectly through a co-ordinating committee which it oversees" (OECD 2006, p. 21). Only in a few OECD countries responsibility was placed with the prime minister's office or some equivalent. This trend shows how difficult it was to implement the guidance of 2001 which had recommended embedding the strategy in high-level government commitment and influential lead institutions in order to ensure a comprehensive approach. As a result, environmental objectives dominate in most NSDSs. In principle, this could be remedied by ensuring broad participation of non-governmental actors which:

> helps to open up debate to new ideas and sources of information; expose issues that need to be addressed; enable problems, needs and preferences to be expressed; identify the capabilities required to address them; and develop a consensus on the need for action that leads to better implementation.
>
> (OECD 2001, p. 27)

But an NSDS with an environmental bias is likely to mainly attract environmental non-government organizations (NGOs). With regard to participation, the

OECD (2006) merely lists consultation processes and institutions which exist in member states without analysing their effective impact on the elaboration of NSDSs, i.e. the selection of goals and indicators or the negotiation of trade-offs and their implicit value judgements.

Third, the adoption of implementation instruments and continuous improvement: the analysis of 2006 shows that not all instruments recommended in 2001 were put in place. In 2001, a high emphasis had been put on linking the targets of an NSDS with budgetary priorities. Information on such links, however, is missing completely in the OECD analysis of 2006 as there is no information on whether NSDSs have an impact on budget formulation. Instead, emphasis in 2006 is put on indicators and targets that should sustain the strategy. In 2001, indicators were mentioned merely for purposes of monitoring. The role of analysis and assessments has also changed: in 2001, analysis needed for elaborating and continuously improving the strategy had been described as "comprehensive and reliable analysis ... of the present situation" which includes "forecasted trends and risks, and the links between local, national and global challenges", "external pressures on a country – such as those resulting from globalisation, or the impacts of global climate change" and "credible and reliable information on changing environmental, social and economic conditions, pressures and responses, and their correlations with strategy objectives and indicators" (OECD 2001, p. 27). In 2006, this is reduced to the recommendation of using integrated assessment tools in order to identify the environmental, social and economic costs and benefits of policies. For continuously improving the strategy, however, it would be fruitful to engage in deeper analysis of linkages between implemented policies at different levels and their (positive or negative) outcomes, as detailed in 2001. Another approach considered essential in 2001 was that NSDSs build on existing processes and strategies to enable "convergence, complementarity and coherence between different planning frameworks and policies" and "to identify and resolve potential conflicts" (OECD 2001, p. 27). Building on existing policies and strategies is mentioned in 2006 only with regards to analysis and assessment, but not anymore as a key ingredient for improving policy coordination.

The conviction that NSDS should have the ambition to push for and facilitate policy change and policy coordination towards sustainable development in its three dimensions breathes through the documents of the OECD DAC (2001) and UNDESA (2002), but it is hard to find in the document issued by the OECD in 2006. How this ambition changed and has been redefined over time will be discussed in the fourth section of this chapter, after a fresh look at current NSDSs in rich and poor countries in the third section.

NSDS in rich and poor countries: a few examples

Although currently the bulk of NSDSs seems to be European, there are also examples of NSDSs in developing countries.[6] A review of the 54 country profiles collected at the website of the global network of national councils for sustainable development and similar bodies (www.ncsds.org) shows that only 19 of them have an NSDS or an equivalent strategy from the environmental realm. About 12 countries are listed where councils for sustainable development have been closed down, among them Australia, Bolivia, the Democratic Republic of Congo, Japan, Lithuania, Mongolia, the United Kingdom and Sweden. Still, about 53 countries have either a council or a committee for policy coordination, in most cases dominated by government representatives. The information presented in the website suggests, however, that only a few of these strategies and councils play an active role in policymaking towards sustainable development.

The selection of cases in this chapter[7] focused on two criteria: first, countries should actively pursue sustainable development policies and have an NSDS or similar strategies with recent updates or related reports. All countries in the sample fulfil this criterion. Second, the cases should reflect different types of NSDSs and institutional settings embodied in these strategies. Bangladesh, Germany, Taiwan and Finland are examples of NSDS documents that exist parallel to strategy processes anchored in ministries and whose real influence on policymaking is either unclear or weak. Canada and Korea are examples for strategies with a specific focus on one dimension of sustainability (environmental impacts, green growth). Costa Rica and Bhutan combine long-term policy learning processes on sustainability with specific national policy frameworks (Bhutan 2020 and Gross National Happiness in one case, and the National Development Plan as the framework where sectoral policies converge in the other). The description of the cases concentrates on the main features of NSDSs as defined in the OECD concept (see bibliography for more details on individual NSDSs).

Countries with NSDSs as separate documents

Bangladesh's National Strategy for Sustainable Development 2010–21 was prepared with support from the UN Development Programme (UNDP) and adopted in 2013.[8] In 2007, the process was started by the Ministry of Environment and Forest which presented a draft strategy to the Cabinet in 2009. Then, responsibility was shifted to the General Economics Division of the National Planning Commission (Government of Bangladesh 2013, p. 3).

The strategy responds to both future development needs and explicitly also to:

> the formidable environmental challenges that Bangladesh faces in the way to development … [including] degraded agro-ecosystem, rivers and wetlands, coastal environment and urban environment, degradation and depletion of ground water, deforestation and desertification in different parts of the country. Equally and perhaps more important are the challenges arising from global climate change induced by the production and consumption patterns of other countries especially the developed and fast growing developing countries that exert multiple impacts on our development. Apart from the domestic exigencies, NSDS fulfils Bangladesh's commitment to the international community to formulate and implement a sustainable development strategy addressing environmental issues.
>
> (Government of Bangladesh 2013, p. 3)

The strategy is separate from but aligned with the Perspective Plan 2010–2021 which aims at transforming the country into a middle-income country – therefore it comes as no surprise that sustained economic growth is the first strategic area of action identified in the strategy, followed by development of priority sectors (which include agriculture, industry, energy, transport and human resource development), urban environment, social security and protection, and environment, natural resource and disaster management. Three cross-cutting areas will be considered by policymaking: disaster risk reduction and climate change adaptation, good governance and gender. The NSDS thus aims at the three dimensions of sustainable development and the inter-linkages between them. Despite this breadth of sectors, monitoring will focus on 29 indicators only (Government of Bangladesh 2013, pp. 141–142).

Governance arrangements reflect a balance between mainstreaming – by locating responsibility with the Ministry of Planning and including a wide number of relevant ministries – and maintaining the expertise and ownership of the Ministry of Environment and Forest. Implementation of the NSDS will be supervised and monitored by the Sustainable Development Monitoring Council (SDMC) which is chaired by the minister of planning. The SDMC has 49 members, including the minister of environment and forest, 3 members of Parliament, 20 secretaries of other ministries concerned and representatives of other state agencies, the private sector and civil society. The sessions of the SDMC will be supported by technical reports prepared by the Sustainable Development Board which has 18 members from different ministries and is located with the Ministry of Environment and Forest. The NSDS features rather weak links with subnational levels: they were heard during local consultations but are not included in implementation.

In 1993 **Finland** was the first country to establish a national commission for sustainable development (Niestroy et al. 2013b). Since then it has gathered much experience with the design, implementation and review of sustainable development strategies. The Finnish National Commission for Sustainable Development (FNCSD) is led by the prime minister and comprises representatives of the executive and the Parliament, of civil society (private sector, trade unions, churches, NGOs) and academia. It meets once every three months and works with subcommittees that elaborate quantitative targets and detailed programmes for action. The FNCSD is supported by an inter-ministerial secretariat for horizontal coordination which gathers 20 representatives of different ministries and other institutions, under the lead of the environment ministry. Despite these coordinating bodies, the trend had been to develop sectoral strategies and programmes which meant that the steering effect of the national strategy was rather low (Lepuschitz 2014, p. 5). In order to remedy this situation, a stocktaking and reformulation process was started which lead in 2013 to the adoption of a new document called *The Finland we Want by 2050 – Society's Commitment to Sustainable Development*. This document establishes eight shared goals which will be operationalized through commitments worked out by government entities and a broad variety of non-governmental actors. Performance indicators are also stated to be part of the document.[9] Whether this process can achieve a new quality in sustainable strategizing and more coherence will be proven by the operational commitments and their implementation in the future.

Germany's sustainability strategy follows a different approach. The strategy was adopted in 2002 and has since been updated twice. Reporting is done on a bi-annual basis by the Statistics Office; the last report covered 21 goals and 38 indicators. The goals are quantified and should be achieved by 2020. The NSDS covers four dimensions of sustainability: intergenerational justice (i.e. resource efficiency, climate protection, renewable energies, biodiversity, innovation, education), quality of life (i.e. economic growth, mobility, agriculture, air quality, health and nutrition), social cohesion (i.e. employment, gender equality, integration) and international responsibility (development cooperation, imports from developing countries) (Bundesregierung 2012, pp. 29–31). Of the 21 indicators, 11 are related to environmental objectives which hardly can be interpreted as an environmental bias, as is clearly the case in Canada. The measures adopted for implementation in 2010, however, show such a bias as 10 out of 12 measures refer to energy and resource efficiency and to emissions reductions (Staatssekretärsausschuss für nachhaltige Entwicklung 2010). The three dimensions of sustainable development employed in the elaboration of the strategy become more visible in the progress reports to which all ministries contribute.

The governance structure of the German NSDS includes overall coordination by the Federal Chancellery, the State Secretary Committee for Sustainable Development which monitors implementation and further elaboration of the NSDS, a Parliamentary Body for Sustainable Development which is responsible for a formal sustainability review of law projects, and the Council for Sustainable Development which consists of 15 representatives from academia, the private sector and civil society with the task to give advice to the federal government and promote public awareness and dialogue on sustainability. The second peer review of the NSDS published in 2013 recognized Germany's "well-developed institutional framework as considerable strengths in the country's ability to deal with these challenges" but also saw weak horizontal and vertical coordination and a lack of vision (Stigsson et al. 2013, pp. 19–20): interministerial work is complicated by the principle of ministerial autonomy, which is reflected by sectoral committees in the Parliament. There is no explicit coordination between the federal NSDS and similar strategies owned by the federal states or cities.

It is expected that the content and the timeframe of the SDGs which was adopted by the UN in September 2015 will be considered in the current review and update process of the NSDS.

By comparison, **Taiwan** seems to stick to the conventional model of the comprehensive NSDS with an environmental focus (National Council for Sustainable Development Taiwan 2013). The NSDS was first elaborated in 1997, as a follow-up to the Rio Summit in 1992, and it was granted legal status in 2002. The latest annual report available was issued in 2013 and it shows that the strategy is rather an action plan, and that reporting focuses on output, not on outcome. Reporting is not done against quantified goals for improving performance, but rather with the intent to induce incremental improvements in the nine sectors covered by working groups. These include energy conservation, carbon reduction and climate change; land and resources; biodiversity; transportation; technology; urban and rural development; health and welfare and education. Since 2004, national awards for outstanding accomplishments in sustainable development are given in order to raise awareness and show practical advantages of changed behaviour. Awards are given to elementary schools, enterprises, civic associations and public agencies. In 2013, debates in the National Council for Sustainable Development focused on the outcome of the Rio+20 Conference, and the working groups were instructed to adjust their programmes to the results of this conference. The programmes are funded through the national budget.

Countries with NSDSs that emphasize one dimension

Canada started with an innovative whole-of-government approach in the 1990s (Volkery et al. 2006) and has arrived at a stage today where sustainable development is again under the responsibility of the environment ministry. In 1995 Canada chose a decentralized model which required 31 government departments and agencies to develop departmental sustainable development strategies – with an environmental focus – which were reviewed annually by the Auditor General. In 2008, however, the system was changed with the Federal Sustainable Development Act which laid the basis for a federal strategy[10] to be developed by the environment ministry with contributions by several other departments. The federal strategy is closely integrated with annual departmental budgetary planning and reporting. The Act instituted an office for sustainable development with Environment Canada as well as several committees and working groups for coordination among the executive. At the subnational level, provinces such as Manitoba and Quebec have passed their own sustainable development acts, and there are also integrated community sustainability plans at local level which are incentivized by a federal programme funded with the gas tax revenue (UNOSD 2012, p. 18).

The same Act also created the position of the commissioner of the environment and sustainable development at the Auditor General. The commissioner "conducts performance audits, and is responsible for assessing whether federal government departments are meeting their sustainable development objectives, and overseeing the environmental petitions process".[11] The National Round Table on the Environment and the Economy which had existed as an independent public advisory body to the government since 1988 was abolished in 2013 by the conservative government. Environment Canada now has a Sustainable Development Advisory Council which is chaired by the minister of the environment and which gives advice to the minister on drafts of the Federal Sustainable Development Srategy. Members are both governmental and non-governmental; they are appointed by, and report directly to, the minister of the environment.

In **Korea** the National Strategy for Sustainable Development (NSSD) adopted in 2006 was replaced in 2008 by the **National Strategy for Green Growth**. The NSSD had built on Korea's National Action Plan to implement Agenda 21 and on the sectoral plans elaborated by the Presidential Commission for Sustainable Development which had been established in 2000. These sectoral strategies had covered energy, water, coastal waters, land, climate change, transportation, conflict management and development cooperation, and were implemented by the responsible departments (Young-Keun Chung & Kumju Hwang 2006). In 2008, however, Korea's strategy underwent paradigmatic reform by replacing sustainable development with green growth – at strategy and institutional levels. With this move, Korea aimed at becoming an "early mover" in addressing climate change, in becoming the first non-Annex I country of the UN Framework Convention on Climate Change (UNFCCC) to set a voluntary emissions reduction target and to institute a "new paradigm to economic development (which) seeks to break away from the conflicting nature of 'green' and 'growth' and achieve economic growth while maintaining environmental integrity" (Korea Country Profile at www.ncsds.org). The strategy covers the years 2009–2050 and its ten policy agendas have a clear emphasis on mitigation policies in energy, transport, building, industry, water use and agriculture. Compared to a standard NSDS, the range of objectives and sectors covered is much narrower. However, the clear focus of the strategy and the considerable public funding attached to it (US$30.7 billion to be spent between 2009 and 2013) may increase its impact considerably (Jones & Yoo 2011). The Five-Year-Plan 2009–2013 outlined government actions (by ministries and local governments) for implementation of the strategy.

Countries with integrated national frameworks for sustainable development

Bhutan is known for the conceptual approach elaborated by King Jigme Singye Wangchuck within the opening and modernization process of the country: the concept of gross national happiness (GNH) first emerged at the end of the 1970s and was laid out in the document *Bhutan 2020: A vision for peace, prosperity and happiness* published in 1999. The vision and the concept integrate human, cultural, economic, institutional and environmental dimensions of prosperity and aim at improving people's satisfaction with life. Bhutan 2020 is implemented through the five year plans, which are elaborated by the Commission for Gross National Happiness, an interministerial body which includes the prime minister, the secretaries of all ten ministries, the president of the National Environment Commission and the secretary for GNH. Further instruments which shall ensure mainstreaming of the GNH principles and objectives are the environmental impact assessment (which includes strategic environmental assessment) and a screening process at all levels of administration to ensure that programmes and measures obey the GNH principles. Screening has real impacts; the Bertelsmann Stiftung reports that it impeded important projects such as applying for World Trade Organization (WTO) membership, building a large hydrological power plant and a mining project (Niestroy et al. 2013a, p. 78). The 38 subindices and 33 indicators of the GNH Index have been monitored twice (2008 and 2010) in order to measure the GNH state.

    Costa Rica is a country which excels in elaborating ambitious policies for sustainable development without focusing on an NSDS as such. Already in the 1970s the country devised an active policy for forest protection and afforestation, given its extremely high deforestation rates. The funding of this policy initially relied on subsidies of afforestation, in the mid-1990s these were substituted by a system of payments for ecosystem services which were first supported by international funding and later by a tax on fossil fuel sales. In 1990, the newly created Ministry of Environment and Energy published a strategy for resource protection and sustainable development which presented a sharp analysis of the challenges for sustainability and formulated ambitious goals, including areas clearly beyond the natural environment, such as energy, water, tourism and health. In the 1990s, the country started to actively support the development of ecotourism, which today is an important part of its economy. In 2007, the country announced its decision to be climate-neutral by 2021. Since 2011, Costa Rica has a National Development Plan (NDP) which explicitly includes environmental protection and territorial planning as one of its four areas of strategic action. The NDP covers four years and is legally binding for all ministries; it is elaborated and monitored annually by the Ministry of Planning and Political Economy (MIDEPLAN). The NDP 2011–14 had 11 goals with one indicator each in five areas (competitiveness; equality and solidarity; security; balance between economic growth and the environment; democratic governance and modernization of the state). The judiciary has a trajectory of deciding against economic projects when they bring a high environmental burden with them, similar to the results of GNH screening processes in Bhutan (Keller et al. 2013, p. 100).

Comparison and conclusion

Comparing these country cases, it seems clear that the catalytic potential ascribed to NSDSs in the early concepts developed by OECD and UN has only rarely been used. In the three developing countries considered in this brief review – Bangladesh, Bhutan and Costa Rica – international cooperation has played an important role in supporting domestic processes towards sustainable strategizing, especially through the United Nations Programmes for Environment and Development respectively (UNEP and UNDP), the Global Environmental Facility (GEF) and bilateral programmes (the Netherlands and Switzerland). The relevance of the strategies and instruments developed, however, depended more on domestic priorities and long-term learning processes than on external steering and support, as is clearly shown by the examples of Bhutan and Costa Rica. Bangladesh, Canada and Taiwan seem to be examples for strategies developed within the environmental realm and therefore are burdened with difficulties of leaving that policy sector and becoming influential in social and economic policymaking. Canada refined its instruments for environmental impact assessment, and still it explores its tar sands and seems to have abandoned climate policy. Finland, Germany and Korea are OECD countries with distinct approaches: Finland and Germany adhere to the classic approach of aggregated sustainability strategies, and the question arises whether their processes, instruments and goals are able to influence priority setting and policymaking in the major relevant policy fields, or whether they turned into a specialized policy process parallel to other processes. Korea instead abolished its SDS in favour of a green growth strategy with a strong focus on greenhouse gas emission reduction and clean technologies.

Thus the question arises whether NSDSs really are tools to enhance strategic decision making and what is needed for effectively using them as an "opportunity to take stock and fix priorities" and as "an occasion to focus debate, build consensus, examine trade-offs and make choices" (Meadowcroft 2007, p. 157). In their analysis of integrated strategies in 15 European countries, Casado-Asensio and Steurer (2014, p. 459) come to the conclusion that in practice integrated strategies "usually fail as integrative governance processes" and "prove to be comparatively weak administrative routines" that are "preoccupied with low-key communication rather than high-profile policy coordination". The following section will shed some light on the governance challenges faced by NSDSs and other integrated strategies in order to explain this failure.

Governance challenges of NSDSs

Integrated policies usually are "grand design policies" with the ambition of improving policy coordination and coherence in order to address complex and persistent environmental problems that "affect several policy sectors, and all levels of governance, are resistant to simple technological fixes and challenge established patterns of governance, policymaking, economic practices, social norms and individual behaviours" (Casado-Asensio & Steurer 2014, p. 438). It is no coincidence that environmental policy analysis has developed a focus on multidimensional problems whose solutions require complex and new approaches as it is a typical feature of environmental problems that (1) their causes are often located outside the direct area of influence of environmental policy, and (2) that economic and social objectives are directly represented in relevant polities and more deeply rooted in relevant institutions and regulations while environmental objectives are not, which makes them much more difficult to deal with.

Sustainable development, however, is not primarily or mainly concerned with environmental problems. Some would say that it is about the linkages and trade-offs between environmental, social and economic objectives, others that it is about the frictions between the natural system and the social system which in turn includes the difficulties of making social and economic objectives and processes compatible with each other (cf. Chapter 1 in this volume by Michael von Hauff et al.). With a view to governance or policy coordination, it makes a difference whether one adopts the perspective of ensuring coherence between three different (and interdependent) dimensions (as exemplified by the concepts described in this chapter) or whether one adopts a co-evolutionary systems perspective in which the social system is characterized by historically and institutionally different ways of combining social and economic objectives, which in turn have different requirements of and impacts on the natural system in which it is embedded (cf. Norgaard 1994; Kemp et al. 2007; Loorbach 2010).

The first approach makes it paramount to design incentives as well as policy instruments and processes that promote coordination and coherence – based on a rather mechanistic understanding of policy processes and related conflicts between objectives and interests. Governance challenges from this perspective (see Table 2.1)

Table 2.1 Governance challenges for sustainable development from a government-centred perspective

Principle	*Governance challenges of sustainable development (SD) strategies*
(1) Common vision and strategic objectives	An SD strategy should define a common long-term vision for SD; the vision for SD should be operationalized with strategic objectives that are SMART (**S**pecific – ideally stating a quantified target; **M**easurable – with SD indicators, see below; **A**chievable – neither too easy nor too demanding; **R**ealistic – to be achieved with the given resources and political circumstances; **T**ime-bound – indicating a start date and target year).
(2) High-level commitment	An SD strategy should be backed by high-level political commitment (from the entire government, from influential lead institutions).
(3) Horizontal integration	The integration of economic, environmental and social issues should be taken into account: in the SD strategy document (e.g. by highlighting links and trade-offs between the three dimensions of SD); in the governance of the SD strategy (e.g. by establishing interministerial bodies that are responsible for implementing the SD strategy).
(4) Vertical integration	An SD strategy should be in line with priorities and implementation activities at other levels of governments (European Union, national/federal, regional, local).
(5) Participation	Different stakeholder groups should be involved in the development and implementation of an SD strategy (participatory activities can be informational, consultative or decisional, and they can make use of different tools and mechanisms, such as permanent councils for SD, ad-hoc stakeholder dialogues, informative/consultative internet actions, etc).
(6) Implementation mechanisms and capacity-building	The objectives of an SD strategy should be addressed with (1) provisions and mechanisms of implementation (budgeting, annual or bi-annual work/action plans) in which political responsibilities are clearly defined; and (2) adequate institutional and/or personal capacities or capacity building activities that are necessary to achieve the objectives.
(7) Monitoring, evaluation and strategy renewal	The effectiveness of an SD strategy in achieving its objectives should be (1) monitored continuously with a set of SD indicators (mostly quantitatively); and (2) reviewed/evaluated in regular intervals (mostly qualitatively). Monitoring and reviewing results/reports should be considered in the continuous adjustment and the cyclical renewal of an SD strategy so that evidence-based policy learning takes place.

Source: Elaborated by the ESDN Office at the Institute for Managing Sustainability, Vienna University of Economics and Business, n.d.

include the need to ensure a shared long-term vision across government and a broad diversity of stakeholders, high-level commitment to SDS, adequate horizontal and vertical integration, participation processes and budgeting as well as procedures for monitoring and strategy renewal.[12]

The governance traps associated with this approach are well known: goals remain too vague and fail to change the compartmentalized nature of policymaking and to reduce institutional inertia and path dependency. In addition, integrated strategies are often driven by environmental actors which – both as environmental departments within ministries or as environmental ministries within government – generally have a weak standing (Asensio-Casado & Steurer 2014, p. 459).

The second approach allows conceiving advances in the sustainability of human societies and their interaction with nature as a result of more specific policies which promote change in specific subsystems and have positive feedback effects on other, related subsystems. The basic difference in the understanding of governance systems is that systems theory views subsystems, first, as units which "enjoy relative autonomy in their development" (Kemp et al. 2007, p. 80), but which are, second, interrelated through "cause-effect-cause loops across different scales and systems, with effects becoming causes of other developments ('positive feedback' in systems terms" (ibid., p. 79). Subsystems such as technology and institutions may shape each other and thus co-evolve, but they do not *determine* each other. Third, change is seen as a transition from one equilibrium state to another by a slow process which is punctuated by periods of radical change.

For governance processes to promote societal co-evolutionary change it follows that attention should focus on supporting the transition from one state of the subsystem to another in a gradual way through network-based processes of decision-making, innovation and experimentation (for a detailed description, see Loorbach 2010). The transition management approach has been developed in the Netherlands where it has been applied to changing the waste management system from a waste-as-waste perspective to a waste-as-a-resource perspective, and for switching energy supply from coal to gas. These changes are partial and incremental if judged from the level of ambition of some of the NSDSs described in this chapter. Still, they describe a different understanding of the dynamics of change. In order to achieve broader society-wide changes, it would be necessary to focus on subsystems that have many linkages with other subsystems and thus may trigger positive feedback effects. One example for such subsystems is the transition from fossil-fuel based energy technologies to renewable technologies which has direct effects not only on greenhouse gas emissions (and thus global warming) but also on air quality, human health and environmental impacts associated with oil, gas and coal exploitation, and indirect effects on the reproduction and stability of political elites and economic power associated to them, to name just a few.

Achieving sustainable development is thus seen as a society-wide process and not as centred on a government that develops a coherent long-term vision and coordination processes that balance out diverging interests and powers. Kemp et al. (2007) identify five main governance problems of transition management in contemporary industrial societies that need to be addressed (see Table 2.2 below) over the long-term in a managed process, in order to "help alter regimes of governance and nested hierarchies in the provision of goods and services through processes of variation and selection – of beliefs, concepts, artifacts and institutions" (ibid., p. 82).

Table 2.2 Governance challenges of sustainable development from a systems perspective

Governance problem	Description	Solution
Dissent	Complex societal problems are characterized by dissent on their nature, priorities and means for solving them; long-term impacts are uncertain.	Continuous and iterative deliberation and assessment; agreement on key parameters for a future system and on non-sustainable aspects of current system.
Distributed control	In pluricentric societies control is distributed over various actors with different beliefs, interests and resources, making unitary action impossible.	Cooperation and inclusive network management concerned with long-term aims and transition processes
Determination of short-term steps	How to achieve long-term change through short-term steps is unclear.	A dual strategy of forward reasoning (trend analysis, forecasts, reflexive experimental learning) and back-casting (identify past experiments, pathways, robust options and derive goals).
Danger of lock-in	Particular solutions that look attractive in the short-term but are not optimal in the long-term.	Develop and use a portfolio of options; regularly review and adapt the portfolio and support given to it.
Political myopia	Transitions in socio-technical systems take one generation or more; transition management must survive several political cycles.	Create a transition arena outside regular political cycles for focus on long-term and on in-depth analysis of the problem and options for its solution; establish a transition agenda that allows the change process to co-evolve with changing circumstances and political wishes.

Source: Kemp et al. 2007, pp. 81–82

The European Sustainable Development Network considers that sustainable development strategies need to move "from grand rigid planning schemes to flexible strategy processes, accompanied by a transition from clear-cut sectoral authorities to cross-cutting competencies, from pure hierarchies to an amalgamation of hierarchies and networks, from top-down control to process and policy assessments, and from knowing to learning".[13] As has been shown it makes a difference, though, whether governance procedures and institutions are conceived as geared towards the implementation of a comprehensive strategy (an ideal-type NSDS) or towards more narrow transition processes in sub-systems with an anticipated wider impact.

In any case, policymakers in the various sectors will have to leave their cozy niches and face a rather steep learning curve for integrated policy approaches, either pushed by integrated strategies or by active transition management. The number of stakeholders involved grows which requires more coordination effort and more time. Successfully concluded negotiations will lead to complex compromises that are only an approximation to first best solutions. Planning for sustainable development thus challenges many features of current political and societal practice. In democracies, the main concern is about political priorities and action conceived within electoral cycles and not on the long term. This implies the risk that policy learning on how to conceive, promote and implement transformative change is endangered by the short-term cycles of political competition, and also the societal consensus on the need and direction of long-term change. This is important as transformative change towards sustainability is not a technological operation carried out by political and economic elites. Instead, it requires continuous investment in social dialogue and support. Autocratic regimes may face considerable difficulty with engaging in such society-wide processes, especially as their economies and societies will become more pluricentric, too, the more their economies and societies are integrated in regional and global markets and communication processes.

Specific governance challenges arise through the need to include the poor and marginalized sectors of the population into this transition process, too. This is not only a problem for developing countries as inequality and exclusion are processes increasingly faced by rich countries as well. In low- and middle-income countries, the challenge has two main dimensions: first, how to ensure that transformation processes towards sustainability do not only address problems of economic efficiency and environmental sustainability, but provide substantial and durable improvements for the lowest income groups of society. Second, how to ensure that additional income available to emerging middle classes does not reinforce non-sustainable consumption patterns prevalent in rich countries (Guarín & Knorringa 2015).

Sustainable Development Goals 2016–2030: a way forward?

In the 1990s, a series of world summits (on topics such as environment, social policy, women, population, human rights) had contributed to raising awareness of the international community that domestic policies needed to be sustained by efforts in global cooperation or governance for achieving welfare gains (Messner & Nuscheler 2007). Development cooperation was seen as a crucial instrument for promoting comprehensive and integrated approaches to development, and thus national strategies and plans for poverty reduction and sustainable development became a favoured instrument in cooperation with developing countries. NSDSs fitted well into this picture. Their real influence on policy implementation, however, remained rather limited as the added value of the strategy documents often was not clear. Often, they were thus perceived mainly as a condition imposed by donors, and sectoral policy programmes and measures remained essentially unchanged (Bojo & Reddy 2002). Thus, despite the relative importance of official development assistance (ODA) for funding public budgets and investment in developing countries, donor-funded strategies did not succeed in mainstreaming integrated approaches, neither in development cooperation nor in developing countries.

Most importantly, donors themselves changed their strategic approach a decade later when they adopted the Millennium Development Goals (MDGs) which privileged poverty reduction as overarching concept and strategic objective and not sustainable development. The MDGs introduced seven quantified global goals in the areas of income poverty, health, education, gender and access to clean water with specific indicators for monitoring progress. An eighth goal specified the supportive action to be delivered by rich countries, in particular mobilising 0.7 per cent of gross domestic product (GDP) for ODA (and thus funding measures for achieving the MDGs). The MDGs were successful in coordinating donor funding. Many positive changes were achieved although it remains unclear how much of these really can be attributed to ODA flows (Rippin 2013; Loewe 2014). The implicit message of the MDGs was that development was a need of the South, and that development cooperation was the main ingredient to make it happen. Certainly policy coherence for development was mentioned in Goal 8, but not much progress was achieved in this area of action (Ashoff 2005).

The MDGs provided an important learning experience for global cooperation: agreement on specific goals and indicators could help to focus and coordinate bilateral and multilateral action. This experience was one important influencing factor in the debate on sustainable development goals that emerged in the preparation process for the Rio+20 conference. Another influencing factor was the disillusionment with the slow implementation of multilateral environmental agreements. In order to make progress in orienting national sustainability policies towards shared objectives and common goals, Colombia and Guatemala proposed in 2011 that negotiating parties should agree on universal SDGs which would reduce poverty in a context of sustainability. Implementation would be based on national plans following national needs and conditions, translating the globally agreed goals into national targets and thus contributing to the achievement of the global goals.

Since the SDGs were adopted by the UN General Assembly in September 2015, countries are faced with the need to devise such national goals and to implement them via NSDSs or more loosely connected sectoral policies and programmes. More focused sectoral transformation strategies are needed, too (Casado-Asensio & Steurer 2014, p. 460), and it is hoped that the pressure to report on SDG implementation progress at the UN will help to trigger them.

This turn to intergovernmental negotiations on universal goals, and global/national implementation, also reflects the changes in economic and political power which occurred during the last decade. The MDGs had been elaborated by a team of UN development experts; developing countries themselves had no say in their elaboration (Rippin 2013). In bilateral negotiations with donors, poor countries often could not object to donors prioritizing specific MDGs in their portfolio. In the meantime, however, the economic and political situation in the developing world has changed: instead of 60 low-income countries, as in the 1990s, the World Bank now counts only 34, and the majority of developing countries are now classified as (either lower or upper) middle-income countries (105).[14] Half of the world's GDP is produced by developing countries, and in 2014 the economic output of Brazil, China, India, Indonesia, Mexico, Russia and Turkey surpassed that of the G7 (IMF 2014).[15] At the same time, developing countries have increased their share in world trade to 40 per cent in goods and 30 per cent in services (United Nations 2012).

In such a dynamically changing world, some sort of global agreement on the need to make economic prosperity inclusive and environmentally sustainable seems more necessary than ever, and more difficult to achieve. There is an opportunity that economic and knowledge resources necessary for such transformative change will be less concentrated in the North than they were in the 1990s which may increase its chances.

Notes

1   Including Germany (federal and federal states level) this would make 25 NSDSs and 38 subnational strategies.
2   See www.sd-network.eu/?k=resources (accessed 4 February 2015). Poland is an unclear case as this website records no NSDS while Jacob et al. (2014) mention Poland as having an NSDS. The website www.ncsds.org which lists national councils for sustainable development mentions 14 NSDSs, 8 of which are from the EU (Belgium, Czech Republic, Estonia, Finland, France, Germany, Hungary and Italy). The other six are Bangladesh, Canada, Fiji, Gabun, Korea and Taiwan.
3   Not even at the website of the recently founded UN Office for Sustainable Development (UNOSD) located in Incheon, South Korea, which has the task "to support U.N. Member States in planning and implementing sustainable development strategies, notably through knowledge sharing, research, training and partnerships" (see www.unosd.org/index.php?menu=17; accessed 2 March 2015).
4   "We encourage regional, national, subnational and local authorities as appropriate to develop and utilize sustainable development strategies as key instruments for guiding decision-making and implementation of sustainable development at all levels, and in this regard we recognize that integrated social, economic and environmental data and information, as well as effective analysis and assessment of implementation, is important in decision-making processes" (United Nations 2012, p. 19).
5   This definition contrasts with the broader definition used by the UN Division for Sustainable Development in 2008. In our view, strategies with an environmental focus such as environmental action plans with no explicit actions in the social and economic areas are necessary elements of a comprehensive NSDS but they cannot replace it. In 2002, in its guidance document, UNDESA (2002, p. 7) had explicitly supported this view: "Since the Rio Summit, the understanding of a sustainable development strategy has moved from a national environmental strategy to a strategy that integrates economic, social and environmental aspects, as the original Rio emphasis".
6   For a discussion of different definitions of rich and poor countries, see the final section of this chapter.
7   The selection is based on the analysis of information contained in the literature (Berger & Gioksi 2009; Jacob et al. 2014; UNOSD 2012; Bertelsmann Stiftung 2013) and websites of the global network of national councils for sustainable development and similar bodies (www.ncsds.org) as well as of individual countries.

8   See www.stakeholderforum.org/fileadmin/files/National-Sustainable-Development-Strategy%202013.pdf (accessed 3 March 2015).
9   It is, however, not easy to find them – they are not made explicit in the short version of the *Finland we Want* document, and neither are they visible on the Findicators website.
10 The first federal strategy covered 2010–2013, the second cycle covers 2013–2016. Environment Canada publishes annual progress reports.
11 See the website of the Office of the Auditor General of Canada, www.oag-bvg.gc.ca/internet/English/cesd_fs_e_921.html (accessed 4 March 2015).
12 See the European Sustainable Development Network's website for a systematic presentation of governance challenges, www.sd-network.eu/?k=basics%20of%20SD%20strategies (accessed 4 March 2015).
13 Quoted from www.sd-network.eu/?k=basics%20of%20SD%20strategies (accessed 4 March 2015).
14 Country groupings as defined by the World Bank, see http://data.worldbank.org/about/country-and-lending-groups#High_income (accessed 3 March 2015). The World Bank relies on gross national income per capita for classification, which does not say much about poverty levels. But if we compare World Bank country groupings with the level of human development achieved by countries according to the Human Development Index the result is not very different: 43 countries have a low level of human development, 95 either a medium or a high level, and 49 a very high level. The boundaries between groups are fluid, as not all high-income countries have a very high human development level. Out of 34 low-income countries, 3 have gone beyond their peers and achieved a medium level of human development.
15 Calculations of the International Momentary Fund are based on purchasing power parities in order to make the welfare level of different economies comparable. As purchasing power varies considerably related to currencies and economic conditions, comparing GDP based on current exchange rates would lead to distorted results.

References

Ashoff, G. (2005): Enhancing policy coherence for development: justification, recognition and approaches to achievement. *DIE Studies 11*, Bonn: German Development Institute / Deutsches Institut für Entwicklungspolitik (DIE).

Berger, G.; Gioksi, N. (2009): Sustainable development strategies beyond Europe. *ESDN Quarterly Report*. Vienna: ESDN, URL: www.sd-network.eu/?k=about%20us%20and%20contact&s=ESDN%20office, last accessed 3 March 2015.

Bertelsmann Stiftung (2013): *Erfolgreiche Strategien für eine nachhaltige Zukunft*. Bielefeld: Bertelsmann Stiftung.

Bertelsmann Stiftung (2014): *Nachhaltigkeitsstrategien erfolgreich entwickeln. Strategien für eine nachhaltige Zukunft in Deutschland, Europa und der Welt*. Bielefeld: Bertelsmann Stiftung.

Bojo, J.; Reddy, R.C. (2002): *Poverty Reduction Strategies and Environment: a review of 40 interim and full poverty reduction strategy papers*, Washington, DC: World Bank.

Bundesregierung (2012): *Nationale Nachhaltigkeitsstrategie. Fortschrittsbericht 2012*. Berlin: Presse- und Informationsamt der Bundesregierung.

Casado-Asensio, J.; Steurer, R. (2014): Integrated strategies on sustainable development, climate change mitigation and adaptation in Western Europe: communication rather than coordination. *Journal of Public Policy*, Vol. 38 No. 3, pp. 437–473.

ESDN Office at the Institute for Managing Sustainability; Vienna University of Economics (n.d.): Basics of SD Strategies, URL: www.sd-network.eu/?k=basics%20of%20SD%20strategies, last accessed 9 May 2015.

44   *Imme Scholz*

Government of Bangladesh (2013): *National Sustainable Development Strategy of Bangladesh,* Dhaka, URL: www.stakeholderforum.org/fileadmin/files/National-Sustainable-Development-Strategy%202013.pdf, last accessed 3 March 2015.

Guarín, A.; Knorringa, P. (2015): Inequality, sustainability and middle classes in a polycentric world. *European Journal of Development Research,* Vol. 27 No. 2, pp. 202–204.

IMF (International Monetary Fund) (2014): *World Economic Outlook October 2014: Legacies, Clouds, Uncertainties.* Washington, DC: International Monetary Fund.

Jacob, K.; Kannen, H.; Niestroy, I. (2014): Nachhaltigkeitsstrategien im internationalen Vergleich. In: Bertelsmann Stiftung: *Nachhaltigkeitsstrategien erfolgreich entwickeln. Strategien für eine nachhaltige Zukunft in Deutschland, Europa und der Welt.* Gütersloh: Bertelsmann Stiftung, pp. 301–571.

Jones, R.S.; Yoo, B. (2011): Korea's Green Growth Strategy: Mitigating Climate Change and Developing New Growth Engines. *OECD Economics Department Working Papers* No. 798, Paris: OECD, URL: http://dx.doi.org/10.1787/5kmbhk4gh1ns-en, last accessed 15 May 2015.

Keller, M.; Niestroy, I.; García Schmidt, A.; Esche, A. (2013): Costa Rica: Ein Pionier für nachhaltige Entwicklung. In: Bertelsmann Stiftung: *Erfolgreiche Strategien für eine nachhaltige Zukunft.* Bielefeld: Bertelsmann Stiftung, pp. 91–115.

Kemp, R.; Loorbach, D.; Rotmans, J. (2007): Transition management as a model for managing processes of co-ecolution towards sustainable development. *International Journal of Sustainable Development & World Ecology* Vol. 14, pp. 78–91.

Lepuschitz, K. (2014): *Sustainability transition in Finland: Society's commitment to sustainable development.* ESDN Case Study N°18. Vienna: ESDN.

Loewe, M. (2014): Millennium plus or Sustainable Development Goals: how to combine human development objectives with targets for global public goods? In: Fues, T.; Ye, J. (eds): *United Nations Post-2015 Agenda for Global Development:Pperspectives from China and Europe.* Bonn: German Development Institute / Deutsches Institut für Entwicklungspolitik (DIE), pp. 201–230.

Loorbach, R. (2010): Transition management for sustainable development: a prescriptive, complexity-based governance framework. *Governance: An International Journal of Policy, Administration, and Institutions* Vol. 23 No. 1, pp. 161–183.

Meadowcroft, J. (2007): National Sustainable Development Strategies: Features, challenges and reflexivity. *European Environment* Vol. 17 No. 3, pp. 152–163.

Messner, D.; Nuscheler, F. (2007): Das Konzept Global Governance: Stand und Perspektiven. In: Senghaas, D. (ed.): *Global Governance für Entwicklung und Frieden: Perspektiven nach einem Jahrzehnt.* Bonn: Dietz, pp. 18–80.

National Council for Sustainable Development Taiwan (2013): *Annual Report on National Sustainable Development,* Taipei. URL: http://nsdn.epa.gov.tw/en/PRINT/INDEX.HTM, last accessed 3 March 2015.

Niestroy, I.; García Schmidt, A.; Esche, A. (2013a): Bhutan: Ein Leitbild der Nachhaltigkeitspolitik. In: Bertelsmann Stiftung: *Erfolgreiche Strategien für eine nachhaltige Zukunft.* Bielefeld: Bertelsmann Stiftung, pp. 61–90.

Niestroy, I.; García Schmidt, A.; Esche, A. (2013b): Finnland: Auf dem Weg zu einem Gesellschaftsvertrag für eine nachhaltige Zukunft. In: Bertelsmann Stiftung: *Erfolgreiche Strategien für eine nachhaltige Zukunft.* Bielefeld: Bertelsmann Stiftung, pp. 117–143.

Norgaard, R.B. (1994): *Development Betrayed: The End of Progress and a Coevolutionary Revisioning of the Future.* Florence, Kentucky: Routledge.

OECD (Organization for Economic Co-operation and Development) (2001): *Strategies for Sustainable Development. Practical guidance for development co-operation.* Paris: OECD.

OECD (2006): *Good Practices in the National Sustainable Development Strategies of OECD Countries*. Paris: OECD.

Rippin, N. (2013): Progress, prospects and lessons from the MDGs. Background Research Paper for the Report of the High Level Panel on the Post-2015 Development Agenda, URL: www.die-gdi.de/uploads/media/Rippin_Progress-Prospects-and-Lessons-from-the-MDGs.pdf, last accessed 9 May 2015.

Staatssekretärsausschuss für nachhaltige Entwicklung (2010): Nachhaltigkeit konkret im Verwaltungshandeln umsetzen. Maßnahmenprogramm Nachhaltigkeit. URL: www.bundesregierung.de/Content/DE/_Anlagen/Nachhaltigkeit-wiederhergestellt/2010-12-06-massnahmenprogramm-nachhaltigkeit-der-bundesregierung.pdf?__blob=publicationFile&v=4, last accessed 4 March 2015.

Stigsson, B.; Suresh P.; Prabhu, J.; Bordewijk, P.; Haavisto, J.; Morgan, V.; Moosa, D.; Osborn, S.-J. Yun (2013): *Sustainability – Made in Germany*. The Second Review by a Group of International Peers, commissioned by the German Federal Chancellery, Berlin: RNE, URL: www.nachhaltigkeitsrat.de/uploads/media/20130925_Peer_Review_Sustainability_Germany_2013_03.pdf, last accessed 4 March 2015.

UNDESA (UN Department of Economic and Social Affairs) (2002): *Guidance in Preparing a National Sustainable Development Strategy: Managing Sustainable Development in the New Millennium*. URL: www.un.org/esa/sustdev/publications/nsds_guidance.pdf, last accessed 25 February 2015.

United Nations (2012): *World Economic Situation and Prospects 2012*, New York: United Nations, URL: www.un.org/en/development/desa/policy/wesp/wesp_current/2012chap2.pdf, last accessed 24 February 2015.

United Nations (2015): Zero draft of the outcome document for the UN Summit to adopt the Post-2015 Development Agenda, URL: https://sustainabledevelopment.un.org/content/documents/7261Post-2015%20Summit%20-%202%20June%202015.pdf, last accessed 6 June 2015.

UNOSD (UN Office for Sustainable Development) (2012): *Draft Issues Paper on Strategies for Sustainable Development. Meeting the Challenges of the Post Rio+20 World*. Incheon: UNOSD.

Volkery, A.; Swanson, D.; Jacob, K.; Bregha, F.; Pintér, L. (2006): Coordinating sustainable development – an evaluation of the state of play. In: Jänicke, M.; Jacob, K. (eds): *Environmental Governance in Global Perspective. New Approaches to Ecological Modernisation*. Berlin: FFU, pp. 210–238.

Young-Keun Chung; Kumju Hwang (2006): *The Korean National Strategy for Sustainable Development. A Background Report*, URL: https://sustainabledevelopment.un.org/content/documents/1394backgroundReport.pdf, last accessed 4 March 2015.

3 From conventional to sustainable project management in development cooperation

Bülent Tarkan

Introduction

A frequent criticism of development cooperation is that it produces only a relatively small amount of tangible success and that many of the financial resources introduced are inefficiently used. In this connection, most of the Organization for Economic Co-operation and Development (OECD) countries fail to achieve the target official development assistance (ODA) quota of 0.7 per cent of gross domestic product (GDP), and no fundamental change in financing efforts can be anticipated in the near future. Moreover, it is questionable how far an increase to the development cooperation budget would actually solve the problem. However, there are the costs, or expenditure, involved in development cooperation. In this connection because of the restraints on increasing financial assistance, optimizing the deployment of expenditure represents the only feasible option for achieving a better distribution of the financial resources. Since development cooperation is extremely project-oriented, this project level offers a useful starting point for optimizing finance flows in development cooperation. It is therefore necessary to standardize project management as far as possible according to the industrial model and to define guidelines to form a basis for the effective and efficient realization of projects. However, these guideline and standardizations cannot be automatically adopted from the industrial sector, as particularly in development cooperation the project set-ups are extremely complex and often have an international bias. Such complexity is further augmented by the challenges of sustainable development, and here the question arises as to how, against this background, effective project management can be sustainably organized in developing countries. This question and appropriate approaches towards a solution will be discussed in this chapter.

The instruments and actions adopted according to special project management methods can, depending upon the sphere of deployment and the complexity of the individual project, involve different substantive points of emphasis and processes. There is, however, always a basic structure underlying these "special" project management methods. Their structure is of a more or less similar nature, which is then expanded or adapted to a specific project. Therefore, there will firstly be an examination of the bases of traditional project management, with the possible fundamental differences in project management in the non-profit versus profit arenas taken as a starting point. From this axis the different phases of traditional project management will be highlighted. This will be followed by an explanation of the particular features in international project management in order to subsequently investigate specifically project management in development cooperation. The study will be concluded with a discussion of the particular challenges relating to sustainable project management in development cooperation.

Bases of traditional project management

Since the concept of a "project" covers an extremely broad spectrum of demarcations, it is necessary to define the major common denominators. According to Kuster et al. (2011), the following common features can be identified amongst the numerous definitions of the concept: "If a one-off, cross-sector plan is limited in time, specifically targeted, interdisciplinary and is so important, critical and urgent that it cannot be accomplished within the existing line organizational framework, but special organizational arrangements have to be made, this can then be called a project" (Kuster et al. 2011, p. 5).

There are just as many demarcations applied for project management as for the concept of a project. By way of example, the definition under Deutsches Institut für Normung (DIN) 69901 should be cited here. According to this standard, project management is understood as the totality of:

* management tasks
* management organization
* management techniques and
* management tools

required for the completion of projects (cf. DIN, 69901, 2009).

Effective project management is of great significance for both non-profit organizations (NPO) as well as for-profit organizations (PO), although this need – to be considered equally important in terms of organizational form – is not always discernible in the same way. In this respect the adopted nomenclature of "profit-oriented" and "non-profit-oriented" enterprises has a crucial bearing. This attempt in the sense of a "negative" demarcation of NPOs from POs was originally developed in business economics, and points on the one hand towards the commercial enterprises working in accordance with strict market rules, and which are endeavouring to avoid efficiency losses, and on the other hand the organizations which are not seeking to achieve any realization of profits and are thus ultimately targeting their efforts without any (market/margin) pressure (cf. in this connection and generally below, Kaestner et al. 2012, p. 24).

The fundamental difference between the two organizational forms of the NPO and the PO is that, unlike the POs, for the NPOs the formal objective is essentially not the generating of profit but the main focus is placed upon target-specific orientation. However, this specific targeting must, just as much as the formal objective, satisfy the principle of economic efficiency. In concrete terms this means that irrespective of whether specific or formal objectives are striven for, the same principle must always apply to both organizational forms: either a set objective with the least possible input of resources or the optimum achievement of success with a set input of resources.

Two fundamental features relating to the organizational forms of the NPOs continue to be relevant. On the one hand, NPOs as a rule have a common, all-embracing objective: to create sustainable development for people and the environment without thereby disregarding the economic dimension. By contrast, POs focus on their self-interest and strive towards a maximization of profit in the economic sense. On the other hand, NPOs often operate in a triangular constellation, i.e. the executive organization or the non-governmental organization (NGO) and the target group exist alongside the donor institution. In connection with commercial organizational forms, there is an entrepreneurial and client relationship. However, this polarization does not entirely reflect the reality: to some extent, in the context of corporate social responsibility (CSR), POs converge towards sustainability and NGOs have as yet not always fulfilled the requirements of sustainable development.

It can nevertheless be claimed that the bases of project management can be appropriate for both organizational forms, since both must comply with the principle of economic efficiency. However, in the case of NPOs – and in particular with regard to smaller project teams and also more complex project requirements including a number of sub-projects – recourse can be had to so-called *agile* processes.

Standard reduction in particular leads to faster visible results and enables greater flexibility in the completion of projects. However, the lower requirements placed upon the management of projects can also produce disadvantages if, for example, new and – in the area of agile processes – inexperienced team members are brought in or the impression of a lack of target focus is created (Kaestner et al. 2012, p. 44). These agile processes are scarcely suitable for project management in development cooperation, since in many cases there are mandatory documentary obligations as a result of the frequent input of public development funds. Moreover, clearly defined completion and target dates are demanded by donors, as well as interim progress reports and other formal impositions. Therefore, there will be no further discussion of agile processes in this study, which will focus much more upon the traditional approach to project management, and specifically upon the universal action model in accordance with DIN 69901.

Dimensions and phases of project management

Traditional project management presents four dimensions (in this connection and generally below, cf. Kuster et al. 2011, p. 10):

1   Functional dimension
2   Institutional dimension
3   Personnel, psychological and social dimension
4   Instrumental dimension.

The **functional dimension** deals with the question of what is to be done within the framework of the project. Here there will be a consideration of the individual work phases/life phases of the project. In connection with the functional dimension, the different phases of an individual project will be discussed in more detail.

The **institutional dimension** essentially involves adequate project organization. How can and should the project, which is positioned outside the line organizational structure, be embedded within the enterprise? For example, do project committees have to be formed in order to always guarantee an institutional link with institutional decision-makers? Beyond this, functions and roles are to be defined and thus competencies and responsibilities have to be regulated.

The **personnel, psychological and social dimension** is concerned with the need to employ the right personnel and where necessary in specific cases to ensure their improved further training. These personnel must be led as a team, whose collaboration and social processes are to be optimally formed and, ultimately, there is a need to develop conflict resolution strategies.

The **instrumental dimension** represents the various techniques and instruments in connection with project management. It includes, for example, information technology (IT)-supported methods, working aids, models and standardized processes.

Returning to the abovementioned functional dimension, we should now examine more closely the different phases within this dimension. The phasing concept is flexible in its application, i.e. there is no mandatorily prescribed number of phases which have to be applied to each project. However, it can be subsumed from the voluminous literature on project management that there is a pervading basic consensus that there is a requirement for an aggregate of different phases in project management. As a rule, it is considered that at least four phases are required for the targeted objective. These include the:

1 Definition phase
2 Planning phase
3 Control phase
4 Completion phase (in this connection and below, cf. for example Hab & Wagner 2013).

These four phases should, however, also always be preceded by an additional phase, the initialization phase, and followed by a so-called utilization phase. In the initialization phase it is a question of assessing whether a plan is worthy of forming a project at all. Consequently, it must then be examined whether the conceived idea is also target-oriented. In this phase it is not a matter of writing a project application, but – through a brainstorming process, for example – of formulating the correct approaches for solving a problem or finding an appropriate alternative.

The definition phase is tantamount to a preliminary study. After a project has crystallized, it is then a question of representing the current actual situation, as well as the objectives and the intended situation, a consideration of feasibility, a risk assessment and a determination of the usefulness of the intended situation. With the help of the preliminary study there can be an initial assessment of whether an approach to the problem as originally conceived is to be considered realistic. The various conceivable solution variants for the plan are to be formulated in the planning phase. A solution variant should subsequently be selected and formulated in detail for the next stage.

At the end of the control phase the project should be appropriately tested as to its functionality. This is followed by the completion phase, at which stage the target group has been assigned and enabled to implement the solution concept. An acceptance protocol has been signed, a post calculation carried out, the project documentation drawn up, the final assessment completed and the project team has concluded its tasks. Finally, a date for the follow-up inspection is agreed. In the ensuing utilization phase, knowledge management in particular can be expanded, since not until this phase can the strengths and weaknesses of the solution variant be recognized.

This brief representation of the individual phases merely offers an introduction to the subject area of traditional project management and a basis for the subsequent essential stages. Project management in the context of development cooperation presents strong international or intercultural components and is to be shaped as a model for sustainable development. These two components are examined more closely below.

International project management

The bases of international project management are formed as discussed above, although additional factors fall under this heading. These aspects will be analysed in greater detail below. In addition to the relevant components in national management, "specific characteristics of other nations and international differences must be taken into account" (Koch, 2012a, p. 49). International project management means that "Irrespective of the respective geographical position of the project locations, projects are always to be started, planned, monitored, controlled and completed subject to new environmental constellations" (Cronenbroeck 2004, p. 99).

The respective project environment – i.e. the factors which can have a direct as well as indirect effect on a project – represents one of the major problem areas in connection with international projects. Therefore, the success of the project is essentially contingent upon the existing environmental conditions and their influence on the project. The environment of a project or an institution is analysed on the basis of a so-called PEST analysis, an abbreviation used to denote the factors which essentially exert an influence on the project or institution but which are themselves not influenced by the project. The factors involved are the Political, Economic, Social and Technological (cf. Koch 2012a, p. 49).

As well as the environment together with its influences, structural differences also represent a problem area. In particular, economic, political and legal structures and systems can make international project management more difficult. And uncertainties resulting from spatial distances and multilateral cooperation are further challenges for international project management. Moreover, expectations and the varying competence levels of the team members, as well as the capacity for cooperation with regard to the adaptation to local circumstances, can be cited as socio-organizational problem areas. Therefore, human factors can be noted as a particular problem area, especially if team members of the project are working in foreign countries and are bound by different cultures there (cf. Cronenbroeck 2004, p.109).

Consequently, in addition to the achievement of concrete objectives, management tasks also require an awareness that the people involved are also an element of the system and that management has to be adapted to the relevant context. And alongside the national and international contexts, there is also an intercultural context to be taken into consideration. This predominantly involves the management of diffrent cultures, irrespective of whether the organization or institution operates domestically or abroad (cf. Koch 2012a, p. 47). According to Koch, the concept of culture "is understood as an indeterminate number of explicit values and standards as well as implicit basic assumptions by societies, subdivisions of society or social groups" (Koch 2012a, p. 54). Cultures can change and are subject to external influences. The prerequisites for intercultural management competency can be attibuted to four levels:

1   Creating a consciousness of one's own cultural orientation and gaining knowledge of its effect on one's own actions,
2   Accepting one's own cultural orientation as something learned and relativizing this within the context of the intercultural environment,
3   Openness towards foreign cultural orientation and being able to recognize this,
4   Linking one's own cultural actions towards foreign cultural orientations with a common action model and integration of this common model into one's own actions.

If these four stages are completed, this enables a capacity to "successfully [introduce actions] into other cultural or cross-cultural contexts" (Koch 2012a, p. 52) or to adopt "a target- or success-oriented" approach (Koch 2012a, p. 56). Intercultural project management thus represents an expansion of traditional project management and, partially, of international project management. This is clearly shown in Figure 3.1.

Cronenbroeck has developed a six-characteristic model for systematization and as practical support for team members in international project management (see Figure 3.2). This shows the points of emphasis and special features of international projects which the project members should consider before and during the project. However, in this respect it should be noted that in each project not all six areas are of equal significance (cf. Cronenbroeck 2004, p. 112).

In the area of **international competence to act** it is evident that, compared to national project management, additional competencies are necessary and that the personal approach represents an important factor. In this connection, individual motivation for taking up an activity in an international project assumes a special

Figure 3.1 Project management relationships
Source: Koch 2012a, p.57

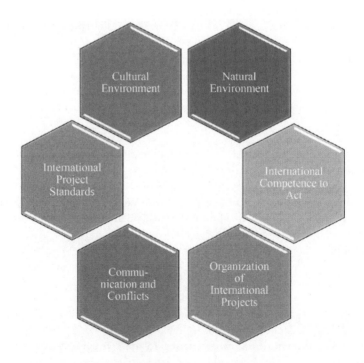

Figure 3.2 The six-characteristic model
Source: Adapted from Cronenbroeck 2004, p. 114

importance. The relevant preparation for "commitment" in the international project team is an essential component here (cf. in this connection and generally below, Cronenbroeck 2004).

The project framework and the project team form the subject of the area of **organization of international projects**. Here, the topics of personnel deployment, structure and management behaviour within the team play a special role.

In the area of **communication and conflicts** the processes, types and means of communication, as well as the special features of international communication, are points of special emphasis. In this connection, the origins, prevention, as well as the strategies and methods, of conflict resolution will also be examined.

Since the framework conditions of international projects vary greatly and standards therefore make work more difficult, and can even obstruct it, **international project standards** are relatively rare. Nevertheless, with this in mind reference will be made to a few international standards.

The **cultural environment** factor is one of the most important in international project management. In this connection, general country-specific features, as well as values and standards, represent the focal points of international project management. This area plays a special role in the individual phases in the management of a project.

The **natural environment** element covers factors such as spatial distances and time zones, as well as geographical and climatic conditions which have to be taken into account when carrying out an international project. In this respect these factors also have a very significant influence upon the project team members.

Project management in German development cooperation – a theory-based approach for explaining success or failure

Compared to traditional project management, project management in development cooperation has a political background. Instead of an enterprise, decisions on the acceptance or rejection of a project are predominantly taken on a political level. German development policy is intended to contribute towards combating poverty, securing peace, democratization, fairer globalization and environmental protection. The objectives should be targeted on a global level, taking sustainable development as a model. The three dimensions of ecology, economy and social factors are defined more precisely as the simultaneous achievement of economic efficiency, ecological viability and social justice. In addition, these are supplemented by the dimension of political stability (cf. BMZ 2008, p. 8).

The objectives of German development cooperation are oriented towards the substance and agreements of international conferences. This includes the Brundtland Report of 1987, which demarcates the model of sustainable development, as well as the results of the Rio Conference of 1992, the 2002 World Summit for Sustainable Development in Johannesburg and Rio+20 (the 2012 UN Conference for Sustainable Development). Furthermore, objectives focus upon the millennium development goals for the period after 2015, and the post-2015 Agenda and the Sustainable Development Goals (SDGs) (cf. BMZ 2015).

Alongside these global objectives, account is also to be taken of dynamic global processes (globalization of the markets, global environmental changes, democratization or state decline) and their significance for the respective project.

In the Paris Declaration and the subsequent agreements in Accra and Busan, it was stressed that the **effectiveness** of development cooperation should be increased. For this purpose ODA was increased, cooperation between the partner countries stepped up and development cooperation measures adapted to the circumstances of the partner country. The intended objective was to strengthen the partner countries and enable them to develop their own strategies and manage projects. Thus the democracy-based **ownership** of the partner country was an additional principle. The partner countries' own responsibility was accorded a higher status as this is treated as the key to the efficiency, effectiveness and sustainability of the projects and in general as the key to development success.

The use of budgetary aid is closely related to the principle of ownership. In this way the partner countries can "set their own priorities ... and use the benefits of development aid more effectively for their own planning" (Kevenhörster & van den Boom, 2009, p. 52). The third principle is based on the **coherence** of the development policy, which means that attention should be paid to development policy objectives in different political spheres. These political spheres should be modified with regard to the target objective, i.e. they should not impede or act against one another (cf. Kevenhörster & van den Boom, 2009, p. 36). An agreement upon the principle of political coherence was achieved in the Millennium Development Goals (MDGs), the Monterry Consensus on Development Financing (2002) and in the Busan Declaration on Aid Effectiveness (2011). Germany has committed to adhere to these principles, for which reason the German Federal Ministry for Economic Cooperation and Development (BMZ) has directed the management of its tasks towards these principles.

The effect and successes of development cooperation must be critically assessed in view of the use of public as well as private resources. As far back as the 1980s the effectiveness of development cooperation had been discussed and a micro–macro paradox discovered. On the micro-level, projects and programmes tended to present positive evaluation results, whereas on the macro-level of development cooperation its the effects were barely apparent or were even negative (cf. Caspari & Barbu 2008, p. 2). Evaluations presented in reports by the World Bank likewise questioned the effectiveness of development cooperation. The two opposing positions represented by Easterly (reduction of ODA) and Sachs (increase of ODA) exist against this background.[1] In their examination of the effectiveness of development cooperation, econometric studies[2] likewise arrive at different conclusions.

Ashoff (2010) cites five areas which may be responsible for a lack of effectiveness in development cooperation, and several causes are cited for each area of responsibility. These areas may be development policy, the partner countries, exogenous factors, the different policies of the donors or development research. As causes for the area of responsibility of development policy, Ashoff cites specific-content or systemic organizational deficits, or negative economic and political system effects of high ODA inflows. A further cause may be the problem of collective action in the development policy system, which will be discussed in greater detail below (cf. Ashoff 2010, p. 33).

However, it should be borne in mind that a comprehensive answer on the effectiveness or quality of the development policy is scarcely possible due to the different research findings and the possible causes. When considering a specific measure, or a project or programme in development policy, it must be taken into account that "Success or failure ... [is] often difficult to establish, since this occurs in a foreign country and cultural environment and as a rule the recipients of aid have no direct relationships whatsoever to the providers of aid (taxpayers in industrialized countries)" (Faust & Michaelowa 2013, p. 15). The effects produced by development cooperation are therefore to be treated in a differential manner with regard to the regions or countries. The framework conditions in the respective project environment should be taken more into account in the planning of projects, the reporting of them and the evaluation (cf. Kevenhörster & van den Boom 2009, p. 87; Faust & Michaelowa 2013, p.13).

The framework conditions also include the intentions of the actors representing both the donor as well as the recipient parties, who are involved with the development projects. In development organizations the career opportunities of the employees are frequently contingent upon the volume of available resources, and not upon the effect of their projects (poverty reduction, for example). Moreover, in the case of specific areas of development cooperation, more tax and donation revenues can be acquired than with less high-profile subject areas, which can nevertheless enable a more efficient use of resources. On the donor side, "in connection with the effectiveness of development cooperation, there is constant reference to the extremely widespread corruption in many developing countries or to exclusive, autocratic and patronage-based structures which can be detrimental to the framework conditions for effective aid" (Faust & Michaelowa 2013, p. 16).

If the new political economy is viewed as a sub-discipline of institutional political economy, the following scenario emerges: the absent or deficient effects of development cooperation can be explained by applying the principal-agent theory, which is based upon information asymmetries. The superior knowledge on the part of the agent (implementer) is used to exert self-interests or in a manner which is not in the interest of the principal (client), although the principal is unable to fully control or prevent this. Mummert (2013) identifies a total of five principal-agent relationships in the planning, implementation and evaluation of development projects: (1) the donor government is the agent of the voters (principals) of the donor country; (2) the implementing organizations (IOs), such as the German Corporation for Technical Cooperation (GIZ) for example, are the agents of the donor state (principal); (3) the IOs (principals) commission an employee or an external adviser (agent) – who in development cooperation is also referred to as an engagement partner (EP) [*Auftragsverantwortlicher* (AV)] – with the development project; (4) either the IO or the employee/external adviser agree upon the implementation of the project with the recipient country, so that the recipient country acts as agent on behalf of the donor (principal); and (5) the recipient government acts as principal vis-à-vis its own bureaucracy whereas the state administration employees, for example, represent the agents.

In the donor countries, politicians have self-interests as well as the IOs. Politicians promote those projects which attract the most votes within their party so that they themselves can remain in office. The IOs endeavour to increase their volume of commissions and to enhance their reputations. Therefore, the level and scope of the budget, or the volume of projects and the frequency of failure play an important role in this process. Projects which are easy to carry out, or measures where failure is difficult to ascertain, are therefore interesting for the IOs, and are conducted to a greater extent. Infrastructure projects are thus of particular interest to the IOs, as their realization can easily be ascertained. By contrast, the effects or the success of institutional reform projects can only be ascertained with difficulty, so that in this case there is more of an attempt to represent results as input-oriented.

Even if the development cooperation provided by the donors is oriented towards the interests of the recipients/target group, there are information asymmetries caused by geographical and political differences. "[T]he recipients [are] not voters in the donor country and therefore have no political leverage with which they can influence policy" (Mummert 2013, p. 57). Only with well-functioning political institutions in the recipient country can the preferences of the voters be communicated via their government to the donors. Patronage-based structures undermine the opinions and interests of the entire electorate in the recipient country, and therefore people's own interests and wishes can scarcely have a bearing upon development policy measures. Therefore, with well-functioning institutions in accordance with the ownership principle, a project should be conducted between the engagement partner and the agent of the recipient country if the latter has no reservations concerning the project. The engagement partner should be able to demonstrate previous experience with the respective country- and culture-specific features in order to establish and sustain such a partnership relationship. In this connection, social standards should ensure that corruption and negative consequences do not occur.

With the principal-agent analysis, as far as the evaluation of development policy projects is concerned the voters/taxpayers and the politicians of the donor country in particular, as well as the IOs, play an essential role. The effect and success of a project are dependent upon the evaluation by the development ministry, and the more important the evaluation is the better are the results achieved in the development cooperation.

> The anticipated profit or loss from the execution of the development policy measure depends ... upon the assumed detection probability of the non-contractual implementation of the project ... The higher the assumed risk of detection is, the more [the IOs] commit themselves and the better the anticipated project results are.
>
> (Mummert 2013, p. 69)

However, evaluations can also support the self-interests of the politicians and the IOs and manipulate voters' decisions. Politicians only use evaluations if they serve to maximize votes, and this be done to the extent that only good results are presented to the public. IOs have similar interests to preserve or improve the commissions they receive, and use evaluations rather for lessons learned processes. Only harmless information, summaries or best practices would therefore be passed on to the public.

Due to the varying evaluation experiences in respect of the effects and successes of development cooperation, as well as the knowledge gained from the principal-agent theory, the framework conditions within which development policy projects and programmes can be implemented acquire an increasing importance. Against this background, over the past few years the methods of project and programme management in development cooperation have undergone many changes. In the following chapter the currently applied method in the sphere of project management will be presented.

Project management method in German technical development cooperation

In development cooperation, projects and programmes are the forms most frequenely used to carry out development policy measures. Due to their own self-critical examinations and the perception of them amongst the public, development cooperation – and technical cooperation in particular – has been transformed over the past few decades. Already at the end of the 1970s the IOs in the sphere of technical cooperation had recognized that projects were being undertaken with active planning and an unclear strategy. These strategies were often pursued with only short-term and unrealistic objectives. In addition, they were in many cases based upon an inadequate situation analysis. The project documentation scarcely enabled an examination of the effectiveness of the projects, and cooperation with the partner countries and other partners, as well as the relationship to the principal, suffered under this kind of project management. Since then, project and programme management has undergone constant change. Recently projects and programmes have also been complemented with purely financing instruments (e.g. budgetary aids).

Cooperation in social and intercultural contexts represents a particular challenge to project management in development cooperation. As a result of the reform process in development cooperation, the forms of cooperation have become increasingly more complex, so that the demands placed upon project managers in the sphere of development cooperation have risen. Since the GTZ, as the original organization for technical cooperation, developed the project management Toolbox Capacity Works in 2009, by way of example we shall focus on the former GTZ, with its instruments, to present the development of different project management methods in technical cooperation.

Five factors are of significance for project and programme management. The approach strategy and the instruments of project management should be **flexible** and adapted to each individual situation. The focus of development cooperation is placed upon the **effect** of development projects and no longer as before upon the results or goal orientation. Therefore, projects should be effect-oriented in their approach. Projects are no longer bound to a close functional task, but relate to activities comprising a larger number of areas. In this case, there is then usually more reference to programmes, and in this way greater effects are to be achieved. And alongside the more complex arrangement of tasks, even more actors are to be brought in. The level of **complexity** is thereby constantly increasing. Tasks are now to be planned, controlled and monitored in cooperation with partners. By way of organization and moderation, different actors with different interests have to be brought together into the **cooperation** process. In development cooperation, the initiation and support of **learning processes** are now the tasks of the project or programme manager.

With the revision of its previous management tools and planning measures, the GTZ has adapted itself to the present framework conditions. From the practical experiences of the GTZ, the "management model for sustainable development", entitled "Capacity WORKS", was developed and introduced in 2009 (cf. Koch 2012b, p. 1). Following the amalgamation of GTZ, DED (Deutscher Entwicklungsdienst or the German Development Service) and InWEnt to form GIZ, Capacity WORKS is also applied in the newly formed GIZ. In this connection, the experiences acquired by DED and InWEnt were channelled into the GIZ's management model, thereby producing a concretization of the concept and an expansion of the applicational opportunities.

The previous management model was updated and expanded in respect of cooperation management. Compared to the former version of Capacity WORKS, a stronger focus was placed upon the topics of "objectives and effects", "differences between cooperation systems and networks", the "formation of all-embracing organizational strategy development" as well as "learning and innovation processes" in terms of knowledge sharing. Various elements of the methodical tools were thereby modified (cf. GIZ 2015, p. 6). In the GIZ, Capacity WORKS is used in the central management processes (project/programme design, realization, evaluation and reporting) (GIZ 2015, p. 2).

According to the GIZ, the concept of "capacity" is understood as "the capacity of people, organizations and societies to sustainably shape their own development and adapt to dynamic framework conditions. This includes the recognition of impediments to development, the development of resolution strategies and then the sucessful implementation of these strategies" (GIZ 2015, p. 4). Therefore, in current development cooperation it is no longer simply a question of acting "correctly" on the political and functional level. For the success of a development policy measure it is likewise crucial "how" action is taken. The methodology, i.e. the path towards the objective, is therefore placed in the foreground. Capacity WORKS is particularly helpful for the shaping of this path, or the orientation towards objectives and effects (GIZ 2015, p. 1).

Objectives are defined as positive situations "at the end of a planned process" (GIZ 2015, p. 30). The set objectives are decided through negotiation processes in cooperation systems between the partners. The resulting common objectives should be clearly formulated, attractive and realistic. Moreover, cooperation should embrace a unified interpretation of the set objectives.

> The module objective (outcome) ... illustrates the effect which is to be real-istically and bindingly achieved within the chronological and financial framework of the measure offered. It describes an intended effect – to be defined – of the measure on the target group, on (regional) public property, structures or policies. The GIZ understands effects as intended or unintended, positive or negative changes to a situation, or a behaviour, as a direct or indi-rect consequence of an intervention.
>
> (GIZ 2015, p. 35)

Therefore, in this connection effects are equated with changes (in society), so that cause–effect relationships play a central role in the work with Capacity WORKS (GIZ 2015, p. 30). With the support of participative processes, the continuous reflection of own actions and the resulting learning experiences, processes of social change can thus be stimulated in the management model.

For complex situations, the model serves for orientation and structuring. In this case, a fixed framework, or fixed approach, is prescribed. The model is character-ized by the various dimensions of the sustainability concept understood by the GIZ: social responsibility, ecological equilibrium, political participation and economic efficiency (GIZ 2015, p. 1). These elements stand in a complementary relationship to one another. Objectives and effects are to be derived from the social environment, and in this connection objectives should be oriented towards the sustainability dimensions. Only then can changes designed for the long term be initiated.

In the beginning Capacity WORKS was only rarely passed on to interested parties by the GTZ, and project successes were also seldom reported to the public with the then new instrument. Today, information on the management model Capacity WORKS is made available by the GIZ in a comprehensive way. For example, on the GIZ homepage there is an e-Learning platform for Capacity WORKS. In 2015 a reference work on cooperation management with Capacity WORKS was published, together with an attachment containing a large number of tools. Brief reports on the successes and approaches to projects and programmes of the GIZ (practice examples), for which Capacity WORKS is used, are likewise accessible on the homepage for interested members of the public.

Sustainability in the project management of development cooperation

In this connection, sustainable development is understood as a development which, according to the Brundtland Commission, is permanent and which "meets the needs of the present without compromising the ability of future generations to meet their own needs" (Hauff 1987, p. 46). Alongside intragenerational and inter-generational justice, it is necessary to assess the three dimensions of ecology, economy and the social dimension as equally ranking and to integrate them into an equilibrium. In the context of sustainable development the different requirements arising from ecology, economy and the social components are to be brought together "with the same right" into a negotiation process with the participating stakeholders, so that they can be considered in a balanced manner with regard to the different vested interests and priorities. Above all, it is necessary that at least as an idealized concept all three dimensions, with their differing concerns, can be considered in a balanced manner "in a joint investigative and cognitive process" as well as in the decision-making process; on the basis of a negotiation process the three dimensions can then be formed into a balanced relationship (cf. von Hauff & Kleine 2014, p. 118).

This participatory approach in the decision-making process is to be applied to (project) management in development cooperation. For further strategic orientation this should be further supplemented – following the four basic principles of sustainability strategies (cf. OECD & UNDP 2002, p. 32) – by the establishment of a robust and transparent coordination agency for a continuously improving process formation. To mobilize financial resources, specific investments and measures for capacity development should be planned and implemented, and monitoring systems initiated for the activities.

It can basically be stated that scientifically based literature on sustainable project management is as yet relatively scant. There is, however, an increasingly growing interest in the subject and there are frequently more references to the relevance of sustainable project management in the fields of education and consultancy. Institutions or project managers are appearing more and more on the internet in the context of sustainability, in order to present their views on sustainable project management, and thereby enabling a further discussion of participation and transparency of methods and instruments.

For example, from the internet perspective of Sustainable Project Management (SPM), a value compass is presented according to which all works of the SPM members are to be guided. This embraces all personal values, e.g. the assumption of responsibility for decisions, actions and their consequences, or the virtues of respect and honour, whereas the economic values draw upon the three dimensions of sustainable development and the value creation chain. Also cited as organizational values are cooperation, participation, transparency and entrepreneurship (cf. SPM 2015a).

In an initial phase, the objective of sustainable project management is that prior to the commencement of a project it must be clarified whether the planned project is relevant for a sustainable, and thus permanent, strategy and whether it conforms to the negotiated sustainability criteria within an enterprise. In addition, value is attached to a transparent and comprehensible approach. It is therefore about results on the one hand and, on the other hand, shaping the process or the function as such in accordance with the model of sustainable development.

Consequently, a project must achieve a specific quality within a given time limit, with available resources and with costs as low as possible, and take into account the three dimensions of ecology, economy and the social dimension. The so-called

"Triple Constraint" expands the guidelines and formulates the objectives of project management from the traditional (time, volume/content, costs), through the progressive (quality, risks, client satisfaction), to sustainable (economic, ecological, social) project management. In addition to a consideration of these guidelines, their interactions should also be recognized (cf. SPM 2015b).

The approach in sustainable project management also corresponds to the approach adopted in traditional or international project management, whereby all stages – or in all the phases of project management – the model of sustainable development is to be integrated. Therefore, a uniform and practical understanding of sustainability should be identified before the start of the project. Subsequently, the individual activities of each project phase are to be examined, as are all the parties responsible with regard to their sustainable actions. It is crucial that a complementary relationship between the three dimensions is achieved, thereby ensuring success over the long term, and that for a transparent approach all relevant stakeholders are included and intragenerational and intergenerational aspects of justice are striven for. In this connection, not only the objective or the result, but also the internal processes, are to be geared towards the model of sustainable development. It is also important that learning effects are possible and that activities can be readjusted, improved or modified. Project management should therefore be dynamic and oriented towards the prevailing conditions.

Development cooperation is subject to different conditions from those existing in traditional or international project management. In developing and emerging countries, in which development cooperation is undertaken, the starting points, framework conditions and concepts applicable to sustainable development are very different.

At the end of the 1990s the concept of sustainability in development cooperation was still very much limited to the permanent effect of development cooperation projects. Scarcely any attention was paid to the model, created in Rio, of a sustainable development with the three dimensions and intragenerational and intergenerational justice. Thus in the European Commission's Green Book sustainability in development cooperation was defined as "the permanence of the results and … the continuance of the results according to the focusing of the aid programmes" (European Commission 1997, p. 8). Similar to the definition used by the KfW, the GTZ at the time defined measures as sustainable "…if the improvements achieved in the partner countries continue to exist after the end of the aid programme" (German Bundestag 1997, p. 27).

Consequently, on the project level there has been reference to sustainable projects or programmes if there has been a long-term impact (cf. GTZ 1996, p. 4). There has been agreement that efforts should continue to be made towards monitoring the sustainable effect of development cooperation measures with regard to their contribution towards sustainable development in accordance with the Rio and Agenda 21 models. Furthermore, the participative character of development policy approaches should be applied more strongly, and intercultural competence promoted amongst the implementing parties. After a new catalogue of criteria for the assessment of projects had been drawn up as far back as the Stockholm

Conference in 1972, a catalogue which provided that with a more sparing use of resources the population should participate more (cf. Bethge et al. 2011, p. 25), in 1998 there followed a resolution by the German Bundestag that the participation of the target group in development policy projects should be established as a criterion of success for development cooperation (cf. Holtz 2000). The Millennium Declaration, the MDGs, the Johannesburg Implementation Plan (2002) and the Paris Declaration can also be seen as breakthroughs for a development policy following the model of sustainable development.

However, it is questionable whether the industrialized countries, whose societies have up until now more or less strongly resisted the sustainability ideal, can make a contribution towards sustainable development in developing countries. The objective of sustainable development in the countries of the South can possibly only be established through a practical implementation of the sustainability ideal in the industrialized countries (cf. König 2011, p. 63).

In practical project work in development cooperation, due to the complex nature of tasks in the development policy context, there is a strong desire for simple and standardized processes. The development policy problems which need to be solved are, however, usually attributable to different causes. Consequently, nor can blueprints or action guidelines for how sustainable project management is to be implemented in development cooperation be laid down on the basis of the heterogeneity of the developing countries, or on the basis of plans, objectives and framework conditions. The comments below therefore represent only recommendations or criteria which may promote sustainable project management in the sphere of development cooperation.

Due to the multifactorial causes of development policy problems, the strategic orientation of a development cooperation project is also to be extended to several factors. Therefore, it is not simply necessary to seek improvements to the global, national and regional framework conditions, but to also implement capacity development measures, i.e. measures to improve the local capacities of people and institutions (cf. Rauch 2012, p. 47). For solving development policy problems, these different factors are also to be taken into consideration in the ecological, economic and social dimensions, which also embrace socio and politico-institutional themes, and are also to be placed within their complementary relationship. A very fundamental question in this connection would then be: "How do these factors attributable to these dimensions relate to one another, with reference to the specific situation and the specific problem to be solved?" (Rauch 2012, p. 48).

The sectoral programmes which have hitherto been carried out in development cooperation are, in comparison to the multidimensional strategies promoted, easier to implement. Multidimensional strategies call for project teams, consisting of experts from various disciplines and which apply multi-sectoral approaches. Rauch therefore recommends:

> Joint, multidimensional thinking and planning, but then taking action whereby distinctions are made between functional sectoral competencies and specific mandates. This should ensure that multidimensionality is not achieved

at the cost of clarity, specialized functionality and clearly defined institutional competencies and responsibilities … Multidimensional solutions therefore always require an interdisciplinary discourse and a dialogue between the various interest groups directed towards a balance of interests.

(Rauch 2012, p. 49)

It is therefore crucial that strategies, which take into account all three dimensions of sustainable development, are adapted to the respective context and are interlinked. The following principle can thus apply: "Integrated thought and analysis, embracing all dimensions and [global, national and regional] levels – acting in a focused and context-related manner" (Rauch 2012, p. 75). The "multidimensional, multi-level approach developed by Rauch should therefore be understood as "a mindset", "which helps to reduce the respective problem in a structured manner, to determine the appropriate strategic focus in a context-related way and to thereby logically coordinate problems" (Rauch 2012, p. 76).

Therefore, objectives, implementation and resources, as well as organization, should be coordinated with the project partners. "The participation of the target group is more than a partnership ritual. The awareness of their problems, resources and culturally influenced approach is an indispensable prerequisite for successful cooperation" (Kevenhörster & van den Boom 2009, p. 93). Only someone who has an actual knowledge of the relevant problems and their causes can formulate context-specific and solution-oriented strategies which implement all dimensions.

In summary, a number of criteria can be ascertained which should be taken into consideration for sustainable project management in development cooperation. Taking as a starting point the model for sustainable development which has existed as a normative concept since the Brundtland Report, a development path can be theoretically posited for shaping strategy.

For sustainable action, not only all three dimsensions of the model of sustainable development have to be taken into account, but also their interdependent relationship (cf. Bethge et al. 2011, pp. 20). Therefore, in sustainable project management account has to be taken not only of the three dimensions within the project (i.e. with regard to the processes or functions of the project), but also in each phase (for example, in the definition, initiation, planning, implementation, control and evaluation phase, and thus – specifically in the analysis – in decision-making and strategy development), and also outside of the project (i.e. in respect of the value creation chain, the result or the outcome or impact) account has to be taken of the applicable intragenerational or intergenerational justice.

Furthermore, in terms of the complementary aspect, a long-term or permanent effect on human development has to be promoted and a dynamic adaptation to the prevailing circumstances and the resulting learning effects implemented. There has to be regular monitoring of whether the project promotes sustainable development with its objectives and measures. In this connection, an essential factor is to conduct project management on the basis of participation, cooperation and the accompanying intercultural competence, along with transparency.

In development cooperation, the concept of Capacity WORKS can be under-stood as an aid, although this must in each case be specifically oriented according to the problems involved, target group, stakeholders, framework conditions and the criteria for sustainable project management. "Achieving sustainable development will require deep structural changes and new ways of working in all areas of economic, social and political life" (OECD & UNDP 2002, p. 27).

Conclusions

The management of projects, and the accompanying standardizations and guide-lines, has now already been developed and established for a considerable time. Particularly in large-scale enterprises, such as the traditional automobile industry, these project management methods have been applied over a long period. And in many medium-sized businesses, corresponding management methods have become indispensable and ought to guarantee that an enterprise operates efficiently. This requirement of efficiency is time and again seen as only applicable to "market-driven" profit-oriented enterprises. However, it has been possible to demonstrate that it makes no difference whether an organization is profit-oriented or not. Both must work efficiently towards their respectively set goals, or they otherwise lose their right to exist. The principle of economic viability can and must be applied to both organizational forms.

It is now apparent that particularly organizations which have a specific-target orientation as a formal objective, and which operate within an international envi-ronment, in many cases have to impose greater demands upon their employees in connection with project management competencies than is the case in traditional forms of industry. Such non-profit organizations are above all to be found in devel-opment work, and in these organizations employees must, amongst other things, constantly prepare for their new country of operation. The six-characteristic model offers a model framework for this, to specifically enable adaptation to and preparation for a country and its population. In addition, it has been possible to demonstrate with the new political economy that for the numerously cited exam-ples of failure on the macro-level, there is no monocausal reason for the poor management of projects or programmes.

It is much rather the specific constellations in development work which do not always allow successes on the macro-level. In view of the strong level of profes-sionalism in German development cooperation, it certainly cannot be claimed that there is deficient or poor management. As examples of this, reference has been made to the GIZ and the approach adopted for development cooperation projects with the support of Capacity WORKS.

However, it remains to be stressed that one dimension of project management in development cooperation should be mentioned which has as yet not achieved the desired level of professionalism. This relates to the sustainable management of proj-ects in development cooperation – an area which has so far been subject to no standardization within the meaning of DIN 69901. It does, however, represent an indispensably necessary framework for the implementation of projects in developing countries. There should continue to be considerations of and critical discussions about the concepts of sustainability as well as development. Even if the concept of sustainability has in the meantime been introduced into the theoretical discussion of development cooperation, its practical implementation must be further reinforced (cf. Bethge et al. 2011, p. 38).

Notes

1   On the range of criticism, see Ashoff (2010, p. 29).
2   For more precise details, see Faust & Leiderer (2008, 2010), Doucouliagos & Paldam (2008 and 2011); Harms & Lutz (2006); Roodman (2007).

References

Ashoff, G. (2010). Wirksamkeit als Legitimationsproblem und komplexe Herausforderung der Entwicklungspolitik. In J. Faust, & S. Neubert (eds), *Wirksamere Entwicklungspolitik* (pp. 27–68). Baden-Baden: Nomos.

Bethge, J. P.; Steurer, N.; Tscherner, M. (2011). Nachhaltigkeit. Begriff und Bedeutung in der NEtwicklungszusammenarbeit. In J. König, & J. Thema (eds), *Nachhaltigkeit in der Entwicklungszusammenarbeit* (pp. 15–40). Wiesbaden: VS Verlag für Sozialwissenschaften.

BMZ (German Federal Ministry for Economic Cooperation and Development) (2008). *Leitlinien für die bilaterale Finanzielle und Technische Zusammenarbeit mit Kooperationspartnern der deutschen Entwicklungszusammenarbeit.* (BMZ Konzepte 165). Bonn, Berlin: BMZ.

BMZ (2015). *Eine Welt ohne Armut und Not. Ziele der internationalen Entwicklungspolitik.* Downloaded on 13.06.2015 from www.bmz.de/de/was_wir_machen/ziele/ziele/index.html?PHPSESSID=0f0c1a7b42e07a742bbf33ef3cb2dbb5.

Caspari, A.; Barbu, R. (2008). Wirkungsevaluierungen: Zum Stand der internationalen Diskussion und dessen Relevanz für Evaluierungen der deutschen Entwicklungszusammenarbeit. *Evaluation Working Papers.* Bonn: Bundesministerium für wirtschaftliche Zusammenarbeit und Entwicklung.

Cronenbroeck, W. (2004). *Handbuch Internationales Projektmanagement Grundlagen, Organisation, Projektstandards, Interkulturelle Aspekte, Angepasste Kommunikationsformen.* Berlin: Cornelsen Verlag.

DIN (Deutsches Institut für Normung) (2009). *Projektmanagement – Projektmanagementsysteme,* Berlin Vienna Zurich: Beuth Verlag.

Doucouliagos, H.; Paldam, M. (2008). Aid effectivness on growth: a meta study. *European Journal of Political Economy, 24*(1), pp. 1–24.

Doucouliagos, H.; Paldam, M. (2011). The ineffectiveness of development aid on growth: an update. *European Journal of Political Economy, 27*(2), pp. 399–404.

European Commission. (1997). *Green Paper on Relations betwenn the European Union and the ACP Countries on the Eve of the 21st Century.* Luxembourg.

Faust, J.; Leiderer, S. (2008). Zur Effektivität und politischen Ökonomie der Entwicklungszusammenarbeit. *Politische Vierteljahresschrift, 49*(1), pp. 129–152.

Faust, J.; Leiderer, S. (2010). Die Effektivität der Entwicklungszusammenarbeit – Ergebnisse des ökonometrischen Ländervergleichs. In J. Faust, & S. Neubert, *Wirksamere Entwicklungspolitik. Befunde, Reformen, Instrumente* (pp. 166–188). Baden-Baden: Nomos

Faust, J.; Michaelowa, K. (2013). Die Politische Ökonomie der Entwicklungszusammenarbeit – Einführung und Überblick. In J. Faust, & K. Michaelowa (eds), *Politische Ökonomie der Entwicklungszusammenarbeit* (pp. 13–28). Baden-Baden: Nomos.

German Bundestag – Ausschuß für wirtschaftliche Zusammenarbeit und Entwicklung (1997). *Stellungnahmen zu der öffentlichen Anhörung des Ausschußes für wirtschaftliche Zusammenarbeit und Entwicklung "Nachhaltigkeit in der Entwicklungszusammenarbeit" am 29.* Oktober 1997. Ausschußdrucksache *13/162.*

GIZ (Deutsche Gesellschaft für Internationale Zusammenarbeit) (2015). *Kooperationsmanagement in der Praxis.* Wiesbaden: Springer-Verlag.

GTZ (Deutsche Gesellschaft für Technische Zusammenarbeit) (1996). *Project Cycle Management (PCM) and Objectives-Oriented Project Planning (ZOPP). Guidelines.* Eschborn: GTZ.

Hab, G.; Wagner, R. (2013). *Projektmanagement in der Automobilindustrie. Effizientes Management von Fahrzeugprojekten entlang der Wertschöpfungsketten.* 4th edition. Wiesbaden: SpringerGabler.

Harms, P.; Lutz, M. (2006). Aid, governance, and private foreign investment: some puzzling findings for the 1990s. *The Economic Journal, 116*(513), pp. 773–790.

Hauff, V. (ed.). (1987). *Unsere gemeinsame Zukunft. Der Brundtland-Bericht der Weltkommission für Umwelt und Entwicklung.* Greven: Eggenkamp.

Holtz, U. (2000). Nachhaltigkeit in der Entwicklungszusammenarbeit. In B. Fahrenhorst, & S. A. Musto (eds), *Grenzenlos – Kommunikation, Kooperation, Entwicklung* (Bde. SID-Berlin Berichte Nr. 13, pp. 54–60). Berlin.

Kaestner, R.; Koolmann, S.; Möller, T. (eds) (2012). *Projektmanagement im Not for Profit-Sektor – Handbuch für gemeinnützige Organisationen,* Nuremberg: Verlag GPM Deutsche Gesellschaft für Projektmanagement e.V..

Kevenhörster, P.; van den Boom, D. (2009). *Entwicklungspolitik.* Wiesbaden: VS Verlag für Sozialwissenschaften.

Koch, E. (2012a). *Interkulturelles Management – Für Führungspraxis, Projektarbeit und Kommunikation.* Konstanz and Munich: UVK Verlagsgesellschaft mbH, Lucius.

Koch, E. (2012b). Capacity WORKS – interkulturell. In E. Koch, & S. Speiser (eds), *Interkulturalität in der internationalen Entwicklungszusammenarbeit* (pp. 1–18). Munich, Mering.

König, J. (2011). Entwicklung und Nachhaltigkeit. Kritische Betrachtung von zwei dehnbaren Konzepten. In J. König, & J. Thema (eds), *Nachhaltigkeit in der Entwicklungszusammenarbeit* (pp. 41–68). Wiesbaden: VS Verlag für Sozialwissenschaften.

Kuster, J.; Huber, E.; Lippmann, R.; Schmid, A.; Schneider, E.; Witschi, U.; Wüst, R. (2011). *Handbuch Projektmanagement,* 3rd extended edition. Berlin Heidelberg: Springer.

Mummert, U. (2013). Multiple Prinzipale, Agenten und Ziele: Konsequenzen für die Entwicklungspolitik. In: J. Faust, & K. Michaelowa (eds), *Politische Ökonomie der Entwicklungszusammenarbeit* (pp. 51–87). Baden-Baden: Nomos.

OECD (Organization for Economic Co-operation and Development), UNDP (United Nations Development Programme) (2002). *Sustainable Development Strategies. A resource book.* London: OECD & UNDP.

Rauch, T. (2012). Strategien und Instrumente nachhaltiger Entwicklung – ein multidimensionaler Mehr-Ebenen-Ansatz. In: K. Fiege, & T. Rauch (eds), *Entwicklungszusammenarbeit gestalten. Inhalte und Methoden für ein erfolgreiches Wirken in einem komplexen Berufsfeld* (pp. 40–81). Berlin: SLE Publikationsserie. Seminar für Ländliche Entwicklung.

Roodman, D. (2007). The anarchy of numbers: aid, development, and cross-country empirics. *World Bank Economic Review, 21*(2), pp. 255–277.

SPM (Sustainable Project Management) (2015a). *Wertekompass.* Downloaded on 26.10.2015 from www.nachhaltiges-projektmanagement.de/cms/index.php/de/werte.

SPM (2015b). *Triple Constraint.* Downloaded on 26.10.2015 from www.nachhaltiges-

projektmanagement.de/cms/index.php/de/knowledge/nachhaltiges-projektmanagement/
11-triple-constraint.
von Hauff, M. (2014). *Nachhaltige Entwicklung: Grundlagen und Umsetzung.* 2nd ed., Munich:
Oldenbourger Wissenschaftsverlag.
von Hauff, M.; Kleine, A. (2014). *Nachhaltige Entwicklung: Grundlagen und Umsetzung.*
München: Oldenbourger Wissenschaftsverlag.

4 Evaluation of sustainable development

Reinhard Stockmann and Wolfgang Meyer

Introduction

The 21st century is facing some formidable challenges. Social inequality is increasing dramatically, in both the developed countries and the less well-developed ones. In addition to that, the gaps between 'rich' and 'poor' countries are widening. Climatic change, demographic trends and migration triggered by terrorism, war and poverty are jeopardizing previously achieved successes. In the course of globalization, the primacy of economy, the creed of open international trade and that of the 'free' play of market forces, is leading to a rigorous natural selection which is oriented solely toward the pursuit of economic gain and resulting in a 'survival of the fittest': only the strongest market players will survive.

The primacy of economy is threatening not only the social equilibrium, the way people live together in societies and the peaceful coexistence of states, but also the ecology of the planet Earth itself. Poverty on the one hand, which leads for example to deforestation, excessive exploitation of soils, overgrazing etc., and on the other hand, the economically motivated plundering of mineral and natural resources (tropical forests, water etc.), uninhibited environmental pollution and the production of substances which are harmful to the environment (e.g. greenhouse gases) are systematically ruining the environment and prejudicing nothing less than the future of the human race.

For these reasons, a balance between social, economic and ecological systems is urgently needed. Political strategies which strive toward such a status have been developed increasingly in the past two decades under the overall control of the United Nations and can be comprised under the generic term '*sustainable development*'. The implementation of political strategies calls for *purposeful, effective measures*. To this end, wide-ranging programmes must be initiated, and they should make a clearly defined contribution to the goals of the strategy. These then need to be divided up into viable projects, which in turn comprise practically implementable packages of measures and are also able to guarantee their effectiveness. At the end, the cumulation of the individual impacts of measures, projects and programmes should lead to appreciable progress as regards the strategies and their goals.

This is where *evaluation* comes into play. Evaluation has set itself the task of assessing the effectiveness of measures and aims by the deployment of scientific methods to enable insights to be gained for the management of projects, programmes and strategies. For the assessment of the *sustainability* of impacts, in other words the permanent changes brought about by interventions which run for a limited period of time only, the instrument of ex-post evaluation was developed.

This chapter concerns itself with the evaluation of sustainable development. First, the two central terms 'evaluation' and 'sustainability' are defined, and then a look is taken at the special requirements imposed on an evaluation of the model of sustainable development at macro level and programmes and projects supporting this model at micro level. After that, the challenges and needs of evaluating sustainability are compared with the state of art of evaluation research and the potentials available here. Especially weak points and potentials for development of evaluation approaches are emphasized. The next section deals with the practical side of regular investigating the effects and impacts of sustainable development. The focus on the macro-level of sustainability reveals that monitoring approaches are poorly linked to evaluation concepts and therefore evidence-based policies toward sustainable development are hindered. While looking at the micro-level of programs and projects, one has to state a broad variety of evaluation use and, at least partly in some policy fields, a well established and systematic usage. This use fulfills different functions in project and programme management as well as in society. However, evaluation use is poorly linked to macro-concepts of sustainable development and the understanding of sustainability is merly limited to durability.

What does evaluation of sustainable development mean?

If this question is to be answered, the terms 'evaluation' and 'sustainability' first need to be clarified. This is all the more important in view of the fact that both terms are nowadays used in a positively inflationary manner with a very wide range of meanings indeed. The word evaluation is often used to designate any kind of assessment, quite independently of what has been assessed, by whom and applying what criteria. Yet these are the very questions that need to be investigated precisely in a scientific definition of evaluation. Evaluations are distinguished by the fact that:

- they refer to a *clearly definable object* (e.g. political intervention measures, projects, programmes, organizations, individuals, processes, products etc.);
- they are conducted by *persons who are specially qualified for the purpose* (experts);
- the assessment is carried out with explicit reference to the circumstance or object to be evaluated and applying precisely stipulated and *disclosed criteria*;
- objectifying *empirical data collection methods* are used in the generation of information;
- *methods involving systematic comparison* are used for the assessment of that information.

Evaluation is thus *part of applied social research*, which aims to make a contribution to the solution of practical sociopolitical problems by attempting purposively and systematically to provide bases for non-scientific decision-making processes (cf. Clemens 2000, p. 215). To do this, evaluation avails itself of the entire spectrum of social science theories, concepts and research methods, and it is rules that are standard in the world of science that apply to the collection of valid and reliable data (cf. Rossi et al. 2004, p. 16).

Applied social research and thus also evaluation research differ from pure research in several ways:

- Evaluations are always usefulness-oriented, i.e. the findings should be useful for decision-making processes and make a contribution to the improvement of societal management.
- Evaluations therefore have a service character; the research objectives are determined by the clients and the research findings utilized by the clients for their own specific aims.
- Evaluations are always associated with assessments, by which it is not subjective value judgements that are meant, but 'technological estimates', in which the values achieved are measured against pre-specified criteria. If for example, on its introduction, it is decided that a study course will in accordance with the resources available be fully subscribed when it has 25 participants, it is primarily a matter of achieving that target and simply ascertaining whether there has been an over- or under-subscription. Whether this result is to be classified as 'good' or 'bad' on a superordinate scale of values is not a thing that an evaluation can determine on the basis of the measurements it makes.

A general definition can be derived from these features: 'Evaluation is the systematic investigation of the merit or worth of an object (program) for the purpose of reducing uncertainty in decision making' (Mertens 1998, p. 219).

Evaluation thus hovers in an area of tension between scientific integrity and usefulness. On the one hand, it is part of empirical social science and has to comply with its rules and standards, so that it can arrive at findings that are reliable and as accurate as possible. On the other hand, evaluation does not merely have a commitment to the gaining of insights; it is also geared to providing findings that are utilizable for the improvement of social praxis, and must accordingly also orient itself toward the existing framework conditions of that utilization and toward the practical necessities.

Like 'evaluation', the term 'sustainability' is multifaceted and controversial in terms of what it actually means. In general terms, we can differentiate between a macro and a micro level in the use of the term (cf. Stockmann 2008, p. 122).

At macro level, the term sustainability describes a societal model in which ecological, economic and social developments are perfectly balanced. This is nothing less than the *vision of an all-embracing social integration*, the aim of which is to make it possible, by means of suitable management rules, to *manage the limited resources rationally* on the basis of a perfect and lasting *fairness of distribution* (cf. Meyer 2012). This integration should take place in three dimensions:

1   *horizontal integration* of the target dimensions ecology, economy and social affairs (the 'three pillars of sustainability');
2   *vertical integration* between global, national and local levels of action ('think globally, act locally', the motto of the first UN Conference on Sustainable Development in Rio de Janeiro);
3   *inter-generational integration* between the needs of today's generation and those of future generations (Brundtland definition).

There is no question but that such a sweeping and abstractly worded Utopia is bound to be interpreted variously by the groups of actors involved in terms of its actual implementation. As a *normative construct* which aims to set general societal targets and establish universal rules for action, the model of sustainable development will remain controversial in the future too. It is, accordingly, questionable whether the call for more substantiation and more precise description of that model, issued in various different forms as it has been, really gets to the heart of the matter. It is in fact much rather the case that that very room for interpretation has been the cause of the widespread acceptance of the model and its astonishing ability to integrate on a global scale. With each interest group and each nation adding its own emphases and 'tweaking' the model to cater to its own wishes, it is comparatively easy to gather beneath this flag. However, this does not solve fundamental conflicts of objectives; it merely shunts them on to the implementation level. At the same time, there is always the risk that 'sustainable development' will degenerate into an 'empty formula' or 'political catchword' which is not really meaningful. The questions of whether or not decisions about measures promote the goal of sustainable development and whether or not they lead to purposeful action at all is the subject of a *normative societal discourse*. Particularly in the case of the most urgent organizational issues, the *reconciliation of interests* which is necessary to create a 'win–win' situation proves to be a tough task, hampered by positions of power and emotional judgements and prejudices. Accordingly, the argument about the content and interpretation of the sustainable development model is likely to go on for a very long time.

Because the model is a controversial normative construct, the policy-makers must breathe life into it with specific strategies for action ('policies'). Whilst sustainability from the macro perspective is a Utopian notion, aiming to integrate human needs and interests over generations in such a way that economic, ecological and social objectives are balanced and global, national and local levels of action connected up, the implementation level often disappears from view. The fact is often overlooked that the macro-concept of sustainability is not a condition that can be created by concrete measures and then assured 'sustainably' in the long term. Neither is sustainable development the result of endogenous evolution; it can only be achieved in an ongoing management process by means of rational and planned human interventions. Thus sustainability at macro level can only be brought about and maintained if there are, at micro level, measures which are effective in the long term and subject to continual verification in respect of their effects on sustainable development. Such measures are packaged into projects and programmes and form the main elements of sustainability strategies, with which the objectives of the model of sustainable development, defined as desirable on a global scale, are to be achieved.

As on the macro level of sustainable development, there are also a large number of different definitions on the micro level of concrete action (see Stockmann 1993, 1996, 2013; Caspari 2004, p. 45). First of all, it is important to emphasize that 'sustainability' in this context can by no means be equated to normatively hoped-for results aimed at achieving the ecological, economic and social objectives of the model of sustainable development. Impacts can occur positively in the context of the aims being striven toward, though those aims do not necessarily have to conform to the maxims of the model of sustainable development. There are also *'side effects'* or *unintended consequences of action*, which can unintentionally jeopardize the success of the measure or cause problems in other areas. And it is at least conceivable that *negative impacts* may lead to long-term or permanent damage which far outweighs the benefit achieved by a measure. This certainly applies with regard to the model of sustainable development: the negative impacts of human action are still far greater than the effects of the positive efforts made to promote a fair and resource-conserving way of managing the world's commodities.

Because of the focus on sustainability, the time dimension shifts to the centre of cognitive interest. This gives rise to special requirements imposed on an evaluation of sustainability, which make it different to other evaluations. If a decision is to follow the premises of the model of sustainable development, it requires forecasts which are as accurate as possible about its long-term impacts. The time horizon to be taken into account is in principle infinite – for the aspiration of attending to the needs of future generations obviously has no temporal limitations. One may have some doubts if the existing evaluation approaches are able to tackle these challenges of sustainable development. This will be discussed next.

Is evaluation able to tackle the challenges of sustainable development?

There is a broad variety of different evaluation approaches which may be used for the purpose of evaluating sustainability. Following the distinction of Stockmann and Meyer (2013, p. 156), one can find seven groups of evaluation approaches:

1   One group of evaluators understand themselves primarily as *researchers* and scientific interests dominate their approaches (Mark et al. 2000; Rossi et al. 2004, Stockmann 2008).
2   Another perspective is taken by approaches who focus on capacity building and empowerment at the 'grass roots' level and such evaluators understand themselves more as *social workers* than as researchers (Cousins & Earl 1995; Whitmore 1998; Fetterman 2000).
3   The third group of approaches has a broader understanding of stakeholders (not only the target group but also employees, beneficiaries and people barred from the outputs) and the idea of 'participatory evaluation' bestrides this way of thinking (Stake 1975; Patton 1986; Guba & Lincoln 1989).

4   Other evaluators understand themselves as *consultances* for the programme or project management and the 'management perspective' of their approaches is aiming on improving steering abilities (Alkin 1969; Stufflebeam 1971; Bamberger et al. 2006).

5   The 'client perspective' of the next group of approaches is even broader: doing evaluation is seen as delivering services to clients and evaluators as *service providers* have to follow the needs and wishes of their clients (House 1978; Scriven 1980; Wholey 1983).

6   Objective-oriented evaluation approaches are primarily doing some kind of *book-keeping* and accountability is the guiding principle of such an evaluation – which is in many cases not an evaluation but a form of monitoring[1] (Provus 1971; Sanders & Cunningham 1973).

7   Closely related to this, one can identify a final group of *administrative initated monitoring and evaluation* approaches such as accreditation systems for universities or school supervisory boards. These approaches share a 'state-regulative perspective', making monitoring and evaluation to a task for the state and its institutions.

The use of evaluation approaches is certainly depending on the topic and issues under observation. In the evaluation of sustainability a distinction must be made between the assessment of effectiveness (analytical level) and the assessment of purposefulness (normative level). For the *assessment of effectiveness*, the foremost question is that of what (lasting) effects were triggered off by an intervention supporting sustainable development. The scientific investigation concentrates on the *allocation of observed or measured changes* and attempts to investigate *causal connections* between the intervention and those changes.

The decision regarding the selection of the 'right' action alternative for sustainable development draws attention to the *normative character* of its assessment: are the measures purposeful for achieving sustainability goals or not? This implies a certain understanding of sustainability in the *intention* of those who are implementing the measures, giving the evaluators the opportunity to make meaningful statements in a *target-performance comparison* about the *achievement of sustainability objectives* with the measures deployed.

As if this task were not already difficult enough, the evaluation of sustainability is also faced with two further challenges. With reference to the coordination of the actions of those involved it is, on the one hand, a matter of paying adequate attention to ecological, economic and social interests, and assessing their relative importance with regard to concrete measures and their impacts. This means that scientific methods and cognitive traditions need to be brought together meaningfully in an interdisciplinary evaluation concept. On the other hand, the global aims should be translated into concrete local actions and these, in an interplay of many minor impacts, should lead to the hoped-for and urgently needed successes at global level. For the evaluation of sustainability this means that complex aggregations and disaggregations of impacts need to be assessed.

This refers again to the three dimensions of the macro-concept of sustainability: approaches used for the evaluation of sustainable development have to cover not only the effects caused by interventions and its durability on a micro level but have also to provide adequate tools for assessing the integration on target, territorial and time dimensions on a macro level. These tasks are key challenges for evaluation approaches and its different perspectives shortly described at the beginning of this part.

By using these aspects for a meta-analyses of evaluation approaches, Meyer (2012, p. 49) came to the conclusion 'that some aspects are covered by almost all approaches, while others are not even handled by a single one'. First, the goal system of a sustainable development programme or project must include the 'three pillars', for example it must make reference to impacts which can actually be reached (or should not be released to avoid negative side effects) in the economical, ecological and the social system. The evaluation approach should therefore be able to handle the key question whether the goal system under observation is able to cover this integration task of different system requirements in a proper way. If an evaluation approach does not analyse the desired system from this perspective, one may not be able to judge about horizontal social integration as a key element of sustainability. In general, all evaluation approaches are assessing goal systems in one or the other way and to include the evaluation of sustainability concepts is easily possible without conflicting with the overall philosophy of the evaluation concept.

Second, looking at the vertical social integration means to focus on the communication and coordination processes within a programme or project and towards the outside world. Evaluating communication systems is especially important because of the existing social, political and geographical distances refering to the differing interests of people living under varying circumstances. Several aspects within a programme framework have to be taken into accout: for example the communication between programme managers and their staff, between programme members and other responsible person or departments of the implementing agency, between different organizations or departments involved in the programme or some parts and so on. While such kinds of internal communication are of certain importants for all kind of programmes and projects, the specific task of sustainable development programmes and projects is embedding their own activities in a framework of other activies towards shared goals of sustainable development. These implies communication and coordination with target groups, stakeholders, clients, sponsors, journalists and so on not only in a local or national context but also on an international and even global level. The direction of coordination is also of some importance: while the process of agenda-setting must be a somewhat 'top-down' process, that is one's own goals must be adjusted with other goals on the local, regional, national and global levels, the process of aggregating impacts is strictly 'bottom-up' – that is moving from the single outcome reached by one measure to effects which can be noticed even on a global scale. It also implies the existence of a sufficient and far-reaching impact chain. All these issues must be targeted by the evaluation approach. At least some of the newer, more integrative approaches based on scientific and management perspective are open for analysing agenda setting and coordination aspects. However, most evaluation approaches are underdeveloped if it comes to the question, how programme and project activities are coordinated towards shared external goals.

Third, the time dimension is very important for sustainable development issues. Short-term successes may be harmed by long-term failures and side effects. This implies the use of some kind of 'sustainability impact assessment' able to capture long-term risks for at least the three basic systems (ecology, economy and society). One of the main aspects under observation must be the 'half lifetime' of impacts achieved by the programme and of side effects which are released by trying to produce such kind of effects. Impact and risk assessment must not only concentrate on probabilities but also on the duration of impacts and risks: It does not make any sense to avoid carbon dioxide production for a period of time if all the while one is producing nuclear waste which pollutes the environment for millions of years by radioactivity. Finally, living in a changing world, one cannot assume constant needs, interests, framework conditions, feedback effects and so on. Sustainable development means change, and change requires adaptation. As described above, there must be some institutionalised mechanisms to asure sustainability on a micro scale of interventions, telling the actors that they have to adapt the existing system to new framework conditions and not to follow the 'old road' into a dead end. Again it must be the task of evaluation to assess all these aspects in a prober way. Hence, the (long-term) time dimension is hardly mentioned in evaluation concepts. Risk assessments are seldom used in evaluations although such methods are already standards in technological and environmental planning processes. Among the evaluation approaches described above, only Stockmann (2008) uses a dynamic model derived from life-course theory and includes a concept for impact sustainability in his approach. In general, evaluation research is merely limited to a narrow programme or project perspective which finishes with the end of the activities under observation.

To sum it up: the existing evaluation approaches are at least able to face some of the challenges associated with an adequate assessment of sustainable development. Most deficits can be found if one is looking beyond the horizont of project and programmes: while evaluation is merely focusing on a narrowly defined undertaking, the broader scope (especially on the time dimension) is merely out of sight. Moreover, as the following section will show, the practice of sustainability evaluation is not on a track towards more advanced evaluation approaches but more or less limited to monitoring.

How is sustainable development investigated in practice?

In general, three context factors are important for the development and implementation of monitoring and evaluation systems for sustainable development (Martinuzzi & Meyer 2016):

1   Sustainable development must be a relevant issue for policy-makers and therefore become a well operationalized policy aim.

2   Monitoring and evaluation must be seen as important and well-institutional-
    ized tools for governance.
3   The discourse on evaluation and sustainable development can be framed on a
    broad societal base or as an expert appraisal. While the first path is paved by
    the ideals of *Aufklärung* and 'social betterment' (and therefore linked to main-
    stream thinking in evaluation), the second one is following the more technical
    discourse in several scientific disciplines on sustainability with certain disposi-
    tion to exclude non-experts (and therefore the majority of people).

On the global level, the concept of sustainable development is still a 'child' of the
United Nations system (especially in the United Nations Commission on
Sustainable Development (CSD), the United Nations High-level Political Forum
on Sustainable Development (HLPF), the United Nations Environmental Program
(UNEP) and the United Nations Development Program (UNDP)). There are no
doubts that sustainable development was and still is a key issue for the UN system.
It shaped global policies and strategies from the very beginning through a series of
international conferences, meetings, workshops etc. Moreover, these activities
involved many national governments, implementation agencies, non-govermantal
organizations, private consultancies, multinational corporates or small and
medium-sized companies in almost all parts of the world.

One important step forward was the Millenium Summit in New York: the 189
member states of the United Nations and 23 international organizations signed the
United Nations Millenium Declaration and committed themselves to help to achieve
eight Millenium Development Goals (MDGs) devided in 21 targets until 2015
(United Nations 2011). This was the first time that the leaders of the world decided
to have a commonly shared goal systems and sustainable development was an important part of it. Its importance was even increased in autumn 2015 when the successor
of the MDGs, the 17 Sustainable Development Goals (SDGs), were endorsed.

The United Nations developed a set of indicators for monitoring the progress
towards the MDGs and established a regulary reporting and reviewing system for
to draw balance and derive lessons learnt. From 1990 to 2015, 60 indicators were
measured and published in global, regional and country reports (eg. United
Nations 2014). To select the indicators, five main criteria were used: relevant and
robust measures, clear to interpret and provide a base for comparison, consistent
and manageable, based on international standards, and constructed as quantifiable
from well-established data sources (UNDP 2003, p. 1). Approaching 2015, some
critical assessments of this monitoring system were published (Manning 2009;
Fukuda-Parr & Greenstein 2010; Fukuda-Parr et al 2013; UN System Task Team
2012; United Nations 2013).

The main advantages and positive side effects of this kind of indicator system,
based on public statistics, are obvious:

> The concept of monitoring concrete goals with statistically robust indicators
> is a clear strength of the framework from the policy and the statistical perspec-
> tives ... The MDG framework fostered the strengthening of statistical systems

and the compilation and use of quality data to improve policy design and monitoring by national governments and international organizations.

(United Nations 2013, p. 3)

While being a conservative approach, the MDG monitoring uses only existing data on highly aggregated level. This causes some inconsistencies between goals, targets and indicators: some goals are not adequately addressed by existing indicators and some of the targets are vaguely formulated, while others have clear numerical yardsticks. The goals, targets and indicators were developed in 2002 but 1990 was taken as the baseline year, making it difficult for some countries to provide adequate data (especially in those with limited statistical capacities). In general, there is a time lag of some years between data collection and data dissemination which affects policymaking. Moreover, the global trends were dominated by a few countries with large population so the global targets were merely interpreted as national ones especially in big countries (United Nations 2013, p. 3).

From a sustainability perspective, the MDGs and its monitoring system can be criticized as follows:

•   Horizontal integration: the MDGs target on economic, social and environmental issues but they do not balance the system needs in a proper way. The social aspects – especially health – dominate and neither the economic system nor the environmental system are adequaltely treated. There are a lot of well-established indicators which are able to cover economic or environmental performances which are not used in the MDG system. Moreover, it relies on an adminstrative initiated monitoring system which is not linked to evaluation approaches or any form of scientific-based systems thinking. As a result, it cannot produce information on causal linkages and system developments.
•   Vertical integration: the MDG monitoring system clearly focuses on a national perspective and also on the global comparability of the data provided by nation states. It does not mention the issue of disaggregating data on regional and local levels, especially to make the data manageable for programs and projects. It does not integrate an evaluation concept which gives information on the effectiveness or purposefulness of measures. Therefore, it is impossible to judge whether progress (or failure) of the global, regional or national trends can be attributed to political decisions, strategies or concrete actions.
•   Time: the MDG monitoring system is able to provide time-series data and the comparability of indicator results is one of its main advantages. However, for impact monitoring it does not cover long-term effects and risk assessments are missing. There are no offical scenario models which try to reflect future impacts or pathways to reach the MDGs. Moreover, there is a lack of action planning, linking activities to goal attainment. Due to the missing evaluation component, there are no hints about the causes of deficits and changes, to enable better joint actions and succesful ways to reach the goals.

There are probably two reasons why the United Nation system did not include a proper evaluation concept in its MDG monitoring: from a political point of view, suggesting an evaluation approach may cause irritation among the member states and can be interpretated as a trial of the UN system's ability master the governance of sustainble development. This is, for sure, a very sensible approach and the UN avoids any action which may be interpreted in this way. From a practical point of view, the UN evaluation activities are concerned with the UN system and as such limited to this (UNEG 2013, 2015). To follow a more open and decentralized approach for the evaluation of sustainable development makes some sense.

Compared to the UN system, the European Union is a much more coherent political body. The broad variety and complexity of policy instruments have led to several feedback mechanisms within the EU system and helped to establish ex-ante policy impact assessment, ex-post programme evaluation, monitoring, auditing, etc. (Martinuzzi 2011). Evaluation is a far developed tool for the EU (eg. European Agency 2005). In terms of action for sustainable development, Europe and especially the EU are often perceived as leading in the world. Without a doubt, the concept of sustainability is to a certain degree integrated into European politics and policies (cf. Martinuzzi & Meyer 2016, pp. 88).

Just to give an example: agricultural policy is still the EU's most important common policy area. The European Agricultural Fund for Rural Development (EARFD) is one of the main policy measures that co-finances rural development programmes by EU member states on national or regional levels. These programmes make extensive use of ex-ante impact assessments (see for example Ernst & Young et al. 2014) and the EU Directorate-General for Agriculture and Rural Development coordinates the European Evaluation Network for Rural Development (for its evaluation practice, see European Evaluation Network for Rural Development 2010) with an aim of establishing good practice and capacity building (Martinuzzi & Meyer 2016, p. 90). Sustainable development is explicitly mentioned in evaluation guidelines published by this network (European Evaluation Network for Rural Development 2006, p. 6). Strategic environmental assessments (SEA) play an important role in these evaluations and have to assess the adequacy of planned measures to promote sustainable development. Ex-post evaluations of EARFD are contracted by the EU on a regular basis and employ counterfactual impact evaluation, GIS-based analysis, benchmarking, economic, environmental and social impact indicators (as an example Grieve & Weinspach 2010). The framing of the Europe 2020 Strategy incorporates this policy area under the headline 'sustainable growth and natural resources'. Nevertheless, the specific challenges for sustainability evaluation are not systematically tackled in this somwhat coherent monitoring and evaluation system.

The EU system for evaluating sustainability can assessed as follows:

- Horizontal integration: there is still a way to go to reach an integrated EU monitoring and evaluation approach which is able to treat ecological, economical and social systems adequately. However, sustainability is at least partly anchored in the existing concepts. But it is mainly treated as a technical issue which needs advanced expertise in technical assessment and not in evaluation.

• Vertical integration: within some areas, evaluation of sustainability is institutionalized on different levels and the cross-level linkage seems to work fairly well. Although there might be room to improve, the vertical dimension is at least recognized and there are some trials to implement the evaluation of sustainability on various levels in an interrelated form.

• Time: the example of rural development programmes shows also some elements of long-term risk assessments and spatial planning. The instrument of SEAs gives some room for integrating other aspects of sustainable development and there are at least some efforts to follow this direction. However, there is as yet no long-term sustainability assessment tool available.

On the national level, sustainability strategies are widespread, especially in Europe and other countries of the well-developed world. In Germany, the sustainability strategy was endoresed in 2002, just in time for the World Summit in Johannesburg. Sustainability is seen as a cross-sectional task and a 'basic principle of German policy' (Bundesregierung 2002, p. 324). The role of government is defined as guiding a societal dialogue and for managing this task; the German federal government has endorsed a 'sustainability council' (Rat für Nachhaltige Entwicklung, see www.nachhaltigkeitsrat.de).

The performance monitoring system (*Erfolgskontrolle*) is quite similar to the MDG system: the main instrument is 38 quantified indicators which are supposed to reflect 21 dimensions of sustainability. A biannual indicator report gives an overview on the development (Statistisches Bundesamt 2014), while progress reports (*Fortschrittsbericht*) will offer a more deeper assessment of the development. The most comprehensive report was published in several languages for the tenth anniversary of the sustainability strategy (Federal Government of Germany 2012). There is no evaluation component systematically implemented and again it is obvious that purposive, goal-oriented action toward sustainable development is not possible soley on the basis of such a small indicator set.

To summarize: evaluation of sustainable development is only weakly established on the macro level. Well-developed indicator-based monitoring approaches dominate but are not linked to evaluation concepts which provide information on the effectiveness and purposefulness of interventions, measures and activities. The next section shows some tendencies of how evaluation approaches are used for development issues on the project and programme levels and how sustainability is included in this kind of use.

How is evaluation used for sustainability programmes or projects?

At the micro level, centre stage of the evaluation is occupied by the programmes and projects which support sustainability strategies or policies at the meso level and are mostly supposed to bring about social changes at macro level which will persist in the mid or long term. Programmes and projects thus constitute the central instruments of political action in order to implement sustainable development. The following presentation of various different forms of evaluation concentrates on this level because it is that occurs most frequently in practice.

The course of programmes and projects can be divided up into different phases, in each of which evaluation takes on a different task. In the development and implementation phases, evaluation supports the programme and project management in planning and management. As information about the progress and the results achieved is gathered, systematized and assessed, aids to decision-making are elaborated for the management. Such evaluations, which supply the management with management-relevant data and assessments, are referred to as formative evaluations.

If a programme or project was carried out or terminated a considerable time before the evaluation, the evaluation has the task of recording the whole range of impacts achieved, be they positive or negative, intended or unintended, and assessing them, and of looking into the causes – the impact relationships. Such evaluations, which are conducted in a summarizing, recapitulating and results-oriented way, are referred to as summative evaluations.

The first thing to be said is that no evaluation can function without gaining *insights*. In research-related evaluations, it is this aim in particular that is to the fore. Evaluations are however also often conducted for the purpose of *control*. In these cases the foremost questions are whether or not the objectives set down in the planning phase have been achieved, and whether or not all the actors have fulfilled their obligations. Insight and control-oriented evaluations ensure transparency, pave the way to an open dialogue and can thus trigger off *learning processes* for the further development of programmes. Finally, evaluation insights can also be used to *legitimize* programmes and measures that have been carried out in the public eye, or in the eye of the funders. It is true that all four evaluation functions are closely interwoven, yet evaluations can be differentiated according to their main purpose.

This classification scheme for objectives can be applied to the evaluation of sustainability. In concrete terms this means that sustainability evaluations can be used to:

- find out whether and at what level (macro, micro) sustainability has been achieved and what the reasons for that achievement or non-achievement were (insight);
- investigate, applying selected success criteria, whether or not the goals laid down in sustainability strategies or programmes have been achieved and whether or not the funds deployed for that purpose were adequate (control);
- tap learning potentials in order to adapt strategies and programmes aimed at creating sustainability to altered framework conditions, rectify shortcomings in planning or implementation, or learn ex-post for the creation of sustainability with the aid of other programmes and strategies (development);
- show whether a strategy or programme was successful in triggering off sustainable development processes, generating sustainable impacts or simply

implementing structures and processes, which also still continue to exist after the end of the funding and implementation phases in order to justify the investments made in the eye of the funder and/or the public eye (legitimation).

Sustainability evaluations mostly serve purposes of control or legitimation: the aim is to show retrospectively (ex-post) that the funds made available were deployed effectively (planned objectives achieved) and that they brought about sustainable impacts. In other words, evaluations of sustainability are often conducted in a summative function and have as their objective the legitimation of programmes, projects and measures which have already been carried out.

Depending on which evaluation objective is to the fore, the whole scope of evaluation approaches presented above may be used. This also applies to the question of how they are conducted. We differentiate here between internal and external evaluations. Evaluations are referred to as *internal* if they are conducted by the same organization as is implementing the programme or project. If this internal evaluation is conducted by the department which is at the same time entrusted with the operative implementation of the programme, the evaluation is a '*self-evaluation*'. If the evaluation is conducted by a different department in the organization (e.g. an evaluation or quality assurance department), it is an internal evaluation but not a self-evaluation (cf. Scriven 1991, p. 159 & p. 197).

External evaluations are conducted by people who do not belong to the funding or implementing organization. As a rule external evaluators thus have greater independence, profound methodological competence and professional evaluation knowledge, and are familiar with the area to which the programme or project belongs. External evaluations can also endow the reformatory forces within an organization with the extra legitimacy and clout they need to set processes of change in motion (cf. Pollitt 2000, p. 72). However, external evaluations may also trigger off feelings of apprehension among the evaluees and lead to defence reactions. Problems may also crop up later in the implementation of the evaluation findings. Internal and external evaluations are often seen *combined*, so that the two views can be brought together and the advantages of both procedures exploited.

With reference to the objectives of the *evaluation*, it should be noted that evaluations in which learning is mainly to the fore are often conducted internally. Insight and control-oriented evaluations are conducted both internally and externally. Evaluations mainly intended to serve the purpose of legitimation are almost exclusively commissioned as external evaluations, so that the greatest possible degree of objectivity and credibility can be attained. Since this legitimation aspect is very often to the fore in sustainability evaluations, they are mostly conducted as external evaluations.

One has to state that there is no particular solution implemented for monitoring and evaluating sustainable development as shown above. Even in development cooperation – where evaluation is well established – standardized concepts are missing. Evaluating sustainable development in projects and programmes of development cooperation is basing primarily on the agreements made in an Organization for Economic Co-operation and Development (OECD)

Development Assistance Committee (DAC) working group on evaluation. OECD DAC developed five principles for evaluation and the fifth one is on 'sustainability'. Hence, evaluations should primarily ask 'whether achievements are sustainable in the longer run' (OECD DAC 1991, p. 10) and thus the evaluation criteria do not cover completely the concept of sustainable development (see Chianca 2008).

As it relates to the micro level of concrete measures, sustainability means that the impacts of an intervention should continue after its conclusion. Since in programmes and projects it is usually a question of introducing innovations which contribute to the achievement of the macro objectives of sustainable development, we can diffentiate between four dimensions at the micro level of sustainability (see Table 4.1).

The first dimension focuses exclusively on how *long-term* the *utilization* of project or programme interventions is, with the innovations (products, services, technical solutions etc.) that have been created continuing to be used by others for their own benefit after the end of funding and support. An example of this kind of sustainability would be the permanent use of a course book in the context of a study course after the authors have withdrawn.

The second dimension centres around the *scope of the impacts*. Here it is a question of the extent to which the innovations spread within the potential user group and whether or not it has been possible to reach new user groups beyond the target group at which the project or programme was actually aimed. In the case of the course book, this would mean that it were used not only at one university but also for similar courses at other universities.

Table 4.1 Four dimensions at the the micro level of sustainability

Dimension	Type	Feature
I	Project–/programme–oriented	The target group and/or provider perpetuates the innovations in its own interest and for its own benefit.
II	Output-oriented	Other groups/organizations have permanently adopted the innovations in their own interest and for their own benefit.
III	System-oriented	By processes of diffusion, the innovations lead to an improvement in the performance of the system as a whole (e.g. the healthcare or education system).
IV	Innovation-oriented	The target group/provider has a potential for innovation with which it can react to altered environmental conditions in a flexible and appropriate way.

Source: Stockmann & Meyer 2013, p. 103; Caspari 2004, p. 67

The *system change* emphasized in the third dimension does not come about until an innovation is being used across the board and implemented as a genuine component part of the entire social system. In this case the course book would be used by all tertiary education institutions with study courses of the kind in question, or its use even prescribed as a regulation for all new study courses of a similar nature (diffusion of the innovation). An improvement in the performance of the system could manifest itself in a significant increase in expertise on evaluation questions on the part of development policy practitioners.

For the fourth dimension, finally, it is the *adaptability of the originally introduced innovation* that is decisive. It is now no longer a matter of a given project or programme being continued unchanged, but of its being flexible and adaptable to the altered requirements of the social environment. For this, appropriate capacity building is necessary in the organizations that provide the funding, with those organizations continuing to observe changes in the framework conditions and the needs of the target group, and being in a position to translate them, with the appropriate institutional backing, into appropriate modifications of the innovations. For the course book, this would mean regular updating of the contents by a firmly anchored course book commission.

With regard to the model of sustainable development and the link to the sustainability of the impacts of the measures carried out to implement the model, it should be noted that, independent of the different normative interpretations of the model, it is effects above all in the third and fourth dimensions of sustainability that should be achieved. This is primarily a question of comprehensive system changes (dimension 3), in which all sectors of society should adapt to the maxims of the model. For management that is 'fit for the future', however, it is also necessary to institutionalize the innovative capacity (dimension 4) and thus achieve a long-term or permanent adaptation of effective measures to the changing social, ecological and economic environmental conditions. Whether the measures developed in pilot projects are perpetuated in their originally planned form (dimension 1) or adopted by other organizations as 'best practice' (dimension 2) is, at best, only meaningful as an initial, very modest contribution toward this actual objective.

Conclusion

While looking at current implementation of monitoring and evaluation of sustainability, one has to state some limitations. As outlined above, evaluation is applied social research with some kind of assessment. Sustainability can be targeted by evaluations in two different ways. On the micro level, sustainability is primarily understood as the duration and the long-term scope of effects. Interventions may cause a lasting use of its products by the target group itself or by third parties. Hence, there is need for a more ambitious concept of sustainability on the micro level if the programme or project are to contribute to the macro-concept of sustainable development (as it is supported by the UN system). Effects caused by interventions must be system- or innovation-oriented and this means that change and its systematic observation and analysis have to be somehow institutionalized.

The main goal is to integrate several different aspects on three dimensions in this macro-concept of sustainability. Horizontal integration means a linking of system needs from the economic, environmental and social system in a well-balanced way. Vertical integration is about the disaggregation of goals from the global to the local level and the aggregation and cumulation of effects from the local to the global level. Integration on the timescale means emphasizong not only on short-term effects but also long-term (side)effects. The main challenges for monitoring and evaluating sustainable development can be derived from this.

There are many different approaches for evaluation which have been established and discussed in a steadily growing evaluation community. Some of these approaches are following the ideal of *Aufklärung* and want to contribute to 'social betterment' from the perspective of empowerment. The main difference is the target group of this empowerment: while some approaches are 'grassroot' oriented, others understand themselves as consultancies for programme or project responsible persons or as part of the scientific community with the task of providing new insights in a more general perspective. All these approaches can be used for different purposes in the evaluation of sustainability but they have to be adapted and further improved for meeting these needs. Hence, the understanding of evaluation in sustainable development context is much more influenced by a 'governance' perspective, primarily in minds of political decision-makers. The main issue here are to control the process of producing effects and to legitimate the resources used for this process. Monitoring and evaluation are much more seen as technological tools and not as part of an interactive social process.

The practice of evaluation of sustainability is therefore limited to an externally provided expert view and merely focused on technical aspects. Performance monitoring is highly standardized and concerns the process of 'controlling' sustainable development. There is a lack of well-developed evaluation approaches (and usage of them) for actively designing and governing these processes in an interactive and dialogue-oriented way of 'learning'.

Evaluation is primarily used on the micro level of sustainability in the context of programme and projects. At this level, the principles of sustainable development are still not well established and 'project thinking' (as well as evaluation) is too narrowly focused on project or programme activities and their direct outcomes. The scope must be broadened toward 'system thinking', especially on the vertical dimension (including impact assessments) and the time dimension (including risk assessments). There are at least some encouraging developments in this direction in evaluation research.

Note

1   Monitoring is a continuous and comparable measurement of indicators without asking for causes, causalities, side effects or impacts. It indicates, for instance, the achievement of goals but does not ask for the reasons why goals are achieved (or not), if these goals are the right ones, or if there are some additional effects beyond the scope of the indicators used. These are tasks of evaluations which are supposed to be linked to such a monitoring system.

References

Alkin, M.C. (1969): Evaluation theory development, *Evaluation Comment* 2 (1), pp. 2–7.

Bamberger, M.; J. Rugh; L. Mabry (2006): *RealWorld Evaluation. Working Under Budget, Time, Data, and Political Constraints.* Thousand Oaks: Sage.

Bundesregierung (2002): *Perspektiven für Deutschland – Unsere Strategie für eine nachhaltige Entwicklung.* Berlin: Presse- und Informationsamt der Bundesregierung.

Caspari, A. (2004): *Evaluation der Nachhaltigkeit von Entwicklungszusammenarbeit. Zur Notwendigkeit angemessener Konzepte und Methoden.* Wiesbaden: VS Verlag.

Chianca, T. (2008): The OECD/DAC criteria for international development evaluations: an assessment and ideas for improvement. *Journal of MultiDisciplinary Evaluation* 5 (9), pp. 41–51.

Clemens, W. (2000): Angeordnete Sozialforschung und Politikberatung. In: Clemens, W. & Strübing, J. (eds): *Empirische Sozialforschung und gesellschaftliche Praxis.* Opladen: Leske+Budrich, pp. 211–233.

Cousins, J.B.; Earl, L.M. (1995): *Participatory Evaluation in Education: Studies in Evaluation Use and Organizational Learning.* London: Falmer Press.

Ernst & Young Baltic AS, the Institute of Baltic Studies and OÜ Hendrikson & Ko (2014): *Ex-ante Evaluation of the Estonian Rural Development Plan 2014–2020.* Final Report. Tallinn: Minstry of Agriculture Estionia.

European Agency for Reconstruction Programming and Quality Assurance Division Evaluation Unit (2005): *Evaluation Guidelines. Revision 1 – May 2005.* Brussels: EU (EAR/2005/30/04).

European Evaluation Network for Rural Development (2006): *Guidelines for Ongoing Evaluation. Rural Development Programmes 2007–2013.* Brussels: European Evaluation Network for Rural Development/European Commission.

European Evaluation Network for Rural Development (2010): *The Evaluation of National Rural Network Programmes.* Brussels: European Evaluation Network for Rural Development/European Commission.

Federal Government of Germany (2012): *National Sustainable Development Strategy. 2012 Progress Report.* Berlin: Federal Government.

Fetterman, D.M. (2000): *Foundations of Empowerment Evaluation.* Thousand Oaks: Sage.

Fukuda-Parr, S.; Greenstein, J. (2010): How should MDG implementation be measured? Faster progress or meeting targets?, *Working Paper No. 63.* Brasilia, D.F.: International Policy Centre for Inclusive Growth.

Fukuda-Parr, S.; Yamin, A.E.; Greenstein, J. (2013): *The Power of Numbers: A Critical Review of MDG Targets for Human Development and Human Rights,* Working Paper Series, May, Harvard, MA: Harvard School of Public Health.

Grieve, J.; Weinspach, U. (eds) (2010): *Capturing Impacts of Leader and of Measures to Improve Quality of Life in Rural Areas.* Brussels: European Evaluation Network for Rural Development/European Commission.

Guba, E.G.; Lincoln, Y.S. (1989): *Fourth Generation Evaluation.* Newbury Park: Sage

House, E. (1978): Assumptions underlying evaluation models. *Educational Researcher* 7 (3), pp. 4–12.

Manning, R. (2009): *Using Indicators to Encourage Development: Lessons from the MDGs,* DIIS Report 2009:01. Copenhagen: Danish Institute for International Studies.

Mark, M.M.; Henry G.T.; Julnes, G. (2000): *Evaluation: An Integrated Framework for Understanding, Guiding and Improving Public and Nonprofit Policies and Programs,* San Francisco: Jossey-Bass.

Martinuzzi, A. (2011): Developing and mapping a community for evaluating sustainable development. In: Raggamby, A.; Rubik, F.; Hardi, P. & Martinuzzi, A. (eds): *Sustainable Development, Evaluation and Policy Making*. Cheltenham: Edward Elgar, pp. 279–296.

Martinuzzi, A.; Meyer, W. (2016): Evaluating sustainable development in a global society. In: Stockmann, R. & Meyer, W. (eds): *The Future of Evaluation. Global Trends, New Challenges, Shared Perspectives*. Basingstoke/New York: Palgrave Macmillan, pp. 81–94.

Mertens, D.M. (1998): *Research Methods in Education and Psychology: Integrating diversity with quantitative and qualitative approaches*. Thousand Oaks: Sage.

Meyer, W. (2012): Should evaluation be revisited for sustainable development? In: Raggamby, A.v. & Rubik, F. (eds): *Sustainable Development, Evaluation and Policy Making. Theory, Practice, and Quality Assurance*. Cheltenham: Edward Elgar, pp. 37–56.

OECD-DAC (1991): *DAC Principles for Evaluation of Development Assistance*. Paris: OECD.

Patton, M. Q. (1986): *Utilization-focused Evaluation*. Beverly Hills: Sage.

Pollitt, C. (2000): *Public Management Reform: A comparative analysis*. New York: Oxford University Press.

Provus, M.M. (1971): *Discrepancy Evaluation*. Berkeley: McCutchan.

Rossi, P.H.; Lipsey, M.W.; Freeman, H.E. (2004): *Evaluation. A Systematic Approach*. 7th edition. Thousand Oaks: Sage.

Sanders, J.R.; Cunningham, D.J. (1973): A structure for formative evaluation in product development. *Review of Educational Research* 43 (2), pp. 217–236.

Scriven, M. (1980): *The Logic of Evaluation*. Inverness: Edgepress.

Scriven, M. (1991): *Evaluation Thesaurus* (4th edition). Thousand Oaks: Sage.

Stake, R.E. (1975): *Program Evaluation, Particularly Responsive Evaluation*. Kalamazoo: Western Michigan University Evaluation Center.

Statistisches Bundesamt (2014): *Nachhaltige Entwicklung in Deutschland. Indikatorenbericht 2014*. Wiesbaden: destatis.

Stockmann, R. (1993): *Die Nachhaltigkeit von Entwicklungsprojekten. Eine Methode zur Evaluierung am Beispiel von Berufsbildungsprojekten* (2nd edition). Opladen: Westdeutscher Verlag.

Stockmann, R. (1996): *Die Wirksamkeit der Entwicklungshilfe. Eine Evaluation der Nachhaltigkeit von Programmen und Projekten der Berufsbildung*. Opladen: Westdeutscher Verlag.

Stockmann, R. (2008): *Evaluation and Quality Management. Principles of Impact-Based Quality Management*. Frankfurt u.a.: Peter Lang.

Stockmann, R.; Meyer, W. (2013): *Functions, Methods and Concepts in Evaluation Research*. Basingstoke/New York: Palgrave Macmillan.

Stockmann, R.; Meyer, W. (eds) (2016): *The Future of Evaluation. Global Trends, New Challenges, Shared Perspectives*. Basingstoke/New York: Palgrave Macmillan.

Stufflebeam, D.L. (1971): The relevance of the CIPP evaluation model for educational accountability. *Journal of Research and Development in Education* 5 (1), pp. 19–25.

United Nations (2011): *Accelerating Progress Towards the Millennium Development Goals: Options for sustained and inclusive growth and issues for advancing the United Nations development agenda beyond 2015*, Annual Report of the Secretary-General, A/66/126. New York: United Nations.

United Nations (2013): *Lessons Learned from MDG Monitoring From A Statistical Perspective*. Report of the Task Team on Lessons Learned from MDG Monitoring of the IAEG-MDG. New York: United Nations.

United Nations (2014): *The Millenium Development Goals Report 2014*. New York: United Nations.

UNDP (2003): *Indicators for Monitoring the Millennium Development Goals. Definitions Rationale Concepts and Sources*. New York: United Nations.

UNEG (2013): *UNEG Handbook for Conducting Evaluations of Normative Work in the UN System*. New York: UNEG.

UNEG (2015): *UNEG Strategy 2014–2019*. New York: UNEG.

UN System Task Team on the Post-2015 UN Development Agenda (2012): *Review of the Contributions of the MDG Agenda to Foster Development: Lessons for the post-2015 UN development agenda*, Discussion Note. New York: United Nations.

Whitmore, E. (1998): *Understanding and Practicing Participatory Evaluation*. San Francisco: Jossey-Bass.

Wholey, J.S. (1983): *Evaluation and Effective Public Management*. Boston: Little Brown.

Part II
Fields of action

5 From governance to good governance

Franz Nuscheler and Veronika Wittmann

The boom of the concept of governance

Prior to the rise of the normative concept of good governance to become the key concept of international development discourse was a rise of the concept of governance in various scientific disciplines. The Social Science Citation Index has since the mid-1990s recorded a steep rise in frequency of the mention of the term in social science and economics publications. A Google search brought to light in 2007 that the term *governance* even more frequently emerged in the production of various scientific disciplines and in political journalism than the also widely used term of globalization.

The suspicion arises quickly that here again a fashionable term, a "catch-all phrase" or a container concept with vague meanings, was born. Good governance had become a trend of the international transformation debate after the end of the East–West conflict. The figure of speech was striking and positive, but the term "good" can be associated with various desires.

An additional confusion was caused by its etymological proximity to the term of government, which implies the hierarchical control of politics, society and economy. When the *Oxford Dictionary* (2015) defines governance as "the action or manner of governing a state, organization etc.", then this proximity and confusability is promoted. The academic use and definition acrobatics could not prevent both terms from often being used interchangeably in everyday political language.

For the purpose of preliminary disambiguation, which has yet to be confirmed by the reconstruction of the governance debate: government refers to the entirety of government institutions and laws, the state monopoly of legislation and the hierarchical decision-making powers of the formally legitimized state apparatus. Governance, however, also recognizes decision-making processes beyond state institutions and activities that cannot be derived from formal and legally defined responsibilities, especially through the involvement of private actors in cooperative decision-making processes.

The reconstruction of the conceptual history also shows that the World Bank is sometimes asserted in retrospect with the origins of the concept of good governance in its 1989 study on the "crisis of governance" in Sub-Saharan Africa (World Bank, 1989), but this was not the starting point of the governance debate. Instead, the boom in growth of the term could be traced back to the academic debate in economics about the control and regulation capacity of the state, notably on findings of the New Institutional Economics and the New Political Economy. In particular, the theories of organization collected many insights and empirical findings which were provided by the Institutional Economics. The governance debate bridged disciplinary classifications.

There have been numerous attempts at a definition of governance that, as a rule, first address the erosion of a state decision-making monopoly in complex control systems and second, address the coordination and cooperation between public and private actors to develop collective decisions which are able to compensate for different interests. This focus on the cooperative action of public and private institutions is in line with the arguments of *Institutional Economics*, including those of the Commission on Global Governance (CGG), which presented in its 1995 report *Our Global Neighbourhood* with the consensus of political and academic representatives from all regions of the world the following definition:

> Governance is the sum of the many ways individuals and institutions, public and private, manage their common affairs. It is a continuing process through which conflicting or diverse interests may be accommodated and co-operative action may be taken. It includes formal institutions and regimes empowered to enforce compliance, as well as informal arrangements that people and institutions either have agreed to or perceive to be in their interest.
>
> (CGG 1995, p. 4)

Governance in the New Institutionalism

In the last four decades several scientific disciplines – in addition to economics, sociology, political science and even history – have been strongly influenced by a New Institutionalism. With this concept James G. March and Johan P. Olsen (1984) initiated not only in political science an "institutionalist turn". This paradigm shift permeated the social and economic sciences, the interdisciplinary organizational and network theories.

The term 'institutions' was already in use in the sociology classics of Herbert Spencer, Talcott Parsons, Max Scheler and Arnold Gehlen and others. The new research approaches have their origins in the research on organization which stressed the social embedding of prevailing value preferences and patterns of legitimation.

There are various definitions which emphasize different aspects. Here, a definition is selected, suggested by John Meyer (2010, p. 2) from Stanford University, who could be described as a social scientist of institutionalism:

> Institutions are in contemporary parlance to be understood as extensive sample or control systems in which the actors, such as individuals, organizations and nation-states are embedded. Institutionalist analyses therefore focus on the factors that generate these patterns and/or on the consequences that these patterns have on players.

Included among the institutions are not only formal organizations, but also less formal regulative social actions such as customs and routines that have been internalized through socialization processes. Institutions not only restrict, but allow through the security of expectations the production of certain behaviours, as can be seen in the function of rules of conduct. Institutions are the foundation of all political behaviour. Without institutions there could be no social organization and no organized politics.

Two, three or four New Institutionalisms?

Textbooks on governance and on the paradigm of New Institutionalism distinguish several academic schools and theoretical approaches.

Historical Institutionalism

Historical Institutionalists in the social sciences are interested in explaining real outcomes in history and tend to perceive institutions as structuring variables for understanding political developments. We quote here the classification of theoretical approaches from Sven Steinmo (2001, p. 1), a confessed Historical Institutionalist and chairholder for Political Science and Public Policy at the European University Institute of Florence:

> Historical Institutionalists are primarily interested in understanding and explaining specific real world political outcomes ... They do not argue that institutions are the only important variables for understanding political outcomes. Quite the contrary, the scholars generally see institutions as interesting variables (or structuring variables) through which battles over interest, ideas and power are fought. Institutions are important both because they are the focal points of much political activity and because they provide incentives and constraints for political actors and thus structure that activity.

A rich source for the ideas of Historical Institutionalists, who have been and still are influential and relevant in history and political science, can be found in an enlightening review of Kathleen Thelen (1999) and in a collection of papers edited by Sven Steinmo et al. (1992).

Rational Choice Institutionalism

Sven Steinmo asserts – together with some other scholars, namely Barry Weingast (1996), Peter A. Hall and Rosemary Taylor (1996) – the following difference between Historical and Rational Choice Institutionalism:

> For Rationalist Scholars, the central goal is to uncover the laws of political behaviour and action. Scholars in this tradition believe that once these laws are discovered, models can be constructed that will help us understand and predict

political behaviour. In their deductive model, rational choice scholars look to the real world to see if their model is right ... rather than look to the real world and then search for plausible explanations for the phenomena they observe.

(Steinmo 2001, p. 2)

In other words: Rational Choice scholars are not interested in a comprehensive understanding of a historical phenomenon, but rather in discovering the rational logic behind the facts and constructing models of behaviour and action.

It is remarkable and somewhat surprising that Sven Steinmo and the prominent Harvard political scientist Peter Hall, in cooperation with Rosemary Taylor (1996), share the view that the New Institutional Economics cannot claim a specific originality because these two schools overlap in many ways. This position of the social scientists is not convincing because the New Institutional Economists originated and dominated the academic debate on New Institutionalism. Peter Hall nevertheless uncovers more theoretical and analytical virtues in a third school.

The Sociological Institutionalism

For Peter Hall and Rosemary Taylor (1996, p. 14), three features render Sociological Institutionalism relatively distinctive to the other New Institutionalisms:

First, the sociological institutionalists tend to define institutions much more broadly than political scientists and do include, not just formal rules, procedures or norms, but the symbol systems, cognitive scripts, and moral templates that provide the "frames of meaning" guiding human action.

Second, the new institutionalists in sociology all have a distinctive understanding of the relationship between institutions and individual action, which follows the "cultural approach".

Finally, the new institutionalists in sociology also take a distinctive approach to the problem of explaining how institutional practices originate and change.

More than an academic sham battle?

In the conclusion of their brilliant comparative analysis and interpretation of the three New Institutionalisms, Peter Hall and Rosemary Taylor (1996, p. 22) concede that these three schools of Institutionalism "share a great deal of common analytical ground".

But are all these debates and controversies an academic sham battle? In these different approaches there is always the behaviour-regulating function of institutions, be it in politics and administration, in business or in social interaction. Institutions structure the behaviour, interests and preferences of actors.

In opposition to Peter Hall, Rosemary Taylor and Sven Steinmo we conclude that the New Institutionalism has won profile and relevance primarily by the New Institutional Economics, whose prophets were ennobled by prestigious Nobel Prizes. This school has also been especially relevant to the theory and comparative analysis of development. Robert H. Bates (2006, 2013), a political scientist of Harvard University, reactivated the academic debate on Institutionalism and emphasized the crucial role of institutions in the development of African economies. This was the message of US President Barack Obama to his African audience when he made a short stop-over in Ghana: do not wait for strong men, but try to build strong institutions! Poor governance means weak institutions.

Governance in the New Institutional Economics

Already in the 1930s, Ronald Coase, who was known for his pioneering contributions and was recently as 1991 awarded the Nobel Prize, countered against the neoclassical credo that in the economic life of modern societies the market cannot cope with all its control and coordination problems and therefore needs institutions which can provide the necessary rules for its functioning.

In the development of economic theory over the last four decades a radical shift of direction has taken place. Although the neoclassical apologists still form the mainstream in teaching and research, more and more economists have questioned the neoclassical theorems and stressed the importance of institutions that were always placed at the centre of public policy science for the functioning of economic systems and for the economic behaviour of individuals and businesses. The fact that two representatives of the New Institutional Economics, namely Ronald Coase and Douglass Cecil North, were awarded in the early 1990s the Nobel Prize, indicates a change of direction in the academic Olympus. This academic nobility was further enlarged by Joseph Stiglitz in 2001, who as a long-time chief economist of the World Bank and an inveterate Institutional Economist allowed the seeds of the New Institutional Economics to flourish in this powerful agenda-setting agency.

It is not possible to display all the ramifications and nuances of the New Institutional Economics, which have been laid out by Richter and Furubotn (1998) in a voluminous textbook. These two authors refer to the emphasis on the costs of transactions as "essential characteristics" of the New Institutional Economics. Transaction costs are costs resulting from the operation of an economic system and in the provision of institutional arrangements. Political transaction costs are the operating costs of a political system or costs incurred in the construction, maintenance or modification of a political order. The transaction cost theory envisaged by Ronald Coase and further developed by Williamson (1996) is based on the assumption that the costs of economic transactions are not always lowest when the transactions are settled through imperfect markets. Rather more important is the institutional arrangement ("institutions of governance"), which by this rule makes transactions more cost-effective.

Two classics of the New Institutional Economics: Oliver E. Williamson and Douglass C. North

The key messages of *the New Institutional Economics* can best be discovered in its two most important economists: namely, Oliver E. Williamson (1996) and Douglass Cecil North (1990, 1993). This concentration is also justified because the two authors not only had a significant influence on the economic theory discourses, but also on the regulatory rethinking of the World Bank, which resulted in their credo: "Institutions matter".

The structuring key question must be: what contribution has the New Institutional Economics made toward the governance concept and possibly also toward the normative good governance concept? It reflects not only on the impact of "institutions of governance" on markets, companies and individuals, but has also developed something of an institutional economic theory of the state and of political organizations. Therefore, it is occasionally associated with the social and economic sciences' generic term of the New Organizational Theory, with which it shares many connections.

In the 1970s, Oliver E. Williamson picked up the early ideas of Ronald Coase and systematized them in his transaction cost theory. For the governance discourse, in which he participated with several contributions, his institutional theory was important. It is the "institutions of governance" which reduce the operating costs of the economic system and the political system. Institutions apply, as is already the case with the New Institutionalists, lasting agreements which have a part in influencing the behaviour of economic agents. These long-term agreements are formal rules, such as constitutions, laws and property rights, patterns of behaviour such as social norms and traditional value preferences as well as organizations in the strict sense, such as government bodies, authorities, political parties and associations.

With this emphasis on the role of formal and informal institutions, the New Institutional Economics is different in one important respect from neoclassical economic theory: the institutions do not play a relevant role in the marketplace and neither should they play such a role; but transaction cost theory, however, derives the needs of institutions from the emergence of transaction costs in imperfect markets.

Williamson (1996) no longer gives much weight – such as do the neoclassical successors of Adam Smith – solely on the "invisible hand" of the market which regulates economic activity in a mysterious way, but on "institutions of governance"; furthermore he also questions the neoclassical rational choice dogma because individual choice behaviour, although the intention, cannot due to missing prerequisites and imperfect information be rational as a result. Although institutional economics shares with the neoclassicals the actor-model of Homo Oeconomicus, it emphasizes decision uncertainty and therefore sets institutions at the side of Homo Oeconomicus, which should give him predictable rules and a greater reliability of expectations.

A "simple theory of the state"

North, in his *Institutions, Institutional Change and Economic Performance* (1990) developed in his own words, a "simple neoclassical theory of the state" – for an economist this was a highly ambitious project. It is based on the idea of a contract between rulers and citizens, and follows the logic that the rulers provide protection and justice, including the protection of disposal and contract rights, in exchange for revenue. Their most important achievement is the implementation of a constitution that also governs the structure of property rights. These property rights also include citizenship.

The state has the right to command and in return for his protection function to enforce the payment of taxes. The rulers are subject to two restrictions on their power and authority: they may be dismissed by rivals that promise the citizens better services. Thereby the opportunity costs, incurred by citizens either through the replacement of the government or by leaving the country ("exit"), play an important role. The second reason lies again in the transaction costs incurred during a power or regime change.

In this economistic shortened "theory of the state", which is not only very "simple" and also oversimplifies complex contexts, transaction costs have a central role to play alongside property rights. Relevant for the construction of governance is the reciprocal contractual relationship: protection of property rights and provision of public goods in exchange for loyalty and tax benefits. The "principals" in the principal–agent contract are the citizens as the original owner of authority, who instruct agents in democracies through an election process to exercise their delegated power, but they can also be dismissed by a "recall" and can be replaced – though with high transaction costs. This Anglo-Saxon theory of the state is strongly built on the contract theory of John Locke.

The persuasiveness of the New Institutional Economics and its cognitive value for governance discourse does not derive from complex theories of the state and democracy but from the discovery of all aspects of the life-shaping power of institutions. Within these "institutions of governance" is an important contribution to a theory of governance which was also reflected in the publications of the World Bank, and in this way greatly influenced international development discourse.

The Harvard expert on African economies Robert H. Bates (2006, 2013) undertook an interesting attempt to use the New Institutionalism and specifically the work of Douglass North for the analysis and explanation of the problems which African economies are facing. Here one can discover a great match between the New Institutionalism, as it was taught by its prominent apologists, and the thinking of the World Bank (2002), as is documented in the *World Development Report* 2002. Here an "institutionalist turn" really took place.

Good governance means, from the perspective of Institutional Economics, succinctly the ability to create frameworks for a market economy, to ensure contract certainty in economic relations, which includes the protection of property, the rule orientation of management and to provide for the functioning of the economic system of necessary public goods. This Institutional Economics is first and foremost about how to achieve a maximum of controllability with a minimum of government.

The new credo of the World Bank: Institutions matter

Douglass Cecil North was awarded with the Nobel Prize in Economics in 1993, on the basis of his economic history research on the cornerstones of neoclassical economic theory. In his most important work, *Institutions, Institutional Change and Economic Performance* (1990), he asked the question already posed by Adam Smith and central to the theory of evolution: why do some nations become rich and many others remain poor? His answer was that:

> Institutions are the rules of the game in a society or, more formally, are the humanly devised constraints that shape human interaction. In consequence they structure incentives in human exchange, whether political, social, or economic. Institutional change shapes the way societies evolve through time and hence is the key to understanding historical change.
>
> (North 1990, p. 3)

For North institutions also have the function of reducing uncertainty in contractual relationships and of creating a regulatory framework for economic activity and social interaction. In his Prize Lecture for the Nobel Prize in Stockholm North (1993) attacked neoclassical economics: "Neo-classical theory is simply an inappropriate tool to analyse and prescribe policies that will induce development. It is concerned with the operation of markets, not with how markets develop". It was those findings which promoted regulatory rethinking and a turn away from neoclassical dogmas also within the World Bank. "Institutions Matter" was now the new credo and the title of a new index operated by the World Bank: the Governance Matters Index.

The *World Development Report* 2002 entitled *Building Institutions for Markets* (World Bank 2002) was not only a commitment prepended by North to institutions, but this commitment also permeated the regulative argument of the report. The Institutional Economics had arrived at the Vatican of international development policy, which also dominated development discourse with claims to truth and displaced the crude monetarism of Milton Friedman, whose students had dominated the thinking and actions of the "eggheads" in Washington in the 1990s.

The success of the "East Asian Miracle" shook neoliberal faith in markets with the empirical power of its spectacular track record. This success was the act of a "strong state" that controlled economic life and understood that to exploit the comparative advantages of integration into the world market, more was needed than the "invisible hand of the market". The neoclassical theory fails to explain the "East Asian Miracle"; the World Bank learned from this experience.

The final farewell to the Washington Consensus with its neoliberal triad of deregulation, liberalization and privatization – that is, "denationalization" – was finalized by the report of the Commission on Growth and Development, which worked under the chairmanship of Nobel laureate Michael Spence, to which 22 high-level representatives from the government and business world belonged.

The "Growth Report" (Commission on Growth and Development 2008) submitted by the Commission in early summer 2008 encouraged the reassessment of the role of the state, which had been looming in the earlier World Development Reports. In the report, the state is again the "policy maker" which sets rules and creates institutions. The summary of the report states:

> Economists know how markets work, and they can say with some confidence how a mature market economy will respond to their policy prescriptions. But mature markets rely on deep institutional underpinnings, institutions that define property rights, enforce contracts, convey prices, and bridge informational gaps between buyers and sellers. Developing countries often lack these market and regulatory institutions. Indeed, an important part of development is precisely the creation of these institutionalized capabilities.
>
> (Commission on Growth and Development 2008, p. 4)

Governance research as a precursor to good governance discourse

The reconstruction of the debate on good governance showed that the concept of governance has appeared in various reasoning contexts, meanings and application fields. Governance concepts were found in the theories of international relations and in the concepts of global governance, in organizational and network theories or in the important White Paper of the European Commission (2001) entitled *European Governance*. Sectoral applications were formed in the burgeoning management theories that use the term governance for reform strategies both in the private corporate sector and in public administration.

"Governance in complex control systems" is more or less pronounced at all political levels of action, from the local to national and regional to the global level. There is already extensive literature on local governance – where civic engagement may develop in various forms – while within the European Union it is most advanced, but also practiced in other regional organizations as regional governance, as well as in the system of global governance.

Methodological approaches can also be distinguished. The term governance has been used first as a descriptive term, trying to respond to socioeconomic and political structural changes and regulatory mechanisms and record the fact that collective decisions can come about in modern societies in non-hierarchical forms of cooperation between public and private actors. Second, it has served as an analytical concept to capture these new forms of coordination and interaction systematically. Third, the concept was given special prominence as a strategic concept that, then in the normative extension to good governance guidance, was supposed to establish guidance for political action.

Lessons for the World Bank from the African "crisis of governance"

It was the World Bank which adopted the insights of the Institutional Economics and introduced the governance concept in the debate on development. It proved once again to be an "agenda-setting agency" with a remarkable power of definition and interpretation. It is striking how quickly the UN Development Programme (UNDP), the Organization for Economic Co-operation and Development (OECD) and the European Union, as well as individual donors, jumped onto this governance bandwagon with development policy statements and then even exceeded the World Bank with political demands for reform.

The World Bank (1989) gave its study on the development crisis in Sub-Saharan Africa a new approach to diagnosing the crisis by blaming the misleading developments, but also the failure of many of their own cost-intensive projects, on a "crisis of governance" or "poor governance". This made it difficult not only for African governments to make their usual attempt to attribute the causes of the plight to the legacy of colonialism and to global economic inequalities, but also relieved the Western donor community from the claim of dependency, and imperialism to be the cause for the misery.

The World Bank identified in its crisis diagnosis a series of home-made politically misleading developments in the institutional environment of states and administrations which impeded the economic, social and political development of many African countries. These negative developments in the post-colonial state were, however, already in the scientific literature on Africa, which had discovered the "weak state" and clientelistic power structures to be obstacles to development and which had long since been accepted as common knowledge.

The World Bank emphasized the following manifestations of bad governance:

- An unreliable legal system that granted both individuals as well as domestic and foreign companies no investment security;
- A weak public management that impeded the implementation of development strategies and the targeted use of external subsidies;
- The insufficient binding of governmental and administrative actions to laws and the accountability of governments for their action and inaction being enforced by rarely elected parliaments and independent courts;
- The lack of transparency in the management and use of public funds and external subsidies that financed up to two thirds of public investment in individual cases;
- Negligence of the imperatives of sustainable development;
- The rent-seeking thinking of elites and especially rampant and crippling corruption in acting like a cancer in all places. Here the influence of the New Institutional Economics on the regulatory thinking of the World Bank becomes particularly evident, because rent seeking and corruption weaken the performance of public institutions.

The World Bank (1989, p. 60) defined governance first in quite a technocratic and economic development manner as "the manner in which power is exercised in the management of a country's economic and social resources for development". This definition was focused on the core area of public administration and the public management of the economy, because the World Bank assumed, in accordance with the Institutional Economics, that only functioning state institutions can implement the necessary macroeconomic reforms.

The World Bank continued to present the economic dimension of governance in the foreground. There was therefore also criticism that it still continued to subordinate the political dimension of good governance to the primacy of economic and administrative efficiency aspects. The director of the UN Research Institute for Social Development (UNRISD) stated at a special conference of the German GTZ – the later GIZ – the following harsh criticism (GTZ 2004, p. 28): "The question of how to build confidence among investors, became the actual content of good governance ... It was forgotten that good governance has something to do with human dignity and values, with the state and society, and not just economics".[1]

United Nations agencies such as UNDP or UNRISD tended to blame the Bretton Woods Institutions for crude economism. It must be remembered that UNDP set its Human Development Reports, which oriented development more on social indicators, against the World Development Reports of the World Bank. In such assessments it must be noted that in the policy departments of the World Bank, hegemonic struggles were fought between economic theory schools. In the 1990s, during which their own studies grappled critically with the ambivalent results of their Washington Consensus macroeconomic structural adjustment policies, the monetarists from the "Chicago School" of Milton Friedman gradually lost their power to the Institutional Economists and Keynesians, with the latter also awarded the Nobel Prize for Joseph Stiglitz. In awarding this prize, which is equivalent to the award of a title of nobility, the academic appreciation is expressed.

The spectacular world conferences of the 1990s, especially the 1992 Rio Conference on Ecology and Development (UNCED), called for development policy adjustments in an international consensus towards a primacy of poverty reduction and sustainable development, which also obligated the Bretton Woods institutions. They responded with new programmes that at least rhetorically bid farewell to old recipes. The UNDP set against the World Development Reports of the World Bank its Human Development Reports, which advocated a different approach to development: development is no longer equated solely with economic growth and instead social indicators (life expectancy at birth, literacy and school-enrollment rates) were placed in the centre.

The problem of the normative "good" in good governance

The World Bank's 1989 Africa study, which is often praised as the birth certificate of good governance, mentions the normative attribute "good" only at the margins or rather incidentally in the foreword of the president. The policy paper on *Governance and Development*, published in 1992, which the expert on constitutional and international law Rudolf Dolzer (2007, p. 18) classified as the "cradle of the new thinking in the paths of good governance" and categorized in the history of a new development paradigm, was very frugal with politically evaluative predicates. This reluctance can be attributed to their statutes (Articles of Agreement) requiring "policy banning".

There was, however, within and outside the World Bank also criticism of the normative attribute "good", which could be enriched quite arbitrarily with demands for political reform. There were then other international organizations such as the OECD and the European Union, and especially individual donor countries (such as Germany, Australia and the USA), which offensively associated good governance with demands for democratic reform. Some scholars therefore critized the "good" in good governance as more or less equated with the values and practices of Western democracies, ignoring cultural differencies (Poluha & Rosendahl 2002).

The World Bank may have shied away from politicizing their governance concept and have avoided whenever possible the term *good governance* for the above reasons. But from the "crisis of governance" or the syndromes of bad governance political demands for reforms derived, outlined though the normative core components of good governance:

- The establishment of the rule of law, which the World Bank gave the highest value, because for the World Bank – in line with the Institutional Economics – legal security for investors and secure property rights are of prime importance for economic development;
- The establishment of functioning administrative structures for improved public sector management;
- The transparency of governmental and administrative action, particularly in the use of its own and external financial resources that require an independent audit;
- The responsibility ("accountability") of the goverments and elected representatives over the citizens;
- The fight against corruption as a particularly predominant system element of bad governance, which the president of the World Bank James Wolfensohn later awarded a special prominence, so that the fight against corruption alongside and together with the rule of law-imperative became a metaphor for good governance;
- Respect for fundamental political and social human rights, which also provide normative orientations for the activities of international organizations.

This combination of good governance with human rights postulates and the possible conditioning of loans often occupied the legal department of the World Bank, which was hiding behind the mandate of political neutrality, but had increasingly to fend off criticism from academics and from some of its stakeholders.

The internal conflict came to a head over the question of whether the World Bank may raise demands for democratic reform or if good governance should be limited to improvements in economic and financial management.

However, it is highly contradictory to demand accountability of those in government, the rule of law and respect for human rights, without questioning the political system. The statute also served as an excuse for the management level of the World Bank to replenish good governance with political norms. The contradiction becomes even more apparent when analysing macroeconomic structural adjustment policies in an ideologically critical way. The demands for market-based structural reforms, for deregulation of the economy and privatization of enterprises were highly political and penetrated deeply into the political insides of political regimes. The statement that the World Bank had with the discovery of the "crisis of governance" become more political implies that it had once been apolitical.

The World Bank was an obstetrician of the governance paradigm. It has made a significant contribution to governance and the normative extension to good governance was promoted in the subsequent period to the central development and transformation of the concept of political reform. However, it must not be overlooked that the New Institutional Economics, to which the World Bank made many connections, had already done a lot of preparatory work and further underscored the scientifically based regulatory credo "Policy Matters".

It also took some qualitative improvements so that a "new model of statehood" could arise, based on "functional state institutions, on respect for human rights, on the emphasis on the rule of law, on economic common sense in politics and on the need of the participation of all classes and social reconciliation and peace" (Dolzer 2007, p. 13). The World Bank established at most the carcass of this new paradigm. The interior equipment was provided later by other international organizations that had no obligation to political neutrality.

The normative profiling of good governance by the donor community organized by DAC

While the World Bank with reference to its apolitical mandate held back with political demands for reform in the name of good governance, other international organizations, particularly those donor countries freed from the constraints of the Cold War, surged ahead with a normative extension of the concept. They made sure that good governance was the key concept and action-guiding programme in the Western donor community, which together with their voting rights also has an influence on the actions of the Bretton Woods institutions.

A programmatic pioneering role was played by the Development Assistance Committee (DAC) of the OECD, in which the major bilateral donor countries (among them, however, only 15 belong to the 27 European Union member states) joined forces and tried at least a coordination of their development activities. In late 1993, DAC adopted the "Orientations on Participatory Development and Good Governance". These orientations first resorted to the core elements already defined by the World Bank: rule of law, improved public sector management and control of corruption. DAC added to these core elements however four highly political demands:

- Participatory development;
- Respect for human rights;
- Democratization;
- Reduction of excessive military spending (although the responsibility of the arms exporters, which were with the exception of Russia mostly DAC members, remained excluded).

Already in 1989, and thus at the same time as the governance discussions within the World Bank, the ministries and implementing agencies of the OECD countries organized through DAC (2015) a resolution on "Development Co-operation in the 1990s" and established what they meant by "participatory development":

> that the vicious circle of underdevelopment that links high population with growth, poverty, malnutrition, illiteracy and environmental degradation can be broken only through economic and developmental strategies and policies which integrate the objectives and requirements of
>
> - Promoting sustainable economic growth;
> - Enabling broader participation of all the people in the productive processes and a more equitable sharing of their benefits;
> - Ensuring environmental sustainability and slowing population growth in those many countries where it is too high to permit sustainable development.

Participatory development linked democracy with a market economy and pinpointed the concept of what had already been understood as development by the modernization theorists. However, disagreements among the delegates from the ministries soon became apparent on what value participatory development should receive in the superordinate concept of good governance. A memorandum of a conference organized by DAC in May 1992 summarized these differences of opinion, which illustrate the difficulties in the implementation of programmatic rhetoric into action concepts, thus:

> On one hand there are good reasons to consider "good governance" as one aspect of "participatory development", namely the extent to which good governance creates a favourable climate and conditions with regard to sustainable development with wide consequences. On the other hand, one could also be of the opinion that the objectives of "participatory development" constitute an essential aspect of "good governance". Likewise, it might be possible and useful from certain points of view, assuming an "administrative/technical"

and a "political" approach of "good governance", thereby these two concepts are closely interdependent.

(Fuster 1998, p. 157)[2]

It is noteworthy that here there is a playing with terms and an argument with verbal reservations ("perhaps possible" and "useful from certain points of view") so it has been possible to bypass a clear statement on the approach of good governance. The ministerial bureaucrats still had difficulties operationalizing the new political guidelines and reconciling them with their administrative routine.

Such difficulties emerged especially in the aftermath of the political imperative of specific development policies and conditionalities in the allocation of funds from the pot of official development assistance or the European Development Fund (EDF). Nonetheless, good governance has become established as a development model since the 1990s and can be found in the completed 2000 Cotonou Agreement between the European Union and the African, Caribbean and Pacific Group of States (ACP), following controversial negotiations on the application of good governance imperatives, inputs in the development of international law and international treaty law.

The guiding principles of good governance are summarized in Figure 5.1.

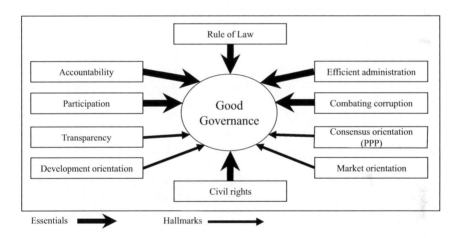

Figure 5.1 Essentials and hallmarks of good governance

The gradual universalization of a normative paradigm

After the global political changes of 1989–1990, all international organizations and national development authorities engaged in development cooperation put the guiding principles of good governance at the centre of their programmes and rhetoric because the deepening criticism of the benefits of development cooperation focused mainly on the allegation that they encouraged corrupt practices and fed kleptocracies with subsidies.

The German BMZ applied the specifications of DAC with some slightly changed principles that reflected the history of German development policy and formed action-orienting guidelines that are still in place today:

- Promotion of the rule of law and good governance;
- Promotion of democratization and improving the human rights situation;
- Participation of the population in political decision-making processes;
- Encouragement of a stronger "development orientation" by the elites by fighting corruption and reducing military spending;
- Support for market-oriented reforms.

The UN Economic and Social Commission for Asia and the Pacific (UNESCAP, 2014, p. 1) answers the question "what is good governance?" in the following way:

> Good Governance has 8 major characteristics. It is participatory, consensus orientated, accountable, transparent, responsive, effective and efficient, equitable and inclusive and follows the rule of law. It assures that corruption is minimized, the view of minorities are taken into account and that the voices of the most vunerable in society are heard in decision-making. It is also responsive to the present and future needs of society.

This comprehensive definition includes that the normative concept of good governance is not only a Western but a universal concept. But it should be realized that the definition does not mention human rights. The autocratic regimes of the region try to ignore the universality of political human rights laid down in international law.

The World Bank with its study on the "crisis of governance" in Sub-Saharan Africa (1989) or at least with its policy paper on *Governance and Development* (1992) opened up the discussion on the importance of governance in the development process. But it has, as the most important agenda-setting agency that has a lot of money and expertise at its disposal, always initiated and promoted paradigm shifts in international development policy: from the trickle-down justification of its growth strategy to the basic needs strategy in the era of its President Robert McNamara, towards the neoliberal Washington Consensus macroeconomic structural adjustment policies of the 1980s and its return to pro-poor growth policies in the late 1990s, by which it had already opened in a tactically clever way the conversion of the donor community to the Millennium Development Goals (MDGs).

The insight that political conditions are essential for the effectiveness of international development policy, that is "policy matters", preceded the theoretically founded insights of the New Institutional Economics that the "invisible hand" of the market does not always control the best, and that the market also needs regulating institutions. Yet, owing to the pledge of its mandate to be politically neutral, the World Bank was not willing to make the leap from governance to good governance and acknowledge the cancer of corruption and the role of infamous kleptocrats in bad governance. It therefore limited its technocratic demands for the reform of public management and shunned the concept of democracy like a plague.

The global political changes of 1989–1990 also released development policy from the geostrategic shackles of the Cold War and led amazingly quickly to the Western donor community and UN organizations replenishing the flourishing governance discourse in a qualitative leap with regulatory standards: rule of law, respect for human rights, democratic participation and market orientation.

These normative standards get to the point of what the OECD meant by "participatory development", and what the European Union enshrined in its international legally binding Cotonou Agreement with 79 ACP countries. This agreement committed the ACP contractual partners, if they wanted to get grants from the EDF, to reforms in the direction of good governance; that is, official development assistance with political conditionality.

This, and then the Millennium Declaration of the UN achieved by a consensus of the international community of states, enhanced the normative model of international cooperation in the early 21st century. The *Journal on Development Studies*, the *Third World Quarterly* (Weiss 2000) and *Oxford Development Studies* (Andrews 2008) led the academic debate. Martin Doornbos (2001) reflected early on the *Rise and Decline of a Policy Metaphor*. At the beginning of the 21st century the concept of good governance was still on the agenda of development policy. However, it is true that the MDGs mentioned good governance rather marginally in Goal 8, even though the Millennium Declaration had stressed it under point V. in a prominent position.

The then UN secretary-general, Kofi Annan, stressed again and again – mainly directed to the African leadership groups, which he himself originated from – that good governance is the bare requirement for the development of the continent. In the African Governance Report of 2005, he wrote under the title *Striving for Good Governance in Africa* (Annan 2005, p. 2):

> Good Governance and sustainable development are indivisible. That is the lesson of all our efforts and experiences, from Africa to Asia to Latin America. Without good governance – without the rule of law, predictable administration, legitimate power and responsible regulation – no amount of funding, no amount of charity will set us on the path to prosperity.

This is a substantial translation of good governance, particularly as penned by the former highest representative of the community of states, who could not easily be accused of playing the role of a bailiff of the West. US President Barack Obama, who also has African roots, gave the African elites during his short visit to Ghana a similar message: Africa does not need strong men, but strong institutions. This is the essence of the debate on good governance!

The limited potential of development cooperation to promote good governance

The econometric impact studies confirmed the assumption that good governance – apart from the desirability of orderly legal and administrative structures and democratic structures – can create the conditions for the greater effectiveness of development cooperation (see Boone 1996). However, these conditions do not exist among the growing number of failing states with precarious statehood, and the donor community is still pretty clueless as to how they might also set these "low-income countries under stress" (LICUS) on their way to good governance. When it comes to knowing what to do, it still remains completely open as to how the target countries will respond to advice and external funding.

Scientific curiosity and the demand of development authorities for information on the extent to which countries are pursuing the mission statement of good governance, or how far they are away from this model, have led to a boom of quantifying index structures which attempt to measure each different development. Most clearly committed to the normative model of good governance is the Bertelsmann Transformation Index (BTI). It investigates, with a differentiated set of 52 indicators, the development of 129 developing and transition countries towards the postulated symbiosis of democracy and market economy.

Western development agencies have developed timetables for the promotion of good governance. The Bush administration established in 2004 the Millennium Challenge Corporation with the declared aim of promoting good governance with foreign aid. The US Congress enacted the African Development Foundation (USADF) with the mission of promoting participatory development. But such endeavours failed because they largely disregarded socioeconomic and sociocultural differences and the findings of development theories and regional sciences. They failed especially in places where bad governance built blockades against reform processes.

It proved impossible to produce frameworks for good governance by a kind of constitutional engineering. This is also the experience of the German political foundations, which get a lot of public money in order to promote democracy in developing countries. Under the challenge of eroding or even collapsing statehood, political strategists insidiously bade farewell to the good governance paradigm. The problem of stabilization of fragile state structures, which lack almost all the qualities of modern statehood, can be demonstrated by the cases of Afghanistan, Somalia or Iraq.

If the objective of democratization is postulated, two basic questions always arise. First, how can democratization be encouraged from the outside, as there is a broad consensus that it must come from within, from endogenous democracy movements and enlightened elites and therefore can at best be supported from the outside? There is a highly controversial debate on the opportunities and limitations of external democracy promotion. The European Commission (2011, p. 5) recommended in its *Agenda for Change* the following "mix and level of aid": "As long-term progress can only be driven by internal forces, an approach centred on political and policy dialogue with all stakeholders will be pursued. The mix and level of aid will depend on the country's situation, including its ability to conduct reforms". Second, can democratization also be the basis for the expected stimuli for economic and social development, or must democracy also be viewed beyond such functional considerations as a desirable goal?

The compendia of data from the World Bank seem to show that it is not democracies, but more or less autocratic states with well-functioning public management autocracies, (especially the East Asian emerging countries where the World Bank discovered the East Asian Miracle), that provide evidence of relatively good economic performance. So the question is whether a concept of good governance enriched with high goals leaves the base of reality and whether the concept of governance of the World Bank, which aims initially to stabilize legal and administrative structures, can claim greater realism (and not only political opportunism). It is also not about the ethics of conviction, but about the ethics of responsibility in the context of realistic possibilities.

If Sub-Saharan Africa is again the focus here, then it was here that the "crisis of governance" was first discovered and this continent had to fight in particular with the infamous eight Ks (wars, disasters, corruption, etc.). Such crises also occurred in other continents and "fragile states" from Haiti to some countries of the Commonwealth of Independent States (CIS), to Afghanistan or Iraq. The Failed States Index 2014 implicitly registered 24 states as such fragile states.

The terrorist attacks of 11 September 2001 (9/11) changed abruptly the activities of the donor community towards the LICUS because they became suspected of being hotbeds of international terrorism. The re-establishment or stabilization of statehood, that is "state-building" and not good governance, became the development target.

Corruption proved to be a major cause of the low performance and viability of states, because it infests politics, public life and potentially rich countries like the African oil exporting countries. It makes individual kleptocracies rich, but the majority of their people destitute; it contributes significantly to the loss of legitimacy and state failure (see Johnston 2005). Both the World Bank (2007) and the International Monentary Fund (IMF 2005) launched programmes on anti-corruption, but achieved little or no success where corruption is worst. This cause of low performance and viability of states has many dysfunctionalities (see Debiel & Gawrich 2013). Combating corruption is a global challenge.

How limited the power of these two powerful financial institutions is to enforce changes in the ruling elites is demonstrated by Angola, whose corrupt government was able to reject a loan offer from the World Bank on condition of controlling corruption because China stepped in with a loan to hedge its oil interests. It has been found that the campaigns of international civil society watchdogs have achieved greater impact through the public politics of shaming because they can put governments and international organizations under pressure to justify their actions.

International comparative indices verify that the African exporters of raw materials in particular are, despite a relatively high per capita income (with the exception of the Democratic Republic of Congo), further behind in the ranking list of the Human Development Index (HDI), the Corruption Perception Index (CPI) of Transparency International and the BTI for the degree of transformation toward democratic conditions (that is: good governance) (see Table 5.1).

Decline of a policy metaphor?

There have always been voices critizing the boom of the good governance paradigm. This prompted Martin Doornboos (2001) as early as 2001 to reflect on the "Rise and Decline of a Policy Metaphor". The criticisms voiced also by some other scholars can be summed up as follows:

- The trite acceptance of the good governance creed has given rise to the suspicion that this formula was a kind of "catch-all phrase", allowing for many sorts of interpretation. The inflationary use of the formula suggested that good governance might be a master-key to a better world and might thus serve as a globally applicable model. This expectation, however, fails to take into account either the various socioeconomic situations and sociocultural differences, or the abovementioned fact that the concept is not helpful in places where bad governance is at its worst.
- It is not unjustified to say that the donor community, having only had limited success with poverty reduction, especially in Sub-Sahara Africa, with the magic formula good governance, has almost exclusively blamed the "governance crisis" in order to distract attention from its own deficiencies and from the impacts of international trade and finance.
- The normative principles of good governance add depth in development theory, which could better explain the cultural obstacles of development. Culture is not a beautiful-but-irrelevant factor, but a driving force of development, both forward and backward.

Table 5.1 Exporters of raw materials on ranking lists of the HDI, CPI and BTI

Countries	HDI 2012 187 countries	CPI 2013 177 countries	BTI 2014 129 countries
Angola	149	153	84
Equatorial Guinea	144	163	..
Gabon	112	106	..
DR Congo	186	154	117
Nigeria	152	144	71
Sudan	166	174	126
South Africa	118	72	28
Botswana	109	30	18
Mexico	71	106	33
Venezuela	67	160	93
Russia	57	127	77

Source: Based on the Human Development Index (UNDP 2014); Corruption Perception Index (2014); BTI (Status-Index) (2014); and IMF (2014)

- The donor community has good rhetoric but no convincing strategy for a peaceful transformation from bad to good governance, particularly in failed states where state building and the mere management of survival is a priority.

This chapter shares the credo that good governance, both for functional reasons underlying the governance thinking of the World Bank, as well as for normative reasons that recognize the achievements of civilization or goals in democracy, rule of law, participation and human rights, represents a desirable overall concept; but it also shares the scepticism that development policy can bring from the outside something that is not initiated and fought for by internal reform movements. Good governance could, however, support these reform movements more if it were less guided by geostrategic and/or commercial interests. Good governance also requires from the donor community the conduct to which it committed itself in the Paris Declaration of 2005, on the effectiveness of development cooperation in the Millennium Declaration of 2000 and in many other declarations of intent. The Sustainable Development Goals (SDGs) of the post-2015 agenda include the normative concept of good governance.

Summary

In the debate on the achievements and disappointments of international development cooperation, and also on the balance of the MDGs, the finding has prevailed that money alone (in the form of official development assistance) cannot overcome the causes of poverty, and rather it can have counterproductive effects if it does not try to change kleptocratic structures. It was the finding of the World Bank that poor governance or bad governance is the root of many African development problems. But for a long period of time it has been hard for the Bank to fill the normative concept of good governance with content. At this point the United Nations in 2000 consensually adopted the Millennium Declaration, the European Union their Cotonou Agreement with the 79 ACP countries, and OECD DAC created its normative orientation. There is no shortage of consensually adopted principles, but there is a shortage of mechanisms to implement and enforce them in the practice of cooperation. The basic principles of good governance, as illustrated above, are: the rule of law; accountability of the governments and politicians; combating corruption as a universal evil cancer; and respect for human rights and democratic principles. The SDGs for the post-2015 period of international cooperation include these principles.

Notes

1   This quotation was translated literally from German to English by the authors.
2   This quotation was translated literally from German to English by the authors.

References

Andrews, M. (2008): The Good Governance Agenda: Beyond Indicators without Theory, *Oxford Development Studies*, vol. 36 (4), pp. 379–407.

Annan, K. (2005): Striving for Good Governance in Africa, *African Governance Report 2005*, Report by the Economic Commission for Africa, Addis Ababa.

Bates, R. H. (2006): Institutions and Development, *Journal of African Economies*, vol. 15 (suppl. 1), pp. 10–61.

Bates, R. H. (2013): The New Institutionalism and Africa, *Journal of African Economies*, vol. 22 (4), pp. 499–522.

Boone, P. (1996): Politics and the Effectivness of Foreign Aid, *The European Economic Review*, vol. 40 (2), pp. 289–329.

BTI (2014): Status-Index, Online: www.bti-project.org/de/atlas/, last checked on 28.01.2015.

CGG (1995) *Our Global Neighbourhood: The Report*, Oxford: Oxford University Press.

Commission on Growth and Development (2008): *The Growth Report. Strategies for Sustained Growth and Inclusive Development*, Washington, DC.

Corruption Perception Index (2014): Corruption Perceptions Index 2014: Results, Online: www.transparency.org/cpi2014/results, last checked on 28.01.2015.

DAC (2015): *Development Co-operation in the 1990s*, Online: www.oecd.org/dac/dacdevelopmentco-operationinthe1990s.htm, last checked on 28.01.2015.

Debiel, T.; Gawrich, A. (eds) (2013): *(Dys-)Functionalities of Corruption: Comparative Perspectives and Methodological Pluralism*, Wiesbaden: Springer.

Dolzer, R. (2007): Good Governance. Genese des Begriffs, konzeptionelle Grundüberlegungen und Stand der Forschung, in: Dolzer, Rudolf; Herdegen, Matthias; Vogel, Bernhard (Hrsg.) (2007): *Good Governance. Gute Regierungsführung im 21. Jahrhundert*, Freiburg/Basel/Wien, pp. 13–23.

Doornbos, M. (2001): 'Good Governance': The Rise and Decline of a Policy Metaphor?, *The Journal of Development Studies*, vol. 37 (6), pp. 93–108.

European Commission (2001): *European Governance*. A White Paper, COM 424, Brussels.

European Commission (2011): *Agenda for Change*, SEC (2011) 1173, Brussels.

Fuster, T. (1998): *Die "Good Governance" Diskussion der Jahre 1989 bis 1994*, Bern/Stuttgart/Wien.

GTZ (2004): *Good Governance und Demokratieförderung zwischen Anspruch und Wirklichkeit*, Eschborn.

Hall, P. A.; Taylor, R. (1996): Political Science and the Three New Institutionalisms, *Political Studies*, vol. 44, pp. 936–957.

IMF (2005): The IMF's Approach to Promoting Good Governance and Combating Corruption – A Guide, Washington, D.C.

IMF (2014): International Monetary Fund. Annual Report 2014. From Stabilization to Sustainable Growth, Online: www.imf.org/external/pubs/ft/ar/2014/eng/pdf/ar14_eng.pdf, last checked on 28.01.2015.

Johnston, M. (2005): *Syndromes of Corruption: Wealth, Power, and Democracy*, New York: Cambridge University Press.

March, J. G.; Olsen, J. P. (1984): New Institutionalism: Organizational Factors in Political Life, *American Political Science Review*, vol. 78 (3), pp. 734–749.

Meyer, J. (2010): World Society, Institutional Theories, and the Actor, *Annual Review of Sociology*, vol. 36, pp. 1–20.

North, D. C. (1990): *Institutions, Institutional Change and Economic Performance*, Cambridge: Cambridge University Press.

North, D. C. (1993): Economic Performance through Time, Prize Lecture for the Nobel Prize in Stockholm, Online: www.nobelprize.org/nobel_prizes/economic-sciences/laureates/1993/north-lecture.html, last checked on 11.11.2014.

Oxford Dictionary (2015): Governance, Online: www.oxforddictionaries.com/definition/english/governance (28.01.2015).

Poluha, E.; Rosendahl, M. (2002): *Contesting "Good" Governance: Crosscultural Perspectives on Representation, Accountability and Public Space*, London: Psychology Press.

Richter, R.; Furubotn, E. G. (1998): *Institutions and Economic Theory: The Contribution of the New Institutional Economics*, Michigan: University of Michigan Press.

Steinmo, S.; Thelen, K.; Longstreth, F. (eds) (1992): *Structuring Politics: Historical Institutionalism in Comparative Analysis*, New York: Cambridge University Press.

Steinmo, S. (2001): The New Institutionalism, in: Clark, Barry/Foweraker, Joe (eds) (2001): The Encyclopedia of Democratic Thought, London. Online: http://stripe.colorado.edu/~steinmo/foweracker.pdf, last checked on 11.11.2014, pp. 1–5.

Thelen, K. (1999): Historical Institutionalism in Comparative Politics, *Annual Review of Political Science*, vol. 2, pp. 369–404.

UNDP (2014): Human Development Report 2014 Sustaining Human Progress: Reducing Vulnerabilities and Building Resilience, Online: http://hdr.undp.org/sites/default/files/hdr14-report-en-1.pdf, last checked on 28.01.2015.

UNESCP (2014): What is Good Governance, Bangkok, Online: www.unescap.org/sites/default/files/good-governance.pdf, last checked on 11.11.2014.

Weiss, T. G. (2000): Governance, Good Governance and Global Governance: Conceptual and Actual Challenges, *Third World Quarterly*, vol. 21 (5), pp. 795–815.

Weingast, B. (1996): Political Institutions: Rational Choice Perspectives, in: *A New Handbook of Political Science*, Oxford, pp. 167–190.

Williamson, O. E. (1996): *The Mechanisms of Governance*, New York: Oxford University Press.

World Bank (1989): *Sub-Sahara Africa. From Crisis to Sustainable Growth*, Washington, DC: World Bank.

World Bank (1992): *Governance and Development*, Washington, DC: World Bank.

World Bank (2002): *World Development Report 2002: Building Institutions for Markets*, Washington, DC: World Bank.

World Bank (2007): *Strengthening World Bank Group Engagement in Governance and Anticorruption*, Washington, DC: World Bank.

6 Challenges for setting–up effective social security systems in developing countries

Beate Bergé

Providing social security as major challenge for the international community and development cooperation

According to article 22 in the Universal Declaration of Human Rights of the United Nations everyone as a member of society has the right to social security:

> Everyone as a member of society, has the right to social security and is entitled to realisation, through national effort and international cooperation and in accordance with the organisation and resources of each state, of the economic, social and cultural rights indispensable for his dignity and the free development of his personality.
>
> (Article 22, United Nations Universal Declaration of Human Rights)

Social security is not only a human right and results in a comprehensive protection against a variety of risks in life, but also forms the prerequisite for a broad-based inclusive growth and the integration of the poverty-striken population into the labour market (ILO 2006; World Bank 2006b).

In the 21st century, social security systems worldwide are under increasing pressure due to growing economic and social imbalances and social tensions (OECD 2011). Only 27 per cent of the global population have access to comprehensive social protection systems; 73 per cent of the world's population is insufficiently or not at all protected (ILO 2014). In times of globalization the needs for far-reaching and comprehensive effective systems of social security rise. At the same time, with increasing global economic integration, economic modernization, accelerated urbanization, migration and individualization, community-oriented and family-based social security systems erode or lose their economic base because of widespread poverty. The challenge thereby is that global competitiveness must be insured by bringing social security needs and economic growth in line.

Thus, social security systems are under pressure for various reasons (ILO 2011a, p. 51). On the one hand social and economic risks increase, while on the other hand traditional systems lose their meaning. Additionally, environmental degradation and climate change threaten livelihoods, especially of the poor, and undermine the functioning of traditional security mechanisms (World Bank 2006a).

Consequently, systems of social security need to be expanded rapidly in terms of covered risks and number of persons protected, with a focus on the poor and so far unprotected underprivileged groups, taking into account the manifold risks they have to face every day to ensure their livelihoods.

Life chances are unequally distributed within the population. Poor and economically weak groups are disproportionately affected by increasing hazards and risks, as they have very limited reliable risk coping strategies (see Chambers 1989). Poor and disadvantaged groups often lack access to productive resources due to multiple socio-economic discriminations. They are more vulnerable and over-proportionately exposed to numerous hazards such as illness, disability, death, widowhood, natural calamities and disasters. These risks represent a serious and constant threat to their livelihoods.

Table 6.1 gives an overview of types and causes of risks in different categories. Depending on the nature of risk, individuals as well as village communities, regions or nations can be affected. Individual survival and risk coping strategies quickly reach their limits when crises such as droughts or floods collectively jeopardize a larger group within a particular region. In such situations, it becomes particularly clear how vulnerable the majority of the population is, as existing social security systems usually only offer comprehensive coverage for privileged members of the public service or formal sector employees.

Table 6.1 Types and causes of risks

Type of risk	Individual risk (micro)	Risk for groups of households or village communities (meso)	National or regional risk (macro)
Nature		Rain, landslide, volcanic eruption	Earthquake, flood, drought, storm
Health risks	Illness, injury, disability, old age, death	Epidemics	
Social risks	Crime, domestic violence	Terrorism, gang activity	Civil war, war, national riots
Economic risks	Unemployment, relocation, crop failure, changes in food prices		Growth collapse, hyperinflation, financial and monetary crisis, external shocks, transition cost of economic risks
		Changes in food prices	
Political risks		Local political unrest	Failure of political reform programmes, bad governance, coup d'état
Environmental risk		Deforestation, environmental pollution, nuclear disaster	

Source: Adapted from World Bank 2000, p. 137

But also for the more privileged groups, the coverage in case of sickness, old age and disability is rather low in many developing countries. In most countries employees and workers lack a minimum protection during unemployment. Unemployment is often synonymous with poverty. The dismissed workers have to take up an income-earning activity in the informal sector with low wages, unsafe working conditions and high income risks. The majority of the poor who earn their livelihood in the informal sector remains largely excluded from the benefits of formal security systems, even though there are particularly affected by the risks listed above. They basically rely on privately organized help or rudimentary social safety nets with only limited outreach and risk coverage.

With the current trend of globalization, the progressive integration of states and economies leads to growing inequalities between countries but also within countries. Inequalities and widespread poverty contributing to social and political instability are a major factor that explain why governments, especially in those countries undergoing a political and economic transformation process, are limited in their capabilities to develop an inclusive social security system (Klemp & Poeschke 2005, pp. 18). Increasing inequalities and social problems are not only explained by globalization and global structural change, but also, as the example of China shows, attributed to modernization, urbanization and internal development processes. This means that on the one hand, the course of globalization and, on the other hand, the government's ability to act, as well as the chosen development path, determine the options and conditions for expanding social security systems.

The conditions for setting-up effective and comprehensive social security systems are highly dependent on the social context, which in turn, is subject to constant change, especially in times of globalization (von Hauff 2005). For the last two decades, the group of developing countries is particularly confronted with far-reaching change processes which exacerbate social pressures and restrict economic, social and political choices. Nevertheless, even under these more difficult conditions, the expansion and the financing of social security systems in poorer countries are possible (ILO 2014, p. 119).

In international development cooperation, the establishment and expansion of social security systems became an important field of activity already in the 1980s. With the negative effects of socially unbalanced structural adjustment programmes, it has become evident that social security cannot only be based on trickle-down effects resulting from economic growth and wealth creation. Not least in the context of the series of terrorist attacks since September 11, 2001 and global fears of a growing international terrorism, the development gaps, growing social inequalities and numerous human rights violations came into a new focus. Under the influence of the global financial crisis and its negative social impact, the elimination of global poverty and social justice obtained a higher priority. Since then, many international reports have highlighted the causes and consequences of growing income inequalities and requested a new fairness in international relations. Based on a new partnership between industrialized and developing countries, social protection and the expansion of social security systems became a priority field of activity in international and German development cooperation and resulted in a (controversial) debate on how to provide social floor protection to all (Löwe 2011).

The International Labour Organization (ILO) and the World Bank have traditionally, or in response to growing criticism of socially unbalanced structural adjustment programmes, led the way in the international debate over the development of social security in developing countries. The ILO aims at a minimum level of social security by establishing social and labour standards without distorting international competition. Already in 1952 the ILO adopted the International Convention No. 102 on Social Security, which defines minimum social security standards in major industries.

The ILO focused at first on the establishment of state-organized social security systems to protect manpower in the formal sector and modern business. However, the ILO increasingly paid attention to workers in the informal sector and favoured systems of social floor protection to all. In the course of the Social Protection Floor Initiative adopted by the UN, "Social Security for all" was on the agenda of the hundredth ILO Labour Conference in June 2011, which resulted in a strong commitment to put this initiative into practice. In this context, the ILO relies on a two-dimensional strategy. As part of the horizontal dimension, the ILO promotes the rapid expansion of social floor protection systems, while as part of the vertical dimension, the level of social protection is to be increased in line with the ILO Convention No. 102 (ILO 2011a, p. 133).

The World Bank gave a higher priority to the promotion of social security in the late 1980s and increased its engagement in this area. Initially, the strengthening of social security nets for vulnerable and risk-prone groups and targeted interventions were in the forefront. Later the World Bank focused on a more comprehensive approach to promote social security. The new approach is mainly based on public investments to help ensure that individuals, households and communities can better cope with their diverse economic and social risks and that those who are particularly at risk and in need of protection are actively supported.

The new role of social security is understood as proactive and includes an integrated social risk management system based on the analysis of risks and their causes. Table 6.2 shows the starting points of such a complex approach and illustrates the wide range of possible instruments for risk prevention, risk reduction and risk management used (BMZ 2009a).

It is clear that risk prevention receives a high priority in risk management. Risk management requires the identification of the origin and economic characteristics of the risks. For example, it must be examined in how far the relevant risks affect individuals, entire regions or the total population. The appropriate combination of risk strategies in a given situation depends on the nature of the risk, the costs and the efficiency of available resources.

Consensus is given that developing and emerging countries themselves are responsible for the design of the development approach, the implementation of poverty eradication policies and the provision of social security. Governments thereby have to balance economic and social goals and have to stress more strongly the benefits of social security for economic growth in order to promote inclusive

Table 6.2 The risk management system of the World Bank

Risk management by	Main approach	Frequently used instruments
Risk prevention	Increased productivity	Basic social services, use of efficient production techniques, vocational training
	Strengthening social cohesion (social capital)	Strengthening the capacity of self-help, participation, empowerment
	Production of public goods	Social and economic infrastructure
Risk reduction (before a damage occurs)	Stabilization of income	Diversification of livelihood, employment promotion, insurance
Risk management (after a damage occurs)	Smoothing consumption	Savings, loans, migration, transfers

Source: Adapted from World Bank 2003

development. Developed countries are responsible for creating a supportive global environment by eliminating social insecurity through structural reforms and peace and the production of international public goods (Kohlmorgen 2004).

Social security in developing countries: A conceptual framework

Social policy, social protection and poverty alleviation

Social security is defined by the ILO as:

> The protection which societies provide for its members through a series of public measures, against the economic and social distress that otherwise would be caused by the stoppage or substantial reduction of earnings resulting from sickness, maternity, employment injury, unemployment, invalidity, old age and death, the provision of medical care, and the provision of subsidies for families with children.
>
> (ILO 1984, p. 3)

In this view, social security is organized primarily by the government or public institutions. The aim should be to safeguard the standard of living caused by the stoppage or substantial reductions of earnings. In the context of developing countries, the definition of social security is generally more broad-based. The focus is not on the coverage of individual standard risks such as sickness, invalidity, old age, unemployment and maternity, but on the vulnerability of the people, i.e. the economic vulnerability of the entire population, which can result from individual economic and social risks or from economic shocks or natural disasters.

According to the German Federal Ministry for Economic Cooperation and Development (BMZ) social protection refers to the entire system of protective measures against risks to assist individuals, households and communities to better manage risks and economic shocks, and to provide support to the critically vulnerable. It includes public interventions such as social insurance, social assistance and social safety nets, and provides room for private and community-based initiatives. The reasons for a broader definition of social security in the development context are varied, but are mostly linked to the fact that the variety of risks has markedly increased in the recent two decades. Social security in a broader sense is associated with the concept of "human security", which is defined by the UN as a life safe from hunger and lack of income, disease, crime and oppression (UNDP 1994). This view embeds social security in the context of a human rights-based development, linking social policy with other policy areas.

The degree of risk exposure and vulnerability is very different. Primarily, the poor population is suffering from high vulnerability and an almost complete lack of social protection. Due to social, economic and political discriminations the poor are often excluded from economic growth and have no access to social protection. In these cases, the poor are threatened by a variety of risks they cannot cope with on their own. There is a high risk for a relatively large population to remain in poverty or to fall back into poverty if no social security system adequately provides social protection in times of crisis. Thus, the central element of social protection in developing countries must be the fight against poverty. This means that the expansion of social security systems should focus on the dual function of social security, that social security should be aimed at reducing poverty and improving the general living conditions over an acceptable minimum level as well as providing protection against social, economic and environmental risks (BMZ 2008).

Overall, it is important to create structures and implement policies which help reduce the economic vulnerability, in particular of the poor and which facilitate the management of multiple risks of life at different policy levels (Garcia & Gruat 2003). Hence, social security should be interpreted as a cross-sectional issue. So far, the provision of social protection is basically understood as redistribution of wealth, incomes and resources. This is in any case an important element of effective social security systems. The World Bank emphasized, however, in its 2006 Development Report, that not only the redistribution of wealth, incomes and resources, but also the equal access of the poor to productive resources and to social services such as education and health is considered to be crucial for inclusive social security systems. When the poor are productively integrated into the labour market they are more likely to tackle livelihood problems on their own by improving their risk management capacities. Against this background social security policies should also entail policies and interventions to increase social justice and equal opportunities, as well as policies to eliminate discrimination in all phases of life of different population groups, notably of the poor.

General objectives in the establishment and expansion of social security systems

According to the current understanding of development, all people should be enabled to live a fulfilling life. Thus, the focus is on human development. All individuals should be able, on their own initiative and using their own skills and abilities, to equally participate in economic and social life. From this perspective, the primary objective of social security systems should be to build up a non-discriminatory environment which meets material and immaterial conditions to tap the full potential of the individuals and to foster the development of their personality. Food security, health, education and employment are thus priority intervention areas to provide basic protection and ensure better labour market participation and risk management capacities of the poor and socially disadvantaged groups. The starting point of social security is therefore the linking of economic, social and, increasingly, environmental policies.

Social security is largely based on the access to productive employment. Thus, the promotion of inclusive growth is a prerequisite for setting-up effective social security systems aimed at protecting the population from manifold income and livelihood risks. In addition to social security systems covering the labour force, systems must also be set up which protect the non-active persons and particularly vulnerable groups which include children, the youth, non-working women, the elderly and people with disabilities. Social protection should thus have an essentially positive impact on the living conditions and on the possibilities of social participation of the people. Primary focus should thus be on protecting the labour force in the informal sector and basic social protection to all.

The role of the state in establishing and expanding social security systems

Arguments occur over which role the state should play in setting-up a sustainable social security system or to what extent state-organized or privately organized social security systems should be prioritized. The answer to the question depends on ideological standpoints and political beliefs and convictions. There is no blueprint for the establishment of social security systems. In the development context, the main problem is that the government must play a central role in organizing social protection, but many countries are still in the process of state formation or subject to transformation processes (Debiel 2005, p. 12). Transformation processes entail political and economic structural changes associated with structural shifts in power relations generating winners and losers of such reforms and creating a new potential for conflicts. In principle, losers could be rewarded with a variety of compensation measures, which leads to the conclusion that the simultaneous strengthening of state and society is the basis for successful social and economic development.

The expansion of social security systems should be built on a combination of complementary social security subsystems and involve many actors and suppliers of social protection, since the state alone would not be in the position to set up a comprehensive social security system with a sufficiently high outreach and coverage. It is now widely accepted that social security systems are to be implemented by a combination of public, non-governmental and private actors which are complementary in providing social protection (Gsänger 1993).

Forms, actors and instruments for providing social security in developing countries

In many developing countries, a comprehensive system of social security does not exist. It is based on a variety of different forms of protection provided by different actors, such as individuals, households, communities, cooperatives, self-help groups, state or private insurance companies which are organized according to different principles. Social protection is thus provided by interacting suppliers of social security at different levels.

Given the dualistic economic structures and different living and working conditions in the formal and informal sectors, social security systems can be differentiated between traditional, informal and formal systems or forms of social security. As illustrated in Figure 6.1, formal systems of social security comprise state- and privately organized schemes. Protection schemes or arrangements developed by households, non-governmental organizations (NGOs) or self-help groups are characterized by a low degree of formalization and can further be differentiated from traditional and informal systems of social security. Both systems are based on the principle of reciprocity, but the latter is less binding and depends on the solidarity within the self-help group.

As a rule, formal systems of social security play a less prominent role in still agrarian economies or in countries with a low level of economic development. Evidence from the industrialized countries shows that with a higher degree of industrialization, modernization, urbanization, privatization and individualization, traditional and informal group-based systems of providing social protection continue to erode and need to be substituted or complemented by formal social security systems. Ideally, formal systems fill the increasing security gap without weakening the

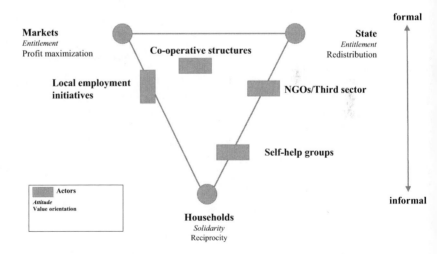

Figure 6.1 Social protection in the field of tension between domestic state and markets
Source: Adapted from Gsänger 1993, p. 96

effectiveness of other still existing self-help mechanisms. In many developing countries the economies are marked by a large informal sector. Therefore it is not surprising that under these circumstances the expansion of formal social security systems, especially state-organized social insurance schemes, is extremely difficult. Outreach and risk coverage is therefore quite low. Those who are living and working in the informal sector often remain excluded from such schemes and even those who are working in the formal sector have only inadequate social protection due to the inefficient management and poor performance of state or private insurance companies and hence due to limited insurance benefits.

A particular conceptual problem of formal systems results from the fact that usually only standard risks can be covered. People often remain unprotected in case of crop failures, natural disasters and general economic risks such as high inflation, as well as in the case of sudden economic shocks like global financial crises. Since a large proportion of the population or entire regions would negatively be affected, these so-called covariate risks can hardly be insured and financed. In addition, corruption and the mismanagement of the insurance companies weaken the performance and profitability of insurance companies and undermine the confidence and trust of insurance holders in formal social security systems also on a long-term basis.

There is no "one-size-fits-all" solution when it comes to developing viable and socially equitable security systems. The key is to develop systems that are adapted to the country-specific needs and conditions. Reform processes in this area can only be effective in the long run if the state, civil society and the private sector cooperate closely. Together they can create a social security system for the entire population that takes account of the interests of all those affected (BMZ 2009a). The different systems of social security offered by various actors need to be complementary and to be integrated into a universal system. It is important, in this perspective, to analyse the comparative strengths and weaknesses of these various forms of social protection.

Comparative strengths and weaknesses of the different forms of social security

The specific economic structures in developing countries with a high share of the informal sector require a "portfolio of social security" which is interlinked and adjusted to the specific needs of the poor and informal workers (Jütting 2004). The different forms of social security have their specific strengths and weaknesses, which simultaneously reflect their limitations in providing social protection. In case of social insurances, for example, the risk of underinsurance is relatively small. The potential for risk diversification, especially in case of a compulsory social insurance, is quite high, whereas the risk of a stoppage of payments even when covariant risks occur is rather low. In contrast, access to these insurances is rather limited since it is linked to an employment in the formal sector and requires a formal working contract for closing an insurance contract. The main weakness is that social insurances generate a lot of administrative work and require effective institutions as well as control mechanisms for the collection, management and administration of contributions and claims.

Similar strengths – but to a lesser extent – can be observed for private insurances. The major advantages over social insurances are lower transaction costs and the better control of misuse of funds and fraudulent claims. The main disadvantage of private insurances is the selective access to benefits, since insurance holders must have a reasonably high and steady income to be able to pay their contributions on a regular basis. The traditional and informal social security systems are in particular advantageous for poor people in terms of the accessibility and the control of misuse of the benefits. The abuse of collective systems is less likely as compared to formal systems as social pressure and sanctions control the access to benefits. However, they only provide inadequate risk coverage and security benefits. They are often insufficient to cover covariant risks.

How far transaction costs can be kept at an acceptable level and to what extent the accumulation of bad risks can be avoided ultimately depend on the design of the social security services. In principle, insurance-based forms of social security provide a high level of social protection, but are not accessible to all. In contrast, the traditional and informal security systems are very accessible, especially for the poor, but offer only inadequate and unreliable protection. This raises the question of how the different forms of social security can effectively be interrelated and designed in such a way that the poor also have access to formal social security systems.

Requirements for a sustainable social security system

In principle, various institutions, organizations or actors can be part of a sustainable social security system. The state alone would not be in the position to provide sufficiently high levels of social protection for the whole population. However, even if the social security system is set-up by various providers of social security, the state plays a central role for ensuring social security to all. Primarily the state, in its capacity as norm-setter, is responsible to build up a just and non-discriminatory social order to create a favourable environment for broad-based and inclusive economic growth as well as to provide a predictable framework for action for private and non-governmental providers of social security. The state must also held to be responsible for organizing a coherent and comprehensive system of social security. This role includes the establishment and support of institutions which provide preventive and reactive protection measures to the population in times of crisis. In this context, the state bears the responsibility to design pro-poor economic, social and environmental policies.

Depending on ideological standpoints the exact role of the state must be defined in providing social security. However, regardless of the ideological positions, ways need to be found to disburden the state. Currently, it is observed that in many countries state weakness is emerging, meaning that the state is not or hardly in a position to fulfil its core functions and provide inclusive social protection. Consequently, the state must regain its capacities to act to launch social reform programmes. This means that the development and expansion of social security systems should be integrated in the process of state formation and be part of building good governance structures. At the same time an effective administration oriented towards the security needs of the population must be set up (Hein 2005). In strengthening social security systems as a strategic element of poverty alleviation policies, the idea took hold that a multi-tier system of social security will be most successful in achieving the objective to provide social security to all.

The following principles can help to design a social security policy from which primarily the poor can benefit, i.e. to implement policies aimed at stabilizing the livelihoods of the poor, to support self-help initiatives, to strengthen social cohesion, to accentuate the insurance principle and to follow integrated social, economic and environmental policies. Taking these principles into account, the state should intervene only as long as private and individual social security mechanisms cannot ensure minimum standards of living. This would correspond to the notion of a subsidiary intervening welfare state. This would also mean that a sustainable social security system should be based on a pluralistic institutional set-up with relatively easy access to various forms of social security for the poor. Following an approach of decentralization, the various social security systems need to be linked at different intervention levels and be combined to an effective risk management system.

The major task of the central government is the creation of a legal framework, the development of social and sector programmes and the provision of financial resources. The regional government is responsible for implementing the sector programmes, while local governments have the responsibility to provide basic services and to mobilize, support and link local organizations and self-help initiatives. The involvement of NGOs helps make the social security systems more effective since NGOs are in close contact with the poor and more familiar with their needs and living conditions. They can therefore reach the poor more directly and lobby social policies for the unprotected poor (BMZ 2008). Integral elements of social security systems are measures to systematically identify and dismantle multiple forms of discrimination and to extend social protection to the hitherto excluded poor by introducing basic social protection schemes, by stepping up micro insurances or introducing innovative programmes linking formal and informal systems of social security (Schubert 2005). In this context, models must be developed which integrate the informal sector workers in the formal social security systems.

Poverty alleviation policies can make a considerable contribution to reduce poverty-related social and economic risks. Since the economic success and the sustainability of self-help and self-organization are also dependent on the facilitated access to gainful employment, education, health and resources, participatory development favouring the productive integration of poor and vulnerable groups into the formal economy is important. Social security is similar to the fight against poverty: a cross-cutting issue that requires an integrated policy approach. An orientation towards the concept of sustainable development and a focus on preventive risk reduction measures forms the basis for a sustainable social security and effective risk management system.

The provision of social security is not free of costs. It is predictable that the financing needs will continue to increase in the future. However, studies show that even economies with a low level of economic development can finance social security systems (ILO 2008). In this context it is important that financial resources and government revenues are mobilized. This includes the development of an efficient tax system and an efficient banking and insurance sector, which is itself an important element of sustainable social security systems. Ultimately, however, the financing of social systems depends on the political will of the government to provide social protection to all. Thus, there is continuous need to make governments responsible for setting-up effective social security systems, especially for those who had so far been excluded.

Contribution of German development cooperation

The establishment and expansion of social security systems have become increasingly important in recent years. They are now regarded as being a crucial strategic part of the structural fight against poverty. The key principle is that every country decides on its policy of social protection in accordance with international conventions, subject to its existing traditional systems of social protection, historical experience, economic and social situations, as well as to its cultural values and social norms (BMZ 2009a).

The main objectives of German development policy in the field of social security are:

- Protection for all, especially the poor, in terms of all relevant risks (increase of coverage and depth of coverage);
- Creation of comprehensive and inclusive social security systems for the entire population, especially for the poor;
- Increase the efficiency and quality and financial sustainability of social security systems;
- Improvement of social justice within the systems.

The primary objective is to create adequate framework conditions for the establishment and extension of effective social security systems. This includes the elimination of structural causes for social risks and the strengthening of the institutional capacities of the different institutions providing social protection as well as of those responsible for the framework conditions. In addition, specific protection measures are implemented catering to their various needs and interests. As social protection is a cross-cutting issue, development policy in this field pursues a multi-level approach across institutions. Social protection projects and programmes with high poverty relevance are implemented at the macro, meso and micro levels and consequently often with several partners. The focus is on poverty alleviation and the extension of social protection systems to the informal sector.

At the macro level the development interventions contribute to the improvement of national framework conditions, i.e. consultation of ministries or government institution institutions concerning the expansion of education and health care systems or pension schemes, also to the informal sector. In addition, decision makers and the staff in the state authorities are trained. It also includes the facilitation of the cooperation between the state, self-help organizations, NGOs and the private insurance industry. Furthermore, it embraces the support of the establishment of mutual insurance schemes, basic protection programmes as well as decentralized health insurance systems. Also the churches and the political foundations are increasingly active in this area (Adam et al. 2002; Liebert 2011). While the political foundations primarily promote social dialogue, social reforms and legal advice, churches rather support grassroots organizations such as savings and credit groups as well as basic services and decentralized health insurance schemes. Priority areas of cooperation in the field of social protection are health, education, employment, social floor protection and old age.

Health

Improved health of the population is not only a consequence of socio-economic development, but a healthy population represents an essential prerequisite for development. The establishment of a comprehensive health care system for the entire population is thus one of the priorities for social protection. This is, on the one hand, to avoid social decline as a result of ill health and, on the other hand, to increase general health conditions, especially for poor groups by improving nutrition, reducing the risk of disease and prevention and treatment of chronic diseases, as well as to improve prevention and treatment of disabilities. Good health and adequate health services simultaneously create conditions for empowering the poor or informal workers to improve their livelihood based on their own initiatives and capacities and so finally be responsible for their social protection. Health improvement is thus an important strategic element of poverty alleviation.

The objective of health policy reforms is to enhance access to affordable health services for the entire population and to establish a comprehensive health care system. The views on how a comprehensive national health system can be set up, however, are very different. Minimum consensus in the context of health is to put a stronger focus on preventive health and health care for the poor. The state is responsible for the nationwide organization of a universal and accessible health care system and must regulate the functional relationships between the various heath institutions and providers of health care services. What is still unspecified is how far the state itself should provide social services (Ramesh & Wu 2005). Many countries have focused on the introduction of national social insurances. They work best in countries which have a high proportion of formal jobs and effective administrative institutions.

For the poor, decentralized protection schemes can be more effective. In many countries undergoing a transition to democratic market economies, health care tends to become more decentralized. In this process, the integration of local providers of basic health services is increasingly important. This applies to local authorities, to non-state actors as well as to the local population and increasingly to private health providers who start having a greater role within the health care system at least on the local level. However, the fragmentation of the health care system should be avoided.

The access of the poor to basic health care services under a national health care system can be improved by eliminating, reducing or differentiating fees according to the patient's income situation. It would also be possible to replace payable fees by vouchers for health care services (Hardeman et al. 2004). In addition to systems with (partial) exemption from costs for the poor, health micro insurance schemes covering specific health risks become increasingly important (BMZ 2009b). In many cases, NGOs serve as intermediaries between the insurance company and the target groups. Professional NGOs usually offer effective organizational structures to reach out to the poor, to collect the contributions, to assess risks and to handle the claims with the insurance company.

A prominent example for the development of an innovative approach to health insurance, which opens the access of the poor to health care services, is the Indian National Health Programme or Rashtriya Swasthya Bima Yojana (RSBY). With the help of a smart card issued by the government, the needy poor obtain access to public health services. Under the RSBY programme insurance services worth RS 30,000 (about € 500 euros) are granted per year for five members of a family. The costs the insured family have to bear amount to RS 30 for the registration fee per year (about 50 cents). The insurance premium of RS 600 per year (about € 10) is paid by the government. The rates for specific medical services are defined. The poor pay by smart card and the sum is deducted immediately from the card's chip. The invoice is sent electronically to the insurance company. This innovative insurance model is considered to be very successful (Nishant & Swarup 2010, p. 268). Both micro insurance and social health insurance schemes such as RSBY have their weaknesses, but they are an increasingly important option, especially in low-income countries, where people are not covered by national health insurances.

Education

Education is crucial for the integration of the labour force in the labour market and is, besides health, an essential prerequisite for the economic and social development of a country. The long-neglected promotion of primary education has become an important element of a comprehensive education system which is considered to be a strategic part of effective poverty reduction (BMZ 2004). The problem is that the rapid quantitative expansion of primary education could compromise the quality of education and vice versa. It is therefore difficult to set a clear priority on broad-based education.

The increase in government spending for the infrastructural expansion of primary schools is no guarantee for higher school attendance rates. In many countries it is not the lack of infrastructure and facilities, but, rather, the high dropout rates that are the main problem. Accordingly, supply-oriented measures must be combined with demand-sided measures embedded in a national education programme. Programmes and measures to improve the quality of primary education are most successful when implemented at different levels and combine different instruments. Important demand-oriented instruments are the provision of school uniforms and teaching materials, the exoneration from school fees, the provision of free school meals and conditional cash payments, i.e. cash payments in return of regular school attendance. The last of these should encourage the parents to send their children to school. The programmes are seen as a compensation for the opportunity costs poor families have to bear when sending their children to school. Both, supply- as well as demand-sided programmes and measures are highly cost-intensive and a considerable burden on the government's overall budget, especially in case of untargeted conditional transfer programmes (Javad 2011). It finally depends on the political will and the priorities of the government as to how fast the education systems can be expanded.

Employment programmes

A huge labour force is a high potential for the economic development of a country as well. However, not only the size of the working population alone determines a country's growth potential. The "quality" of the workforce, which can be increased by investments in nutrition, health and education and training, is crucial for economic growth.

In most developing countries the agricultural sector is on the decline while the industrial as well as the service sector increase requiring other and higher qualifications of workers and the employees. Thus, a large proportion of the poverty-affected population lack necessary qualifications and cannot be integrated into the formal labour market for structural reasons. They have to seek employment opportunities in the informal sector, because in many countries no or only a rudimentary protection against unemployment exists. Comprehensive unemployment insurances or, alternatively, social assistance schemes covering the entire labour force or poor population are often too expensive.

In this context, employment programmes better targeted to the poor are an important instrument to ensure a basic standard of living. Already existing employment insurances usually protect only the formal employees in the public or private sector. In these cases, public employment programmes can be a substitute for unemployment insurances for the working poor. The 100-day programme in India guarantees to the rural poor at least 100 days of work in public investment projects implemented during the agricultural off-season. However, it should be noted that the employment programmes only favour the population in working-age and who are physically able to work. The groups unable to work such as old, sick or disabled people cannot benefit from those programmes and still rely heavily on their family and informal networks. Furthermore, often the paid wages are far too low to eke out a living. Therefore, targeted conditional cash transfer programmes to extreme poor households as part of a basic social protection to all strategy gained importance (Leisering et al. 2006). These transfer programmes are promoted by the ILO's Global Campaign on Basic Social Protection to All (ILO 2011b).

Cash transfer programmes

Basic social protection programmes can be understood as effective tools to reduce temporary or structural poverty, to implement social protection as a human right and to simultaneously stimulate economic growth and development as well as to contribute to political stability.

In that context, social cash transfers are increasingly seen as a means of providing basic social protection (Schubert 2005). However, there is an ongoing controversial debate over the effectiveness of this tool to fight poverty and social insecurity. It is recognized, if used intelligently, that cash transfers can be an effective instrument with which to implement the human right to social security and to stimulate economic growth and long-term development at the same time. However, it is necessary to note that such programmes only fight the symptoms; they do not tackle the root causes of problems. Nevertheless cash transfer programmes are being widely adopted by governments in developing countries to tackle extreme poverty. Instead of transfers in kind (typically in the form of food), poor households receive a small cash subsidy to help cover their basic needs.

A distinction can be made between different types of social cash transfers (Löwe 2008). The debate over cash transfers primarily focuses on the question to which extent the payment of social transfers should be means tested or be subject to conditions. Proponents of means-tested social transfers argue that scarce state resources should target the neediest, should avoid windfall gains and should not undermine work incentives by paying substitute incomes. The conditioning of cash transfers can help achieve developmental policy objectives if, for example, the payment of social transfers to poor households is linked to school attendance of their children. Opponents of means testing claim that targeting is complicated and costly and does not adequately reach to the needy.

Multiple criteria can be used for the means testing. Eligibility criteria could be the housing condition of a household. No fixed roof for example could serve as a proxy indicator as part of a means test being used. Furthermore, it is possible to target groups of selected categories of households such as single mothers or of selected poor regions (geographical targeting). In case of community-based targeting, the community, to whom social transfers are to be paid, decides over the transfers. The self-targeting is a self-filtering mechanism through which the non-needy are discouraged to profit unjustifiably from the transfers and waive the benefits. This is common in employment generation programmes, where heavy physical labour is paid very low and is therefore not of interest for better-off households.

Experience shows that social transfer programmes can successfully be used to help cushion risks and to reduce chronic poverty. Even in low-income countries these programmes can effectively be implemented. However, those programmes linked to health, nutrition and education services, as well as access to legal aid and information about rights, and which help households to secure sustainable livelihoods, have the greater potential to tackle poverty and transform lives. If poverty is the result of a lack of education, skills and jobs combined with precarious livelihoods, then tackling poverty effectively ultimately depends on cash transfers being part of an integrated approach to social protection and providing poor people with routes out of poverty (Schubert 2005).

Old-age provision

Overall, there is a considerable variety of national social and private insurance programmes for old age. The following types can be differentiated: state-managed pension or pension funds (e.g. national provident funds), social insurance programmes, special old-age schemes for formally employed and privileged groups and social assistance programmes for the elderly needy and private life insurances (Kurz 1999). With the exception of social assistance programmes, the above types of pension schemes are more likely to benefit formal employees or privileged groups. Outreach and coverage of risks are usually dependent on the size of the formal sector or the number of contributors, the performance of public and private suppliers of social security and available financial resources.

The introduction of a national provident fund is usually the first step in establishing a system for the provision of old age. They are seen as a possibility to provide a minimum income to individuals or certain groups of aged people at least during a transitional period until a more comprehensive old age security system is established. The savings accumulated on individual accounts are in many cases far too low to secure a living in old age. In addition, the amounts paid can be misused, especially if they are paid as a lump sum at the end of working life. It is widely accepted that formal systems need to be expanded while preserving the family-based and informal security systems. The World Bank advocates a growth and market-compatible three-pronged programme. The first pillar consists of a state-funded minimum old age pension based on a pay-as-you-go principle. The second pillar is based either on a statutory occupational pension or individual forced saving. The third pillar is a voluntary supplementary private insurance. This three-pillar model attempts to achieve various objectives such as the redistribution of incomes and the formation of savings capital, as well as securing already achieved life standards also through individual self-provision efforts.

In contrast, the ILO promotes a four-pillar model. The four pillars are, first, a tax-financed basic protection for those in need, second, an income-based and contributory social insurance based on a pay-as-you-go principle, third, a privately operated mandatory insurance, and fourth, a supplementary voluntary insurance. The ILO favours a stronger role of the state in setting-up an effective old age security system and calls for solidarity between different income groups within the systems. The ILO is basically against a system where pension rights are dependent on individual savings. This would not be in line with established norms of social security. Pensions must therefore be determined and guaranteed (Gsänger 2001). Ultimately, the differences between these two models essentially depend on the fixed level of the basic pension and to what extent the solidarity principle can also be anchored in the World Bank model.

It must be ensured that the population in poverty and informal workers have access to old-age pension schemes (Van Ginneken 1999). In this context, the Self-Employed Women's Association (SEWA) in India is considered to be one of the pioneers in this field. As one of India's largest NGOs, the old-age pension scheme of SEWA is considered as the best-known example of an attempt to introduce forms of social security based on the insurance principle in the informal sector. SEWA has established an integrated insurance scheme for their members including an insurance package, which protects women against various risks, while it also contains a life insurance policy. The life insurances potentially offer supplementary welfare benefits and provide a second pillar of age security for the poor (BMZ 2008).

Learning experiences in shaping the social security systems in developing countries

Previous learning experiences in the design of social security systems can hardly be generalized and only to a certain extent be transferred to other countries (EU 2010). Nevertheless, they can be summed up as follows:

- Social security systems can make a significant contribution to reducing risk and vulnerability of the poor and can thus contribute to overcoming poverty and inequality traps. Targeted basic social protection and public employment programmes can reach a large proportion of the population.
- The establishment and expansion of social security systems require political will, national ownership and a social consensus that contribute to the acceptance of social policy measures (redistribution) and strengthen the willingness of better-off groups to finance the programmes by taxes and contributions.
- When the financing of a system of social security is not be possible due to the limited availability of financial resources, individual programmes can be carried out and lay the foundation for a more comprehensive system of social security.
- Successful programmes are tied to institutional and administrative conditions which may still be set up during programme implementation. In any case, the successful implementation of programmes requires a clear defined division of roles and responsibilities as well as a good cooperation and coordination between the various actors, effective coordination mechanisms, transparency and accountability.
- Through pilot projects, phased implementation and reliable evaluations and impact analyses strengths and weaknesses of the programmes and schemes can be identified and programmes can be adjusted accordingly.
- Experience shows that disincentives and windfall gains, for example within cash transfer programmes, are less than previously expected. Microfinance systems offer additional benefits and can be used as a platform for the development of contributory social security systems. It should be noted that the poorest of the poor are excluded from these systems and social transfer systems are more suitable for this group.

- The expansion of social security systems can contribute to achieving long-term development objectives and is not only limited to risk and crisis management. Social security should therefore be considered as part of the overall national development strategy and must be intertwined with other policy and funding areas so that existing synergies can be exploited.
- Social protection promotes gender equality, strengthens the influence of women and reduces social exclusion.

Conclusions

Social security is a human right and a prerequisite for sustainable economic development, social justice and successful poverty reduction. One of the main challenges for developing and emerging countries is the increasing social security gap. The need to build social security systems is rapidly rising. Developing and emerging countries are faced with the problem that changed conditions of life, social inequalities and risks, for example by climate change, primarily hit the poor and vulnerable. Thus, the focus must be on the poor and vulnerable groups and aligned with effective risk management strategies for better risk prevention, risk reduction and the support of risk coping strategies. Since especially in poorer developing countries, a large proportion of the working population is employed in agriculture or the informal sector, it is necessary to find adequate solution to effectively extend social security also to those living and working in the informal sector. Furthermore, additional financial resources must be mobilized to provide comprehensive inclusive social security systems. Emerging markets continue to face the particular challenge that, due to a rapid aging of the population, the establishment and expansion of old age provision schemes must be given a higher priority top avoid eventually compromising overall economic growth prospects.

References

Adam, E.; von Hauff, M., Jon, M. (2002): *Social Protection in Southeast & East Asia*, Friedrich-Ebert-Stiftung, Singapur.

BMZ (2004): *Grundbildung für alle als internationales Entwicklungsziel – Eine zentrale Herausforderung für die deutsche Entwicklungspolitik*, Bonn.

BMZ (2008): *Mit Mikrofinanzierung aus der Armut: Der deutsche Beitrag zur Entwicklung nachhaltiger Finanzsysteme*, Bonn.

BMZ (2009a): *Förderung sozialer Sicherung und sozialer Sicherungssysteme*, BMZ-Positionspapier, Bonn.

BMZ (2009b): *Kleine Beiträge – große Sicherheit, Mikroversicherungen in der Finanzsystementwicklung, Mikroversicherungen als Arbeitsbereich der deutschen Entwicklungspolitik*, Bonn.

Chambers, R. (1989): Vulnerability, Coping and Policy, *IDS Bulletin*, Vol. 2, pp. 1–7.

Debiel, T. (2005): Fragile Staaten als Problem der Entwicklungspolitik, *Aus Politik und Zeitgeschichte*, B 28–29, pp. 12–18.

EU (2010): *Europäischer Entwicklungsbericht 2010, Soziale Sicherung für eine inklusive Entwicklung*, Brussels.

Garcia, A.B., Gruat, J.V. (2003): *Social Protection: A life cycle continuum investment for social justice, poverty reduction and development*, ILO, Geneva.

Gsänger, H. (1993): Soziale Sicherungssysteme für arme Bevölkerungsgruppen, *Schriftenreihe des Deutschen Instituts für Entwicklungspolitik*, Band 106, Berlin.

Gsänger, H. (2001): Wie fördert man die soziale Sicherung im Süden?, *Der Überblick*, Vol. 37(1), pp. 17–25.

Hardeman, W.; Van Damme, W.; Van Pelt, M.; Ir Por, Van, H.K.; Meessen, B. (2004): Zugang zu medizinischer Versorgung für alle? Über Nutzungsgebühren und einen „Gesundheitsfürsorgefonds" (Health Equity Fund) in Sotnikum, Kambodscha, *Focus Asien, Schriftenreihe des Asienhauses Nr. 18*, Essen, pp. 35–52.

Hein, W. (2005): Vom Entwicklungsstaat zum Staatsverfall, *Aus Politik und Zeitgeschichte*, B 28–29, pp. 6–11.

ILO (2006): *Changing the Paradigm in Social Security: From Fiscal Burden to Investing in People*, Geneva.

ILO (2008): *Can Low-Income Countries Afford Basic Social Security?* Social Security Policy Briefings, Paper 3, Geneva.

ILO (2011a): *Can Low-Income Countries Afford Basic Social Security?* Social Security Policy Briefings, Paper 3, Geneva.

ILO (2011b): *Social Security for Social Justice and a Fair Globalization: Recurrent discussion on social protection (social security) under the ILO Declaration on Social Justice for a Fair Globalization*, Report VI, Geneva.

ILO (2014): *World Social Security Report 2014/15: Building economic recovery, inclusive development and social justice*, Geneva.

Javad, A. (2011): *Social Cash Transfers: a Useful Instrument in Development Cooperation? Potentials and Pitfalls*, Friedrich Ebert Stiftung, Berlin.

Jütting, J.P. (2004): Soziale Sicherung Entwicklungsländern: Herausforderungen und Lösungsansätze, in: Betz, J., Hein, W. (Hrsg.), *Soziale Sicherung in Entwicklungsländern, Neues Jahrbuch Dritte Welt*, Opladen, pp. 105–120.

Klemp, L., Poeschke, R. (2005): Good Governance gegen Armut und Staatsversagen, *Aus Politik und Zeitgeschichte*, B 28–29, pp. 18–25.

Kohlmorgen, L. (2004): Globalisierung, Global Governance und globale Sozialpolitik, in: Betz, J., Hein, W. (Hrsg.), *Soziale Sicherung in Entwicklungsländern, Neues Jahrbuch Dritte Welt*, Opladen, pp. 59–82.

Kurz, S. (1999): *Soziale Sicherung in Entwicklungsländer, Das Beispiel einer Alterssicherung in Indien*, Regensburg.

Leisering, L.; Buhr, P.; Traiser-Diop, U. (2006): *Grundsicherung als globale Herausforderung, Studie im Auftrag der GIZ*, Eschborn.

Liebert, N. (2011): *No Social Justice without Social Protection*, Friedrich-Ebert-Stiftung, Dialogue on Globalization, Berlin.

Löwe, M. (2008): *Basic Social Protection: Positions of key development actors*, German Institute of Development, Berlin.

Löwe, M. (2010): *Neue Strategien der sozialen Sicherung: Der Mikroversicherungsansatz*, Deutsches Institut für Entwicklungspolitik, Analysen und Stellungnahmen 4/2010, Berlin.

Löwe, M. (2011): *Soziale Grundsicherung, Positionen wichtiger entwicklungspolitischer Akteure, Studie für Brot für die Welt*, Stuttgart.

Nishant, S.; Swarup, A. (2010): *The RSBY: National Health Insurance in India*, New Delhi.

OECD (2011): *Growing Income Inequality in OECD Countries: What Drives It and How Can Policy Tackle It?*, Paris.

Ramesh, M.; Wu, X. (2005): Neuorientierung des Verhältnisses öffentlicher und privater Träger der Gesundheitsversorgung in Südostasien, *Focus Asien, Schriftenreihe des Asienhauses Nr. 23*, Essen, pp. 23–34.

Schubert, B. (2005): *Grundsicherung in der Entwicklungszusammenarbeit, Studie im Auftrag der GTZ*, Eschborn.

UNDP (1994): *Human Development Report*, New York.

Van Ginneken, W. (1999): Social Security for the Informal Sector: A New Challenge for the Developing Countries, *International Social Security Review*, Vol. 52, Issue 1, pp. 49–69.

von Hauff, M. (2005): Globalisierung und soziale Sicherung – eine unvereinbare Beziehung?, *Focus Asien, Schriftenreihe des Asienhauses Nr. 23*, Essen, pp. 13–23.

World Bank (2000): *World Development Report 2000/2001, Attacking Poverty*, Washington, DC.

World Bank (2003): *Social Risk Management: The World Bank's Approach to Social Protection in a Globalizing World*, Washington, DC.

World Bank (2006a): *Natural Disaster Hotspots – A Global Risk Analysis*, Washington, DC..

World Bank (2006b): *Weltentwicklungsbericht 2006, Chancengerechtigkeit und Entwicklung*, Washington, DC.

World Commission on the Social Dimension of Globalization (2004): *A Fair Globalization: Creating Opportunities for All*, Geneva.

7 Sustainability and education[1]

Gerd Michelsen and Daniel Fischer

In this chapter we discuss the relationship between education and sustainable development. This relationship is one that has two sides: on the one hand education is the indispensable condition if sustainable development is to be successful. But, on the other, the idea of sustainability is also a magnifying glass revealing how the challenges of our era can only be met if education itself changes. Sustainable development provides an innovative and highly relevant approach to rethinking general education at the beginning of the 21st century. We discuss below the origin and development of the concept of education for sustainable development, its defining characteristics, and then present innovative examples of its implementation.

The relationship between education and sustainable development

Sustainable development is about such pressing global challenges as climate change, biodiversity loss, marine pollution, unemployment and the unjust division of wealth between developed and developing countries. It is also a concept crucial to a future-oriented energy policy, the achievement of social justice and understanding our responsibilities for the life chances of future generations. In the normative idea of sustainability, different societal ideas and beliefs about justice, liberty and self-determination, universal well-being and responsibility towards future generations are all interrelated. Sustainability is seen as an important objective by governments, businesses, non-governmental organizations, municipalities, meeting at national and international conferences, where different interests often play an influential role. When there is talk of sustainable development, there are often references to the definition in the Brundtland Report: "Sustainable development is development that meets the needs of the present without compromising the ability of future generations to meet their own needs" (WCED 1987, p. 54).

A sustainable development involves comprehensive and far-reaching transformations and fundamental shifts in perspective. There is consensus in academia that these changes can only be brought about through drastic changes in lifestyle and the dominant patterns of production and consumption. Such fundamental changes require individuals to adopt new attitudes and develop a greater awareness, which can only be accomplished by systematic learning provided by the educational system. Education is thus an integral component of sustainability processes (de Haan 2004), and sustainable development will not be possible without changing learning processes (Vare & Scott 2007).

The key importance of education is emphasized in Agenda 21, the most important document of the first United Nations Conference on the Environment and Development (UNCED) in 1992: "Education is critical for promoting sustainable development and improving the capacity of the people to address environment and development issues" (Agenda 21, Section 36). Education should promote a change in public awareness that enables individuals to become responsible and engaged citizens helping to develop (global) society in a sustainable way. It can do this by raising awareness for sustainability problems and helping learners acquire the knowledge and competences necessary to deal with these problems (Michelsen et al. 2011).

Educational processes should promote a greater awareness of issues concerning the sustainable development of society and develop competences allowing individuals to participate in coming up with innovative solutions to the economic, social, technological and cultural problems threatening the Earth's ecosystem. If learners are to acquire the necessary competences and seriously engage with sustainability issues, then a shift in perspective leading to a reorientation of the educational system is crucial. This insight has led to discussions since the 1990s about the concept of education for sustainable development (cf. de Haan & Harenberg 1999).

Education for sustainable development opens up new perspectives on traditional educational subjects. An education oriented towards a respect for human dignity and democracy is thus extended to include recognition of the natural bases of life on Earth. Years ago the educationalist Wolfgang Klafki wrote that by dealing with "key problems of the epoch", educational processes should give everyone a possibility to understand their world and help shape its development (Klafki 1995). These key problems need to be approached, and to be supplemented and given greater focus, from the perspective of sustainability. They belong to a general education that does not only involve the acquisition of knowledge but also the development of competences allowing an individual to critically appraise problematic situations and take the necessary action to ameliorate them.

It was in the context of these developments that in 2002 the United Nations declared the UN Decade of Education for Sustainable Development (2005–2014). The Decade was a further impetus to conceptualizing and implementing education for sustainable development as having an important role to play in shaping the sustainable development of societies around the world. From today's vantage point it can be seen that the many activities undertaken around the globe during the Decade of Education for Sustainable Development accomplished much in changing the role and understanding of education for sustainable development. If education for sustainable development was at first seen as a "niche activity" in the larger educational system, then this viewpoint has changed significantly over the past few years. Education for sustainable development is now seen as an innovative concept that can give teaching and learning in different educational sectors a new meaning and importance. It is an approach that offers the possibility of rethinking the purpose of education and raising its quality. Increasingly, discussions now center on a holistic systemic approach based on the assumption that education for sustainable development and the idea of sustainability are not only important for educational processes but also for changing educational institutions, whether they are daycare centres, schools, universities or institutions of further education.

Origins of education for sustainable development

Since the end of the 1990s the concept of a sustainable development has increasingly been a part of discussions in the field of education. Education for sustainable development has its origins in environmental education. A more recent strand is the concept of global learning, which emerged from the tradition of development education and today plays an important role in the conceptual debate about education for sustainable development. Both concepts shared the goal of enabling people to address problems of non-sustainability and to contribute to a sustainable development.

From environmental education to education for sustainable development

For almost 40 years the theoretical relationship between ecological crises and education has been debated. Experimental projects in educational practice have been undertaken and, repeatedly, programmatic educational policy initiatives have been launched, and research activities carried out. *Environmental education* has been on the international agenda since at least the 1970s (Michelsen 2001). Numerous international conferences, many of which were sponsored by the UN and its organizations, had the goal of establishing environmental education in different educational sectors. These efforts took place against a background of discussion world-wide about the threats and dangers posed by human beings to the natural conditions of life on Earth, not least triggered by the report of the Club of Rome with the title *Limits to Growth* (Meadows et al. 1972). This seminal report clearly showed that global change required a new quality in dealing with human-environment problems and the development of human society. A first milestone in this period was the first UN Educational, Scientific and Cultural Organization (UNESCO) conference in 1977 on environmental education in Tiflis, Georgia (UNESCO 1978). This conference had a decisive influence on the understanding and further development of environmental education, which was understood as an integrative component of continuous lifelong educational processes going beyond school-based education. General goals in environmental education include raising awareness, gaining knowledge, changing attitudes, acquiring skills and enabling participation. Together with the urgent question as to the role of education, it became clear that one could no longer speak of education in the sense of adapting or changing behaviour but instead it was understood that education was about the development of educational processes that would place greater emphasis on the responsibility of the individual in shaping the development of societies.

Triggered by the publications and events mentioned above, the discussion about the role of education in sustainable development found a provisional high point at UNCED in Rio de Janeiro in 1992. In almost all chapters of the Agenda 21 plan of action adopted at the conference, the importance of education is emphasized, with *Chapter 36* in particular focusing on promoting public awareness and education as well as listing recommendations for action. With this second milestone, the discussion of the role of education and sustainable development was given a major document that has since been a reference point for educational policy initiatives and activities in a national context.

The important role given to education in the Agenda 21 was reaffirmed ten years later at the World Summit for Sustainable Development in Johannesburg in 2002. A third milestone was the proposal at the conference to implement a World Decade of Education for Sustainable Development, which was then adopted by the General Assembly of the United Nations for the period 2005–2014 (UNESCO 2005). The goal of the Decade was to contribute to the implementation of Agenda 21, as agreed upon in Rio and reaffirmed in Johannesburg, and to establish the principles of sustainable development in national educational systems world-wide.

The fourth milestone is seen in the adoption of a regional strategy of Education for Sustainable Development of the UN Economic Commission for Europe (UNECE)[2] (UNECE 2005) by the environmental and education ministers of the member states in 2005 to introduce and promote education for sustainable development in the countries of UNECE and so to support the realization of a vision of a region committed to sustainable development. The UNECE defined its understanding of education for sustainable development in its strategy as follows (2005, p. 1):

> Education for sustainable development develops and strengthens the capacity of individuals, groups, communities, organizations and countries to make judgements and choices in favour of sustainable development. It can promote a shift in people's mindsets and in so doing enable them to make our world safer, healthier and more prosperous, thereby improving the quality of life. Education for sustainable development can provide critical reflection and greater awareness and empowerment so that new visions and concepts can be explored and new methods and tools developed.

Even before the UN Decade came to an end, it was recommended at the UN Earth Summit Rio+20 in 2012 to promote education for sustainable development in a suitable form beyond the Decade. In the autumn of 2013 UNESCO launched the Global Action Program 2015–2019 as a follow-up programme of the UN Decade. This fifth milestone was an important impulse for the international implementation of education for sustainable development. The goal of the Global Action Program is to continue to actively integrate education for sustainable development in all educational sectors, thus accelerating the process of sustainable development. The emphasis is on the development and intensification of specific measures (UNESCO 2014).

Table 7.1 International milestones of an education for sustainable development

International milestone	Major activity
First milestone	1977: Tiflis Conference
Second milestone	1992: Agenda 21, Chapter 36
Third milestone	2002: Resolution by the UN to implement a World Decade of Education for Sustainable Development (2005–2014)
Fourth milestone	2005: UNECE Strategy "Education for Sustainable Development"
Fifth milestone	2013: Resolution of UNESCO for a Global Action Program for 2015–2019

As a follow-up to the UN Decade of Education for Sustainable Development, the Global Action Program on Education for Sustainable Development (2015–2019) has been in effect since 2015, with UNESCO as lead agency. The programme focuses on five priority action areas:

- The first action area has to do with policy support creating a favourable climate that will allow education for sustainable development to achieve its potential in changing educational systems. This goal involves integrating the education for sustainable development concept in educational and sustainability policy-making as well as in the national and international guidelines of these sectors.
- The second action area is about the holistic transformation of learning and teaching environments. Sustainability should not only be taught, it should be learned directly at the site of learning and training. The goal is to change the values and structures of educational institutions so that their administrations are also sustainable.
- The third action area is found in the development of competences among teachers and trainers. Education for sustainable development should be integrated in teacher training and professional development so that teachers and trainers can become change agents able to implement sustainable development in educational practice.
- In the fourth action area the emphasis is on empowering and mobilizing young people by involving them in the development and implementation of political strategies in the field of sustainable development.
- The promotion of sustainable development at a local level is the fifth action area of the Global Action Program. Networks need to be created, deepened and expanded in local communities so that a variety of different actors can come together to discuss issues pertaining to sustainability and participate in opportunities to learn more about them. The networking of these actors contributes to the success of sustainable development in local communities and improves the quality of educational services.

In order to develop these five action areas, the actors in education for sustainable development world-wide should first be encouraged to voluntarily implement the Global Action Program and create partner networks as well as build a global forum for regular meetings to collaborate on joint projects.

In addition to the Global Action Program, education for sustainable development has also been integrated into the 2030 Sustainable Development Goals (SDGs), which build on the Millennium Development Goals (MDGs) of the UN for 2001–2015 to advance the process of sustainable development. Education for sustainable development is furthermore to be found in a number of different global frameworks and conventions on issues ranging from climate change and biodiversity to sustainable consumption and production.

From development education to global learning

The global learning approach, which emerged in the 1990s from development education (Bourn 2008c, p. 2; Overwien 2009, p. 71), was developed at the same time as the concept of education for sustainable development (Bourn 2008a, 2008b; Scheunpflug 2001; Selby & Rathenow 2003). "If at the heart of development education was the problem of the unfair distribution of wealth between the North and the South and its just sharing" (Overwien & Rathenow 2009b, p. 12), then global learning, just as education for sustainable development, can be understood as a concept that integrates the learning goals of development, human rights, environmental and peace education (Scheunpflug 2001, p. 92).

Global learning is defined as "the response of education to the development of a global society" and "thus reacts to the learning challenges that arise in relationship to the increasing globalization of the world" (Scheunpflug 2001, p. 87). At the core of this concept is the issue of "global justice and the economic and social possibilities of human coexistence on Earth" (Scheunpflug 2001, p. 92).

The key task of global learning is, according to Scheunpflug, to empower individuals to understand global processes – which includes "understanding not understanding" – and shaping global processes, that is "searching for active possibilities to solve problems and to actively initiate them" (Scheunpflug 2001, p. 93; cf. Scheunpflug 2008). Overwien and Rathenow list the following goals of global learning: systemic awareness; awareness of different perspectives; the willingness to accept responsibility for the preservation of the Earth; an awareness of global involvement and the willingness to accept responsibility; and open-mindedness for new developments (Overwien & Rathenow 2009a, p. 122). The Development Education Association (DEA) has defined the following goals for global learning:

> enabling people to understand the links between their own lives and those of people throughout the world; increasing understanding of the global economic, social and political environmental forces which shape our lives; developing the skills, attitudes and values which enable people to work together to bring about change and to take control of their own lives; working

to achieve a more just and sustainable world in which power and resources are equitably shared.

(DEA 2006 cited in Bourn 2008c, p. 3)

Global learning should thus enable individuals to acquire the knowledge they need for a fulfilled and sustainable life in a global society and develop the competences they need to achieve this goal (cf. Asbrand & Scheunpflug 2005; Bourn 2008b; Hartmeyer 2007, p. 281; Overwien 2009; Scheunpflug 2001).[3]

> Global learning strengthens the ability and willingness to recognize globality and promotes the competence for developing a sustainable life and democratic participation in the development of a sustainable society. Through promoting the acquisition of knowledge, motivation and ethical guidelines, as well as initiating corresponding learning processes, global learning should enable people to actively take part in the shaping of a global society and responsibly contribute to the sustainable development of one's own community.
>
> (Janecki 2009, p. 83)

In this context, Seitz also comments that global learning is above all "development of the personality in a global perspective" and so is oriented to the central question about which competences a person needs "in order to lead a successful and at the same time responsible life under the conditions of an imperiled global society" (Seitz 2009, p. 44).

There is a broad spectrum of views on the relationship of sustainable development and global learning (cf. Janecki 2009; Scheunpflug & Asbrand 2006): Some argue that education for sustainable development is a higher level concept, beneath which global learning can be found (cf. Overwien 2009; Overwien & Rathenow 2009a), while others see education for sustainable development as the latest version of global learning (Adick 2008, p. 128), and still others describe education for sustainable development and global learning as concepts on a par in that they both refer to a sustainable development (cf. Nestvogel 2002; Scheunpflug 2001).

The concept of education for sustainable development

Towards a general understanding of education for sustainable development

Education for sustainable development is now understood as encompassing more than just environmental education with a few social aspects added in for good measure. It combines approaches of environmental education and development education, education for peace, healthcare education, as well as civics and political education (BLK 1998, p. 25). The contents and main focus of each of these different approaches to education are related to each other from the perspective of a sustainable development. Education for sustainable development thus attempts to contribute to an understanding of complex interrelationships that cannot be appreciated with the approaches of environmental education or development education alone. However, the concept of education for sustainable development is also associated with fundamentally new perspectives. While specialized pedagogies such as environmental education are mainly considered to make an educational contribution to tackling a problem, education for sustainable development has become – to a much greater degree than its predecessor – an autonomous and innovative concept of education. It claims not only to be able to contribute to achieving the vision of a sustainable development but also to initiating and promoting individual educational processes. These two educational goals stand in a classic tension with each other: on the one hand there is the right of the individual to autonomy and self-determination in developing his or her own particular inclinations, talents and interests; on the other, there are political and economic needs that must be met if society is to provide the specific skills needed to successfully cope with the specific challenges it faces. It is thus a constant challenge to find a balance between the demands of society and those of education that allows a discussion about educational processes without instrumentalizing education in the sense of an affirmative implementation of a societal agenda. For education for sustainable development, this tension can be characterized as follows: to what extent should education have as its major goal the solution of sustainability problems (and so attempt to meet societal needs) as opposed to the empowerment of individuals (and thus serve an individual and personal goals)? One position strives to protect students from being politically coopted to achieve specific objectives. This position also rejects the use of measurable sustainability indicators (for example, sustainable consumption or energy use among students) as criteria to determine the effectiveness of education. The counter-position argues that education for sustainable development will fail to achieve its objectives and could become irrelevant if it is unable to make precisely these kinds of contributions to promoting sustainable development.

This is a critical question for education for sustainable development and as such has been intensively and controversially discussed in international forums. More recently however a third position has emerged, one that represents an attempt to reconceive the two poles not as mutually exclusive opposites but as two sides of the same coin. There is now general agreement that there are two kinds of education for sustainable development, known as ESD-1 and ESD-2. Vare and Scott (2007), who first made this distinction, argue that education for sustainable development should and must do both. It must enable people to advance specific and generally consensual changes towards sustainable development (ESD-1) as well as encourage individuals to critically question positions widely seen as valid and help them to clarify open questions (ESD-2). Such a mediating position includes more recent efforts to identify so-called key competencies that have a general importance cutting across normative positions, both for the individual achieving a good life and for a sustainable development in society (cf. Fischer & Barth 2014).

Education for sustainable development as a separate and distinct concept

The implementation of education for sustainable development shows that it is now a separate and distinct concept. With regard to teaching methods and learning

FROM	TO
Scenario of Threat ▪▪▪▶	Modernization Scenarios
Moralizing ▪▪▪	Values Clarification Approaches
Behavioral Change ▪▪▪	Decision-Making
Transmission ▪▪▪	Deliberation and Dialogue
Knowledge Orientation ▪▪▪▶	Experimenting with Change

Figure 7.1 Reconceptualization of education for sustainable development

goals it is a considerable development from the traditional approaches of environmental and development education and training.

From threat to modernization scenarios

A crucial change in perspective involved in the approach of education for sustainable development is the shift "from a threat to a modernization scenario" (de Haan 2006, p. 5). This means that we must do more than simply problematize different sustainability issues or policy areas; we must also actively search for possibilities to address them by changing and shaping development. That this is not an easy task can be seen in discussions about sustainable consumption or about the transition to renewable energy in Germany, both of which remain very strongly characterized by the problem of non-sustainability. In a forward-looking modernization perspective, alternatively, the question is what would be new and proactive ways to promote sustainable consumption or renewable energy. This would have less of a focus on ideas and approaches involving a problem orientation and aiming at merely combatting and putting an end to non-sustainable consumption. Instead answers to the question should be found as to how human needs can be satisfied, not materially through consumption but immaterially. How, for example, can the need for identity and social belonging be satisfied not by following seasonal fashions in clothing but instead through the undertaking of projects and activities together with others (see Schlegel-Matthies 2002).

From moralizing to value clarification approaches

Sustainable development is not a descriptive concept; it is explicitly normative. It does not describe how the world is but how it should be. And so values play an important role. Values such as justice, dignity and the preservation of natural resources play a key role in sustainable development, and thus are also at the focus of education for sustainable development (cf. Stoltenberg 2009). But what role should these values play in education?

In Europe these values were made the starting point for educational work, in particular in environmental education and health education, in an early phase beginning sometime around the 1980s. In this so-called "normative" phase, the goal was to have learners, after exposure to scientific findings on the state of the Earth, develop environmentally friendly values and behaviours (cf. Sandell et al. 2005, p. 162). Following the problematizing schemata, ecological topics were presented in teaching and learning processes as sources of danger or as a threat. This approach was revised in the concept of education for sustainable development. It is now less about teaching values and much more about having learners question their own attitudes and received values by confronting them with the idea of sustainability.

From behavioural guidelines to competent decision-making

In the 1990s education for sustainable development turned away from the teaching of specific attitudes and behaviours. In a report on the BLK programme, Transfer 21, in which education for sustainable development was piloted in Germany, this problem was criticized in connection with research findings in environmental education:

> It seems then to be imperative to abandon the misconceived causality between teaching in a subject area in school – here environmental education – and the modification of everyday behavior. Since a lesson plan designed in such a way is always suspected – and rightly so – of being more about manipulation and indoctrination than about critical reflection, autonomy and the freedom to decide how to live.
>
> (de Haan & Harenberg 1999, p. 42)

Such an educational programme aimed at changing the behaviour of learners would be in educational "bad faith", not to mention being an attempt at indoctrination. There is, in general, no justification for attempting to enforce any educational norms and objectives that have not been "developed jointly and approved in participative processes" (de Haan & Harenberg 1999, p. 42). From this line of argumentation it follows that "only the regulative idea of sustainable development, not its context-dependent operationalization" (Künzli & Kaufmann-Hayoz 2008, p. 14) can be the basis of an educational programme in sustainable development. Such a context-dependent operationalization would also include behavioural learning goals promoting sustainable consumption lifestyles (e.g. buying fair trade products). This objection should by no means be understood as a demand for educational practice to only work with abstract concepts instead of specific phenomena. Education requires didactic reduction, practical experimentation and exemplification (Wagenschein 1997). This criticism is instead directed at the appropriation of education (and educational institutions) to take on the task of "teaching to the public those standards and measures considered right by science or government" (Müller 2000, p. 9). The predominant position today in the German debate about sustainability-related interventions in education is that they find "their limits in enabling individuals to act in a sustainable and fair manner" (de Haan et al. 2008, p. 123).

There is another justification for criticism of making behaviour modification a goal of education for sustainable development (de Haan & Harenberg 1998). The exponential output of research today, in this objection, has led to a heterogeneous stock of knowledge, which is rapidly changing as a result of new scientific findings. This is associated with uncertainties and a low half-life of current knowledge about the state of global problems and their possible solutions. In an approach to education oriented towards a vision of sustainable development, the goal must be to enable learners to retain the ability to act under changing conditions and actively take part in advancing sustainable development.

In the German discussion about education for sustainable development, the primary learning objective is formulated in the concept of *gestaltungskompetenz* (shaping competence), which characterizes "the forward-looking ability to actively participate in the modification and modelling of societies in which one lives so that they are sustainable" (de Haan & Harenberg 1999, p. 62). In other words, *Gestaltungskompetenz* is understood as the ability:

> to apply knowledge about sustainable development and recognize problems of non-sustainable development. This means being able to draw conclusions from both analyses of the present and studies of the future about interrelated ecological, economic and social developments and use these to make decisions and implement them at individual, social and political levels, thus realizing sustainable development processes.
>
> (Programm Transfer-21 2007, p. 12)

This abstract concept contains a number of different sub-competences.[4]

Education for sustainable development with its goal of *Gestaltungskompetenz* is also an important response to the international debate about competencies triggered by the PISA (Programme for International Student Assessment) studies of the Organization for Economic Co-operation and Development (OECD) on international educational standards. In this regard as well, education for sustainable development can be seen as a concept that has a relevance going far beyond its importance for issues of sustainability.

From transmissive to deliberative communication processes

Earlier approaches to education were mostly oriented to the teaching of scientific findings and specific values, attitudes and behaviours. The concept of education for sustainable development can be seen, in contrast to earlier approaches, as a concept of the pluralist tradition of environmental and development education approaches (cf. Sandell et al. 2005). The goal is no longer to induce learners to adopt predetermined viewpoints or attitudes. Instead the focus is on discovering the different positions articulated in discussions about sustainability, examining presuppositions and their consistency, and exploring democratic ways of solving conflicts and problems. This critical reflexivity is explicitly embedded in teaching–learning arrangements.

In this critical and communicative orientation, education for sustainable development should also be seen as an approach to political and civic education. After all, the future-oriented dimension of education for sustainable development does not only refer to an individual taking on responsibility for the future. It is also about people critically reflecting on the social and political impacts – both present and future – of their behaviour, especially from a global perspective, and the ability to become productively involved with others in creating a sustainable future. The focus is not only on changing personal lifestyles, not just on reducing our "ecological rucksack" or our "ecological footprint", but also and above all on public engagement for renewable energy, for reducing carbon dioxide emissions, for the protection of biodiversity and the preservation of the rainforests, to name just a few examples.

Part of the goal of political and civic education in the context of sustainability, in addition to developing the competences already mentioned, is critically examining lobbyism in the government and making business interests more transparent as well as analysing media reporting. In this context, television talk shows are particularly relevant in showing how propaganda is disseminated, public opinion shaped and particular interests advanced in the media. In his 2009 book on the making of public opinion, Albrecht Müller has shown that the most important decisions are actually made in small circles and groups: "They are characterized by a self-serving mentality in their own interest. The public are rarely consulted, because those at the top are aware of their own power to shape public opinion. Feedback is not necessary. The people are not needed for decision-making" (Müller 2009, p. 37). Education for sustainable development thus has to address key political concepts such as power, interest, conflict, compromise and democracy. A strong argument can be made that over the last few decades civic engagement played an important role in making sustainability policy more progressive. Political and civic education for sustainable development is not only critical of existing structures but also examines participation, constructive decision-making as well as engagement in political parties, trade unions and non-governmental organizations.

From a focus on knowledge to a focus on opportunities to take action

The focus on education *about* the environment was common to earlier approaches in environmental education. This fact-based approach to studying ecological problems was often heavily criticized. One of the main criticisms was that environmental education differed from the science of ecology in that its subject matter was not the teaching of natural science but instead examining the issues, problems and conflicts of interest in the human use of nature (Breiting & Mogensen 1999). In northern Europe this criticism led to making the goal of a sustainability oriented education the systematic development of democratic action competences (cf. Jensen & Schnack 1997), with the term "action" expressly referring to the ability to bring about changes and find solutions. The concept of competence is also fundamentally relevant to action, as competences without consequences for everyday life and professional practice are practically meaningless. *Gestaltungskompetenz*, the most influential competence for sustainability in Germany, implies the possibility to take action – it is always about becoming "active". We should keep in mind however a particular aspect of action: it includes its negation. In other words, competence models in the context of education for sustainable development more than ever call for the *omission of an action*: that is, using less energy, reducing mobility or purchasing fewer imported products. And finally another strand in the discussion on education for sustainable development is that action is not the natural consequence of the acquisition of knowledge, attitudes and values. Instead the idea is to stimulate learning processes by means of a learner's own experiences of taking action, thus reversing the dictum "from knowledge to action" to the maxim "from action to knowledge" (Kruse 2013).

Criticism of the concept of education for sustainable development

In a manifesto launched by Latin American and the Caribbean countries (see Guimarães & Sato 2005), the UN Decade, and the concept of education in general, was accused of being Eurocentric. The postcolonial movement criticizes that the relations between developed and developing countries are structured by the colonial past and have led to an inequality on political, social and economic levels between countries of the Global North and South (Danielzik 2013). Critics argue that in education for sustainable development these historical power and domination relations have not been sufficiently discussed, which has had as a consequence the continued stabilization of unequal relations. As a result, postcolonial critics have demanded that the European norm be decentralized and habitual Eurocentric perspectives be changed to include non-European worldviews. The importance is now recognized of critically examining not only one's own positions but all knowledge produced in the North, as this knowledge is not produced under equal conditions of global equality but represents positions of power. In education for sustainable development there is also a glaring lack of materials that would support learners in freeing themselves from these knowledge structures and questioning existing power relations. Moreover, educational institutions do not give enough space to students to learn about alternative perspectives. It is, as a result, crucial to initiate a process of active unlearning (Danielzik 2013).

Implementation of education for sustainable development: Examples from selected educational sectors

Since the beginning of discussions about education for sustainable development in the early 1990s, efforts have been made world-wide to integrate their elements in all formal, non-formal and informal educational sectors (cf. Michelsen 2006). The state of implementation of education for sustainable development in a changed educational practice in Germany is discussed for two educational sectors: schools and higher education, and illustrated by two case examples.

School

The greatest progress in integrating education for sustainable development has taken place in the school sector. Education for sustainable development is now established in the curriculum guidelines of almost all the different types of secondary school and increasingly references are made to education for sustainable development in school programmes and development plans. Moreover, a wide variety of projects for the sustainable development of school life, school buildings and grounds as well as school operations have been carried out. In addition to saving resources, these projects also involve student start-ups and international exchange programmes with the goal of promoting education for sustainable development (BMBF 2009, p. 18).

The recommendations of the Standing Conference of the Ministers of Education and Cultural Affairs of the States in the Federal Republic of Germany (KMK) and the German UNESCO Commission (DUK) in June 2007 gave an important impulse to further improve the general conditions for education for sustainable development (KMK/DUK 2007). Another milestone was the successful implementation of the Transfer 21 programme, the successor to the BLK Program 21: Education for Sustainable Development launched in 1999 (see above). The central vision of Transfer 21 was to orient school education to the concept of sustainability and the development of *Gestaltungskompetenz*. New educational material was developed for all school areas and further schools were involved. "The program that ended in July 2008 reached a total of 2,586 schools in the participating federal states. The goal of ten per cent of all schools was thus exceeded" (BMBF 2009, p. 18).

The Transfer 21 schools were part of a greater endeavour to establish the sustainability concept in Germany and were joined by UNESCO project schools, the Environmental Schools in Europe and the GLOBE schools. The relatively large number of projects recognized as official contributions to the implementation of the UN Decade on education for sustainable development coming from schools also shows that education for sustainable development is well established in this educational sector. Measured by the total number of projects, schools are the most strongly represented among all educational sectors.

The growing availability of educational material has made it easier for teachers to integrate issues of sustainable development in their lessons. It is however still a challenge to integrate education for sustainable development in teacher education and development programmes (cf. KMK/DUK 2007, p. 6).

Case example: BINK

Following its adoption at the World Summit on the Environment and Development in Rio de Janeiro in 1992, one of the main tasks of Agenda 21 for the international community of nations was to change non-sustainable patterns of consumption moving into the 21st century. The goal of the project BINK (Educational Institutions and Sustainable Consumption, www.consumerculture.eu)

was to find examples of educational institutions promoting sustainable consumption among young people and to further develop them in a framework of education for sustainable development. This involved developing a model relating formal and informal learning to sustainable consumption in educational institutions, linking them to organizational development processes, and making sustainability experienceable. Educational institutions were selected as a target group because they affect the consumer behaviour of young people in two ways. For one, their educational services can make a contribution to critically reflecting on consumer behaviour and lead to a greater awareness of sustainability. For another, they are also places of consumption themselves, for example in campus cafés or the cafeteria.

In the BINK research project an approach was developed to systematically link formal and informal learning about sustainable consumption (Fischer 2013). Based on this model, measures were then developed that would help to establish a culture in the partner schools that would promote the consumer competence of young people and enable them to develop a lifestyle of sustainable consumption. The main question of the project was how learning opportunities in informal learning spaces outside the school and university classroom could become an "experiential space for learning about sustainability" (Stoltenberg 2000) for both structured and incidental learning about sustainable consumption. This approach takes the principles of experiential learning and perspective-taking as the conceptual framework of an education for sustainable development.

Change processes towards a culture of sustainable consumption in educational institutions require that the approach be participative and account for specific organizational contexts. As a result, collaboration with practitioner partners took the form of participative intervention planning (Matthies 2000). This participative and transdisciplinary process with practitioner partners led to the formulation of goals and ideas for specific measures to learn about sustainable consumption (Homburg et al. 2013). Practitioner partners in the project were not only students from schools or universities and colleagues at the educational institutions but also actors at the place of consumption (cafeterias and kitchens), external experts and prominent individuals such as the chef Sarah Wiener. This meant that a fund of practice-related knowledge about the local context of the institution, as well as different perspectives on consumption, was represented in this project. The result was a package of measures for each institution consisting of a number of different interventions related to different aspects of consumer culture and located in settings of informal learning. The operationalization, implementation and evaluation of the measures were carried out by the practitioners, who were accompanied by academic researchers serving as moderators and organizers in the project team.

The results of empirical research undertaken in connection with the project show that there are some important differences between those young people that actively took part in BINK and those that did not. The participants were significantly more upset by poor working conditions and how society handles this problem; they found the environment and justice to be significantly more important when shopping, and they were in general significantly more confident that consumer decisions can initiate changes towards a sustainable development (Barth et al. 2013). The greatest influences of consumer culture on what young people learn about sustainable consumption, what possibilities they believe they have as consumers to exercise influence, and what personal relevance sustainable consumption has for them personally have two organizational characteristics: the status of educational goals relating to sustainable consumption and the perception of change at the institution towards sustainable development. The results of the study support the approach developed in the BINK project to address sustainable consumption through an approach of making the holistic development of consumer culture a goal at the educational institution by means of changes both inside and outside of the classroom.

Higher education

The *Higher Education and Sustainability Memorandum*, adopted by the German Rectors' Conference (HRK) in 2010 jointly with the German UNESCO Commission (DUK/HRK 2010), gave momentum to sustainability-related activities in higher education by recommending core university tasks such as research and knowledge transfer, teaching and degree programmes be oriented to sustainable development.

Numerous higher education institutions offer degree programmes in which issues of sustainable development are treated. In a study based on self-reports by higher education institutions, de Haan (2007) distinguishes three different groups of sustainability-related degree programmes: programmes with sustainability-related degree majors or concentrations, those with special modules related to sustainability or elective courses (54.6 per cnen); degree programmes in sustainability (30.8 per cent); and degree programmes with individual modules related to sustainable development (14.2 per cent). In addition, multi-institution degree programmes and modules are offered through networks of higher education institutions, an example being the Education for Sustainable Development network of the universities of applied sciences in Baden-Württemberg (BMBF 2009, p. 19).

An increasing number of universities are now adopting environmental management schemes and environmental auditing systems (Fischer et al. 2015), while some universities have even gone a step further and are publishing sustainability reports (cf. Sassen et al. 2014).

The discussion about education for sustainable development in higher education as well as its implementation on an institutional level is primarily driven by actors from non-governmental organizations or by groups cooperating, often internationally, on an informal basis. A point of criticism is that the professional activities of many individuals in higher education are still the result of informal and personal engagement (Adomßent & Henze 2013).

There can thus be no question of extensive engagement in education for sustainable development in higher education. A 2010 study of university mission statements revealed that only a quarter of the universities and 28 per cent of the universities of applied science are committed to sustainable and environmentally responsible practices (Meyer-Guckel & Mägdefessel 2010). However, "it is possible to speak with cautious optimism of a degree of consolidation of sustainability oriented engagement in higher education" (Adomßent 2010, p. 34).

Case example: The first semester module Science Bears Responsibility at the Leuphana University Lüneburg

If higher education is to meet the demands of the 21st century, then it must encourage individuals to take both personal and social responsibility in a globalized world. Whether this can actually be realized depends on the programmes of study offered in higher education following the Bologna reforms. The module Science Bears Responsibility at Leuphana University Lüneburg provides an illustrative example of how this goal can be accomplished. It is the starting point for a bachelor's programme of study that aims at developing social responsibility and *Gestaltungskompetenz* in its students (cf. Otte et al. 2014).

What questions will tomorrow's problems bring? This question opens the module Science Bears Responsibility for 1500 first semester students and invites them to critically reflect on the vision of sustainable development. As part of an interdisciplinary introduction to science, the module is embedded in the so-called Leuphana Semester. Inspired by the Anglo-American tradition of the college, the focus is on offering young students a more general education in addition to their disciplinary training to serve as a transition from school to university by cultivating critical thinking, personality development and democratic citizenship (cf. Axelrod 2002). The so-called Responsibility module anticipates a transdisciplinary approach students will use later in their studies to work on social problems in a way that individual disciplines would only be able to provide an insufficiently.

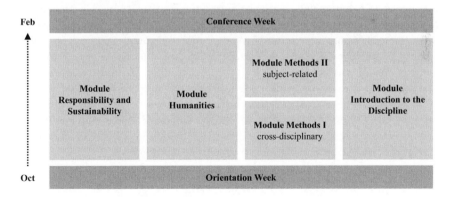

Figure 7.2 An overview of the modules of the Leuphana Semester

Source: Based on Michelsen 2013, p. 1508

This module brings together students in the Leuphana Semester in interdisciplinary learning groups and aims at providing a fresh look at its subject matter, one not yet formed by a particular discipline. Ideally over the course of a student's studies this competency grows, allowing them to participate in an interdisciplinary and transdisciplinary discourse based on individual disciplinary competence (cf. Mittelstraß 2005). In order to cultivate interdisciplinary shifts in perspective, the Leuphana Semester is immediately followed by the Complementary Studies Programme, which offers interdisciplinary electives from the second to the sixth semester.

How does the Science Bears Responsibility module accomplish this interdisciplinary introduction to science? And what are the formats available for students to engage in sustainable development? The focus of the module shows that responsibility and sustainability are conceptually related as an extension of the concept of justice. While the principle of sustainability serves as a normative anchor for the concept of responsibility, conflicts over sustainability can be analyzed by enquiring into the *accountability* and *attributability* of an agent. Attention is also paid to the question *who* can work towards sustainable developments and just institutions and how they can do so.

The module consists of the following elements:

- A lecture series and accompanying tutorials provide a framework for the content of the module.
- They introduce the many dimensions of the topic of sustainable development and equip first semester students with what they need to orient themselves in the transdisciplinary debate about sustainability.
- Roughly 60 project seminars each with 25 participants examine a particular aspect of the general topic in greater detail, allowing – in the sense of "learning by research" – the students to undertake initial exploration of a research field.

In small-sized projects the students test their own hypotheses and then present their findings to a university-wide audience during the Conference Week at the end of the semester. The integration of sustainability in higher education can thus be much more than merely raising the topic as one issue among many in individual lectures or seminars. Teachers and learners alike are required to engage in new contents and methods. This integration can take place at different levels. The Leuphana Semester at the Leuphana University Lüneburg and its module Science Bears Responsibility shows an approach that combines innovative teaching-learning methods with the subject of sustainable development, opening up new forms of university teaching. In the Science Bears Responsibility module small student teams work on exemplary solutions to sustainable development.

An outlook from the perspective of the younger generation

The Global Action Program on education for sustainable development begun in 2015 seeks to involve young people as so-called change agents in sustainability processes (see above). But what is the interest and engagement of young people in Germany for sustainability? Answers to this question can be found in the Sustainability Barometer, the results of a joint study between Greenpeace Germany and the Leuphana University Lüneburg.[5]

The data of this representative survey show that among 15 to 24 year olds there is a high level of awareness for issues of sustainable development. When asked about the basic principles of sustainable development, there is broad agreement. However, when the survey respondents had to choose what was more important, economic and the social values were considered of equal value, while ecology was ranked behind the economy and much farther behind social issues. Young people see, on a general level, a particular need to take action against poverty, to promote equal rights and peaceful coexistence. In comparison, overcoming ecological challenges such as biodiversity loss, marine pollution, the lack of clean drinking water in many parts of the world or even climate change are considered of secondary importance. For Germany the issues highest on the agenda are the provision of satisfying jobs, eradicating poverty and the use of renewable energy.

Young people are very much aware of issues relating to sustainable development. But what are their attitudes to these challenges? The study reveals there are five distinct ways young people relate to sustainability (see Table 7.2).[6]

These five types show that the awareness of sustainable development is now wide spread among the younger generation. However, it has so far had little impact on their willingness to act accordingly.

It would not though be correct to speak of a disinterested or passive generation. On the contrary, we have observed a rising level of engagement among young

Table 7.2 Five types of sustainability orientation among young people

Sustainability orientation	Description	Percentage 2014
Affinity for sustainability	Motivated and ready to act, potential change agents	32%, decreasing tendency compared to 2011
Resistant to sustainability	Unable to become enthusiastic about environmental and sustainability issues	16%, decreasing tendency compared to 2011
Acts sustainably but without intrinsic motivation	Acts in a sustainable way but without an intrinsic motivation to do so	16%, increasing tendency compared to 2011
Interested in sustainability without changing behaviour	High motivation and intention but without consequences for actual behaviour	20%, increasing tendency compared to 2011
Apathetic about sustainability	Has the intention to act in a sustainable way but unable to find the motivation	15%, unchanged tendency compared to 2011

Source: Based on Michelsen et al. 2015a

people over the last few years. Only 6 per cent of the younger generation does not show any kind of engagement. For the other 94 per cent there is a spectrum of engagement from easily done individual activities such as waste reduction, energy saving or company boycotts to more intensive varieties such as networking, participating in initiatives or active protest.

It is also clear that the forms of engagement have changed. Even if younger generations are still engaged in the environment, religion, social issues or emergency services, the modalities and motivations of their participation are changing. Activities are becoming shorter term and are related to projects with a visible impact. Traditional forms of voluntary work as an activity that also demands self-sacrifice and has less direct benefit for the individual are becoming less important.

A major challenge in the next phase of education for sustainable development in the context of the Global Action Program will thus be to react to these changing conditions of the awareness and engagement of young people. The challenge is to develop a variety of different kinds of educational programmes that will enable learners to make a contribution to a sustainable development on their own terms.

The good news is that young people are ready and willing.

Notes

1   This article is based on course material "Education for Sustainable Development" developed for the Kaiserslautern University of Technology as well as the article "Education for Sustainable Development", which was published in fall 2015 in the publication series on sustainability by the Hessische Landeszentrale für politische Bildung. The authors would like to thank their colleagues in the Institute for Environmental and Sustainability Communication (INFU) as well as at the Institute for Integrative Studies in the Faculty of Sustainability at the Leuphana University Lüneburg, all of whom contributed to the development of the study materials, as well as Paul Lauer for the translation into English.

2   UNECE is an agency of the Economic and Social Council of the United Nations and one of five regional commissions of the UN, with members including the USA and Canada, all European countries as well as countries such as Kirgizstan and Uzbekistan.

3   One current of thought in global learning is oriented to evolutionary theory and seeks to help learners in acquiring competences to deal with uncertainty and complexity in a globalized society. There are also action theory approaches that "often are based on a holistic view of the world and human beings and formulate normative goals and content for global learning to be achieved through education, as for example showing solidarity in action, tolerance, empathy, a holistic worldview etc." (Asbrand and Scheunpflug 2005, p. 473).

4   De Haan et al. (2008) provide a list of sub-competencies in anticipatory thinking, interdisciplinary thinking, perspective-taking, handling incomplete and overly complex information, participation, cooperation, coping with individual dilemmas in decision-making, supporting others and showing solidarity, motivating oneself and others, and reflecting on both individual and cultural ideals and in taking moral action.

5   The Sustainability Barometer studied the sustainability awareness of the younger generation aged between 15 and 24 years old by means of a nationwide representative survey in Germany of over 1000 young people. Datasets exist for the years 2011 and 2014 (cf. Michelsen et al. 2012, 2015a, 2015b).

6   The five types are the result of a statistical procedure (cluster analysis) applied to questions on sustainability-specific motivation, the formation of an intention to take action

and the specification of an action (following Rost et al. 2001). The five types are thus composites of bundles of cognitions and specific actions.

References

Adick, C. (2008). *Vergleichende Erziehungswissenschaft: Eine Einführung.* Stuttgart: Kohlhammer.

Adomßent, M. (2010). Hochschule und Nachhaltigkeit. Eine kritische Bestandsaufnahme. *ZEP – Zeitschrift für internationale Bildungs-forschung und Entwicklungspädagogik, 33* (4), pp. 33–34.

Adomßent, M.; Henze, C. (2013). Hochschulbildung für nachhaltige Entwicklung – eine Bestandsaufnahme. In N. Pütz, M. K. Schweer & N. Logemann (eds), *Bildung für nachhaltige Entwicklung. Aktuelle theoretische Konzepte und Beispiele praktischer Umsetzung* (Psychologie und Gesellschaft, Vol. 11, pp. 159–181). Frankfurt am Main: PL Academic Research.

Asbrand, B.; Scheunpflug, A. (2005). Globales Lernen. In W. Sander (ed.), *Handbuch politische Bildung* (pp. 469–484). Bonn: Bundeszentrale für Politische Bildung.

Axelrod, P. D. (2002). *Values in Conflict. The university, the marketplace and the trials of liberal education.* Montréal: McGill-Queen's University Press.

Barth, M.; Fischer, D.; Michelsen, G.; Rode, H. (2013). Konsumlernen in Bildungseinrichtungen: Befunde aus einer empirischen Studie. In G. Michelsen & D. Fischer (eds), *Nachhaltig konsumieren lernen. Ergebnisse aus dem Projekt BINK („Bildungsinstitutionen und nachhaltiger Konsum")* (pp. 165–184). Bad Homburg: Verlag für Akademische Schriften.

BLK (Bund-Länder-Kommission für Bildungsplanung und Forschungsförderung) (1998). *Bildung für eine nachhaltige Entwicklung. Orientierungsrahmen.* Bonn: BLK.

BMBF (Bundesministerium für Bildung und Forschung) (Hrsg.) (2009). Bericht der Bundesregierung zur Bildung für eine nachhaltige Entwicklung. Berlin. Available at: www.bmbf.de/pub/bericht_fuer_nachhaltige_ entwicklung_2009.pdf.

BMU (Bundesministerium für Umwelt, Naturschutz und Reaktorsicherheit) (1992). Agenda 21. Konferenz der Vereinten Nationen für Umwelt und Entwicklung im Juni 1992 in Rio de Janeiro. Dokumente. Berlin.

Bourn, D. (Hrsg.) (2008a). *Development Education: Debates and dialogue.* London: Institute of Education University of London.

Bourn, D. (2008b). Development education: Towards a re-conceptualisation. *International Journal of Development Education and Global Learning 1* (1), pp. 5–22.

Bourn, D. (2008c). Introduction. In D. Bourn (ed.), *Development Education: Debates and dialogue* (pp. 1–17). London.

Breiting, S.; Mogensen, F. (1999). Action competence and environmental education. *Cambridge Journal of Education, 29* (3), pp. 349–353.

Danielzik, C.-M. (2013). Überlegenheitsdenken fällt nicht vom Himmel. Postkoloniale Perspektiven auf Globales Lernen und Bildung für eine nachhaltige Entwicklung. *ZEP – Zeitschrift für internationale Bildungsforschung und Entwicklungspädagogik, 36* (1), pp. 26–33.

de Haan, G. (2004). Politische Bildung für Nachhaltigkeit. *Aus Politik und Zeitgeschichte,* (7–8), pp. 39–46.

de Haan, G. (2006). Bildung für nachhaltige Entwicklung – ein neues Lern- und Handlungsfeld. *Unesco heute, 53* (1), pp. 4–8.

de Haan, G. (2007). *Studium und Forschung zur Nachhaltigkeit.* Bielefeld: Bertelsmann.

de Haan, G.; Harenberg, D. (1998). Nachhaltigkeit als Bildungs- und Erziehungsaufgabe. Möglichkeiten und Grenzen schulischen Umweltlernens. *Der Bürger im Staat, 48* (2), pp. 100–104.

de Haan, G.; Harenberg, D. (1999). *Bildung für eine nachhaltige Entwicklung. Gutachten zum Programm*. Bonn: Bund-Länder-Kommission.

de Haan, G.; Kamp, G.; Lerch, A.; Martignon, L.; Müller-Christ, G.; Nutzinger, H. G. et al. (2008). *Nachhaltigkeit und Gerechtigkeit. Grundlagen und schulpraktische Konsequenzen*. Berlin: Springer.

DUK & HRK (Deutsche UNESCO-Kommission & Hochschulrektorenkonferenz) (2010). Hochschulen für nachhaltige Entwicklung. Erklärung der Hochschulrektorenkonferenz (HRK) und der Deutschen UNESCO-Kommission (DUK) zur Hochschulbildung für nachhaltige Entwicklung – Ein Beitrag zur UN-Dekade „Bildung für nachhaltige Entwicklung".

Fischer, D. (2013). Bildungseinrichtungen als Konsumkulturen. In G. Michelsen & D. Fischer (eds), *Nachhaltig konsumieren lernen. Ergebnisse aus dem Projekt BINK („Bildungsinstitutionen und nachhaltiger Konsum")* (pp. 131–164). Bad Homburg: Verlag für Akademische Schriften.

Fischer, D.; Barth, M. (2014). Key competencies for and beyond sustainable consumption. An Educational contribution to the debate. *GAiA, 23* (S1), pp. 193–200.

Fischer, D.; Jenssen, S.; Tappeser, V. (2015). Getting an empirical hold of the sustainable university: A comparative analysis of evaluation frameworks across 12 contemporary sustainability assessment tools. *Assessment & Evaluation in Higher Education, 40* (6), pp. 785–800.

Guimarães, M.; Sato, M. (2005). *Manifiesto por la educación ambiental*. Río de Janeiro.

Hartmeyer, H. (2007). *Die Welt in Erfahrung bringen: Globales Lernen in Österreich: Entwicklung, Entfaltung, Entgrenzung*. Frankfurt am Main: IKO Verl. f. Interkulturelle Kommunikation.

Homburg, A.; Nachreiner, M.; Fischer, D. (2013). Die BINK-Strategie zur Förderung nachhaltigen Konsumverhaltens und nachhaltiger Konsumkultur in Bildungsorganisationen – Weiterentwicklung auf der Basis einer formativen Evaluation. In G. Michelsen & D. Fischer (eds), *Nachhaltig konsumieren lernen. Ergebnisse aus dem Projekt BINK („Bildungsinstitutionen und nachhaltiger Konsum")* (pp. 185–213). Bad Homburg: Verlag für Akademische Schriften.

Janecki, G. (2009). Ansätze zur Vernetzung von Globalem Lernen und Bildung für nachhaltige Entwicklung. In T. Lucker & O. Kölsch (eds), *Naturschutz und Bildung für nachhaltige Entwicklung: Fokus: Globales Lernen* (pp. 81–99). Bonn-Bad Godesberg: Bundesamt für Naturschutz.

Jensen, B. B.; Schnack, K. (1997). The cction competence approach in environmental education. *Environmental Education Research, 3* (2), pp. 163–178.

Klafki, W. (1995). Schlüsselprobleme als thematische Dimension einer zukunftsbezogenen Allgemeinbildung – Zwölf Thesen. *Die Deutsche Schule,* (3), pp. 9–14.

KMK& DUK (Ständige Konferenz der Kultusminister der Länder in der Bundesrepublik Deutschland & Deutsche UNESCO-Kommission) (2007). Empfehlung zur „Bildung für nachhaltige Entwicklung in der Schule". Available at: www.kmk.org/fileadmin/veroeffentlichungen_beschluesse/2007/2007_06_15_Bildung_f_nachh_Entwicklung.pdf.

Kruse, L. (2013). Vom Handeln zum Wissen – ein Perspektivwechsel für eine Bildung für nachhaltige Entwicklung. In N. Pütz, M. K. Schweer & N. Logemann (eds), *Bildung für nachhaltige Entwicklung. Aktuelle theoretische Konzepte und Beispiele praktischer Umsetzung* (pp. 31–57). Frankfurt am Main: Peter Lang.

Künzli David, C.; Kaufmann-Hayoz, R. (2008). Bildung für eine Nachhaltige Entwicklung – Konzeptionelle Grundlagen, Legitimation, didaktische Ausgestaltung und Umsetzung. *Umweltpsychologie, 12* (2), pp. 9–28.

Matthies, E. (2000). Partizipative Interventionsplanung – Überlegungen zu einer Weiterentwicklung der Psychologie im Umweltschutz. *Umweltpsychologie, 4* (2), pp. 84–99.

Meadows, D. L.; Meadows, D. H.; Zahn, E.; Milling, P. (1972). *Die Grenzen des Wachstums*.

Bericht des Club of Rome zur Lage der Menschheit. Stuttgart: Deutsche Verlags-Anstalt.

Meyer–Guckel, V.; Mägdefessel, D. (2010). Vielfalt an Akteuren. Einfalt an Profilen. Hochschulleitbilder im Vergleich. Available at: http://stifterverband. info/presse/pressemitteilungen/2010/2010_08_24_hochschulleitbilder/hochschulleitbilder_im_vergleich _zusammenfassung.pdf.

Michelsen, G. (2001). Umweltbildung – Umweltberatung – Umweltkommunikation. In F. Müller-Rommel (ed.), *Sozialwissenschaften* (pp. 125–152). Berlin: Springer.

Michelsen, G. (2006). Bildung für eine nachhaltige Entwicklung: Meilensteine auf einem langen Weg. In E. Tiemeyer & K. Wilbers (eds), *Berufliche Bildung für nachhaltiges Wirtschaften. Konzepte, Curricula, Methoden, Beispiele* (pp. 17–32). Bielefeld: Bertelsmann.

Michelsen, G. (2013). Sustainable development as a challenge for undergraduate students: the module "Science bears responsibility" in the Leuphana bachelor's programme. Commentary on "a case study of teaching social responsibility to doctoral students in the climate sciences". *Science and Engineering Ethics, 19* (4), pp. 1505–1511.

Michelsen, G.; Siebert, H.; Lilje, J. (2011). *Nachhaltigkeit lernen. Ein Lesebuch.* Bad Homburg: Verlag für Akademische Schriften.

Michelsen, G.; Grunenberg, H.; Rode, H. (2012). *Greenpeace Nachhaltigkeitsbarometer – Was bewegt die Jugend?* Bad Homburg: Verlag für Akademische Schriften.

Michelsen, G.; Grunenberg, H.; Mader, C. (2015a). Engagement durch Bildung für nachhaltige Entwicklung: das Weltaktionsprogramm von Quantität zur Qualität. Vorab-Veröffentlichung aus dem Nachhaltigkeitsbarometer 2014. Hamburg: Greenpeace. Available at: www.leuphana.de/fileadmin/user_upload/Aktuell/images/ Startseitenbeitraege/2015/nachhaltigkeitsbarometer-bildung-20150522.pdf.

Michelsen, G.; Grunenberg, H.; Mader, C.; Barth, M. (2015b). Engagement der jüngeren Generation heute: Faktoren – Potentiale – Konsequenzen für Nachhaltigkeit. Vorab-Veröffentlichung aus dem Nachhaltigkeitsbarometer 2014. Hamburg: Greenpeace. Available at: www.greenpeace.de/sites/www.greenpeace.de/files/publications/ nachhaltigkeitsbarometer-auskopplung-engagement-jugend-20150818.pdf.

Mittelstraß, J. (2005). Methodische Transdisziplinarität. *Technikfolgenabschätzung – Theorie und Praxis, 14* (2), pp. 18–23.

Müller, A. (2009). *Meinungsmache. Wie Wirtschaft, Politik und Medien uns das Denken abgewöhnen wollen.* München: Droemer.

Müller, U. (2000). Der Mensch im Mittelpunkt. Bildung für nachhaltige Entwicklung benötigt die Klärung des Bildungsbegriffs. *Politische Ökologie, 15* (Sonderheft 12), pp. 8–11.

Nestvogel, R. (2002). Zum Verhältnis von „Interkulturellem Lernen", „Globalem Lernen" und „Bildung für eine nachhaltige Entwicklung". In C. Wulf & C. Merkel (eds), *Globalisierung als Herausforderung der Erziehung: Theorien, Grundlagen, Fallstudien* (pp. 31–44). Münster: Waxmann.

Otte, I.; Prien-Ribcke, S.; Michelsen, G. (2014). Hochschulbildung auf der Höhe des 21. Jahrhunderts. In C.-G. v. Müller & C.-P. Zinth (eds), *Managementperspektiven für die Zivilgesellschaft des 21. Jahrhunderts. Management als Liberal Art* (pp. 183–203). Wiesbaden: Springer Fachmedien.

Overwien, B. (2009). Globalisierung und Globales Lernen. In T. Lucker & O. Kölsch (eds), *Naturschutz und Bildung für nachhaltige Entwicklung. Fokus: Lebenslanges Lernen. Ergebnisse des F+E-Vorhabens "Bildung für nachhaltige Entwicklung (BNE) – Positionierung des Naturschutzes"* (pp. 63–80). Bonn: Bundesamt für Naturschutz.

Overwien, B.; Rathenow, H.-F. (2009a). Globales Lernen in Deutschland. In: B. Overwien & H.-F. Rathenow (eds), *Globalisierung fordert politische Bildung: Politisches Lernen im globalen Kontext* (pp. 107–131). Opladen: Barbara Budrich.

158   *Gerd Michelsen and Daniel Fischer*

Overwien, B.; Rathenow, H.-F. (2009b). Globalisierung als Gegenstand der politischen Bildung – eine Einleitung. In B. Overwien & H.-F. Rathenow (eds), *Globalisierung fordert politische Bildung: Politisches Lernen im globalen Kontext* (pp. 9–21). Opladen: Barbara Budrich.

Programm Transfer-21 (2007). *Orientierungshilfe Bildung für nachhaltige Entwicklung in der Sekundarstufe I. Begründungen – Kompetenzen – Aufgabenbeispiele.* Berlin.

Rost, J.; Gresele, C.; Martens, T. (2001). *Handeln für die Umwelt – Anwendung einer Theorie.* Münster: Waxmann.

Sandell, K.; Öhman, J.; Östman, L. (2005). *Education for Sustainable Development. Nature, school and democracy.* Lund: Studentlitteratur.

Sassen, R.; Dienes, D.; Beth, C. (2014). Nachhaltigkeitsberichterstattung deutscher Hochschulen. *Zeitschrift für Umweltpolitik und Umweltrecht, 37* (3), pp. 258–277.

Scheunpflug, A. (2001). Die globale Perspektive einer Bildung für nachhaltige Entwicklung. In O. Herz, H. Seybold & G. Strobl (eds), *Bildung für nachhaltige Entwicklung. Globale Perspektiven und neue Kommunikationsmedien* (pp. 87–99). Opladen: Leske + Budrich.

Scheunpflug, A (2008). Why global learning and global education? An educational approach influenced by the perspectives of Immanuel Kant. In D. Bourn (ed.), *Development Education: Debates and dialogue* (pp. 18–27). London.

Scheunpflug, A.; Asbrand, B. (2006). Global education and education for sustainability. *Environmental Education Research*, 12(1), pp. 33–46.

Schlegel-Matthies, K. (2002). Das Modell der Salutogenese als Handlungsanleitung für haushaltsbezogene Bildung? – Fragen und Folgerungen. *Haushalt und Bildung* (3), pp. 24–33.

Seitz, K. (2009). Globales Lernen in weltbürgerlicher Absicht: zur Erneuerung weltbürgerlicher Bildung in der postnationalen Konstellation. In B. Overwien & H.-F. Rathenow (eds). *Globalisierung fordert politische Bildung: Politisches Lernen im globalen Kontext* (pp. 37–48). Opladen: Barbara Budrich.

Selby, D.; Rathenow, H.-F. (2003). *Globales Lernen: Praxishandbuch für die Sekundarstufe I und II.* Berlin: Cornelsen-Scriptor.

Stoltenberg, U. (2000). Lebenswelt Hochschule als Erfahrungsraum für Nachhaltigkeit. In G. Michelsen (ed.), *Sustainable University. Auf dem Weg zu einem universitären Agendaprozess* (pp. 90–116). Frankfurt am Main: Verlag für Akademische Schriften.

Stoltenberg, U. (2009). *Mensch und Wald. Theorie und Praxis einer Bildung für nachhaltige Entwicklung am Beispiel des Themenfeldes Wald.* München: Oekom.

UNECE (United Nations Economic Commission for Europe) (2005). UNECE-Strategie über die Bildung für nachhaltige Entwicklung. Angenommen von der hochrangigen Tagung der Umwelt- und Bildungsministerien am 23.03.2005.

UNESCO (United Nations Educational, Scientific and Cultural Organization) (1978). *Intergovernmental Conference on Environmental Education. Final Report of the Tbilisi Conference.* Paris.

UNESCO (2005). *United Nations Decade of Education for Sustainable Development (2005–2014).* International Implementation Scheme. Paris.

UNESCO (2014). *Roadmap zur Umsetzung des Weltaktionsprogramms "Bildung für eine nachhaltige Entwicklung".* Paris.

Vare, P.; Scott, W. R. (2007). Learning for a change: Exploring the relationship between education and sustainable development. *Journal of Education for Sustainable Development, 1* (2), pp. 191–198.

Wagenschein, M. (1997). *Verstehen lehren. Genetisch – Sokratisch – Exemplarisch* (11. Ed.). Weinheim: Beltz.

WCED (World Commission on Environment and Development) (1987). *Our Common Future.* Oxford.

8 Fair trade

An alternative trading concept

Michael von Hauff

Introduction

For many years international trade has experienced a progressive dynamism world-wide, one effect of which is a positive influence on trading profits. This creates a basis for many endeavours towards further expanding and promoting international trade, a topical example being the Transatlantic Trade and Investment Partnership (TTIP). However, a consideration of the international structure and development of trade reveals a significant imbalance between individual countries and within the populations of many countries. The share of the profits from international trade is to some extent reflected in extreme inequality. If this situation is studied in the context of the sustainable development paradigm, to which the international community committed itself at the 1992 conference in Rio de Janeiro and which was put into concrete terms within the Agenda 21 framework, this development in international trade cannot be described as sustainable.

This raises the question of what role is to be adopted by the World Trade Organization (WTO). As an independent institution, the task of the WTO is to implement agreed measures and to monitor the national trade policies accordingly. In this connection it has authority to enforce its basic principles, and its central basic principle is aimed at a worldwide realization of free trade. However, in addition to this fundamental objective, the WTO Preamble contains an agreement which is highly relevant in connection with fair trade:

> The Parties to this Agreement,
>
> ***Recognizing*** that their relations in the field of trade and economic endeavour should be conducted with a view to raising standards of living, ensuring full employment and a large and steadily growing volume of real income and effective demand, and expanding the production of and trade in goods and services, while allowing for the optimal use of the world's resources in accordance with the objective of sustainable development, seeking both to protect and preserve the environment and to enhance the means for doing so in a manner consistent with their respective needs and concerns at different levels of economic development.

> *Recognizing* further that there is a need for positive efforts designed to ensure that developing countries, and especially the least developed among them, secure a share in the growth of international trade commensurate with the needs of their economic development,
>
> *Being desirous* of contributing to these objectives by entering into reciprocal and mutually advantageous arrangements directed to the substantial reduction of tariffs and other barriers to trade and to the eliminations of discriminatory treatment in international trade relations,
>
> *Resolved,* therefore, to develop an integrated, more viable and durable multi-lateral trading system encompassing the General Agreement on Tariffs and Trade, the results of past liberalization efforts, and all of the results of the Uruguay Round of Multilateral Trade Negotiations,
>
> *Determined* to preserve the basic principles and to further the objectives underlying this multilateral trading system.

This agreement sets normative targets, although challenges such as improved standards of living, full employment, optimum use of scarce resources and the objective of sustainable development have as yet not been adequately resolved worldwide. The pertinent question here is "why?". In the context of international trade, many developing countries have until now been marginalized, or largely excluded. This applies to the majority of African, as well as to some Asian and South American, countries. And also in ambitious developing countries which at least participate to some extent in world trade, certain sections of the population – such as small-scale farmers – are excluded.

Up until now, international trade has essentially been conducted between the industrialized nations. Even in developing countries such as Brazil, South Africa, China and India, which are often seen as future economic powers, in many cases only specific sections of the population reap the rewards. The overwhelming majority of the populations do not participate, or only participate marginally, in the profits from international trade. There are various reasons for this, and a distinction should be made between exogenous causal factors (trade barriers) and endogenous factors (poor infrastructure, inadequate education systems).

However, unequal trading terms have led to consumers in industrialized countries becoming increasingly aware of the economic, ecological and social conditions experienced by many people in developing countries. In this connection the fair trade seal offers consumers the opportunity to actively influence a fairer distribution of trading profits. The price of fairly traded products, which is often above the world market level, is aimed at securing for producers in developing countries a fair remuneration for their work and thereby enabling them to enjoy a commensurate standard of living.

The fair trade movement began in the USA after the Second World War, and in 1946 the Ten Thousand Villages non-governmental organization (NGO) started importing handicraft products from Puerto Rico. These products were then sold through its privately owned church network. The first Fair Trade shop opened in the USA in 1958, at a time when the differentiation between the countries geared towards a free market economy and those oriented towards a planned economy became further pronounced. A third group was then added: the group of less developed countries, i.e. the developing countries, for which the term "Third World" emerged. At this time there arose an awareness of producers in the developing countries who were disadvantaged in international trade. In Germany the fair trade movement developed in the 1970s, likewise resulting from criticism of the dominant paradigm of international trade.

The fair trade movement is therefore a reaction to the following criticism: global trade was oriented towards the lowest prices for goods, with no regard for ecological and social standards. The trading system thereby benefited the stronger and disadvantaged the weaker trading partners, so the objective was – at least partially – to create a fairer basis for trade. Within the last 40 years various organizations and actors have therefore developed a concept of fair trade.

In particular, the numerous organizations actively involved in fair trade criticize the discrimination against producers working in the agricultural sector in developing countries. For a variety of reasons, they scarcely have an opportunity to sell their products on the international markets, particularly on the markets of the industrialized countries. Fair trade is thus an important concept for development policy in the industrialized countries, which is promoted both by national governments and national development organizations as well as by the EU. It also forms part of the sustainable development paradigm, and as such is therefore a sustainable development concept.

First this chapter presents a few important development trends in world trade, demonstrating how international trade is characterized by serious imbalances. The concept of fair trade is then introduced. Finally, the effects of fair trade, particularly from the development economics perspective, will be outlined and evaluated. In this respect the effects will be presented in the three-dimensional context of sustainable development, i.e. by considering the ecological, economic and social aspects. Finally, major findings are summarized once again in the concluding section.

Position of the developing countries in world trade

The concept of fair trade has its basis in the development of conventional trade. Therefore, the starting point will be a few selected development trends in trade, with particular emphasis on the situation in the developing countries. So the question is whether, and to what extent, the developing countries are integrated into international trade. In this connection, the level of free trade and the various forms of trade barriers between industrialized and developing countries are of particular significance.

A fundamental problem of the current international trading system is that there is no neutral "world government" which is responsible for harmonizing national foreign and trade policies, coordinating these policies and assuming a democratic supervisory function (Krugman & Obstfeld 2009). This deficit leads to conflicts of interest, causing the global economy to be permeated with a high level of imbalance. Nor can it be anticipated that this imbalance will or can in the future be reduced by the WTO.

To a large extent, trade is characterized by trade barriers. Since the mid-1970s non-tariff trade barriers have increasingly applied, while tariff barriers such as customs duties have become less significant. In reality, a main reason for this is that since the 1970s the customs duties have been continually phased out in the individual General Agreement on Tariffs and Trade (GATT) rounds and "substituted" by non-tariff trade barriers. These include subsidies, anti-dumping procedures, as well as ecological and social standards, which the foreign producers and their products have to satisfy.

Advocates of the concept of fair trade are particularly critical of the protectionist measures of the industrialized countries, as these restrict the involvement of developing countries in international trade. The concept of fair trade is thus intended to offer producers (predominantly small-scale farmers) from developing countries the opportunity to participate in international trade.

It can be concluded that the structure of the world trading system has so far not contributed towards an integration of the large majority of developing countries. These have primarily cited exogenous factors as essentially a conglomeration of causes. However, globalization per se should not be held responsible in the context of the exogenous causes. Stiglitz, for example, sees the problem in the form of globalization. According to him, the "invisible hand", which Adam Smith emphasized as a controlling mechanism, does not work; at least for the developing countries (Stiglitz 2002, pp. 36 ff.).

In principle, trade can make a universal contribution if conducted within fair framework conditions. However, this requires a restructuring of the prevailing regulatory framework. On the global level, trade barriers must be lifted, particularly for goods that are advantageous for developing countries, which, however, cannot be used because of the obstacles to trade imposed by the industrialized countries. In the Human Development Report 2005, the unequal treatment of the individual developing countries and the methods of solving problems are shown in very differentiated terms (UNDP 2005).

On the microeconomic level, producers in developing countries must be better integrated into the supply chains, although this does not seem to be possible in the context of the structure of the world trading system. Globalization is therefore misdirected and has transformed the individual national economies into a world economy in which a great imbalance is prevalent (Stiglitz & Charlton 2005, p. 11). In this case as well, it can once again be concluded that the WTO is scarcely able to solve the problem, since – apart from the objectives in the Preamble – it really has no mandate.

Nevertheless, in this connection the internal causation factors of inadequate development, particularly in rural areas of developing countries, should not be disregarded. It is not enough simply to impute responsibility for the imbalanced world trade structure solely to the industrialized countries. Governments in many developing countries can be reproached for serious failings, which include, inter alia, a limited availability of human capital, insufficient production capacities in both quantitative and qualitative terms, an inadequate infrastructure, unsatisfactory healthcare and education systems, inadequate diversification of economic sectors, limited access to social services, inadequate access to information and communication technologies and the availability of only weak institutions. To this extent it can be concluded that both the exogenous and endogenous factors have contributed towards the imbalance in trade.

Figure 8.1 shows that in Asia there are only a few countries, such as Japan, Korea, China and also to an increasing extent India, which make a significant contribution to Asian world trade. The other regions, such as Africa and even South America, have as yet only participated to a minor extent in world trade. Figure 8.1 also shows the strength of intra-European trade. Nevertheless, it is anticipated that there will in the future be a change to the distribution of world trade: In the view of many experts, the five BRICS states (Brazil, Russia, India, China and South Africa) will assume significantly more important roles in world trade, although in these countries only a relatively small proportion of the population will benefit from this.

To summarize, it can be concluded that the unequal trade structures in the development of international trade have led to a strong imbalance. An analysis of world trade based on empirical findings shows that in recent decades only a few countries have managed to successfully integrate into trade relationships. In this respect there is controversy over whether internal or external factors are primarily

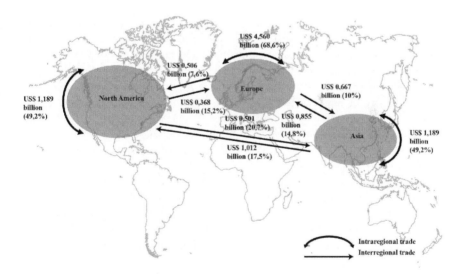

Figure 8.1 Main flows of world trade within the triad (2013)

Source: Based on data from WTO 2014, p. 25

responsible for causing this situation. However, the controversy contributes little towards finding a solution to the problem. Approaches to finding a solution should much rather be along the lines already mentioned: removing obstacles to trade in favour of the developing countries and the inclusion of small-scale producers as well into the global supply chains. Over the years the Doha negotiations have clarified the problems to a great extent and show what heavy weather the developing and industrialized countries are making of finding solutions (Stiglitz & Charlton 2005, p. 57). The developing countries must themselves solve the internal causation factors, if necessary with the assistance of development policy measures.

The concept of fair trade

Over the years the existence of numerous actors and organizations involved in fair trade has led to the development of various definitions for the concept. In 2002 members of the International Federation of Alternative Trade organization (IFAT), now the World Fair Trade Organization (WFTO), to which both producers as well as organizations importing fairly traded products belong, agreed upon the following definition:

> Fair-Trade is a trading partnership, based on dialogue, transparency and respect that seek greater equity in international trade. It contributes to sustainable development by offering better trading conditions to and securing the rights of marginalized producers and workers – especially in the south.
>
> (WFTO 2014)

Fair trade is primarily intended to support small-scale farmers in developing countries and give them the opportunity to participate in international trade. They essentially find themselves in a situation in which they only profit to a minimal extent from the production of their wares, and as a rule have no access to the infrastructure in order to transport the goods to the appropriate market and sell them there. They are therefore dependent upon intermediaries, who collect the goods locally from a large number of small-scale farmers and are able to offer the importer a larger quantity of the goods in demand. For the small-scale farmers, the intermediary is the sole source of information as far as the market price and market activity are concerned.

Thus the intermediary finds himself in an advantageous position: the small-scale farmers are reliant upon him and therefore receive only one-sided information. Consequently, they have access to insufficient information with regard to the market price and quality requirements. The objective of fair trade is to ensure the direct export of the products to the industrialized countries, cutting out the intermediary. To further reinforce the position of the small-scale farmers, the linking-up of several producers into cooperatives is an additional component of the concept of fair trade. Figure 8.2 links the principles of partnership with the three-dimensionality of sustainable development.

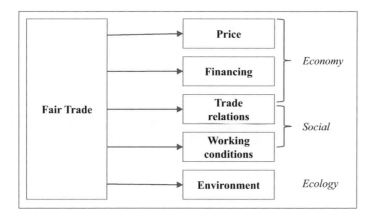

Figure 8.2 Components of the concept of fair trade
Source: Adapted from von Hauff & Claus 2013, p. 93

To some extent, the conditions under which fair trade is conducted between importers and producers vary amongst the different organizations. Nevertheless, the concept is based upon fundamental principles, which are accepted by and striven for by all organizations. The concept of fair trade consists of the three well-known dimensions: ecological (preservation of nature and ecosystems for later generations), economic (more responsible use of economic resources with the aim of increasing prosperity) and social (development of a society in which all members participate equally) (von Hauff 2014, p. 15).

The concept is based on the following characteristics:

- the adaptation of the prices for the products to the living conditions of the producers,
- the support of the producers in the financing of their projects,
- the reliable trading relationship between the importers in the North and the producers in the South,
- the social contract working conditions on the plantations and the production facilities in the producer cooperatives,
- the observance of certain environmental standards to improve the environmental situation and the preservation of useable farmland in developing countries.

The composition of the "fair price" is one of the central criteria of the concept, whereby the price for fair trade products is fixed differently by the various organizations. An introduction to the Fair Trade Labelling Organisation (FLO) system of price formation and to the import organizations El Puente and GEPA (Gesellschaft zur Förderung der Partnerschaft mit der Dritten Welt mbH or The Fair Trade Company) is presented below (von Hauff & Claus 2013, p. 122).

$$FTP = COSP + DFC + MD + OD + FIP$$

Where: FTP is fair trade price; COSP is the cost of sustainable production; DFC is direct fair trade costs; MD is market differential; OD is organic differential; and FIP is fair trade investment premium. The COSP includes the production costs – a calculation undertaken by the producers – as well as a margin, which is incorporated because many small-scale farmers are unable to precisely calculate their production costs. The additional "buffer" ensures that the real production costs are covered, and the costs of certification (verification that standards are maintained, award of fair trade label) are included in the calculation under the DFC heading. The market and quality differential (MD) then becomes effective whenever qualitative improvements lead to higher costs. An organic price premium is guaranteed for organic farming products. This premium becomes part of the FTP in the form of the FIP (around 15 per cent of the production costs) and is linked to the production costs (von Hauff & Claus 2013, p. 122).

However, it is worth considering that the markets for many products which are sold by way of fair trade are to a large extent already saturated. A typical example is coffee. Therefore, the fair trade suppliers have to compete with the conventional suppliers of goods. Due to the higher prices, it is not easy to win over price-conscious consumers to buy fairly traded products. The small selection of products, as well as the low level of flexibility with fluctuating quantities in demand, represent additional problems in the marketing of fairly traded products. Furthermore, the existence of labels and certificates for biological, organic, ethical and fairly traded products leads to uncertainty amongst consumers. One consequence of this is that purchasers are often less prepared to pay a surcharge for the products (Giovannucci & Kroekoek 2003, p. 21).

Comparing the international sales trend for fair trade products, Germany is positioned in third place, behind England and the USA. However, if the population of the individual countries is taken into account, the turnover has to be calculated and shown on a per capita basis. Using this method, in 2011 Ireland heads the list, with an average per capita turnover of EU€ 34.68. Switzerland is in second place with a per capita turnover € 33.04, above England with a per capita turnover of € 23.71. Germany is in 14th place with a per capita turnover € 4.90 (Fairtrade International 2012, pp. 1–20). Figure 8.3 shows the sales for the 18 most important sales markets in absolute figures and per capita values.

There are currently 991 producer organizations in 66 countries which are certified by the FLO (see Figure 8.4). These organizations are spread over the regions of Latin America (538), Africa (299) and Asia (154) (FLO 2011, p. 12). Worldwide there are around 1.2 million producers actively engaged in fair trade. If family members are added to this, there are at least 6 million people who live from the fair trade system. Figure 8.4 shows the geographical distribution of the certified producer organizations and the number of members.

In addition to the pure marketing of the products, through the concept of fair trade the actors also attempt to fulfil a political objective, thereby adopting a position on current realities in world trade policy. For example, the fair trade organizations working together under the FINE (FLO, IFAT, NEWS and EFTA) cooperation used the Sixth WTO Ministerial Conference in Hong Kong as an

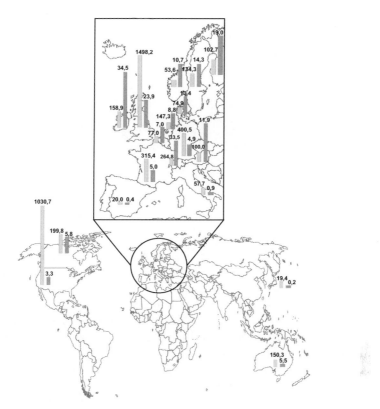

Figure 8.3 Sales of fair trade products in the 18 major sale markets (on the left absolute
values in millions € and on the right per capita values in €)

Source: Based on data from Fairtrade International 2012, p. 12

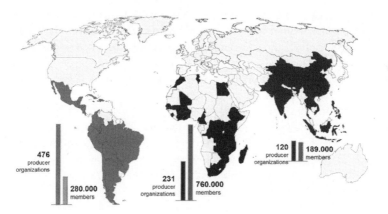

Figure 8.4 Geographical distribution of the certified producer organizations and their
members in 2009

Source: Based on data from FLO 2011, p. 12

opportunity to comment on the current round of negotiations with a position paper and issue demands to the negotiating partners. Following this presentation of important features of the concept of fair trade, the next section will consider the effects of fair trade.

The effects of fair trade

The effects of fair trade should be considered more closely in the context of the model of sustainable development. Dietz pointed out this correlation back in 2000 (Dietz 2000, p. 191). These findings should be highlighted by recording the ecological, economic and social effects on the basis of case studies from various developing countries. Comments are predominantly based on the studies by Oxford Policy Management and the Sustainable Market Group, studies by Hopkins (2000), Immhof and Lee (2007), as well as the regional studies by Kogo (2000), Chandra (2000) and Rodriguez (2000).

In 2012 the extensive study "Assessing the Impact of Fair Trade on Poverty Reduction through Rural Development" was published by Centrum for Evaluation for TransFair Germany and the Max Havelaar Foundation Switzerland (CEval 2012). Mention should also be made of the survey study of the effect of fair trade by Nelson and Pound (2009). These two studies are predominantly regional studies. As yet there has been no "blanket coverage study" presenting a comprehensive analysis of effects, and nor will there be such a study in the future. The following observations will focus on specific effects which can be attributed to the three dimensions of sustainable development.

Ecological consequences

First, there will be a consideration of the ecological consequences arising from the production process of agricultural products. The change in cultivation methods and the avoidance of pesticides and environmentally harmful fertilizers represent an important contribution towards the environmental situation in the developing countries. For example, organic farming is regionally promoted in the collaboration between the Raos community in Honduras and fair trade organizations. Cultivation methods and fertilization are reorganized where necessary, and organic fertilizers are therefore manufactured and used.

The switch to organic farming is promoted by the fair trade organizations, and awareness of organically manufactured products and demand for them is increasing. Fair trade enables producers to acquire further training in and to implement ecological demands. For example, the switch to organic fertilizers involves a relatively low level of expenditure, since fertilization with chemical substances is often considerably more expensive. And, small-scale farmers are frequently also untrained in how to correctly measure out chemical fertilizers, resulting in overfertilization which causes higher costs, a lower crop yield and, over the long term, contamination of the soil.

In this connection, targeted guidance by the fair trade companies, for example in the form of local seminars or workshops, makes an important contribution towards increasing ecological as well as economic efficiency. By switching to organic farming, farmers not only improve the environmental conditions in their region, but can also prevent production methods which are detrimental to health. This also protects the soil and maintains and promotes its productiveness over the long term. A further benefit is that the demand for organically grown products is rising, in both industrialized as well as developing countries. In addition, they receive as an incentive a premium from the fair trade companies.

However, it should be taken into account that, as far as ecological demands are concerned, diversification of the cultivation of agricultural products is often inadequately undertaken. Producers frequently only market one of their products through fair trade. This is particularly evident in the case of coffee, the classic example of a fair trade product. Due to the higher price the producers obtain for their products, they are induced to expand their output volume and to restrict the production of other agricultural products on their fields. Nevertheless, diversification is extremely important both for the quality of the soil as well as for the independence of the producers. Furthermore, in the context of the increasing water shortage in many regions, the recycling of used water is now an important action point (CEval 2012, pp. 64–70).

In sum, specified ecological standards have to be achieved for the admission of cooperatives onto the FLO register. The producers are supported by the fair trade organizations in the implementation of the environmental standards. Targeted advice and access to information are therefore essential factors for success in the introduction of ecological standards. The costs resulting from this are offset by a higher selling price for the products.

Economic consequences

The economic consequences can be differentiated according to various criteria. One essential aspect is facilitated market access for the producers. An easily quantifiable effect of fair trade is the rising income of the producers (Nicholls & Opal 2005). The guaranteed prices and the added social premium produce an income which is above the subsistence minimum. Producers also have an opportunity to obtain more information about the market mechanism and, if they wish, to also develop a trading relationship for themselves. The prefinancing of the products and the long-term trading relationships enable producers to undertake the necessary investments to increase production or productivity, and the organization of cooperatives means that producers receive a higher proportion of the added value.

Studies demonstrate that amongst producers the proportion of products sold through fair trade varies. Whereas for some producers this proportion amounts to only a low percentage of the output volume, other producers sell almost all of their goods to the fair trade companies. Steinrücken shows that the resulting profit for producers from fair trade essentially depends upon the proportion of products which they are able to sell through fair trade. His example of coffee can be used for all other products offered for sale under the fair trade banner (Steinrücken 2003, p. 13). Fair trade always results in a benefit for producers whenever the profit produced from the sale of the products exceeds the profit which the producer would have achieved from selling via conventional trade.

Through fair trade, production capacities can be expanded, and new products and designs developed. Furthermore, improved quality control makes a positive contribution. According to a study by Hopkins (2000) on the projects of the fair trade company OXFAM, the rejection rate for the products can thereby be considerably reduced. Through an acquaintance with fair trading systems, the aim is to give producers the opportunity to also be able to sell their goods via conventional trade at a later date.

For example, through fair trade exporters firstly acquire a better understanding of how the coffee market operates, which can be helpful in the production phase and subsequent marketing through other trading channels (Jones et al. 2000, p. 24). By participating on the world markets, consumer demand can be better understood and market competence acquired. In this connection it should be noted that only a small proportion of producers actually succeed in accessing the conventional markets, and over the long term many producer groups are reliant upon the fair trade organizations.

The cooperatives which enter into a partnership with the fair trade organizations must nevertheless fulfil certain criteria and are selected according to specific considerations. The minimum price and the fair trade premium are linked to the units of a product sold. However, it is often impossible to eliminate the free rider problem, since this represents a fundamental problem within the organizational form of the cooperative. This means that not all members of the cooperative are active to an equal extent, although they nevertheless profit fully from the benefits provided by the cooperative. At worst, there are also members in the cooperative who play a completely passive role. As far as the link between cooperative and fair trade is concerned, it should be pointed out that there is better access to information and, associated with this, an improved basis for negotiations with traders (fair trade organizations as well as conventional purchasers of products) (Develtere & Pollet 2005, p. 21).

The fair trade organizations profit from a lasting trade relationship with producers, as the producers also profit from the fair trade organizations which they know about. Taking into account the additional costs, for outsiders this aspect is the major obstacle to creating a partnership with the fair trading companies. The cooperatives, which are already in a position to market their products through fair trade distribution channels, thereby have an advantage. Fair trade assumes a protective function for producers, which can be useful for market introductions. However, it does not represent a lasting measure for future trade, since it does not solve problems but merely distances them from the producers.

In their study on poverty reduction in Bolivia, Immhof and Lee (2007, pp. 56–62) also examined the influence of fair trade on producers who are not themselves involved in fair trade. As already briefly mentioned, only a small proportion of producers can enter into a trading relationship with fair trade organizations. These producers receive a higher price for their products. In the case of the coffee market, there is a large number of producers compared to a relatively small number of local intermediaries. So if some producers participate in fair trade, the supply of coffee for local intermediaries will be reduced. These intermediaries will then be forced to pay the producers a higher price in order to continue acquiring the volume required. In this case, all small-scale farmers will on average earn more. However, this presupposes that all additional influencing factors remain constant. If the entire volume of goods cannot be sold to the producers integrated into fair trade systems, this will result in a negative effect. For example, the higher price which the producers receive for fair trade may encourage them to produce more.

In summary, it can be concluded that in developing countries as a result of fair trade the producers are exposed to both positive and negative economic consequences. One important influencing factor is the dependency of producers upon the fair trade organizations. If the cooperatives sell most of their goods to these organizations, the level of dependency is very high and may have negative consequences for the producers. On the positive side, it should be stressed that, through collaboration with fair trade organizations, the producers in developing countries have an opportunity to tap into new markets.

Likewise, through the development and new acquisition of machinery and equipment, as well as the improvement of workplaces and the further development of the organization, the capacity and productivity of the production plants can be increased. In the evaluation by CEval, stable prices and long-term trade relationships are particularly highlighted as positive factors. In the case of coffee production in Peru, it is demonstrated that during periods of low coffee prices, it is only fair trade producers who are able to continue making a living from their product (CEval 2012, pp. 35–44).

Social consequences

The higher selling price of the products, which the producers are guaranteed through fair trade, leads to higher wages for the farmers and workers on the plantations. In an ideal case scenario, the additional fair trade premium is invested in joint projects, such as the reconstruction or further development of the infrastructure, or the improvement of living conditions of small-scale farmers. This can include, for example, the financing of schools, the improvement of the housing conditions of small-scale farmers or the establishment of health centres. As a rule, it does not make sense to distribute the bonus directly to the individual producers. If only a portion of the goods produced is sold through fair trade, the proportion of the fair trade premium for the individual producers is relatively small. Nevertheless, a positive factor for the producers is the higher and secured income.

The projects initiated by the fair trade organizations have a positive effect on the living conditions of the beneficiary producers. One such effect is the improvement of health-related and working conditions of small-scale producers and workers. It should, however, be pointed out that it is always only some of the small-scale farmers in a particular region who profit from these benefits. Therefore, outside the cooperatives there can arise feelings of isolation and envy on the part of those producers who do not benefit, and income disparities can become even greater.

A question which often arises is whether the promotion of fair trade really benefits the most disadvantaged producers. The need for quality and reliability, in combination with the conditions on the international markets, is to some extent in conflict with the resources which poor people in the developing countries have at their disposal (Tallontire 2002, p. 13). The poorest people lack access to capital and other production factors, and therefore tend to have no opportunity to participate in fair trade and to profit from it.

By eliminating intermediate trade, dependency upon the actors is prevented. The producers receive the entire sales proceeds, whereas in intermediate trade a certain portion is paid over to the intermediate traders. Nevertheless, many fair trade companies are partly dependent on intermediate trading organizations, which are not substitutable locally. Not only do they enable access to a broader product spectrum and a simplified means of importing products, but they also help to overcome linguistic and cultural barriers. The direct trading partner of the import organizations is not always the producer, but sometimes the exporter or the further processing company. Consequently, the objective of eliminating intermediate trade cannot always be achieved. It is, however, possible to reduce the amount of purchases through intermediate traders, whereby a higher proportion of the selling price goes to the individual producers.

By incorporating International Labour Organization (ILO) standards within the framework of the fair trade concept, child labour and discrimination against women are countered, for example. Whenever these standards are implemented in the various producer organizations, great progress thereby becomes evident. Particularly in handicraft production, a large proportion of the work is carried out at home, and through fair trade organizations centres can be set up where the products are manufactured.

Better monitoring of quality and working conditions is thereby guaranteed, in order to eliminate the employment of children for example. At the same time, the producers can also benefit from a better working environment. Some organizations also offer concepts or improvements for already existing systems to support social services. Main areas of focus here are wage security and social security based upon collectively agreed conditions. Additional benefits can be health services and pension payments.

However, the implementation of these standards is not always easy, as producers in the developing countries often have to rely upon help from their children. Thus, taking as an example cotton production in India, the CEval study reveals during the harvest period around 28 per cent of children did not attend school. It is also pointed out in this study that children receive a daily wage of Rs150 (€2.13), whereas an adult worker receives Rs200 (€2.84) (CEval 2012, p. 25).

Nicholls and Opal also emphasize: "Other direct impacts of fair trade on farmers include gender empowerment and an increase in investment in education" (Nicholls & Opal 2008, p. 205). However, in this connection it must be pointed out that many of the studies come to the conclusion that there is still a large deficit in gender equality within the fair trade organizations. Although the requirements of fair trade include improvements in the situation of women, the incorporation of these aspects is still unsatisfactory in the case of most fair trade organizations.

In a large number of cooperatives and associations the proportion of women, particularly in decision-making positions, is very small. It should also be taken into account that the increased integration of women into the production and distribution processes also results in an additional burden within organizational structures, since women are also responsible for the household and childcare. The conception of the roles of men and women does not permit women just to work simply as farmers, i.e. it is taken as a matter of course for women to also carry out housework.

In some developing countries the realization of an increasing employment of women is not insignificantly influenced by the cultural conception of the woman. For example, in some cultures women are not permitted to work together with men. In this connection, the establishment of production centres especially for women is particularly important. Another example of the unequal treatment of the sexes can be identified in the contrasting payment of men and women, although it must be taken into account that payment is not specifically gender-based for the same activity.

The requirements of fair trade stipulate that further and advanced training programmes are carried out within the organizations. This takes places with the support of the fair trade organizations. The further training programmes are particularly aimed at improving the quality controls and marketing for the products. In some cases the producers are even given the opportunity to participate in seminars in industrialized countries. To support producers locally and in the production plants, some fair trade organizations provide qualified personnel who explain the concepts of fair trade to the producers and demonstrate methods for fulfilling the standard.

For the producers, participation in seminars and training measures has an additional positive effect. This enhances their competitiveness on the international markets and their self-esteem can also be raised in this way. Additional contributing factors are the increased awareness created for the small-scale farmers through the training programmes, as well as the visits by fair trade organizations and customers. Through the protected environment offered to producers in the cooperatives, they are able to acquire knowledge, improve their production processes and build up self-confidence. Although on the one hand this can prepare them for an independent existence on conventional markets, there is also a risk on the other hand that their progress will be divorced from the reality of market activity (Immhof & Lee 2007, p. 81).

Improvement potential for the fair trade concept

In summary, a few fields of activity can be identified in which there is clearly still improvement potential for fair trade. There continues to be a considerable need for action regarding equal rights for men and women, as well as in communication, the level of individual ideas on the part of the producers, and in respect of the concept of fair trade. The basis of trust, upon which the partnership is to be founded, can thereby also be improved. As in the industrialized countries, it is also necessary in the developing countries to ensure that the concept is accorded sufficient transparency.

In considering the three dimensions of the economy, ecology and society, it can be concluded in summary that the concept of fair trade delivers extremely positive ecological, economic and social results for the producers. The question nevertheless arises as to how the sustainability of the individual measures is to be evaluated. Supported by the implementation of ecological and social standards, the sustainability of working conditions and environmental protection can be achieved. In economic terms, it is doubtful whether the targeted objectives satisfy these requirements.

It is clear that in some cases it has so far only been possible to implement the objectives of fair trade in the cooperatives of the developing countries to an inadequate extent. In this connection, it can be pointed out that in the ecological sphere the diversification of the cultivation of agricultural products does not always adhere to the principle of ecological sustainability. An example in the social sphere is discrimination against women. The proportion of women employed in producer organizations, particularly on the decision-making levels, remains very low. If women have the opportunity in the producer organizations to contribute towards family income, this is usually accompanied by a double burden in the form of running a household as well as undertaking paid employment.

Nor has the problem of overcoming dependencies yet been satisfactorily solved with regard to the structure of some cooperatives. Nevertheless, through the trading relationships between the cooperatives and the fair trade organizations there is a possibility that the overall environment will be positively influenced. The formation of such relationships in a region can lead to the position of local traders being weakened and the producers likewise having to pay a higher price in order to acquire a certain quantity of products. Fair trade thereby functions as a competitor, stimulates competition and can, ideally, eliminate a significant market failure through a demand monopoly.

Finally, it should also be mentioned that the partnerships between fair trade organizations and the small-scale farmers in the developing countries are fraught with strong contradictions. The fulfilment of standards conceived by the fair trade organizations, which are a matter of course in the industrialized countries, can lead to considerable difficulties amongst the disadvantaged producers. Achievement of these standards can be a very laborious process, and the task of the fair trade organizations is to act in a supporting manner in this connection. However, the role of these organizations is not simply advisory or to act as partners, as it is absolutely essential to constantly monitor compliance with the fair trade standards and conditions. This monitoring or supervision of producers in the developing countries by employees of the fair trade organizations from industrialized countries can cause mistrust. Against this background, it is sometimes difficult to build up a good partnership based on trust.

Current developments in fair trade

An examination of the recent development trends in fair trade firstly reveals that the international financial and economic crisis has not led to a fall in sales of fair trade products. On the contrary, the sales figures have further increased since the outbreak of the international financial crisis. In 2013 total sales of fair trade products amounted to €5.5 billion, corresponding to a growth rate of 15 per cent compared to the previous year. In this connection it should be taken into consideration that over recent years new actors began trading with fair trade products. The fair trade label makes it easier for commercial enterprises to include fair trade products in their range of goods, and therefore numerous supermarkets, discounters and mail order firms now offer fair trade products in their range of goods in order to conduct business without having any closer links to the fair trade concept.

This clearly shows that fair trade products are an increasingly important element in mainstream commerce. On the one hand this could open up a significantly larger and widely spread clientele, although on the other hand the complaint from the core proponents of the concept is that the essential approach of "fair trade as an alternative to conventional trade" thereby becomes lost. And it is also evident that even traditional fair trade organizations are departing from their original charitable intentions. They are also visibly adopting a stronger commercial orientation, which is consequently also increasingly geared towards profit (Davies & Ryals 2010, p. 317).

The following observations will be restricted to a few specific sectors, which can likewise be attributed to the recent development trends.

Sale of fair trade products in developing countries

One important and clear development in recent years is that fair trade products are also sold to an increasing extent in developing countries. For example, the South African supermarket chain Pick n Pay introduced Fair-Trade-Café into its range, and since then additional products have been offered to consumers in South Africa. Moreover, fair trade products are now also being sold in countries such as Brazil, Kenya and India.

For many producer groups the spread of fair trade products to the markets of developing countries is of major significance, as consequently their distribution structure is not unilaterally aimed towards marketing their products in industrialized countries. Therefore, in those developing countries wishing to offer fair trade products on their internal markets, there are various efforts to promote regional marketing (Forum Fairer Handel 2012, p. 2). Up until now, "producer services" have been coordinated by Fair Trade International, whereby local personnel support has been carried out locally.

176 *Michael von Hauff*

Certification in the non-food-sector

While fair trade has for a long time been geared towards foodstuffs and handcrafted products, in recent years a number of products have been added which are attributable to the non-food sector. One initiative is the collaboration of Fairtrade International with the Forest Stewardship Council (FSC). The objective is to support small-scale forest operations. The FSC certification confirms that forests are managed in accordance with social, ecological and economic standards. Such certification ensures that the national and international rights of workers are respected.

Additional non-food sectors are (von Hauff & Claus 2013, p. 233):

> *Emissions trading:* A new instrument within the fair trade system is emission rights trading, which as an instrument of environmental policy is based on the cap-and-trade principle. According to the concept of emissions trading, each emitter of greenhouse gases (state, enterprises) is over a specific period only permitted to release the volume of harmful substances for which it holds the emission rights. The idea within the fair trade system is to give enterprises in industrialized countries the option to acquire emission rights directly from their suppliers in the developing countries. The launch of "insetting" (whereby sale and purchase take place within a commercial chain) opened up an additional source of income for producers in the developing countries.

> *Oil fuels and agrofuels:* Oil fuels and agrofuels are a new branch of the fair trade product range. In a collaboration with Migrol, Gebana AG in Switzerland offers the first fair trade biofuel worldwide. The fuel is based on soya oil, and is sustainably cultivated and offered for sale by small-scale farmers in southwest Brazil.

> *Textiles sector:* In 2004 fair trade standards for cotton were drawn up by the FLO umbrella organization, and on this basis cotton was produced in compliance with these standards. For this, the producers were guaranteed a fixed minimum price and a FTP. All textile goods consisting of fair trade cotton are awarded the label "Fairtrade Certified Cotton".

> *Promotion of mining workers:* To improve the living, working and environmental conditions in traditional gold mines, processing plants and mining communities, the Alliance for Responsible Mining (ARM) and the FLO developed the first Fairtrade/Fairmined Standard for Gold at the beginning of 2010. Standards were developed which comprise the social and ecological criteria such as occupational safety, accident prevention, traceability of the supply chain, freedom of trade unions and the proper and sustainable use of the FTP.

> *Ethical financial investments:* Likewise in the financial sector, a new services sector was formed to comply with the principles of fair trade. Noteworthy elements are ethical financial investments and a fair foreign exchange market.

Oikokredit and Shared Interest are members of the WFTO, and make fair loans available to disadvantaged producers in developing countries. It should also be emphasized that in 2008 Oikokredit ran a campaign called "Fair Finance – Fair Trade". The "Shared Interest" organizations also offer further training measures to provide the target groups with a better understanding of the workings of the financial market.

Fair trade in the services sector

Additional current developments focus on delivering the concept of fair trade to the services sector as well. In 1999 the organization Tourism Concern was formed, with the objective of creating an international network. And in 2002 the organization Fair Trade in Tourism South Africa was formed, with the accompanying trademark FTTSA. A project by the Church Development Service (Evangelischer Entwicklungsdienst – EED) promotes sustainable, i.e. environmentally and socially acceptable, tourism. The specialist unit "TOURISM WATCH" was set up for this purpose.

Even more products and product groups are to be incorporated into the fair trade concept in the future. The development of the fair trade standards for wood and gold led to the original product sphere of fair trade, namely agricultural products, being extended to products sourced from certified raw materials. Consequently, even more people in the developing countries are able to benefit from fair trade.

Conclusions

In its Preamble the WTO makes a clear reference to the new paradigm of sustainable development, which in turn represents the basis for the concept of fair trade. However, if one considers the structure and development of international trade, this aspiration in the WTO Preamble does not exist in reality. Even today there are still many developing countries which are largely excluded from international trade. This particularly applies to the many millions of small-scale farmers who, even in the developing countries which are catching up, such as Brazil, South Africa, China and India, are excluded from international trade. As has been demonstrated, there are both exogenous as well as endogenous causation factors here. The WTO appears not to be geared towards, or is not able to bring about, the reduction of imbalances between industrialized and developing countries in international trade, particularly for agricultural products. The Doha rounds of negotiation have not yet produced the desired breakthrough.

The concept of fair trade evolved as a reaction to the imbalances in international trade, from which – as already mentioned – small-scale farmers are particularly excluded. Globalization, which has intensified over the last few decades, has reinforced on the one hand the dynamics of international trade, and on the other hand the critical awareness of consumers in industrialized countries, which has focused in particular on the living conditions of small-scale farmers in developing countries.

The first activities under the fair trade banner occurred towards the end of the 1940s in the USA, and in subsequent years the concept of fair trade established itself in many industrialized countries. The concept is based on the three-dimensionality of the paradigm of sustainable development: small-scale farmers should cultivate their agricultural products in an environmentally compatible manner, they should obtain a price for their products which enables them to enjoy a reasonable standard of living, and through cooperatives they should jointly bring their products onto the market and through joint revenues improve their social environment. This becomes possible, for example, by building health care centres, schools and community centres.

The analysis of the ecological, economic and social effects demonstrated that it has been possible to achieve major objectives of the concept of fair trade for the target groups. In this connection, important findings have been obtained, particularly from case studies. There are currently 827 producer organizations in 60 countries which are certified by the FLO: 231 producer organizations are located in 21 countries in the Africa/Middle East region; there are 120 organizations in 12 Asian countries and the majority of producer organizations (476) are situated in 20 countries within the Latin American and Caribbean territories (FLO 2011, p. 12).

A total of 1.2 million small-scale farmers and workers operate within the framework of the fair trade system. If family members are also included, there are over 6 million people who profit from the fair trade system. The FLO estimates that around 20 per cent of all products manufactured by certified producers are sold under the fair trade banner. However, it is difficult to calculate how great the potential of fair trade is, i.e. what proportion of this potential has as yet been realized. However, the few figures which are available show that a large number of people already profit from the fair trade system. In this respect an upward trend has developed over recent years, which can be explained, inter alia, by the fact that large retail chains are also increasingly offering fair trade products for sale. However, the consequences of this trend for the fair trade system cannot yet be assessed.

Nevertheless, if one compares people in the agricultural sector in developing countries to the total number of small-scale farmers in developing countries who are established in the fair trade system, together with their relatives, this represents only a small proportion who profit from the fair trade system. Therefore, many farmers are excluded from this system, which to some extent creates differences between insiders and outsiders. Furthermore, there is potential for improvement in the fair trade system, such as support for women, which has been highlighted above. A concluding assessment suggests that the fair trade system has established itself as a successful instrument of development cooperation. Since it cannot be anticipated that in the near future the WTO will achieve the objective it sets itself in the Preamble, the legitimacy of this concept will continue for a long time to come.

References

CEval (Centrum for Evaluation) (2012): *Assessing the Impact of Fair Trade on Poverty Reduction through Rural Development: Final Report Fairtrade Impact Study*. www.fairtrade-

deutschland.de/fileadmin/user_upload/ueber_fairtrade/fairtrade_wirkt/2012_12_12_
Final_Report_Fairtrade-Impact-Study.pdf.

Chandra, R. (2000): Regionalstudie Südasien. In: Misereor-Brot für die Welt – Friedrich-
Ebert-Stiftung (ed.): *Entwicklungspolitische Wirkungen des Fairen Handels*, Beiträge zur
Diskussion, Aachen, pp. 211–226.

Davies, I.; Ryals, L. (2010): The Role of Social Capital in the Success of Fair Trade. *Journal
of Business Ethics* 2(96), pp. 317–338.

Develtere, P., Pollet, I. (2005): *Co-operatives and Fair-Trade*, Leuven.

Dietz, H.-M. (2000): Die Wirkungen des Fairen Handels bei seinen Partnern im Süden –
Einführung und Kommentierung der regionalen Studien, In: Misereor-Brot für die Welt
– Friedrich-Ebert-Stiftung (Hrsg.): *Entwicklungspolitische Wirkungen des Fairen Handels*,
Beiträge zur Diskussion, Aachen.

Fairtrade International (2012): *For producers, with Producers – Annual Report 2011–2012*,
Bonn.

FLO (Fair Trade Labelling Organisation) (2011): Growing Strong Together – Annual Report.
www.fairtrade.net/fileadmin/user_upload/content/2009/resources/FLO_Annual-
Report-2009_komplett_double_web.pdf, Bonn.

Forum Fairer Handel (2012): *Fact-Sheet: Der Faire Handel in Deutschland*. www.forum-fairer-
handel.de/fileadmin/user_upload/dateien/politik/factsheet_jpk_ffh_2012.pdf.

Giovanucci, D.; Kroekoek, F.-J. (2003): *The State of Sustainable Coffee: A Study of Twelve Major
Markets*, International Coffee Organization.

Hopkins, R. (2000): *Impact Assessment Study of Oxfam Fair Trade. Final Report.*
www.komment.at/dokumente/download.

Immhof S.; Lee, A. (2007): *Assessing the Potential of Fair Trade for Poverty Reduction and Conflict
Prevention: A Case Study of Bolivia Coffee Producers*, Seco (Schweizerisches Staatssekretariat
Wirtschaft), University of Basel.

Jones, S.; Fair Trade (Oxford Policy Management; Sustainable Markets Group) (2000):
Overview, Impact, Challenges. Study to inform DFID's support to Fair Trade, Oxford, London.

Kogo, K. (2000): Regionalstudie östliches Afrika. In: Misereor-Brot für die Welt – Friedrich-
Ebert-Stiftung (ed.): *Entwicklungspolitische Wirkungen des Fairen Handels*, Beiträge zur
Diskussion, Aachen, pp. 227–248.

Krugman, P.; Obstfeld, M (2009): *Internationale Wirtschaft – Theorie und Politik der
Außenwirtschaft*, 8th ed., Munich.

Nelson, V.; Pound, B. (2009): *The Last Ten Years: A Comprehensive Review of the Literature on
the Impact of Fairtrade*; University of Greenwich, London.

Nicholls, A.; Opal, Ch. (2005): *Fair Trade – Market – Rhythm Ethical Consumption*, London.

Nicholls, A.; Opal, Ch. (2008): *Fair Trade – Market – Driven Ethical Consumption*, London
(reprinted 2008).

Rodriguez, A. (2000): *Regionalstudie Zentralamerika. Entwicklungspolitische Wirkungen des
Fairen Handels*, Beiträge zur Diskussion, Aachen, pp. 249–269.

Steinrücken, T. (2003): *Funktioniert „fairer" Handel? Ökonomische Überlegungen zum alternativen
Handel mit Kaffee*, Diskussionspapier Nr. 32 der TU Ilmenau, Ilmenau.

Stiglitz, J. (2002): *Die Schatten der Globalisierung*, Berlin.

Stiglitz, J.; Charlton, A. (2005): *Fair Trade for All – How Trade Can Promote Development*,
Oxford.

Tallontire, A. (2002): Challenges facing Fair Trade: Which way now? *Small Enterprise
Development* 13(3), pp. 12–23.

UNDP (United Nations Development Programme) (2005): *Human Development Report
2005*, New York.

von Hauff, M. (2014): *Nachhaltige Entwicklung – Grundlagen und Umsetzung*, 2nd edition, Munich.

von Hauff, M.; Claus, K. (2013): *Fair Trade*, 2nd ed., Munich.

WFTO (World Fair Trade Organisation) (2014): Definition of Fair Trade; http://wfto.com/fair-trade/definition-fair-trade.

WTO (World Trade Organization) (2014): *International Trade Statistics 2014*, OECD Publishing, Geneva.

9 Tourism in developing countries

Matthias Beyer, Heike Dickhut, Diana Körner and Wolfgang Strasdas

Introduction

For more than 60 years international tourism has continued to expand and diversify uninterruptedly as an industry, making it one of the most important economic sectors in the world, with significant growth prospects. However, rapid tourism development often comes along with negative environmental, social and cultural side-effects. Especially emerging destinations are under a high risk of suffering from these negative impacts. Sustainable tourism development, which takes into consideration the environment and host communities, whilst ensuring viable, stable economic operations, aims at avoiding or at least minimizing negative impacts through tourism and can strengthen long-term competitiveness of a destination. Sustainable tourism is not a special form of tourism or a product, but rather a concept, which seeks to encompass all forms of tourism (UNEP 2014). It has been defined by the United Nations World Tourism Organization (UNWTO 2015) as: *"Tourism that takes full account of its current and future economic, social and environmental impacts, addressing the needs of visitors, the industry, the environment and host communities"*.

The importance of sustainable tourism has recently been recognised at global level. At the UN Conference on Sustainable Development Rio+20 in June 2012 heads of state formally adopted the 10 Year Framework of Programmes on Sustainable Consumption and Production (10YFP). The 10YFP is a global action framework to enhance international cooperation on sustainable consumption and production (SCP) by supporting the implementation of policies and activities at regional and national levels. Due to the increasing economic importance of tourism for developing and developed countries, sustainable tourism (including ecotourism) has been recognized as a key vehicle for sustainable development by world leaders and as such has been integrated as one of the five initial programmes under the 10YFP (UNEP 2014). The 10YFP Sustainable Tourism Programme officially incorporates sustainable tourism into a political platform facilitated by the UN system, which is the result of the committed work tourism stakeholders undertook globally over many years since the United Nations Conference on Environment and Development in Rio in 1992.

Table 9.1 highlights the major milestones in international cooperation on sustainable tourism and states the respective outcomes (political papers, declarations, programmes, etc.).

Table 9.1 Major political milestones of sustainable tourism

Year	Milestone	Outcomes relevant for tourism
1992	United Nations Conference on Environment and Development, Rio de Janeiro, Brazil	Rio Declaration on Environment and Development Agenda 21 (defining sustainable development)
1996		Agenda 21 for the Travel and Tourism Industry: Towards Environmental Sustainable Development
1997	International Conference of Environment Ministers on Biodiversity and Tourism, Berlin, Germany	Berlin Declaration on Biological Diversity and Sustainable Tourism
2000	Millennium Summit, New York, USA	Millennium Development Goals (MDGs)
2002	World Summit on Sustainable Development, Johannesburg, South Africa	Joint Programme of Implementation, concrete steps for implementing Agenda 21 UNWTO sets up the Sustainable Tourism for Eliminating Poverty (ST-EP) initiative
2003	First International Expert Meeting of the Marrakech Process, Marrakech, Morocco	Start of the Marrakech Process
2006	UNEP Governing Council, Dubai, United Arab Emirates	Launch of the International Taskforce on Sustainable Tourism Development (ITF-STD) as part of the Marrakech Process
2008	IUCN World Conservation Congress, Barcelona, Spain	Introduction of the Global Sustainable Tourism Criteria (GSTC)
2010	UN Summit on MDGs, New York, USA	United Nations Steering Committee on Tourism for Development (UN-SCTD) is inaugurated
2011	First Annual Meeting of the Global Partnership for Sustainable Tourism, Costa Rica	Official launch of the Global Partnership for Sustainable Tourism (GPST) as successor to the ITF-STD
2012	UN Conference on Sustainable Development, Rio+20, Rio de Janeiro, Brazil	The Future We Want: 2 paragraphs on Sustainable Tourism 10YFP: Sustainable Tourism Programme as one of five programmes
2014	World Travel Market (WTM), London	Official Launch of the 10YFP Sustainable Tourism Programme
2015	Annual Meeting of the Global Partnership for Sustainable Tourism, Namibia	Transition of the Global Partnership for Sustainable Tourism (GPST) to the 10YFP Sustainable Tourism Programme

Source: Adapted from UNEP 2014

This chapter gives an overview of the importance of tourism for developing countries, while assessing their relevance for the German outbound market. Further the major economic, ecological and socio-cultural impacts of tourism are described, with a focus on developing countries. The role of tourism in development cooperation is outlined, together with Germany s involvement and the most relevant fields of action. Finally, this chapter seeks to highlight possible synergies with other development fields and discusses bottlenecks and challenges, together with a series of strategic recommendations for tourism development in developing countries.

Facts and figures of tourism in developing countries

Global tourism development and trends

The tourism industry is one of the largest and most important economic sectors worldwide. In 2014 global receipts were estimated to be around US$7.6 trillion per year (UNWTO 2015; WTTC 2015). This number represents around 9.8 per cent of the world's consolidated gross domestic product (GDP) providing approximately 277 million jobs. Therewith almost every eleventh job is linked to tourism (WTTC 2015). Moreover, in 2014, total exports from international tourism escalated to $1.5 trillion, accounting for approximately 6 per cent of the global export volume of goods and services, with a share of about 30 per cent for services alone (UNWTO 2015). These numbers refer to the total contribution of tourism to the global economy, taking into account all direct, indirect and induced effects. Solely regarding the direct effects, tourism contributes to the world's GDP with $2.4 trillion (approximately 3 per cent) and to employment with 105 million jobs (WTTC 2015), whereby the largest contribution refers to intraregional tourism (71 per cent), while only 29 per cent results from long-haul travel (Aderhold et al. 2013).

Furthermore, with a growth of 3.6 per cent in 2014, tourism grew faster than the wider economy and outperformed growth in the majority of leading economies, for example automotive, public services, retail and financial services. It was only exceeded by booming sectors like consumer electronics and technical tools (WTTC 2015). Regarding the forecast of the World Travel and Tourism Council (WTTC) for the next ten years total tourism GDP is predicted to maintain this rate and grow on average by 3.8 per cent per year in the timespan from 2015 to 2025 (WTTC 2015).

The favourable increase in receipts from tourism is intrinsically linked to constantly increasing international tourist arrivals. In 1990 only 436 million international tourist arrivals were recorded worldwide. More than two decades later, in 2014, the number of international arrivals grew up to 1,138 million persons. According to the forecast of the UNWTO, tourism will grow – with an average of 43 million a year worldwide (3.3 per cent) – to nearly 1.4 billion in 2020 and 1.8 billion in 2030. Of these worldwide arrivals in 2020, 1.2 billion will be intraregional and 378 million will be long-haul travelers (Aderhold et al. 2013; UNWTO 2014).

Currently, almost half of all international tourist arrivals come from Europe, making up for the largest share of all arrivals worldwide (583.6 million or 40.9 per cent). This is followed by Asia and the Pacific (263.4 or 30.3 per cent), the Americas (181.5 or 22 per cent), Africa (55.8 or 5.9 per cent) and the Middle East (50.4 or 4 per cent) (UNWTO 2015). International tourist arrivals basically grew in all regions. However, the strongest growth has been noticed in the Americas with a growth rate of 8.1 per cent (UNWTO 2015).

The importance of tourism for developing countries

Especially in developing countries tourism is of major importance. In 80 per cent of all developing countries tourism is one of the top five sources of foreign exchange, being even the main source in almost one third of them (GTZ 2007). This particularly applies to small island states (SIDSs) and least developed countries (LDCs), in which the share of tourism to the foreign exchange earnings may account for over 50 per cent (GIZ 2014). For some LDCs, such as Cambodia, Laos or Cape Verde, tourism development has been especially dynamic since the turn of the millennium with an average annual growth of 11 per cent (UNWTO 2008).

Over the past decades tourism to developing countries has expanded continuously. Especially long-haul travel has increased over the last 20 years, so that developing countries could significantly enhance their market share in this segment. In consequence the change in the distribution of international tourist arrivals between advanced countries and developing countries has been extremely dynamic since the turn of the century (GIZ 2014). In 2012, developing and emerging countries received 485 million tourist arrivals (leisure and business travelers) accounting for 47 per cent of the global market shares (1.81 billion arrivals), while in 1997 their market share was only at 25 per cent (UNWTO 2014). The growth rates in these countries were on average significantly higher than the ones in developed countries (Strasdas & Zeppenfeld 2015). The major reason for this development is strong economic growth in the emerging countries (in Asia, Latin America and Central and Eastern Europe) and associated with that domestic and outbound tourism is rapidly increasing (UNWTO 2011).

This impressive development shows that tourism constitutes a promising and future-orientated industry for developing countries. Forecasts expect that the popularity of developing countries as tourist destinations will even exceed the advanced economies and represent 57 per cent of the global tourism market share until 2030 (GIZ 2014).

The significance of developing countries for the German outbound market

Travel and tourism to developing countries is also of great significance for the German outbound market. In 2011 every fifth German (in total 8.4 million citizens) travelled to a developing country for their main holiday, contributing to a respective market share in Germany of 16 per cent (compared to 6 per cent in 1991) (Aderhold et al. 2013; GTZ 2007). About two-thirds of these holidaymakers (5.8 million) went to nearby predominantly Islamic developing countries in the Mediterranean region, including Turkey and North African destinations such as Egypt, Tunisia and Morocco. The remaining 2.6 million visited more distant developing countries in Asia, Latin America/Caribbean and Sub-Saharan Africa (Aderhold et al. 2013). Table 9.2 shows the top ten destinations in developing countries of German outbound tourists in 2011.

Table 9.2 Top ten German tourist arrivals on developing countries, 2011

Destination	Number of arrivals (millions)
Turkey	4.557.460
Egypt	964.599
China	637.015
Thailand	619.133
Kenya	563.200
Tunisia	270.668
Brazil	241.739
India	240.235
South Africa	235.777
Morocco	219.576

Source: Based on Aderhold et al. 2013

Reasons for the general increase of the market share of journeys to foreign countries outside of Europe include among others: improved framework conditions (increased income, higher educational level, more leisure time, price reduction of airline travel etc.), increased travel experience, high prestige value of long-haul travels and the facilitated access to media reports or travel literature about foreign countries (Aderhold et al. 2013). Furthermore, the market potential for leisure travel to developing countries has increased over recent years and reflects an overall high level. It is expected that developing countries will remain attractive travel destinations for Germans in the future (Aderhold et al. 2013). According to a survey among German tour operators and tourism boards, tourism to the People's Republic of China, Vietnam, India, Turkey and South Africa will increase most significantly. In addition a general trend has been noted towards environmentally and socially responsible tourism as well as travel experiences which offer the chance to meet the local population and learn about their everyday life (Aderhold et al. 2013).

The greatest challenges in the future of German outbound travel to developing countries as seen by the tour operators will be the development of convincing offers and pricing. Particular emphasis needs to be placed on meeting certain quality standards against a backdrop of pricing pressure and security issues (GIZ 2014).

Impacts of tourism in developing countries

Economic dimension of impacts

As an industry with virtually uninterrupted growth rates and as a major contributor to world trade – 5 per cent of direct GDP and over 30 per cent of the world's exports of services – tourism is one of the main sources of foreign exchange income for developing countries (OECD et al. 2013). Directly and indirectly tourism represents about 8 per cent of the global workforce with a substantial multiplier effect. One job in the core tourism industry creates about one and a half additional jobs in the tourism-related economy (ILO 2011). Depending on the tourism structure, the size of the economy, the stage of development and the political framework, the positive economic effects of tourism in a developing country can vary substantially (Aderhold et al. 2013). A major challenge within the tourism industry is the fact that it is based on generally simple, low-paid, seasonal jobs, having a high fluctuation and gaps between the level of skills of local and foreign workers (GTZ 2007).

Despite these challenges developing countries show favourable conditions, due to unique natural and cultural attractions, to offer direct and indirect employment in tourism. This is particularly the case for the poor(er) and marginalized proportion of the population, especially in rural areas (housing 70 per cent of the developing world's extremely poor people). Tourism is consumed "on location", enabling easy market access and lower trade barriers (GTZ 2007). Employment of the poor in tourism businesses, the establishment of micro, small and medium enterprises (MSMEs) as well as community-based enterprises, supply of goods and services to tourism enterprises by the poor, direct sales of goods and services to tourists, the redistribution of proceeds from taxes or levies on tourism income and profits, as well as voluntary support giving are some of the ways tourism successfully contributes to poverty alleviation. Recognizing this force of employment, tourism is increasingly being addressed in poverty reduction plans issued by developing country governments (UNEP 2014; UNWTO 2009).

To evaluate the actual economic benefit of tourism in LDCs, the net foreign exchange balance is of importance as an indicator of developing countries' expenses for their touristic offer, which can be either generated through external effects (payment of interest to foreign credit and capital lenders, foreign human resources, marketing campaigns abroad, reliance on foreign tour operators, infrastructure development), internal effects (import of food and goods) or invisible effects (related to social and ecological mitigation costs). The amount of foreign exchange which leaves the country to finance imported services is referred to as "leakage". It varies between 5 per cent in Mexico or Turkey and 50 per cent in microstates such as the Caribbean (Aderhold et al., 2013).

In many cases developing countries are not taking sufficient advantage of efficient supply chain management in order to provide economic interlinkages and an enabling environment for trade opportunities between tourism and other related sectors, for example agriculture, handicraft and creative industries (UNEP 2014).

Although the vast majority of tourism businesses are MSMEs, the market is largely dominated by transnational corporations, leaving developing countries with little to no control over tourism development and limited "trickle-down effects" on local economies (GTZ 2007; UNEP 2014). For these reasons mainstream offers (all-inclusive packages) should be complemented with a range of other tourism-related products which foster a favourable market environment for different local tourism providers. Nevertheless mainstream models do not exclude positive direct and indirect effects on local economies, all depending on the country's capacity to provide directly for goods and services and the necessary skilled workforce (GIZ 2014).

SIDSs represent a specific group of developing countries with particular social, economic and environmental vulnerabilities (tourism and fisheries constituting the backbone of their economy) and a high degree of leakages (as high as 56 per cent). They struggle with limited resources, sensitive environments and distance from markets due to remote geographical locations. This leads to dependency and vulnerability, especially if touristic monocultures develop, which require the import of food and other goods. Depending on the circumstances, each SIDS handles these challenges differently, for example Cape Verde imports around 80 per cent of its food supplies, contrasting the Mauritian hotel sector which purchases more than 90 per cent of food items locally (UNEP 2014). Leakages from tourism directly translate to the degree of poverty reduction of tourism in a destination. At best, between one fifth and one third of overall tourist expenditure in a destination is captured by "the poor" from direct earnings and supply chains (UNEP 2011).

In many cases tourism positively spurs infrastructure developments and access to peripheral regions and the poor in the locality. Necessary public infrastructure, such as roads, airports, energy and water supply systems or sewage facilities would often not exist without tourism. However, the local population actually does not always benefit to the full extent from these new developments which are not necessarily implemented in the areas where they are most needed, but in those areas with most tourism demand (Aderhold et al. 2013).

Ecological dimension of impacts

The majority of tourism attractions in developing countries, such as pristine natural landscapes, rich wildlife, unique heritage sites and vibrant indigenous cultures are intrinsically linked to biodiversity (CBD n.d.). Of the world's biological and genetic resources, 80 per cent are found in developing countries (GIZ 2014), with SIDSs having an exceptionally high number and proportion of endemic species (UNWTO 2012). Developing countries make up the majority of the Parties to the Convention of Biodiversity (CBD), with many of these emerging countries being mainstream tourism destinations with over 5 million international arrivals per year (South Africa, Peru, Mexico and Brazil) (CBD n.d.; UNWTO 2013).

The ecological effects of tourism can be broadly grouped in direct and indirect impacts. Direct impacts relate to land use change, the exchange and extinction of species through for eample disturbance and introduction of alien species, harvesting of flora and fauna by tourists, alteration of landscapes and ecosystems of entire regions, biotic exchange and disruption of natural systems. Increased levels of emissions through leisure-related transport are seen as indirect impacts which can affect landscapes, ecosystems and sceneries, harming flora and fauna (UNEP 2014). Coastal environments (crucial for SIDSs) are particularly sensitive to these factors. Many examples exist where mismanaged tourism development has destroyed coastlines and put at risk the welfare of wildlife, vegetation and consequently also humans. For example one of the reasons for the devastating consequences of the 2004 tsunami in South-Southeast Asia was the lack of protecting mangroves which had been cleared to make way for tourism (Aderhold et al. 2013).

Despite potential threats, tourism can also provide major benefits for the environment in a destination and be a contributor to conservation efforts. Increased interest in the conservation of species and ecosystems can raise the environmental awareness of tourists and locals alike. Tourism can open up new sources of funding for conservation purposes, particularly relevant for protected areas, for which tourism often provides the only financing means. Entrance fees, concessions, taxes, corporate sponsorship and donations have been proven successful funding sources for many protected areas, for example the Madikwe Game Reserve in South Africa yielding $95,000 yearly from the operation of ecolodges as part of a public sector and private business concession. Ecotourism has been identified as the major means to foster a respectful tourism development in sensitive ecological areas (UNEP 2014). The supply and demand structures differ from those of mainstream, conventional tourism and are more environmentally friendly, contributing to the sustainable valorization of natural areas (GTZ 2007).

Increasingly tourism businesses and destinations recognize the positive potential which lies in environmentally sound tourism operations and management. Energy efficiency projects and waste management initiatives positively affect the bottom line within short payback times, create jobs and preserve the attractiveness and competitiveness of a destination (UNEP 2011). Nonetheless many hotels and leisure facilities in developing countries still have little to no waste water and garbage treatment systems in place. This poses not only threats to the natural environments but also bears health and safety risks. Conflicts of interest can occur when it comes to consumption of scarce resources, for example high water usage of tourism can be in direct competition with agriculture and local water needs. Tourism facilities are frequently disproportionately high in energy consumption and many tourists lack environmental awareness and responsible behaviour, giving little consideration to their water and energy consumption, waste disposal and choice of transportation when on vacation (Aderhold et al. 2013).

Climate change, driven by greenhouse gas (GHG) emissions, is one of the major threats to the international tourism industry, directly concerning the world community's future living conditions. The choice of increasingly remote places, growing average travel lengths and energy-intense transport modes are factors that impact on GHG forecasts. Tourism contributes to 5 per cent of global carbon dioxide emissions (40 per cent related to aviation), causing various types of direct impacts, such as changes in the length and quality of tourism seasons and weather extremes leading to increased operating costs and business risks. Additionally indirect climate change impacts will increasingly affect fresh water availability and quality, the properties of lake and river systems (water levels and temperatures), coastal erosion, ocean acidification or the spread of diseases. Tourist mobility will be influenced in the future due to higher transport costs as well as growing environmental awareness of the environmental consequences of travel (OECD & UNEP 2008). Developing countries are at the core of the debate, as many of them, especially SIDSs, have been identified as major hotspots of future negative climate change affects (UNEP 2014). Travel to developing countries, with its positive benefits and effects on the destination, almost automatically involves long-haul travel by plane. Facing the need for climate protection this predicament makes (long-distance) air travel the "Achilles heel of sustainable tourism development" (GIZ 2014).

Socio-cultural dimension of impacts

The socio-cultural impacts of tourism on host societies and cultures in developing countries cannot be generalized. Many of them are subjective and indirect effects which are difficult to measure and often appear much later in relation to the tourists' visit on site. Tourism can affect social structures, traditions and local livelihoods in different ways. This can happen either through increased competition for resources and land, price increases for locals or social changes, triggering crime, health issues, devaluation of traditions and other problems such as sexual and commercial exploitation (UNEP 2014).

Tourism in developing countries has often been referred to as modern-day cultural imperialism. Conflicts of land use might occur when tourism investors buy large areas of land, no longer granting locals access to these areas. Displacements can take place through market mechanisms and psychological pressure. Expropriations or expulsions have been reported in developing countries, often linked to purposes of nature conservation projects, but ultimately for tourism development. The basis of existence of many locals is threatened and social structures can be destabilized (Aderhold et al. 2013; GTZ 2007).

Mismanaged tourism development can lead to a loss of traditions and a commercialization of cultural heritage, staged authenticity and the risk of harming the religious–cultural background of a destination. Migratory processes are another reason for the loss of family and community structures. New social stratums form (through employment in tourism), but at the same time irreparable social distortions might occur, such as children being sent to beg on the street so they miss out on primary education (Aderhold et al. 2013). Especially in developing countries, contact with wealthy tourists can cause feelings of economic inferiority among locals, which might lead to criminality and hostility towards foreigners. Locals are confronted with tourists over long periods of time, whereas tourists encounter locals for brief cultural exchanges. Unintentionally tourists can act in a way which causes offense to local cultures, religious traditions and might involve the degradation of cultural sites and potential illegal vending of archaeological pieces or objects of art.

The degree to which negative socio-cultural impacts are likely to occur depends on three main conditions. First, the development status of the destination determines the degree of destabilization. This is especially of importance for small, rural, indigenous destinations, which are very different to the tourists' culture and sensitive to change. Second, the type of tourism determined by the scale of development (land consumption and number of tourist arrivals) plays a role. Well-planned slower developments are more favourable, giving locals enough space for adaptive strategies. The inter-linkage of the tourism structure and activities with the region is a key prerequisite, avoiding acculturation (cultural adaptation), opting for open forms of tourism such as backpacking or organized trips to indigenous population over all-inclusive resorts. Comfort standards play an important role in this regard, minimizing clashes between luxurious tourism facilities on the one side and more basic living conditions in the developing world on the other side. The third aspect is the mode of governance of the tourism development. Participative and independent tourism development (from planning to own businesses) is the only means to strengthen local identity and culture and limit the cultural dominance of tourism. It enables cultural independence, stability and the ability to use the positive force of tourism (Aderhold et al. 2013; Strasdas & Zeppenfeld 2015).

Despite negative influences, tourism often leads to a cultural revitalization through the enhancement of cultural values and traditions, strengthening the sense of culture and identity. Due to its informal structure, tourism, unlike many other sectors, has the potential to provide opportunities for migrant workers and those with social and capability disadvantages (UNEP 2014). Tourism can offer important new career opportunities, especially for women, who constitute 60–70 per cent of employees of the sector, and young people (50 per cent of the global tourism work force), as well as other disadvantaged groups, allowing for social inclusion (ILO 2011). Also it can hinder migration from rural areas and contribute to the stabilization of local communities. Revitalization of traditional branches of trade such as agriculture, fisheries or handicrafts is often another positive side-effect associated with tourism.

In countries with a painful past (civil wars, colonial times), tourism can help people come to terms with history. Encounters with locals can help educate and sensitize individuals from developed countries. Tourists' observations can also help the documentation of infringements of human rights (Aderhold et al. 2013), however, child labour, prostitution and sex tourism are other negative side-effects of international tourism. Income disparities foster prostitution in developing countries, often involving under-aged girls and boys or even young children. Tourism stakeholders are increasingly collaborating for the protection of children from sexual and commercial exploitation. The End Child Prostitution in Asian Tourism (ECPAT) Code has addressed the problem on a global scale, with more than 1,200 signatory tourism companies from 52 countries (UNEP 2014).

Tourism in German development cooperation

The role of tourism in development cooperation: Brief historical outline, main stakeholders and major international processes

As a diverse and interlinked industry, tourism has a wide range of direct and indirect stakeholders at the global level:

- Global tourism partnerships/networks
- Multilateral organizations and foundations
- Bilateral organizations
- Private sector businesses and tourism organizations
- Intergovernmental organizations (IGOs)
- Non-governmental organizations (NGOs)
- Education and training bodies

When it comes to the main actors in German development cooperation, Deutsche Gesellschaft für Internationale Zusammenarbeit (GIZ) GmbH, former Gesellschaft für Technische Zusammenarbeit (GTZ) and KfW development bank are the main implementing organizations and contractors on behalf of the Federal Ministry of Economic Cooperation and Development (BMZ). They cooperate with NGOs, political foundations and church organizations (e.g. Bread for the World). The aim of German development cooperation through BMZ in the field of sustainable tourism is to harvest the opportunities tourism provides for developing countries, while reducing its negative impacts. The protection of human rights in destinations and support in the introduction, implementation and monitoring of minimum social and environmental standards are other important priority areas for the German government. Therewith BMZ contributes to the achievement of the Millennium Development Goals (MDGs), especially to Goal 1: to eradicate extreme poverty and hunger (through sustainable economic development) and Goal 7: to ensure environmental sustainability (through environmental and climate protection and biodiversity conservation) (GIZ 2014).

In 2011 the BMZ published the strategy paper *The Contribution of Tourism to Sustainable Development and achieving the Millennium Development Goals* (BMZ 2011), highlighting its position regarding cooperation with international organizations such as UNWTO, the United Nations Commission on Sustainable Development (CSD) and the CBD. Tourism is not seen as a principal area of focus, but is granted an important role with future potential for German development cooperation, especially with regard to Germany's contribution to the achievement of the MDGs, the economic and cultural development of destinations, the promotion of decentralized flows of income and value chains and the strengthening of local cultures (BMZ 2011; GIZ 2014).

The engagement of German development cooperation in the field of tourism can be traced back to the 1960s and 1970s, when the first tourism initiatives in the framework of German development cooperation emerged, aiming at the promotion of tourism to developing countries. In this early "traditional tourism promotion" phase the focus was principally on infrastructure-related measures (hotel loans), marketing activities (such as financial support to attend trade fairs), combined with consulting for tourism businesses and capacity building (e.g. funding of hotel management schools). From the 1980s to the early 1990s, a nearly complete withdrawal from tourism promotion took place, due to harsh criticism related to rapid tourism growth in developing countries as a result of previous development initiatives which showed little concrete results. Due to a lack of a comprehensive tourism development approach, German development cooperation withdrew from tourism promotion in developing destinations.

The United Nations Conference on Environment and Development in Rio de Janeiro in 1992 triggered a worldwide sustainability debate which led to a revival of tourism activities in German development cooperation. Sustainable tourism development was introduced as a new guiding principle with a strong focus on ecological dimensions. Since 2000 tourism has secured itself a place on the international development agenda, with many development organizations pursuing tourism development projects directly or indirectly. The focus has shifted from community-based tourism and niche products to a wider tourism approach concerning ecological and social standards and development partnerships with the private sector (GTZ 2007). Germany, through the BMZ, has played an active role in supporting various initiatives which came out of the Rio movement.

The Marrakech Process (2003–2011), a bottom-up multi-stakeholder approach, was initiated in response to the call of the World Summit on Sustainable Development (WSSD) in Johannesburg in 2002 to increase international cooperation to support the development of the 10YFP on SCP. Sustainable tourism (including ecotourism) was one of the main SCP development areas addressed by the International Task Force on Sustainable Tourism Development (ITF-STD). This task force supported a variety of initiatives to promote sustainable tourism development (capacity building, policy recommendations and guidelines, new partnerships and networks) and was institutionalized in the form of the Global Partnership for Sustainable Tourism (GPST) in 2011. Germany, through BMZ, was a member of GPST since its beginnings, and in this function supported the organization in various ways, for example by hosting the 3rd Annual Conference of the GPST, which was held in Bonn in 2013. The GPST was one of the most important international sustainable tourism development initiatives, coordinated by the United Nations Environment Programme (UNEP) and UNWTO (GIZ 2014).

A further important milestone in international tourism development cooperation was the release of the CBD Guidelines on Biodiversity and Tourism Development (based on the CBD Guidelines), in which the German Federal Ministry of the Environment, Nature Conservation, Building and Nuclear Safety (BMUB) played a major role among other international actors. Germany participated in the 12th Conference of Parties in South Korea in 2014 which discussed the further implementation of the Strategic Plan for Biodiversity (2011–2020), noting the significance of the CBD Guidelines on Biodiversity and Tourism Development and laying out a number of initiatives (CBD 2014; GIZ 2014). 2012 marked the year in which sustainable tourism was for the first time officially anchored on a political platform facilitated by the UN system and was proposed as one of six major areas of activities under the 10YFP. Parallel to the official launch of the programme in November 2014, the GPST smoothly transitioned to the 10YFP Sustainable Tourism Programme. The 10YFP is based on four programme areas:

- Integrating SCP patterns in tourism-related policies and frameworks;
- Collaboration among stakeholders for the improvement of the tourism sector's SCP performance;
- Fostering the application of guidelines, tools and technical solutions to improve, mitigate and prevent tourism impacts and to mainstream SCP patterns;
- Enhancing sustainable tourism investment and financing for SCP.

Besides the official lead and co-lead, the 10YFP Secretariat is supported by a Multi-Stakeholder Advisory Committee (MAC), which plays a major role in advocating, advising, introducing new activities and linking ongoing activities to the Programme of Work, as well as supporting the initial projects under the 10YFP. Germany, through the BMUB, is one of the 22 members of the MAC (mandate of two years) (UNEP & UNWTO 2014).

Main fields of action and current activities projects

As of 2013 GIZ was implementing 40 regional and supraregional projects on behalf of BMZ of which tourism was either the primary component or one of several thematic areas. Project expenditures reached EU€7.3 million in 2013. The focus of the projects is on the promotion of economic development and environmental protection in developing countries in Africa, Eastern Europe, Asia and the Middle East (GIZ 2014).

Political and good governance approaches and instruments

The promotion of good governance and the creation of a stable political framework is one of the main objectives of the German development cooperation. Good governance generally means governance that is based on democracy and the rule of law. Governments must ensure the implementation of universal criteria, such as political participation, transparency, compliance with human rights, and guarantee its citizens a certain level of security and prosperity. Although the image of and the demand for a tourism destination do not depend directly on good governance, insufficient protection of human rights, undemocratic governance or serious security and health risks can have a negative effect on competitiveness. Therefore the existence of political frameworks and institutions that meet the standards of good governance are very important both for tourism in general and for German development cooperation's involvement in tourism in particular.

Many of the partner countries of German development cooperation that serve as major tourist destinations have been undergoing complex political and economic transformations, with examples including a number of tourist destinations in North Africa (most notably Tunisia and Egypt); Myanmar, a country on the verge of a lengthy socio-political transformation process; and the countries of the Balkans, which have been developing into market economies. These countries will need particularly strong international support in the future to strike a proper balance between reform processes and the resulting changes while maintaining a stable political, economic and social environment, which will enable them to remove potential obstacles to recent and expected developments and to pave the way towards sustainable tourism (GIZ 2014).

Regarding tourism, one major focus of development cooperation's activities is on human rights and its compliance with minimizing the negative effects of tourism on disadvantaged and marginalized groups, including women (promotion of gender equality), children (protection against sexual and economic exploitation), migrant workers (legalization and assimilation), indigenous people (rights to self-determination) and people with disabilities. In 2014, the GIZ Sector Project "Sustainable Development through Tourism" started a comprehensive international study on human rights and tourism on behalf of BMZ to provide a systematic overview of this complex issue and to suggest possible strategies to prevent human rights violations.

German development cooperation has also been working with ECPAT Germany to sensitize actors in the tourism sector to issues of sex tourism, HIV/AIDS and child prostitution through awareness-raising and training activities. Other important links between good governance and tourism include employment rights and mandatory social standards, opportunities for political participation for the local population and land use rights. In this context political participation needs to be understood as an indispensable element for achieving good governance, sustainable development, gender equality and poverty reduction in the framework of development cooperation projects. Formal and informal rights to consultation and decision-making for local actors regarding development policy activities are intended to ensure successful outcomes (i.e. participation as an instrument).

One of the most-advocated approaches to achieving the participation objective in tourism in recent years is that of community-based tourism, which is aimed at an active and comprehensive political and economic participation of the local population in tourism development. However, experience shows that its implementation through tourism projects is hampered by methodological and structural deficiencies similar to those generally faced in development projects. A major problem is that the term "participation" is only vaguely defined and often used ambiguously in different contexts. In some cases participation of the local population begins too late, or at a stage when essential decisions have already been made. Also, since participation concepts are often insufficiently integrated into the project planning process the general participation objective has so far done little to change the basic organizational framework of development projects. Moreover it must be taken into account that many community-based tourism projects focus too much on the integration of the local population without considering sufficiently the sides of the tourism supply and demand, and therefore fail their expected results and impacts.

Economic and employment approaches and instruments

As described above, tourism is one of the largest and fastest growing business sectors of all, both globally and also in regard to developing countries, generating foreign exchange and creating employment. It therefore must be considered as a major factor in terms of economic development in the developing and emerging world, not least as a promising option to reduce poverty effectively (GIZ 2014; GTZ 2007). This rising importance of the tourism sector for national economic growth in a large number of developing countries is mainly due to the pristine nature and landscapes and the cultural diversity found in many of those countries. Beautiful beaches, spectacular mountain ranges, tropical rainforests and a pleasant climate are among the attractions that cause large movements of people worldwide and therewith significantly contribute to the high tourism potential of a destination. Because many of those natural and cultural attractions are located in remote rural areas, tourism is especially capable of supporting and advancing regional economic cycles and promoting rural development. In addition, tourism is a service-based sector and one of the most manpower-intensive industries, with little potential for labour to become automatized and substituted by technology (GIZ 2014). Because of these characteristic features, tourism provides a variety of income and employment opportunities.

Nevertheless, the desired income and employment effects in favour and for the benefit of poor population groups do not necessarily evolve and adjust by themselves. What kind of economic effects may finally be achieved through tourism and to what extent the local population might profit largely depend on the scope and composition of the value chain established in the particular destination and on how local people are integrated into it. The tourism value chain is especially complex and provides many opportunities to produce broad-value added effects. In addition to the direct economic effects generated by the intrinsic tourism components and activities (accommodation, transport etc.), linkages with the wider economic environment (e.g. agricultural cultivation, food production, local handcrafts promotion etc.) indirectly contribute to the creation of further economic value by providing specific components of the tourism product (multiplier effect).

To fully develop the economic potential of tourism in a sustainable way, development cooperation and policy strives to support tourism activities based on the concept of a "green economy", as was postulated at the UNCSD in 2012 as one of the guiding themes relevant for successful sustainable development. This "green economy approach" describes "a way of doing business" which increases the quality of human well-being and secures social equity, while at the same time reducing environmental risks and ecological scarcities (UNEP 2015).

German development cooperation uses the so-called "value chain approach" as a poverty reduction strategy to establish sustainable and diversified economic structures in tourism destinations through and within tourism. The approach mainly aims "to integrate poor and marginalized population groups in the value chain and to rebalance the distribution of income within the value chain in favor of these groups" (GIZ 2014). It furthermore strives to develop, diversify and improve the quality of local production and service structures. A major focus of its work has been on MSMEs which represent the majority of private businesses in the partner countries. Activities not only focus on economic aspects, but also take social and ecological issues into account, such as energy consumption of the activities offered or the observance of human rights, fair working conditions etc. The operational level activities fostered by development cooperation include: provision of technical support in the establishment of business relationships, training and capacity development, process-orientated standards, support in the establishment of networks and cooperation structures and consulting on strategic marketing (GIZ 2014).

To determine reasonable and targeted measures for the purpose of sustainable tourism development a detailed analysis of the tourism value chain must be conducted in the areas under focus. The identification of weaknesses and potentials of individual components of the chain allow for qualified strategies and recommendations in the areas, in which poverty reducing and sustainable economic effects are most likely to be achieved (Aderhold et al. 2013; GIZ 2014). Furthermore, the effectiveness of the value chain is directly related to the amount of goods and services of appropriate quality and the number of skilled people available in a destination. Because of that, attempts of German development cooperation in tourism promotion are not limited to niche segments but also more strongly integrate other segments, such as mass or luxury tourism, to more optimally use the potential which tourism provides for poverty reduction (GIZ 2014; GTZ 2007).

The economic potential of tourism must be explored in relation to other relevant economic sectors of a country or region. Often tourism is considered as the ultimate solution for income generation in rural and peripheral areas without estimating its actual potential, which might not be sufficient to meet the economic needs to contribute to poverty reduction in a suitable and substantial way (Strasdas & Zeppenfeld 2015). Furthermore, total economic dependence on the tourism sector and the establishment of touristic monostructures should be avoided, as tourism might be subject to short-lived trends and fluctuations in demand (GIZ 2014).

Environmental and ecological approaches and instruments

Considering the tourism industry's role as a victim and polluter when it comes to environmental issues, development cooperation aims to contribute to the protection of natural resources and reduce ecological risks, especially focusing on thematic areas such as biodiversity conservation, climate change and climate protection, as well as resource efficiency. As natural resources serve as fundamental sources of living and human well-being, environmental problems are closely related to (other) developmental issues such as poverty reduction. The challenge is to develop tourism in harmony with environmental considerations, thus minimizing tourism's negative impacts and simultaneously maximizing its positive contributions, for instance to nature conservation or climate protection and not least the quality of life of local people. One precondition is to economically and ideally value the natural and environmental assets, which are so important for tourism, and to recognize these values in tourism planning.

Development projects and services concerning the protection of biodiversity mainly concentrate their support on a sustainable development and management of tourism in protected areas, as the potential for land use conflicts between tourism and nature conservation is comparatively high in those areas. The extent of damage depends much on how tourism is managed in such areas. If tourism development is managed sustainably, its impacts might be limited because compared to other industries, tourist activities have the advantage that they are non-consumptive, which means that they do not withdraw goods from nature. Due to this characteristic feature of tourism it meets at best the prerequisites to fulfill the so-called concept of "conservation through sustainable use". Moreover, tourism and nature conservation may be seen as "allies", as they can cooperate with each other to their mutual benefit and peacefully coexist side by side. Both are interested in achieving conservation goals to provide maximum benefit for protected areas and for tourism. In this respect, the Guidelines on Biodiversity and Tourism Development (SCBD 2004) represent an important instrument concerning the implementation of tourism in ecologically valuable sites and protected areas.

Based on this "conservation through sustainable use" strategy, German Development cooperation applies measures to promote sustainable tourism development, striving to foster appropriate preventive action and to avoid potential conflicts of interest between nature conservation and tourism. Measures in protected areas include for example: tourism zoning, visitor management and information and creation of appropriate infrastructure, as well as visitor monitoring. Nature tourism has been identified as a possibility to promote sustainable tourism development in such sensitive areas under protection (=ecotourism), as it provides a concept demanding specific environmental and social outcomes, contributing to the valorization of natural areas. In addition, sustainable tourism is promoted as an instrument to generate income and financially support protected areas and nature conservation. Especially in developing and emerging countries, which are generally high in biodiversity and whose protected areas are chronically underfunded, tourism may provide additional sources of financing. To support the implementation of strategies and measures, development cooperation offers consultancy services to the partner countries to provide local actors with strategic, methodological and practical support.

Depending on the degree a destination and its tourism enterprises are affected by environmental impacts, appropriate strategies in the areas of disaster, risk and environmental management must be considered. An increasing number of destinations and tourism enterprises recognized the related problems and have already started to take action initiating a variety of projects and activities to counteract the results of climate change and resource consumption. For example, water consumption through a combination of technical, operational and creative policies will be considerably reduced.

In the pursuit of an economic transformation towards a green economy, German development cooperation supports tourism players in the partner countries in their process of climate change adaption and mitigation efforts. An emphasis is put on the development and implementation of strategies and specific measures to reduce GHG emissions, for example the promotion of renewable energy or the increase of energy efficiency, within the sector and to adapt tourist destinations and local enterprises at site to respective impacts, which help them to reduce their vulnerability, for example measures for coastal protection. Consulting on environmental management for destinations and tourism enterprises is also an important service provided by development cooperation, which encourages the introduction of environmental management systems, the development of environmental standards and thus implementation of environmentally sound technologies and innovations. For example, sustainable water and waste water management in hotels and leisure facilities might be able to reduce water consumption by using a combination of technical, operational and design measures without loss of comfort.

Further activities include feasibility studies on resource- and climate-related issues in tourism, systematic advice on aspects of resource and climate protection in projects and in policy and investment programmes in the area of tourism, consulting on environmental management for tourism enterprises, planning and implementation of dialogue processes on resource and climate policy in tourism and activities to raise public awareness of aspects of resource and climate protection in the partner countries (GIZ 2014).

Socio-cultural approaches and instruments

One of the most important approaches to develop and design tourism in developing countries in a socially more sustainable way is the enhanced participation and co-determination of the local population. Tourism development promoted by foreign investors often not only neglects the economic interest of local communities but further enhances the cultural dominance of tourism at a site. Against this, participative and co-determined tourism development offers local groups the opportunity to design tourism activities (to a certain extent) according to their own culture and habits, or at least more strongly protect them (Strasdas & Zeppenfeld 2015).

Participation fosters a better linkage of tourism activities with its surrounding environment and therewith helps to recognize and at best to avoid socio-cultural conflicts (acculturation, cultural changes, degradation of historical sites, rising prices etc.) in a tourism destination, for example by having local people and/or communities participate in the planning and implementing process of tourism development and integrate them in decision-making (a bottom-up approach). On the one hand this gives people an active and influential role in the process (ownership) and on the other hand it supports them to develop respective competencies and skills (empowerment). Besides this political participation, which refers to local people "having a word to say", participation can also be of an economic nature, implying that local people economically benefit from the tourism business established or at least will be compensated for inevitable use restrictions with alternative income possibilities through tourism, for example in and around protected areas.

Tourism activities and projects can be carried out with different degrees and intensities of participation of local communities, both in respect to planning-related co-determination and regarding economic shares. The degrees of participation in tourism development range from one in which the entire community or parts of it (e.g. a number of families) would conduct their entire planning and implementation of a tourism project themselves, making their own decisions, to a level in which the community or parts of it only participate passively, for example through the receipt of benefits without being involved in the tourism development process, in which decisions are made by others. An intermediate level would, for example, include contractual agreements or a joint venture between a community or an individual member of a community with outside investors or other business partners (Strasdas 2002).

To what degree and intensity participation should happen depends on specific circumstances in the community at site as well as on their interest, expertise and abilities. It therefore must be considered and weighed case by case to produce the maximum benefit for the local people involved. In order to empower the locals to represent their interests and needs by themselves they have to be incorporated in the development process at an early stage of the project to be implemented. One of the most commonly used approaches in development cooperation to support participation on local and community levels during the implementation of tourism projects is the concept of community-based tourism (CBT). This is a specific attempt to tackle social problems, especially linked to tourism, through tourism and ultimately to contribute to poverty reduction, especially in rural and peripheral areas.

CBT is considered as a form of tourism in which a significant number of local people have significant influence on and substantial control over the development and management of tourism in their region. Furthermore, the major proportion of benefits remains within the local area and its economy (Häusler & Strasdas 2003). The main objectives of CBT projects are to provide the local population with opportunities to politically and/or economically participate in tourism development and management. In most cases, CBT is implemented in the scope of a specific development cooperation project together with a local partner organization in the region. With the support of an external consultant, the tourism potential of the wider community will be identified, infrastructure will be optimized and respective tourism activities will be created. Ideally, every community member is provided with a certain task or assignment and has a share in the income through tourism.

In practice the CBT approach is often difficult to implement and fails to achieve its objectives and the desired outcomes. Though there are some successful examples of CBT projects, the approach often entails problems and many other projects reveal deficits, especially because of the questionable economic viability of tourism activities. Further problems and deficits may encompass the lack of basic requirements of a tourism destination, for example connectivity and accessibility, due to missing (public) infrastructure, insufficient attractiveness and tourism potential of the area, lack of tourism know-how and poor professionalism on behalf of the development expert, insufficient market research and know-how and lack of target group orientation etc. Furthermore, social tensions might occur within the community if benefits are not equally distributed among the community members. A lack of tourism experience and know-how by community members might cause overextension.

To avoid misguided planning and false investment decisions, a rapid destination assessment is often used in the first development stage to analyse relevant key factors (tourism potential, tourism products, infrastructure, local conditions, competition and impeding factors) for local and regional tourism development projects and assess their economic viability. This assessment allows the collection of quick information on whether the community or municipal areas provide an enabling environment for tourism development. An initial stakeholder analysis and face-to-face interviews with key players form the basis of a rapid destination assessment, together with a benchmark analysis of comparable competitor destinations (GIZ 2014).

The subject of participation and the CBT approach are closely related to the issue of education and capacity building, which also plays a significant role in development cooperation as it is a constitutional element and prerequisite for a sustainable development process and empowerment of local people to successfully participate. Because of its complex supply chain and links with various other economic sectors, tourism heavily depends on a reasonable level of education and training among the population (GTZ 2007).

Development cooperation might contribute to the building of the necessary capacities and skills in the field of tourism and therewith helps to ensure that adequately trained local staff are available for tourism businesses. In response to the strong demand for training programmes on issues of sustainable tourism from partner countries and from internal and external experts in German development cooperation, the GIZ Sector Project "Sustainable Development through Tourism" was commissioned by BMZ in 2013 to implement a human capacity development (HCD) programme which involved, among other things, the development of a conceptual framework for training programmes in this area (GIZ 2014).

Conclusions

Conclusions and bottlenecks

Tourism has grown faster in the last 60 years than most other industries. The changes in the distribution of international tourist arrivals between advanced countries and developing countries have been extremely dynamic, especially since the turn of the century. 2015 was the first year in which developing countries record more international tourist arrivals than the advanced countries, and it is safe to assume that their market share will further increase in future years.

The rapid growth of the tourism industry and the worldwide commitment to sustainable economic development agreed on at the Rio Conference back in the early 1990s have played a major role in the German development cooperation's decision to advance the implementation of sustainable tourism in its partner countries. For a long time ecological and environmental issues played a predominant role within the global approach to foster sustainable tourism, while economic impacts, opportunities and requirements were widely underestimated or ignored. Especially in recent it has been observed that this perception has changed and the economic dimension of tourism has come to the fore. Currently the tourism sector is understood increasingly as a strategic instrument for poverty alleviation and reduction, as well as a key factor for regional and local economic prosperity for many destinations.

For German development cooperation, tourism is not an explicit field of action. Due to its economic importance and its many linkages to a variety of major issues of development policy, it has been playing an important role in many partner countries and projects, such as in projects concerned with sustainable economic development and poverty reduction, rural development or environmental, climate and biodiversity protection. It is important to note that the purpose of this involvement is not to promote the tourism sector itself, but rather to achieve economic, ecological and social development effects through and within tourism. For this reason, the activities referred to here in this chapter are not limited to the niche segments of the market, but include all forms of tourism, even and especially the mass tourism market.

However, even though a broader acceptance and recognition of tourism as an important field of activity already exists, its potential for fostering positive development effects and avoiding or minimizing negative impacts (e.g. on the environment) are still underestimated within German development cooperation. Many development experts lack the necessary awareness for taking tourism as a serious development option into account or do not have the required technical expertise for setting up effective tourism interventions and projects in an appropriate manner. As a consequence, tourism projects sometimes fail to achieve the desired results or they are supported inefficiently by distributing limited resources across too many activities without analysing in advance their feasibility and potential for bringing positive impacts. Although the GIZ sector project "Sustainable Development through Tourism" functions as an entity which is dealing exclusively with tourism, it does not have sufficient financial and human means for greater interventions and for serving comprehensively as a hub or knowledge platform for development projects that are directly or indirectly engaged in tourism. It still seems to be difficult to internally communicate the numerous linkages and synergies between tourism and the other fields of activity of development cooperation and to convince important stakeholders of the benefits which could be achieved through an increased engagement in this sector.

Due to these reasons development cooperation's opportunities for using tourism as a promising instrument for economic prosperity as well as cultural and ecological conservation in developing countries have not yet been tapped sufficiently. This appears to be one of the major bottlenecks, in particular taking into account that tourism for many developing countries represents the most or one of the most important economic sectors. Nevertheless, the existence of a BMZ position paper on *The Contribution of Tourism to Sustainable Development and achieving the Millennium Development Goals* (BMZ 2011), as well as the publication of the technical handbook *Tourism Planning in Development Cooperation* by GIZ (2014), are clear signals towards a more holistic and strategic approach at the policy and operational level that are expected to lead to a reinforced engagement in tourism.

Recommendations and outlook

Based on the above-mentioned conclusions and identified bottlenecks, we can provide some essential strategic and operational recommendations how the general performance of tourism as an important field of action within development cooperation can be further improved in the future.

Strategic recommendations include:

- Fostering increased awareness-raising efforts to promote the importance of tourism as a promising field of activity of development cooperation among policy makers and development cooperation experts.
- Establishing communication structures among those projects, advisors and experts who are dealing with tourism within development cooperation to foster a better knowledge and experience exchange as well as mutual technical support.
- Improving the institutional integration of the field of tourism within development cooperation by creating linkages and strengthening synergies to other fields of action (e.g. private sector promotion, climate change, biodiversity, resource efficiency, social standards, good governance).
- Expanding the promotion and application of existing approaches, tools and instruments for sustainable tourism development among projects, advisors, experts and local (public and private) stakeholders (e.g. sustainable tourism policies and control instruments, socio-economic impact analyses, value chain analyses, participatory development approaches for sustainable tourism strategies, supply chain management approaches).
- Encouraging active communication of existing HCD training modules on sustainable tourism, aiming to encourage projects, advisors, experts and local (public and private) stakeholders to improve their technical skills and expertise in this field.
- Fostering consideration of the BMZ position paper on *The Contribution of Tourism to Sustainable Development and achieving the Millennium Development Goals*, as in 2015 the MDGs expired and UN member states finalized the Sustainable Development Goals (SDGs) that will replace them.

Operational recommendations include:

- Integrating the local population into the touristic supply chain is the key to economic benefit for the respective community. Therefore the expansion of political consulting to facilitate the integration of poverty reduction strategies through tourism into policies and public action plans is required. Moreover, capacity building is crucial in order to enable the local communities to identify worthy cultural elements and choose the right channel to market them.
- Encouraging process-oriented support from the tourism private sector in implementing pro-poor approaches and establishing linkages to other sectors.
- Expanding joint activities to resolve existing market access constraints for MSMEs and deficits in tourism education (with a focus on women and low-skilled workers).
- Supporting destinations to link sustainable destination planning with sustainable fiscal and government investment policies, access to finance (especially for MSMEs) and increasing local involvement.
- Enhancing capacities of governments and tourism policy makers to attract both domestic and foreign investors to invest increasingly in sustainable tourism based on investment-friendly (e.g. subsidies, tax incentives) and at the same time sustainability-oriented policies, regulations and guidelines.
- Encouraging public–private partnerships, joint ventures etc. to increase the likelihood of private investments.
- Expanding climate change strategies as well as mitigation and adaption activities, especially in the most vulnerable destinations. Regional and country-specific approaches can provide immediate solutions and incentives for multi-hazard, disaster and water management tools, especially for endangered regions such as in the Caribbean and Asia-Pacific.
- Overcoming the green gap (between the public's increased awareness on one side and the remaining unwillingness to consume more sustainably on the other side) has to be tackled with effective communication and transparent certification. The private sector needs to be incentivized to focus on sustainable product development, which triggers demand in the market.
- Integrating regulations on biodiversity conservation and natural area protection into tourism policies should be given more attention in the future. Especially in developing countries, strong institutional guidance is needed to foster a structured approach. Integrated land use planning, together with the creation of transregional conservation areas, is an important means to strengthen collaboration among major stakeholders to create synergies and diverse tourism products. Enforcement of sustainable management of protected areas (e.g. through zoning, visitor guidance, information centres and visitor monitoring) is essential.

Over the last 20 years the general concern and engagement among main stakeholder groups towards sustainable tourism policies and practices has increased substantially. Evidence about the causes, risks and consequences of unsustainable forms of tourism has been obtained, and apart from particular remaining questions, for example about climate change impacts on and through tourism and evidence of child labour, which still need to be addressed, a significant number of studies, approaches, methods, instruments and guidelines already exist which are suitable for mainstreaming sustainable tourism. However, due to missing implementation on a wider scale, an extensive change in the tourism industry concerning its sustainability requirements has not been achieved yet. This is because too many direct and indirect, public and private actors (including the consumer) still lack awareness, resulting in reluctance and unwillingness to act. In this context, development cooperation by external stakeholders will play an essential role in the future, helping to overcome existing gaps and constraints, to foster appropriate approaches, to encourage strategic relationships and multi-stakeholder processes, as well as to implement the activities required for a sustainable management of tourism in developing countries.

References

Aderhold, P.; Kösterke, A.; Laßberg, D. v.; Steck, B.; Vielhaber, A. (2013): *Tourismus in Entwicklungs- und Schwellenländer: Eine Untersuchung über Dimensionen, Strukturen, Wirkungen und Qualifizierungsansätze im EntwicklungsländerTourismus – unter besonderer Berücksichtigung des deutschen Urlaubsreisemarktes*. Studienkreis für Tourismus und Entwicklung e.V. Seefeld.

BMZ (Bundesministerium für wirtschaftliche Zusammenarbeit und Entwicklung) (2011): *Der Beitrag des Tourismus zur nachhaltigen Entwicklung und zur Erreichung der Millenniumsentwicklungsziele: Ein Positionspapier des BMZ: Strategiepapier 2*. Bonn. Available: www.bmz.de/de/publikationen/reihen/strategiepapiere/Strategiepapier301_02_2011.pdf.

CBD (Convention on Biological Diversity) (2014): *Decisions Adopted by the Conference of the Parties at its Twelfth Meeting*. Available: www.cbd.int/doc/decisions/cop-12/full/cop-12-dec-en.pdf.

CBD (n.d.): *Tourism for Development and Nature Conservation – Resources for Tourism Planners and Practitioners*. Available: www.cbd.int/doc/publications/development/brochure-tourism-en.pdf.

GIZ (Deutsche Gesellschaft für Internationale Zusammenarbeit GmbH) (2014): *Tourism Planning in Development Cooperation: A Handbook. Challenges – Consulting Approaches – Practical Examples – Tools*. Author: Matthias Beyer. Available: www.giz.de/fachexpertise/downloads/giz2014-en-tourism-handbook.pdf

GTZ (Deutsche Gesellschaft für Technische Zusammenarbeit) (2007): *Tourism as a Field of Activity in German Development Cooperation: A Basic Overview, Priority Areas for Action and Strategic Recommendations*. Authors: Beyer, Matthias/ Häusler, Nicole/ Strasdas, Wolfgang. Eschborn. Available: www.giz.de/fachexpertise/downloads/giz2012-en-tourism-field-of-activity.pdf.

Häusler, N.; Strasdas, W. (2003): *Training Manual for Community-based Tourism*. InWent – Internationale Weiterbildung und Entwicklung gGmbH. Zschortau, Germany.

ILO (International Labour Organizaton) (2011): *Poverty Reduction through Tourism*. Available: www.ilo.org/wcmsp5/groups/public/@ed_dialogue/@sector/documents/publication/wcms_154936.pdf.

OECD; UNEP (Organization for Economic Co-operation and Development; United

Nations Environment Programme) (2008): *Climate Change and Tourism Policy in OECD Countries*. Available: www.oecd.org/cfe/tourism/48681944.pdf.

OECD; UNWTO; WTO (United Nations World Tourism Organization; World Trade Organization (2013): *Aid for Trade and Value Chains in Tourism*. Available: www.wto.org/english/tratop_e/devel_e/a4t_e/global_review13prog_e/tourism_28june.pdf.

SCBD (Secretariat of the Convention on Biological Diversity) (2004): *Guidelines on Biodiversity and Tourism Development*. Montreal, Canada.

Strasdas, W. (2002): *The Ecotourism Training Manual for Protected Area Managers*. German Foundation for International Development (DSE) – Zschortau.

Strasdas, W.; Zeppenfeld, R. (2015): *Nachhaltiger Tourismus*. Studienbrief. Fernstudium Nachhaltige Entwicklungszusammenarbeit. Technische Universität Kaiserslautern.

UNEP (United Nations Environment Programme) (2011): *Tourism – Investing in energy and resource efficiency*. Available: www.unep.org/resourceefficiency/Portals/24147/scp/business/tourism/greeneconomy_tourism.pdf.

UNEP (2014): *Stock Taking – Towards the Development of the Sustainable Tourism Programme of the 10YFP*. Available: www.unosd.org/content/documents/606stock_taking_10yfp_tourism_final.pdf.

UNEP (2015): *What is an 'Inclusive Green Economy'?* Available: http://web.unep.org/greeneconomy/what-inclusive-green-economy

UNEP; UNWTO (United Nations World Tourism Organization) (2014): The 10YFP Programme on Sustainable Tourism. Available: www.unep.org/10yfp/Portals/50150/downloads/Brochure_10YFP_Tour.pdf

UNWTO (United Nations World Tourism Organization) (2008): Developing Countries lead Dynamic World Tourism Growth. Press release, Berlin/Madrid, 6 March 2008, in: Strasdas, W.; Zeppenfeld, R. (2015): *Nachhaltiger Tourismus. Studienbrief. Fernstudium Nachhaltige Entwicklungszusammenarbeit*. Technische Universität Kaiserslautern.

UNWTO (2009): *Tourism Contributing to Poverty Alleviation*. Available: http://step.unwto.org/sites/all/files/docpdf/tourismcontributingtopovertyalleviation2009.pdf.

UNWTO (2011): *Tourism Towards 2030. Global Overview*. Madrid, Spain.

UNWTO (2012): *Challenges and Opportunities for Tourism Development in Small Island Developing States*. Available: www2.unwto.org/en/publication/challenges-and-opportunities-tourism-development-small-island-developing-states-0.

UNWTO (2013): *Sustainable Tourism for Development Guidebook*. Available: http://icr.unwto.org/en/content/guidebook-sustainable-tourism-development.

UNWTO (2014): *UNWTO Tourism Highlights, 2014 Edition*. Available: http://mkt.unwto.org/publication/unwto-tourism-highlights-2014-edition.

UNWTO (2015): *UNWTO Tourism Highlights, 2015 Edition*. Available: www.e-unwto.org/doi/pdf/10.18111/9789284416899.

WTTC (World Travel & Tourism Council) (2015): *Travel & Tourism Economic Impact 2015 – World*. London, UK.

10 Urban sustainability

Priorities for international cooperation

Frauke Kraas and Mareike Kroll

Introduction

As a direct result of the "urban transition", cities have progressively gained importance as living space for more than half of the world's population, in addition to their political, economic and cultural functions. These urbanization processes are associated with certain risks, but also offer enormous potential for sustainable development.

At this point, the regional differences of urbanization are becoming essential. The most important drivers of urbanization are economic and demographic growth processes. However, environmental, sociocultural and political factors also play an essential role. The causes of worldwide urbanization, which occurs at regionally differing rates, can only be outlined in general terms. Because urbanization levels in the countries of Europe and North and South America had already reached around 80 per cent in 2015, urban growth will primarily occur in Africa and Asia in the coming decades with an expected growth between 2015 and 2050 from 40 per cent to 56 per cent and 48 per cent to 64 per cent respectively (UN 2014). Due to these differences in development, cities in different countries face greatly different challenges. Most important for urban sustainability – on the global to local scale – will be the concepts and strategies of urbanization in the regional contexts.

The urbanization process in African and Asian countries is accompanied by complex transformation processes. Urban growth is still strongly associated with megacities, which exert a strong attraction as regional, national or even international centres. But growth is increasingly shifting also to cities with more than 1 million inhabitants (UN 2014). When regulatory processes are lacking, or insufficient, and expansion is rapid, urbanization processes are associated with various risks. Waste and emissions from industry, the service sector, and households can lead to significant pollution of air, water and soils; locational disadvantages for the urban economy arise from overloaded infrastructure; a lack of sufficient workplaces results in a pronounced increase in the proportion of populations affected by poverty, which in turn can cause strong socioeconomic disparities with an increasing chasm between poor and wealthy populations (Mertins 1998).

Through the (partial) loss of regulatory capacity, informal and illegal structures gain in importance. Juxtaposed with these shortcomings are a variety of different advantages that are conducive to sustainable development in cities: through higher density, land consumption and energy use can be curbed. Cities, as centres of innovation, attract business enterprises. In addition, they typically offer better social services such as superior education and health systems for the population. Through the increased availability of information and through activities of non-government organizations (NGOs), urban populations can actively participate in political decision-making processes.

Urban sustainability: Definition, goals and dimensions

The concept of sustainable development assumes that it can be applied across space, time and society, and accordingly it should also be applicable to urban circumstances. Agenda 21 was the first global attempt to develop and implement an urban sustainability programme in 1992, followed by the Habitat II meeting 1996 focusing on sustainable settlements (Vojnovic 2014). Megacities were named as one of six key trends that will play a pivotal role in determining the future of humanity (BMBF 2003, p. 7). After all, cities are a central building block for global sustainable development (Hardoy et al. 2001, p. 339) as:

•   More than half of humanity lives in cities and urban areas and, in general, the countries with the highest levels of urbanization (e.g. USA) are also the ones with the highest resource consumption and waste and emission outputs.
•   Worldwide, cities exhibit the highest resource consumption and waste production due to the high concentration of industry and population. In addition, an above-average proportion of high-income earners live in cities, and this section of the population tends to have higher resource consumption.
•   As a consequence, urban policies and development have a significant impact on the extent of future resource use and the generation of emissions worldwide. Accordingly, measures of resource conservation and emission reduction in cities can have significant positive effects on global trends.

Urban sustainability or sustainability in urban areas?

The terms "urban sustainability" and "sustainability in urban areas" are often used interchangeably in similar contexts. However, these two perspectives have different connotations: the concept of "urban sustainability" has a theory-based, system-oriented perspective of the system "city", in which an equilibrium state is aspired. The investigation of "sustainability in urban areas", in contrast, takes place from a process- and actor-oriented perspective that takes into consideration interactions, process rates and divergence of interests of different stakeholder groups and is intended to foster concerted action of institutions, stakeholders and citizens under the joint imperative of sustainability (Kraas 2005, p. 35).

Furthermore, the terms "sustainable city", or "sustainable urbanization", should be understood in a metaphorical sense, as cities as such cannot be sustainable. Though cities can increase their degree of sustainability, for example through increased energy efficiency or improvements of public services, they are always connected to other local and global ecological and economic systems. Ultimately, the primary cause of many urban problems is related to the high population densities, lifestyles and economic activities of urban populations through their comparatively high demands on resources. Hence, on a structural level, cities can at best be designed so that the needs of the population are satisfied in a less non-sustainable way (Satterthwaite 1999, p. 97). In addition, quality and quantity of non-sustainable influences vary so strongly that generalizations are not easily made.

Definitions

Although the guiding principle of a sustainable city is prevalent and embedded in many local, national and international policies, visions and programmes, a generally binding definition for urban sustainability or sustainable cities has yet to be formalized. Thus, although the idea of a sustainable city is very attractive, it is also very complex and difficult to operationalize, because of the multi-dimensionality of the concept and its use in different scientific disciplines. Hence, despite the development of many initiatives on urban sustainability and the different laws in which sustainability goals have been stipulated, it is difficult to assess to what extent progress has been made in the last decades (Williams 2009, p. 129).

An often-cited definition of a sustainable city is provided by the Environment Programme and the Human Settlement Programme of the United Nations (UN-Habitat/UNEP 2001, p. 4):

> A sustainable city is a city where achievements in social, economic, and physical development are made to last. It has a lasting supply of environmental resources on which its development depends, using them only at a level of sustainable yield. A sustainable city maintains a lasting security from environmental hazards that have the potential to threaten development achievements, allowing only for acceptable risk.

The definition of UNEP and UN-Habitat is based on the three pillar model, and the political dimension is not taken into consideration. Accordingly, the sustainable city constitutes a new moral space, in which social values are changed, and durable social, economic and ecological relationships are established (Whitehead 2003, p. 1186). However, in this sustainability definition, the spatial focus on the urban system is rather weak and its regional and global linkages are not considered. Hardoy et al. (2001, p. 354) formulated a very extensive, widely accepted definition that articulates the different goals of sustainable development in an urban context.

In order to safeguard the satisfaction of ecological, economic and social needs for future generations, the following basic conditions have to be met according to Hardoy et al. (Kroll & Kraas 2013):

- For ecological sustainability, the use of finite resources has to be minimized, for example through the application of more efficient technologies and recycling. Regenerative resources have to be used sustainably.
- Cultural, historical and natural capital in cities has to be preserved as they are not replaceable and therefore also not renewable. Examples include heritage buildings and historic city centres that contribute to the identity of a culture, and parks and open spaces that offer leisure and recreation functions.
- The existing social and human capital has to be preserved and further developed for future generations. This type of capital includes sustainable social relationships (trust, reliability, help and support), as well as institutional structures. Social and human capital generally refers to the transfer of knowledge, experience and cultural heritage of a nation or social group.

At its core, the concept reconciles "development" at the local, regional and global levels with the "environment": "For cities, sustainable development is about developing systems of governance that can reconcile meeting 'development' goals with the 'environment'" (Hardoy et al. 2001, p. 338). This summary, on the one hand, clarifies the importance of political institutions for regulatory processes and, on the other hand, demonstrates how difficult it is to reconcile urban development with environmental concerns. Many cities with strong socioeconomic development exhibit environmental sustainability deficits, either on the local or global level through externalization of environmental costs. Because of the dependence of urban areas on the resources of their hinterland, these environmental impacts extend beyond the boundaries of cities (Allen 2009, p. 2).

The spatial perspective is emphasized more strongly in Allen's (2009) approach to urban sustainability, which adds both the sustainability of the built environment and political sustainability to the three established dimensions: the character and planning of the urban built environment may significantly influence the implementation success of sustainability goals in the social, economic and ecological dimensions. Ultimately, these processes are regulated at the political level: political sustainability addresses the quality of regulatory processes, the relationships between different actors and the opportunities for civil society participation. This approach enables a stronger differentiation and a more precise operationalization of individual dimensions.

Due to differences in perspectives and understanding of sustainability, thus there is no clear definition for sustainable city or sustainable development in urban areas. There are also no clear statements on the consequences of the spatial focus on the system "city". Nevertheless, it is becoming apparent that cities not only pose special challenges, due to their multifaceted concentration processes and complex structures, but also offer more opportunities for the implementation of sustainable (or more appropriately: less non-sustainable) structures and processes than peripheral areas. However, for the same reason, cities are also more susceptible to most sustainability risks.

In general, in planning and development practice, many environmental, economic, social, political, demographic, institutional and cultural goals are subsumed under the guiding principle of sustainable development that most city administrations and organizations can claim to be operating sustainably in at least one sector (for example sustainable agriculture, sustainable industrial development, sustainable livelihood systems, sustainable development projects), even if their actions are to the contrary in other sectors. For example, environmental quality is increasing in many cities of the Global North, because resource- and pollution-intensive production is outsourced to other countries.

Urban structures and processes are also the subject of multifaceted negotiation processes. The creation of "sustainable cities" is not a technocratic exercise in city planning and design, but part of a complex socioeconomic regulation process. Thus, is not about reciting universal principals of urban development, but about analysing different pathways through which, in different locations and at different times, social, economic and environmental strategies of urban development emerge. Further, the question of who profits most from these formulated strategies must be addressed (Whitehead 2003, p. 1202). Sustainability principles have to be implemented differently in their respective urban contexts. Asian cities exhibit, for example, different structures and problems than European and North American cities, because globalization-related transformation processes take hold with different spatial and temporal patterns (Sorensen 2004, p. 5).

The dimensions of sustainable urban development

Building on the theory-oriented investigation of urban sustainability, the individual dimensions of urban sustainability need to be discussed in more depth. However, throughout this analysis, one must bear in mind that the terms "social urban sustainability" or "economic urban sustainability" have yet to be explicitly defined. Because individual sustainability dimensions do not occur in isolation from one another, the following discussion will focus on specific conflicting goals between individual dimensions of sustainable urban development and, in order to broaden conceptual understanding, the analysis will make use of a number of specific examples.

Environmental urban sustainability

Environmental urban sustainability, defined as the protection, resilience and adaptation of physical and biological systems (Pugh 1996, p. 1), includes both spatial and sectoral components. With reference to the *spatial* component, Satterthwaite (1999, p. 82) emphasizes:

> To progress towards the achievement of sustainable development goals, the environmental performance of cities has to improve not only in terms of improved environmental quality within their boundaries but also in terms of reducing the transfer of environmental costs to other people, other ecosystems, or into the future.

This demand places city administrations in very difficult political situations, because they are only responsible for citizens within their city limits. An improvement of a city's environmental conditions, in combination with a decrease in the externalization of environmental problems (global planetary boundaries), is often associated with higher costs and/or financial cuts in the short or long term. In addition, cities can experience a loss of attractiveness in the global competition for investments, businesses and residents, when different types of capital are used for the benefit of other regions or their hinterland.

Regarding improvements in individual *sectors*, such as waste water, waste disposal or energy consumption, particular difficulties can be associated with upgrading antiquated settlement structures. For historic cities, it can be problematic to increase the energy use efficiency of urban structures (buildings, settlement patterns, transport systems) that were established over several centuries of low energy prices. In contrast, in cities with high urbanization dynamics (for example South Asia), in which the development of infrastructure can still be influenced, modern technologies can be applied much more easily to improve energy efficiency or environmental protection to avoid negative path dependencies. Theoretically, in today's fast growing cities, the construction of new energy-efficient infrastructure could be mandated through the establishment of a corresponding institutional and regulatory framework, for example houses with low heating or cooling demands (Satterthwaite 1999, p. 82). However, financial limitations of the public sector, as well as private households, and law enforcement in the private sector, are the main challenge for the implementation of sustainable strategies. In addition, urbanization dynamics in many cities have outpaced city planning and the need for sustainable systems is not always recognized.

Ecology and economy: The concept of environmental transition

As shown by the below example of the "brown" and "green" agenda, solutions to urban environmental problems are often also linked to economic and regulatory factors. McGranahan and Songsore (1994) developed a model that takes into consideration the high correlation of urban environmental problems with the level of economic development of a city, as well as the socioeconomic status of its population (for example consumption patterns). In the concept of *"environmental transition"*, the relationships between economic (social) development and the environment are outlined (in simplified terms) in three developmental stages as follows:

1   In the first stage, levels of development and income are low, and problems, pertaining to the "brown" agenda, occur primarily at the scale of neighbourhoods.
2   In the second stage, as the economy is growing, problems of the "brown" agenda are addressed with increasing success, but cities experience a rise in air and water pollution.

3   In the third stage, with a high level of economic development, problems of the "green" agenda become pressing. Environmental problems now also radiate into the urban hinterland and as far as the subglobal level.

While the majority of cities in the Global North can be ascribed to the third stage, many cities in the Global South are transitioning between the different stages. Through the restructuring of the globalized economy, not only do these developmental stages overlap, but often occur even at the same time within a city (Pugh 1996, p. 154).

In the concept of environmental transition, the economy is viewed from a systems perspective in the context of sustainability. Accordingly, a sustainable urban economy pursues the maximization of economic wealth, while simultaneously preserving other types of capital, on which it depends (particularly human and natural capital). Especially in cities with large socioeconomic disparities, the status of the individual cannot be disregarded, whereby an urban economy can only be considered sustainable if it facilitates a certain level of material wealth, or at least basic material security, for all individuals in a society.

Ecological and social urban sustainability: Environmental health or a healthy environment?

Within the two target dimensions of sustainable ecological and social development, conflicts are common and are reflected in the discourse between the so-called "brown" and "green" agendas. The field of environmental health is the central theme of the "brown" agenda, which addresses how urban residents, and in particular those living in poverty, can be equipped with adequate water supplies, waste water disposal, sanitation facilities and waste disposal at present and in the future, within the overarching objective of reducing the spread of infectious diseases. The "green" agenda is concerned with the long-term global conservation of ecosystems and hence "ecosystemic health" (McGranahan & Satterthwaite 2003, p. 263). Problems may arise as a result of the implementation of both agendas. For example, increasing the quantity and quality of the water supply, in order to improve environmental health for marginalized city residents, involves an increase in resource consumption and therefore would be discordant with the goals of the "green" agenda. These "irreconcilabilities" often emerge especially when goals are considered in isolation. However, in a more comprehensive assessment, important relationships between healthier, more secure urban environments and the reduced exploitation of natural capital become apparent. For example, through the improvement of water management, both agendas can be served. When system efficiency is improved, and leaks and water pollution are avoided through regular maintenance, improved access to water for a larger proportion of the population is not inevitably accompanied by an increase of total consumption (for example water loss, due to damaged lines, amounts to 30–40 per cent in cities like Delhi). In addition, through graduated tariff systems, costs can be distributed more equitably amongst different income levels and incentives for reduced consumption can be established. With regard to sanitary installations, intelligent technologies or the utilization of reclaimed waste water can lead to substantial savings.

Social sustainability

Definitions for the social dimension of sustainability are currently also not based on scientific consensus. On the one side, from a cultural perspective, norms and values are regarded as social capital, and on the other side, the satisfaction of basic needs, or quality of life and equity within a society, are principal concerns.

In the context of the first perspective, the term cultural sustainability, which combines both static and dynamic elements, is used: accordingly, common values, perceptions and behaviours need to be developed within societies which facilitate the achievement of sustainable development goals. This concept is based on the premise that cultural heritage and indigenous knowledge harbour great potential, for example for the preservation of natural resources. Social sustainability is seen as an auxiliary precondition for environmental sustainability, because natural capital is used in a social context, in which rules and values of the social fabric determine the intergenerational and intragenerational distribution of natural resources. However, the concept of cultural sustainability is even more difficult to operationalize than social sustainability, because culture is not static and consequently, it is often not evident which type of heritage should be preserved (Hardoy et al. 2001, p. 351).

The most widely distributed definitions are those that emphasize the value of social capital or social conditions that enable or support the fulfilment of human needs (Hardoy et al. 2001, p. 351). Such a definition was advanced by Polèse and Stren (2000, p. 16):

> development (and/or growth) that is compatible with the harmonious evolution of civil society, fostering an environment conducive to the compatible cohabitation of culturally and socially diverse groups while at the same time encouraging social interaction with improvements in the quality of life for all segments of the population.

In this definition, the term *quality of life* is introduced in the context of social sustainability:"Quality of life is a person's subjective perception of their position in life in relation to the culture and value systems, in which they live, and with regards to their goals, expectations, standards, and concerns" (WHO 1993, cited in Rennerberg & Lippke 2006, p. 29). The subjectivity of the term is thus amplified through its relativity, because people measure their standard of living through comparison with that of their neighbourhood. Accordingly, the term *relative poverty* also refers to the comparison with the respective social environment or national average.

The subjectivity and relativity of social sustainability impede the operationalizability of this dimension. The sustainable livelihood approach, for instance, provides a suitable example for a more in-depth exploration of the various aspects of social capital in order to better understand the multi-dimensionality of (sustainable) lifestyles through the linkage with other kinds of capital (Vedeld et al. 2012). With increasing socioeconomic disparities in many cities, the concept of social sustainability increasingly deals with the reduction of social inequalities. Income inequality, as the simplest indicator for measuring social inequality, adversely affects all of society, the economy, and the environment (UN 2013, p. 3). According to Allen (2009), urban social sustainability refers to equitable, inclusive and culturally adequate measures for the promotion of equal rights through ecological, physical and economic capital to secure an adequate way of life.

Political urban sustainability

Due to the plurality of opinions and the variety of actors involved in decision-making processes, democratic systems seem to generally exhibit more favourable preconditions for the implementation of sustainable development. At the urban level, the participation and involvement of a wide section of the population can be realized more easily than at the national level, because cities are spatially confined "systems". However, growing disinterest in urban development policy and declining voter turnout are observed in many countries because local governments tend to be perceived as rather powerless actors in the often charged negotiations between state and economic interests (Hall & Pfeiffer 2000, p. 53). However, municipalities can certainly influence their attractiveness as business locations through increased opportunities for education and professional development, as well as improvements in the quality of life.

Competing interests are a key component of urban democracy. In the area of sustainable development, issues associated with the interactions between competing interests raise important questions regarding the best strategies for solving conflicts between individual sustainability dimensions at international, national, regional and transnational levels.

(Good) urban governance: The implementation of sustainable development

In order to implement the principle of sustainable development, certain regulatory mechanisms have to be in place at different levels and in different sectors. This concept has gained traction under the term "governance".

Governance

The following widely cited definition of the United Nations Development Programme (UNDP) summarizes the key points:

> Governance can be seen as the exercise of political, economic and administrative authority in the management of a country's affairs at all levels. It comprises the mechanisms, processes, and institutions through which citizens and groups articulate their interests, exercise their legal rights, meet their obligations, and mediate their differences.

(UNDP 1997, p. 2)

Politics is perceived as a multi-level system from the local to the global with a myriad of different actors (Benz 2004, p. 5). This results in a "new" reality of complex governing processes and collective action in societies. Although governments persist and are accepted as the central political institutions, it is at the same time acknowledged that processes and structures are also influenced by other actors. Additional groups of actors come primarily from the private sector and civil society (UN-Habitat 2002, p. 12). Civil society actors include for example NGOs, unions, research institutions, religious groups and the media. An essential aspect of the governance concept is the role it plays in establishing a balance of interest between different groups of actors through leadership and regulation processes. In addition, "governability" emphasizes a dynamic processual character, because decisions are often based on complex relationships between actors with different priorities that change over time.

Thus, the increasing relevance of the governance concept can be attributed to new and extended scopes of action for a wide variety of actors, as well as the complexity of "new" political processes and structures in the international system.

Good governance

The term good governance was adopted in the mid-1980s in political practice and included both normative and partly ideological content. Good governance is primarily understood as a programme for the improvement of government leadership in national and international systems. The World Bank used the concept of good urban governance to define criteria for efficient, constitutional and citizen-orientated practices of state and administration, which are used as preconditions for the extension of credit to countries of the Global South. The term was also used by neoliberal governments to describe a concept that favours the reduction of government regulation and services in favour of private and civil society actors. According to the ideology of the minimal state, most public services need to be privatized (Benz 2004, p. 18). Ultimately, good governance also involves "structures and processes of control and coordination by means of a complex combination of hierarchy, procedures, and networks, or of regulations, incentive mechanisms and agreements in the cooperation of actors from government and society" (Benz 2004, p. 19).

Different organizations of the United Nations list eight essential characteristics for good governance:

> Good governance is, among other things, participatory, transparent and accountable. It is also effective and equitable. And it promotes the rule of law. Good governance ensures that political, social and economic priorities are based on broad consensus in society and that the voices of the poorest and the most vulnerable are heard in decision-making over the allocation of development resources.
>
> (UNDP 1997, p. 3)

In addition, a long-term perspective for governance and human development needs to be established.

(Good) urban governance

In the area of urban governance, the governance concept is explicitly applied to issues of urban development and urban policy (Einig et al. 2005, p. 1), as many cities in the Global South are experiencing a progressive loss of governability, which undermines planning and regulatory capacities of local authorities and the organization of urban operations (Coy & Kraas 2003, p. 39). Megacities are especially affected through their growth processes and multilayered dynamics. Social fragmentation and polarization processes, with expanding informal settlements, on the one hand, and growing demands of a wealthy upper class, on the other, can endanger the socioeconomic stability of a society.

Enormous differences in the economic performance and structure of cities within and between countries cannot only be attributed to their material and financial resources (Hall & Pfeiffer 2000, p. 225). Differences in urban development can be partially explained by differences in the regulatory quality of institutions and administrative systems in different cities, which can either promote or discourage private sector development. The quality of regulation is closely connected to social structure and market forces that are embedded in economic globalization processes (Kraas 2000, p. 287). However, it also has to be taken into consideration that government operations have become increasingly more complex in recent decades, and consequently, especially in fast growing cities, urban governments face significant challenges. In the past, the political and economic coordination of development projects were of primary concern. However, since the introduction of the concept of sustainable development, the social and environmental dimensions have been added and have gained prominence. Modern urban systems are characterized by complex interdependencies and interactions of different institutions, actors, functions and spatial levels, and therefore require progressive institutions and new spheres of interaction between government and urban society (UN-Habitat 2009, p. 73).

Thus, urban governance essentially comprises the same, or similar, components as governance, however with a focus on urban space as a geographic entity:

> Urban governance is the sum of the many ways individuals and institutions, public and private, plan and manage the common affairs of the city. It is a continuing process through which conflicting or diverse interests may be accommodated and cooperative action can be taken. It includes formal institutions as well as informal arrangements and the social capital of citizens.
>
> (UN-Habitat 2002, p. 14)

The concept becomes more explicit when the adjective "good" is added to the term and thereby obtains a normative component. *Good urban governance* can be succinctly defined as "desired standards of practice of urban governance"

(UN-Habitat 2002, p. 13). This definition explicitly includes the safeguarding of basic needs such as safe shelter, food, drinking water and sanitary facilities for all strata of the population, as well as access to basic social services such as education and health facilities (UN-Habitat 2002, p. 14). These aspects correspond with those of the social dimension of sustainable development. Hall and Pfeiffer therefore also link good urban governance with the concept of sustainable development: good urban governance is the "driving political force that keeps individual aspects of sustainable development in balance and integrates them in the different areas of policy" (Hall & Pfeiffer 2000, p. 217).

In order to realize positive urban development outcomes, individual actors and institutions in a city have to reliably take on responsibility: "Sustainability as a principle, good governance as its implementation – these are the two inseparable aspects of a positive urban development" (Hall & Pfeiffer 2000, p. 217). In addition, Hall and Pfeiffer (2000, p. 218) identify several guidelines which should be followed in order to reach the goal of positive urban development: based on the principle of subsidiarity, decisions need to be made, or services need to be provided, at the lowest level of government that can perform functions efficiently and effectively. This principle is closely linked to the demand for decentralization, which affords citizens more autonomy and control. An important precondition is a functioning feedback system, which includes good coordination of decision-making processes and consultation between the different levels of government. Solidarity between municipalities can ensure that sufficient resources are available to all municipalities through equalization payments of state governments, in order to fulfil their functions and thus safeguard fundamental rights for all citizens.

However, good governance also means that governments concentrate their efforts on the most urgent tasks and collaborate in some areas with civil society organizations. This collaboration can involve NGOs and community-based organizations (CBOs) that have taken on the task of improving services or setting up social networks and should include, as a basic precondition of good urban governance, the active participation of citizens. Also, the private sector can be integrated in order to achieve common goals. Further, good cooperation between central and local government levels is important for the allocation, distribution and stabilization of funds and goods. Lastly, governments need to set clear priorities, whereby health and education (especially of women, as a key group) should play a special role (Hall & Pfeifer 2000, p. 221). These guidelines are similar to those advanced by UN-Habitat and are embedded in the guiding principle of the "inclusive city".

Concepts of sustainable urban development

How can the theoretical reflections on urban sustainability be translated into the reality of cities? In order to answer this question, different guiding principles of sustainable urban development which help to put sustainability objectives into more concrete terms have to be examined as well as essential implementation strategies (Kroll & Kraas 2013; WBGU 2016).

Guiding principles of urban development

In order to implement the multidimensional concepts of sustainable development, it is necessary to first develop guiding principles and objectives for the respective urban context in order to flesh out the conceptual approach with more concrete details. In development planning, a guiding principle generally is:

> a desired future state formulated as an aspirational goal, which can be achieved through appropriate actions. The time horizon remains open-ended. All measures need to be coordinated towards the formulated guiding principle. The details of the guiding principles are intentionally not precisely defined, in order to avoid a conflict of goals during the implementation of a guiding principle(s). They should not plan a final state, because living in space and time constitutes an ongoing process. Because guiding principles are oriented towards an aspirational, improved state, they enjoy high political acceptance.
>
> (Brunotte et al. 2002, vol. 2, p. 325)

Furthermore, *guiding principles for urban development* are "intrinsically conclusive model conceptions for an ideal structure with regard to urban development and urban space that is in accordance with social ideals and conditions" (Brunotte et al. 2002, vol. 2, p. 325). Against the backdrop of increasingly pluralized urban societies, which give rise to a multitude of values, norms and lifestyles, guiding principles can be an important anchor point in the search for a fundamental consensus and can be an action-guiding orientation framework. Once established, the effective communication of guiding principles should occur in order to raise awareness in the population, as a precondition for their implementation.

For some time prior to the initiation of the sustainability debate, guiding principles were already shaping urban development and, through their often-persistent spatial entrenchment, they still influence urban structures and processes today. Two examples are the dispersed city and the car-friendly town. In Western Europe, the *guiding principle of the dispersed city* was established as the most influential model after the Second World War. This concept was based on the spatial separation of the basic functions of daily life (e.g., living, working, transportation), which was influenced by the garden city movement, the Charta of Athens and other trends. The motivation for a separation of functions, as laid out in the Charta of Athens, was primarily justified with the increasing environmental pollution in residential areas, due to the close proximity of industry. As a result of this guiding principle, a rigid assignment of function and space was implemented in many cities, which resulted in a growing distance between, for example, places of residence and work. Also, land consumption increased especially after the 1960s, which was associated with increasing residential suburbanization and the establishment of industrial estates (Heineberg 2011, p. 865). In the 1960s, the guiding principle of the car-friendly town emerged since suburbanization was primarily facilitated by mass motorization. This concept had a large influence on urban development not only in the US, where motorization was already well advanced, but also in many other countries (Heineberg 2014).

Guiding principles of sustainable urban development

Since the 1990s, the discussion on sustainable development has produced a myriad of potential objectives for urban planning, such as the "cultural", the "democratic", the "ecological" or the "compact" city, or more recently the "resilient", the "green" or "the low carbon" city. The different guiding principles can all, more or less unambiguously, be attributed to the four dimensions of sustainable development, whereby political guiding principles have so far played a conceptually subordinate role (Kroll & Kraas 2013).

Environmental guiding principles

The multilayered aspects of environmentally sustainable urban development find their expression, in a condensed form, in the guiding principle of the "resource-efficient city". This concept aims to create a cyclic urban metabolism with balanced material flows, where inputs closely correspond with outputs, through the efficient use of energy and resources (Rogers 1995, p. 61; Schmitz 2001, p. 9). The environmental guiding principle is further differentiated by Haughton (1999), who identifies three strategies that would advance environmentally sustainable urban development in the western US:

1   The guiding principle of the "*self-reliant city*" focuses on minimizing the negative impacts that cities have on their hinterland through the reduction of general resource consumption, the use of local and renewable resource potentials, the minimization of waste flows, and the replacement of waste exports to the hinterland with local waste treatment.

2   The guiding principle of the "*redesigning city*", which combines environmental and urban development aspects, is the most widely used approach amongst western city planners: in this concept, environmental problems of cities, such as high traffic volumes due to long commuting distances, urban sprawl due to low building density in (suburban) residential areas, and inefficient energy use due to climatically inappropriate construction methods, are primarily attributed to poorly adapted urban design. Appropriate measures include, at the regional level, more intensive land use and, at the local level, adequate insolation of houses for the protection from cold and heat, which both can lead to a substantial increase in energy saving potential. This approach not only aims towards a more natural design for cities, but also emphasizes how, in social and economic terms, human activities can lead to more dynamic, creative cities with increased potential for development.

3   In the concept of the "*fair share city*" environmental goals are linked with economic principles by assigning an economic value to the natural environment. From an economic perspective, the cost-free and unlimited availability of natural resources is a fundamental reason for their overuse. Because ecological carrying capacity is limited, resources that flow into the production processes have to be assigned a monetary value. Prices for goods and services

that are calculated too low would ultimately lead consumers to economic decisions that are detrimental to the environment. This concept is meant to ensure that natural capital is traded on an equitable basis and that exchange processes neither degrade the environment, nor disadvantage urban societies and economies. In addition, through adequate mechanisms, the transfer of natural capital, such as the industrial use of river water, can be compensated for. The concept of the "fair share city" also comprises components of the "self-reliant" and the "redesigning city". As shown by the four guiding principles introduced above, the concepts are always multi-dimensional and do not exclude socioeconomic aspects.

Economically oriented guiding principles

The guiding principle of the "economic city" aims to ensure durable productivity, competitiveness and economic participation. This not only requires the expansion of technical infrastructure but also human capital formation (Schmitz 2001, p. 9). Several authors further differentiate: Hall and Pfeiffer (2000, p. 414) emphasize that a "*competitive city*" needs to promote the urban economy in two areas: 1) municipalities can create a favourable local business environment through effective urban planning, the supply of a qualified workforce, clear framework legislation and further economic measures, which would in turn support the service sector, in particular, as an important source of income for a large portion of the urban population; and 2) municipalities can strengthen the competitive position of local producers in the global market.

The scenario of the *telematics city* is also strongly tied to economic structure. However, in this approach, the technological developments, which are responsible for creating the information society in the countries of the Global North, play the key role. This scenario is based on the premise that the centrality of cities is being transformed through the opportunities of interactive communication, primarily through the internet, but also through a shift from physical products towards information and knowledge as the primary goods produced by cities. On the one hand, traffic flows are minimized through tele-workplaces at home, as well as through online shopping and tele-shopping. Also, citizens can be included in urban information systems and planning processes via the internet. On the other hand, modern technologies can also generate new social patterns of behaviour that are not always desirable.

Similar to the scenario of the telematics city, the guiding principle of the "*intelligent city*" is also based on technological innovations with a rather top-down approach: this approach primarily pursues the development of intelligent solutions, such as energy conversion, transportation and environmental protection technologies, for the improvement of resource productivity and local environmental conditions (Schmitz 2001, p. 9). Human capital is therefore an essential factor for the development of the "intelligent city". The relatively new concept of the "*smart city*" points into a similar direction and combines aspects of the "intelligent city" and the "creative city": a city can be considered as smart when combining technology-based support, coordination and monitoring functions with participatory approaches (Letaifa 2015). However, definitions of the "smart city" differ, some mainly focusing on information technologies.

Socially oriented guiding principles

According to the guiding principle of the "*social city*", citizens need to be integrated in society; that is to say, they need to be able to independently secure a livelihood, to be provided with adequate housing and to have access to social infrastructure (Schmitz 2001, p. 9). As an important starting point, this guiding principle takes on poverty of urban population groups across time and space (Hall & Pfeiffer 2000, p. 419). In its pursuit for solutions to urban problems, the concept is less focused on the establishment of a guiding principle and more on the development of effective strategies in order to integrate unemployed, underemployed and underpaid residents into the urban economy through capacity- and skill-building concepts. The goal is a "*liveable city*" (Hall & Pfeiffer 2000, p. 422), which includes different facets of urban quality of life, in particular in the areas of infrastructure, housing, transportation and land use.

Although quality of life is perceived differently by each individual, urban development planning still faces the challenge of designing more lively and attractive cities in order to enable, or deepen, the identification of all residents with their city. Globalization is thought to lead to the homogenization of cities in certain realms (for example urban architecture characterized by homogenous high-rise developments). This results in the reshaping of national and cultural forms and structures, which have long functioned as iconic elements that maintain the identity of a city and could potentially lead to the loss of urban identity. Because the perception of quality of life is highly subjective, a proportion of residents in all cities will experience problems with unsatisfactory quality of life regardless of their development status and income level: as quality of life increases, so do (unmet) demands in accordance with the hierarchy of needs.

Politically oriented guiding principles

Because of the predominance of the three pillar models of sustainable development, political guiding principles have until now played a subordinate role. However, as a result of the discussion around good governance, the political dimension is steadily gaining attention (WBGU 2016). With the *guiding principle of a strong urban autonomy*, Hall and Pfeiffer (2000, p. 405) have developed a primarily politically determined model of sustainable urban development. This guiding principle is based on two premises: 1) a democratically legitimated government; and 2) a certain degree of decentralization of administrative structures, which gives cities sufficient authority for the regulation of economic and social development. The transfer of competences to the municipalities, which involves increasing financial and legislative autonomy, expands the municipal scope of action. The process of administrative decentralization differs greatly between countries. An important prerequisite is the establishment of an urban policy framework, which regulates the appropriate allocation of authority (with a clear division of competences and responsibilities) and directs the equitable distribution of financial resources. Although the transition from the conventional, central municipal administration towards a more flexible, decentralized municipal management is often pursued, it does not constitute an easy process, especially in the cities of the Global South.

The guiding principle of the "*democratic city*" essentially takes up the same idea and emphasizes the principles of decentralized administration, transparent decision-making structures and expanded possibilities for public participation, which are intended to find their expression in a new planning culture (Schmitz 2001, p. 9). Similarly, the UN campaign on urban governance, in their guiding principle of the "*inclusive city*", identifies the implementation of the principles and norms of good urban governance as an important objective. At its core are mechanisms of inclusive decision-making for the resolution of conflicts of interests (UN-Habitat 2002, p. 15). In the "*responsible city*", individual institutions, organizations and citizens assume responsibility in everyday life for the improvement of urban quality of life, but also take on specific tasks during extreme events, such as natural disasters (UN-Habitat 2002, p. 15).

Guiding principles for urban development

Guiding principles for urban development constitute a further important category. They can also be understood as guiding principles that span the different dimensions, because the structures of the built environment also influence the economic, environmental, political and social quality of cities – and vice versa. The task of politics is to regulate this process of urban development such that a balance between the different dimensions can be achieved. The city government has three important instruments for urban planning and design at their disposal: infrastructure policy, finance policy (taxes and subsidies) and land use policy (Hall & Pfeiffer 2000, p. 434).

In Germany, sustainable urban development is based on three principles of spatial organization (Heineberg 2014):

1   Density of urban development (the "compact city"): the goal is to create more compact urban structures with high-quality housing through fully utilizing and expanding the land use potential of existing buildings and vacant land (renovation, restoration and conversion, as well as urban densification), in order to minimize urban sprawl.
2   Mixed-use developments (the "city of short pathways"): the concept involves mixing of functions in individual urban areas through integration of living and working environments, as well as education and recreation facilities. This principle also includes the social blending of different income groups, household types and lifestyle groups.
3   Polycentrality: the principle focuses on the mitigation of development pressure on the hinterland, as well as the distribution of development amongst certain cities in the hinterland, which need to be interconnected through efficient public transport systems.

These three principles set social and urban development targets that aim to counteract social segregation and polarization and to reduce motorized private transport.

These urban development principles have to be linked with the different one-dimensional guiding principles, depending on the context of individual cities, in order to realize an integrated concept of sustainable urban development; applied on their own, individual guiding principles cannot be very effective. Ultimately, guiding principles are not about the creation of an ideal sustainable city per se, but about reconciling the different aspects of the target dimensions of sustainable urban development, from the type of construction, through government structures and dominant production systems, to patterns of consumption, waste generation and administration systems (Satterthwaite 1999, p. 6).

Strategies of sustainable urban development

The guiding principles of urban development strive towards the overarching goal of integrating social and environmental systems, which can only be achieved through sustainable resource use. For more than three decades, engineers, economists and natural and social scientists have been working on technologies and strategies in order to make the transition from a resource-intensive to a resource-light and more environmentally compatible economy a reality (Wuppertal Institut 2005, p. 165). These efforts essentially follow the principles of efficiency (improved resource productivity), consistency (use of renewable resources) and sufficiency (reduced consumption).

The *efficiency strategy*, as a technical solution, focuses on the minimization of material and energy use per production unit. The input–output ratio, or in other words the ratio between input of capital, labour, resources or prefabricated goods and the production output, can be improved through the increase of resource productivity and the improvement of organizational structures (Grunwald & Kopfmüller 2006, p. 76). Ideally, economic growth can be decoupled from increasing resource use through the dematerialization of economic activity, in order to enable long-term economic growth within the limits of ecological carrying capacities. However, more efficient resource use also implies that resources can only be used up to a level where they still are able to regenerate. In urban areas, for example, this can refer to the use of groundwater within its capacity to regenerate or balanced land use systems. Central to the efficiency strategy are approaches that (further) develop resource-efficient technologies for production and product use (for example high-efficiency power plants, water- and energy-efficient washing machines, or the three-litre car), which include production strategies that utilize repurposed waste or increase product lifetimes.

Furthermore, different concepts have been developed, in order to quantify the material intensity of products and services, as well as the consumption patterns of different population groups. Among them are also approaches of the "ecological backpack" (Stengel 2011) and the "ecological footprint" (Rees 1999).

An increase in efficiency alone is however not sufficient for sustainable development, because the resource savings can easily be eclipsed by the resources required to feed a growing global demand for goods and services, especially through industrialization processes in the countries of the Global South.

The *consistency strategy* also pursues a technological solution, but with a focus on renewable resources. By aiming towards improved compatibility of nature and technology, qualitative aspects of environmental consumption are in the foreground. Based on this strategy, the flows of energy and materials produced by human economic activity need to be organized in a more environmentally compatible manner and adapted to resemble processes of a natural metabolism (Grunwald & Kopfmüller 2006, p. 77). Accordingly, industrial processes should not disturb the natural metabolism, but the two should preferably complement or even augment one another. When this is not possible, environmentally hazardous materials should be directed into fail-safe, independent technological cycles or should be phased out. The design of environmentally compatible cycles should be so "intelligent" that no waste is produced, by using the residuals of one production step as the raw material for the next (Stengel 2011, p. 131). For example, the waste heat of power plants associated with energy production can be used for district heating (Wuppertal Institut 2005, p. 166). In addition, the consistency strategy reflects a holistic perspective in that it considers the different subsystems as part of an entire system; accordingly, subsystems need to be managed in a compatible and integrated way. For the urban metabolism concept, this implies an interference-free coexistence of different subsystems, such as water cycle, transportation, industry and recreation. Thus, the main focus of the consistency strategy is on the more environmentally compatible use of materials and energy, and the strategy is less concerned with the reduction of material flows.

The *sufficiency strategy* views consumer behaviour from a social perspective; the term sufficiency in this context can be roughly equated with "frugality" or "moderation". This does not inevitably imply abstention from consumption but rather the orientation of consumption along criteria of environmental, social and economic sustainability. Simple examples include the purchase of reusable instead of disposable products, the purchase of durable energy-efficient products or travelling shorter distances for holidays, for example to the shores of the North Sea rather than the South Pacific Ocean for German citizens. Thus, according to the rationale of the sufficiency strategy, it is only changes in consumption structure, whether on a voluntary or state-ordered basis, that can have substantial effects on resource consumption, even without technological changes in the production process (Stengel 2011, p. 140).

All in all, it becomes apparent that sustainable development can only be achieved through the interaction of all three strategies, because each of them not only has its own significance, but also its own limitations: "While efficiency secures the rational use of resources, sufficiency advocates their economical use. Consistency strategies enable economic activities that are compatible with nature and are therefore indispensable for the continued existence of a growing human population" (Wuppertal Institut 2005, p. 167). Currently, more than half of the global population lives in cities. This can have significant advantages, especially in relation to the strategies discussed above, because due to their compact form and spatial organization, cities offer large potential for efficient resource use and the establishment of more environmentally compatible and more tightly integrated material cycles. Through effective management and by raising awareness of sustainability issues, cities also offer large potential for facilitating the environmentally sustainable behaviour of citizens, for example in the area of energy consumption and waste separation.

Nevertheless, it needs to be taken into consideration that the implementation of these strategies will only achieve somewhat limited results, as resources are still required for the development of efficient technologies. The consistency strategy is so far only applicable in limited areas, and both approaches are ineffective for certain environmental problems (for example overfishing of oceans). Especially through a growing population and increasing consumption needs, worldwide resource exploitation will rise more than their use can be curbed through efficiency or consistency strategies (Stengel 2011, p. 133).

Conclusions

Opportunities and risks for sustainable urban development are directly related to the risks and opportunities of urbanization. The discussion around a theoretical approximation of urban sustainability has shown that, through the spatial focus on urban systems, implications arise that are specific to sustainable development in urban environments. Viewing urban systems as metabolic entities with their own input–output relationships, for example, offers a good starting point for sustainability research in urban settings. The implementation of sustainable development in cities requires adequate regulatory mechanisms in a political multilevel system with the involvement of different groups of actors; this approach was discussed under good urban governance (WBGU 2016).

In order to make the abstract concept of sustainable development tangible for the public, sustainability goals, which are developed for respective local contexts, need to be made more concrete through the establishment of guiding principles, such as the guiding principle of the "fair share", the "liveable" or the "compact city". For long-term success with the reconciliation of conflicting priorities between environment and societal development, three approaches were introduced: the efficiency, the consistency and the sufficiency strategies. Through the discussion around different regional examples, it becomes apparent that different approaches have to treat the different sustainability dimensions in a holistic and integrated manner.

An important basis for making progress towards sustainable urbanization will be a more holistic understanding of research and planning, as well as a change in perspective that will include a more comprehensive consideration of the multitude of actors and their motives. This implies a deeper understanding of the multilevel driving forces and their interconnections. The strengthening of social coherence and local identity, with a concurrent growth in public responsibility and ownership of civil society networks and institutions, can only be achieved through a change in public awareness and an expansion of public participation.

In view of evolving globalization processes and effects, urban groups of actors will more than ever have to cooperate in strategic alliances and networks in order to enhance synergies, to avoid double-investing through a division of responsibilities and, in the context of urban development policies, be able to react to increasing global-urban competition. Conversely, the specific contribution of cities to shaping global development processes in a more sustainable manner should not be underestimated. Cities and urban societies concentrate experience and expertise, which are valuable resources that can be applied to the development of flexible, innovative and reliable approaches to problem solving. They open up opportunities for mutual learning and "city to city" dialogues. Effective components of a (more) sustainable globalization, especially in triangular partnerships (North–South–South), are knowledge transfer, in the sense of exchanging successful strategies and best practices, capacity building for necessary problem-solving skills and intercultural convergence.

References

Allen, A. (2009): Sustainable cities or sustainable urbanization? *UCL Palette 1.* www.ucl.ac.uk/sustainable-cities/results/gcsc-reports/allen.pdf (last accessed 21.10.16).

Benz, A. (2004): Governance – Modebegriff oder nützliches sozialwissenschaftliches Konzept?, in: Benz, A. (ed.): *Governance – Regieren im komplexen Regelsystem. Eine Einführung,* Wiesbaden, pp. 12–28.

Brunotte, E., Gebhardt, H., Meurer, M., Meusburger, P., Nipper, J., Martin, C. (2002): *Lexikon der Geographie.* Band 1–4, Heidelberg, Neckar.

BMBF (2003): *Die urbane Wende: Forschung für die nachhaltige Entwicklung der Megastädte von morgen,* Bonn.

Coy, M.; Kraas, F. (2003): Probleme der Urbanisierung in den Entwicklungsländern, *Petermanns Geographische Mitteilungen 1,* pp. 32–41.

Einig, K.; Grabher, G.; Ibert, O.; Strubelt, W. (2005): Urban governance, *Informationen zur Raumentwicklung 9/10,* pp. I–IX.

Grunwald, A.; Kopfmüller, J. (2006): *Nachhaltigkeit,* Frankfurt am Main.

Hall, P.; Pfeiffer, U. (2000): *Urban 21. Der Expertenbericht zur Zukunft der Städte,* Stuttgart.

Hardoy, J.; Mitlin, D.; Satterthwaite, D. (2001): *Environmental Problems in an Urbanizing World. Finding solutions for cities in Africa, Asia and Latin America,* London.

Haughton, G. (1999): Environmental justice and the sustainable city, *Journal of Planning Education and Research March 18 (3),* pp. 233–243.

Heineberg, H. (2011): Stadtgeographie, in: Gebhardt, H. et al. (eds): *Geographie,* München, pp. 858–879.

Heineberg, H. (2014): *Grundriss Allgemeine Geographie: Stadtgeographie,* 4. Auflage, Schöningh, Paderborn.

Kraas, F. (2000): Verlust der Regierbarkeit: Globalisierungsprozesse und die Zunahme sozio-ökonomischer Disparitäten in Bangkok, in: Blotevogel, H.H. et al. (eds): *Lokal verankert – weltweit vernetzt,* Stuttgart, pp. 285–291.

Kraas, F. (2005): Urban sustainability – sustainability in urban areas: Basic considerations, in: Gaese, H., F. Kraas, Mi Mi Kyi (eds): *Sustainability in Rural and Urban Environments. Proceedings of the First German-Myanmar Workshop in Yangon/Myanmar,* 17–21 November 2003. Cologne, pp. 31–42.

Kroll, M., F. Kraas (2013): „*Urban Sustainability – Urbane Nachhaltigkeit*". Studienbrief EZ 0510 im Fernstudiengang Nachhaltige Entwicklungszusammenarbeit. Technische Universität Kaiserslautern². 137 Seiten.

Letaifa, S. (2015): How to strategize smart cities: Revealing the SMART model, *Journal of Business Research 68*, pp. 1414–1419.

McGranahan, G.; Satterthwaite, D. (2003): Urban centers: An assessment of sustainability, *Annual Review of Environment and Resources 28*, pp. 243–274.

McGranahan, G., Songsore, J. (1994): Wealth, health, and the urban household: Weighing environmental burden in Jakarta, Accra, Sao Paulo, *Environment 36 (6)*, pp. 4–11, 40–45.

Mertins, G. (1998): Limitationen einer nachhaltigen Großstadtentwicklung in Ländern der Dritten Welt, *Tübinger Geographische Studien 119*, pp. 297–323.

Polèse, M.; Stren, R. (2000): *The Social Sustainability of Cities. Diversity and the management of change*, Toronto.

Pugh, C. (1996): *Sustainability. The environment and urbanization*, London.

Rees, W. (1999): Achieving sustainability: Reform or transformation? in: Satterthwaite, D. (ed.): *The Earthscan Reader in Sustainable Cities*, London, pp. 22–52.

Rennerberg, B.; Lippke, S. (2006): Lebensqualität, in Renneberg, B., Hammelstein, P. (eds): *Gesundheitspsychologie*, Heidelberg, pp. 29–33.

Rogers, R. (1995): Städte für einen kleinen Planeten, *ARCH+ 6*, pp. 58–64.

Satterthwaite, D. (1999): Sustainable cities or cities that contribute to sustainable development?, in: Satterthwaite, D. (ed.): The Earthscan Reader in Sustainable Cities, London, pp. 80–106.

Schmitz, S. (2001): Nachhaltige Stadtentwicklung – Herausforderungen, Leitbilder, Strategien und Umsetzungsprobleme. In: *Petermanns Geographische Mitteilungen 5*, pp. 6–15.

Sorensen, A. (2004): *Towards Sustainable Cities. East Asian, North American and European perspectives on managing urban regions*, Aldershot.

Stengel, O. (2011): *Suffizienz. Die Konsumgesellschaft in der ökologischen Krise. Wuppertaler Schriften zur Forschung für nachhaltige Entwicklung*, Volume 1, Wuppertal.

UN (2013): *The Millennium Development Goals Report 2013*, New York.

UN (2014): *World Urbanizations Prospects. The 2014 Revision. Highlights*, New York.

UNDP (1997): *Governance for Sustainable Human Development*. A UNDP policy document. New York.

UN-Habitat (2002): *The Global Campaign on Urban Governance, 2*. Edition, Nairobi.

UN-Habitat (2009): *Planning Sustainable Cities. Global Report on Human Settlements 2009*, London.

UN-Habitat/UNEP (2001): *Sustainable Cities Programme 1990–2000. A decade of United Nations Support for Broad-based Participatory Management of Urban Development*, Nairobi.

Vedeld, P.; Jumane, A.; Wapalia, G.; Songorwa, A. (2012): Protected areas, poverty and conflicts. A livelihood case study of Mikumi National Park, Tanzania, *Forest Policy and Economics 21*, pp. 20–31.

Vojnovic, I. (2014): Urban sustainability: Research, politics, policy and practice, *Cities 41*, pp. 30–44.

WBGU (2016): *Humanity on the Move: Unlocking the Transformative Power of Cities*. Berlin.

Whitehead, M. (2003): (Re)Analysing the sustainable city: Nature, urbanisation and the regulation of socio-environmental relations in the UK, *Urban Studies 7*, pp. 1183–1206.

Williams, K. (2009): Sustainable cities: Research and practice challenge, *International Journal of Urban Sustainable Development 1 (1–2)*, pp. 128–132.

Wuppertal Institut (2005): *Fair Future. Begrenzte Ressourcen und globale Gerechtigkeit*, Bonn.

11 Industrial and commercial zone planning according to the requirements of sustainable development

Michael von Hauff and Klaus Fischer

Introduction

In industrialized and developing countries there are many opportunities to implement and integrate the requirements of Agenda 21 in politics, society and the economy (von Hauff 2014). On the national level (in countries with federal systems, on the level of the individual states as well), in the municipalities and on the level of individual enterprises and organizations there are various approaches and concepts which are adopted and implemented to varying degrees. Up until now, relatively little attention has been paid to sustainability research and practice on the action level in industrial or commercial zones.[1] However, the importance of the sustainable design of industrial zones, covering aspects of both municipal as well as entrepreneurial sustainability, is becoming increasingly relevant for the long-term viability of municipal economic locations.

In this context, it is that level of industrial zones in particular which offers a high sustainability potential. Compared to individual entrepreneurial activities, industrial zones – benefiting from the spatial proximity and the common interest in locational development geared towards the future – allow sustainability measures extending beyond individual enterprises to be implemented (Fischer et al. 2015). A commitment on the regional level which focuses on sustainability opens up the possibility of combining common resources and skills and creating more opportunities than are available to the individual enterprises, particularly small- and medium-sized ones. Current challenges, such as the demographic as well as climate change and the rising costs of energy and raw materials resulting from an increasing scarcity of resources, can be better met by cooperating on sustainability extending measures beyond individual enterprises.

In this respect it is worth noting that the concept of sustainable industrial zones is relevant to both newly planned and existing zones as well as to transitional areas (former military areas or industrial wastelands). Whereas in existing industrial zones the concept can be introduced retroactively, in the case of prospective industrial zones it can be incorporated right at the planning stage. In many countries aspiring development, such as Vietnam or Myanmar, the large number of new industrial zones, now being planned or already being built, present great opportunities to integrate the concept of sustainability into the planning from the outset. This can prevent the need for a subsequent retrofitting and upgrading.

A predecessor of the concept of sustainable industrial/commercial zones is that of eco-industrial parks, which have already been discussed and implemented in some developing countries since the mid-1990s (Wilderer 2002). Eco-industrial parks, however, mainly focus on preserving the environment. Sustainable industrial zones, by contrast, are based on the concept of sustainable development, thus including more than just the ecological aspects of sustainability. The sustainability approach gives equal consideration to these three dimensions: ecological, economic as well as social sustainability and considers all of them to be of equal importance. Consequently, a sustainable industrial or commercial zone explicitly addresses all three dimensions and their manifold interrelations. As mentioned before, the paradigm of sustainable development has already gained attention and is being implemented in the form of specific concepts or strategies at global, national, regional and municipal levels as well as at the level of individual enterprises. Its specific application to an entire industrial zone has only recently begun and is still in its infancy as a result.

The following section introduces the theoretical basis underlying the concept of the sustainable industrial zone. The discussion focuses in particular on specifying the three dimensions: the ecological, economic and social. Another aspect deals with the difference between partial and integrated approaches to sustainable industrial zones. The chapter then develops initial deliberations on a certification system for sustainable industrial zones, and moves on to exemplify some methods and instruments for developing sustainable industrial/commercial zones and delineates some case examples from Germany, which were developed in the course of two research projects addressing various industrial and commercial zones.[2] A summary of the major findings concludes the chapter.

Theoretical basis for sustainable industrial zones

The theoretical section can be subdivided into three levels. First, there is the question of generally classifying the problem areas and potential fields of action for sustainable industrial zones. This is based on the three dimensions of sustainable development. The next question relates to the differentiation between the so-called partial and integrated approaches to sustainable industrial zones. Whereas partial approaches tend to relate to individual measures, integrated approaches represent a consistently comprehensive concept of a sustainable industrial zone. Finally, initial deliberations on a certification system for sustainable industrial and commercial zones are presented.

Theoretical basis according to the three dimensions of sustainable development

First, it must be clarified which requirements are presented by the paradigm of sustainable development to the concept of sustainable industrial zones. The first step is to define the content of the three dimensions of sustainable development in the context of sustainable industrial zones (von Hauff 2012):

Ecological sustainability

In many different ways, the use of natural resources has already reached a level of over exploitation. The need to reduce this excessive use of natural resources has a large impact on the production as well as the consumption of manufactured products. Thus, ecological sustainability is of great significance to the manufacturing industry in general, but also applies to certain services such as transport and logistics, which have a large, potentially negative, impact on the environment. The aim of ecological sustainability is to preserve the ecologic systems or the stock of ecological capital. The essential need for this sustainability arises from the fact that natural resources form the life support system for all human activities, particularly economic ones. Apart from directly or indirectly providing valuable natural resources, the environment – or the ecological system – also functions as a sink for human made emissions. According to the Brundtland Commission Report (WCED 1987), the generations living today have a duty to leave future generations a world offering resources to satisfy their needs to the same degree available to current generations.

For example, one of the key fields of action in an industrial/commercial zone is the supply of power and the demand for energy. A comprehensive energy concept for an entire industrial zone can incorporate a number of alternatives, however. For example, if the companies in an industrial zone agree on a mutual energy concept, renewable energy sources have "better odds" because of the more advantageous cost structure compared to a single enterprise selecting its power supply. The term "eco-efficiency" or "energy efficiency" is therefore used when positive effects are achieved both ecologically and economically.

Progress in the development of a sustainable industrial zone, in keeping with the paradigm of sustainable development, requires a balanced consideration of the other two dimensions. Consequently, it is also necessary to specify the content of the economic and social dimensions. Economic and social sustainability must be discussed at the same time as ecological sustainability.

Economic sustainability

An understanding of economic sustainability can be gleaned from welfare economics. Neoclassical welfare economics is focused on the maximization of the material well-being of the individual (per capita income). Social welfare is a complex term that goes well beyond the quantitative dimension of the material possessions of an individual or society to include a subjective evaluation of the living conditions (quality of life). This is an expansion on the material dimensions such as work, income and consumption to include intangible dimensions such as liberty, social equality and social consensus (Feser 2008). The extended term "social welfare" consequently goes beyond the social product or per capita income indicators. One tool for measuring the quality of life, for example, is the Index of Sustainable Economic Welfare (ISEW) (Cobb 1989, p. 401).

For example, an important field of action in the context of sustainable industrial zones is an efficient (sustainable) transportation infrastructure or network. This refers to efficient transportation connections for freight traffic (delivery and shipping of goods) as well as for the employees in the industrial/commercial zone. The primary focus is on reducing the number of trips and travel times which results in cost savings for the freight forwarder as well as for the employee. Naturally, this has an impact on the company's bottom line as well as on the employees' real income.

Social sustainability

In addition to ecologic and economic efficiency, there is also a need for social effectiveness. This refers to the preservation of social capital. Coleman, Bourdieu and Putnam define social capital as the social structure of a society (Haug 1997). This presupposes a transparent system of rights, applicable to everyone, and qualified justice, healthcare and education systems for all members of society.

Similar to real capital and natural capital, the individual citizens and the community shall also benefit from the social capital. The question is how to preserve social capital and how to ensure that future generations will be able to profit from the current capital stock. However, because the transfer of a society's social capital to the next generation is possible only to a limited extent, each generation must be able to establish or expand its own social capital.

For example, the social structure of the industrial/commercial zone can be examined in the context of the social structure of a society. The first characteristic is an agreement to build-up networks and trust between the enterprises and further actors (for example local authorities or neighbourhoods), followed by coordinating common management aspects within the industrial/commercial zone. In this way, a community spirit and common identity can be established. This spirit is extremely important for the coordination process between the companies located in the business zone, as well as between the business zone and the local community. Other possible fields of action for social sustainability, for example, are "humanization" measures, continuing education options and leisure activities offered in the industrial or commercial zone. In this context, we refer to the development and expansion of intangible resources.

In addition, there are fields of action that contribute to the improvement of the social standard of living for employees. One such field of action, for example, is the availability of childcare services. If they are provided in industrial/commercial zones, the challenge of balancing work and family, especially for women, is much easier to manage which helps to reduce stress on the parents. At the same time, it increases their productivity. A service such as this one enables employees, who previously chose to stay out of the work force, to reenter, thereby benefiting both the individuals and the companies in the zone.

Looking on the three dimensions or the kinds of capital does not provide any information, however, on the relationships between them. There is still a question as to the optimal management of the three kinds of capital in a way that leads to an optimum human well-being. Therefore it is essential to analyse and then emphasize the complementarity among the kinds of capital. In this respect it is noted that there has been comprehensive treatment in literature of the interrelationships between environmental and economic capital already. By contrast, in economic writings the importance of social capital in regard to the other kinds of capital is widely neglected.

Theoretical basis according to the difference between the partial and the integrated approach

This section clarifies the distinction between two development trends representing different intensities and framework conditions for the concept of the sustainable industrial zone. This involves an ideal-typical differentiation, which can be broken down further into different classifications:

- The characteristic feature of the partial, or weaker, approach to a sustainable industrial zone is the preference to strive for and implement obvious and quickly exploitable potentials. The actors mainly adopt a technical approach and mostly consider individual aspects, such as joint sewage disposal or joint advanced training measures for the employees in the industrial zone. This usually raises the question of what the initial sustainable development measures ought to be in order to produce a direct benefit.
- While this process improves the status quo, from the long-term perspective only moderate improvement in terms of sustainable development can be discerned. Thus, it is also characterized as the "concept of relative decoupling" (for example improving the efficiency of economic activities without looking at their total impacts in sum). Single measures contribute to the ecological and/or social dimension of sustainable development, without fundamentally changing the industrial zone, i.e. in terms of a comprehensive transformation process according to the principles of sustainable development.
- The integrated, or stronger, approach is geared towards a comprehensive transformation process, whereby many individual measures of sustainable development (see below) are combined and harmonized. This can only be striven for and achieved by adopting a long-term strategy. In this context, reference is made to an absolute decoupling or, respectively, taking into account the absolute socio- and eco-effectiveness of the economic activities in the area. When focusing on sustainability, all or at least a large part of the potential fields of action for sustainable development of a zone are integrated into the strategy, whereby the implementation of the fields of action is established through specific criteria based on objectives and timescales.

For industrial zones, the advantage of the partial approach is, that it is very suitable as a starting point for sustainable development and thereby also enabling the persons responsible (for example the industrial zone management) to gain initial experience. The disadvantage of this approach can be seen in the fact that a selection process arises which aims at finding easy solutions. Often, these solutions only have a minor effect upon the ecological and social dimension.

Furthermore, this approach conceals the risk that the persons responsible within the industrial zone do not acquire an understanding as to which requirements are essential for a sustainable transformation process in terms of the integrated approach. The partial approach also frequently neglects to recognize that developing sustainable industrial zones requires a longer-term process. To achieve this long-term process, the fields of action and the timescales for the implementation of the measures have to be determined.

Additionally, developing a system of indicators for evaluating the effect of the measures is of central importance (see Chapter 4). One example of such an indicator is how the volume of reprocessed sewage in the industrial zone has developed over time and which quality the reprocessed water possesses after purification. Another example is that of joint advanced training measures. The question is to which extent they are offered and taken advantage of through the companies and their employees. If specific objectives and timescales cannot be adhered to, the plans are to be suitably adapted in the particular cases where it is justifiable.

It is also worth noting that the design of a specific sustainability concept for zone needs to consider the relevant framework conditions on site. Among other things, some of the following aspects are relevant here:

- whether predominantly large or smaller industrial zones are involved (number of enterprises),
- whether more industrial or service-providing enterprises are established,
- whether predominantly small- and medium-sized, or large, enterprises are involved,
- how the transportation connections are set up,
- which internal or external obstacles there are in regard to implement a sustainability concept.

In sum, the distinction of the partial from the comprehensive approach makes it clear that, in the understanding of the concept of sustainable development, priority is to be given to the comprehensive approach. However, this requires a high level of specialist knowledge, creativity and commitment from the persons responsible (industrial zone management and persons with responsibility in the municipalities) and can be promoted by a certification system, which will be outlined below.

Approach for a certification of sustainable industrial zones

Certification systems are one of several possible instruments to promote the implementation of sustainable industrial zones. As they deliver concrete, action-guiding targets combined with the incentive to gain a certificate, they can be quite effective in supporting first steps as well as comprehensive approaches towards increased sustainability in industrial/commercial zones.

Due to this characteristic, certification systems are not only suitable for industrial countries, but they can also guide the design of sustainable industrial zones in developing and emerging countries. In any cases, the local and national specifics need to be considered. The development of certification systems in the context of sustainable industrial zones is quite an unexplored field. First approaches address sustainability criteria regarding the building infrastructure of industrial quarters and thus mainly emphasize constructional aspects (cf. DGNB 2013). Below, the outline of a possible basic structure for a more integrated system for the certification of sustainable industrial zones is presented (for a detailed presentation, see Fischer et al. 2015). In order to achieve a comprehensive concept such as this one, the following aspects were seen as relevant for the conception of the certification system:

- Pursuing a management-orientated, action-guiding approach which allows the defining of concrete measures and the support of their effective as well as their efficient realization. For that reason, the system should be based on the principles of a comprehensive total quality management (TQM) approach.
- Understanding sustainable development as a path of continuous improvement in accordance with current knowledge (for example about ecological limitations) and state-of-the-art technology.
- Differentiating and conceptualizing the various levels of relevant actors and fields of action (for example the levels of single companies, the entire zone, the respective municipality or even an entire region).
- Referring to existing sustainability requirements and indicators, for example developed in previous research about sustainability in industrial areas (see below) and making them operational.
- The certification system should be open and adaptable for other existing certification systems for enterprises or municipalities. This would promote the benefits of possible synergies and reduces the effort for certificate acquirers, thereby increasing their acceptance of the process.

Furthermore, the certification systems should cover different life cycle phases of industrial and commercial zones as well as the aspect of their overall "organizational ability" (for example in the sense of cooperation and networks as well as common projects building and sustaining social capital). Existent approaches certifying "green" or sustainable buildings and industrial quarters do not address these aspects yet. It becomes clear from these aspects that sustainable development in industrial zones is understood as a continuous process which embraces not only individual measures but, in particular, joint efforts. Thus, the logic of the certification system supports a shift from individual, uncoordinated actions to coordinated joint actions by the enterprises established in an industrial zone as well as between these enterprises and further local/municipal actors.

On the one hand, the sustainability measures that cannot be implemented from an individual economic perspective – since the personnel and financial resources are often lacking, particularly in the case of small- and medium-sized enterprises – can, on the other hand, more readily be achieved through a pooling of resources by several enterprises and by a cooperation between private economic and public actors.

Model framework of the approach

As a basic model for integrated management and continuous improvement we propose the EFQM (European Foundation for Quality Management) Excellence Model (EFQM 2012). It aims to support the development of organizations and offers an extensive management framework which is being used by more than 30,000 European enterprises. The EFQM criteria model consists of nine criteria, five of which relate to the so-called "enablers", dealing with how an organization performs in the fields of leadership, strategy, people, partnerships and resources, as well as with regard to processes, products and services. The other four criteria ("results") represent some of the key performance indices of the organization as well as its outcome for employees, customers and society. According to the model's assumptions, learning, creativity and innovation processes lead to an improvement on the enablers' site, in turn improving the results of the organization (EFQM 2012). The logic of the EFQM model only provides the foundation for the intended certification approach. In order to adapt the model framework to the certification for sustainable development in industrial zones, its structure as well as some of the criteria needed to be adjusted according to context. For that reason, previous research on criteria and indicators for sustainability in industrial zones was used.

The proposed certification system comprises a total of four levels:

1   The actors or measures level: municipality, individual company and inter-company cooperation.
2   The criteria level: criteria of enablers and results.
3   The cooperation level in conjunction with a three-stage system, reflecting the "degree of maturity" of the joint organizational ability with regard to sustainability-orientated measures in the zone.
4   The life cycle level, which encompasses different phases of an industrial zone's life: development, existence and revitalization/transition.

In the following sections, the four levels of the certification system are presented briefly. For an overview of the whole certification system, see Figure 11.1.

Actors and measures level

In industrial zones, sustainability measures can be initiated and introduced by various actors. A basic distinction can be made between three actors or measures levels, whereby in reality numerous interactions between the three levels take place: municipality, individual company and inter-company cooperation. Municipalities have the opportunity to develop a sustainability strategy for an industrial/commercial zone, thus promoting ecological, economic and social criteria in the new conception, as well as reshaping or furthering development of the area. There are various promotional opportunities, from offers of energy supply from regenerative energy sources through to conceptions for better infrastructural integration of the

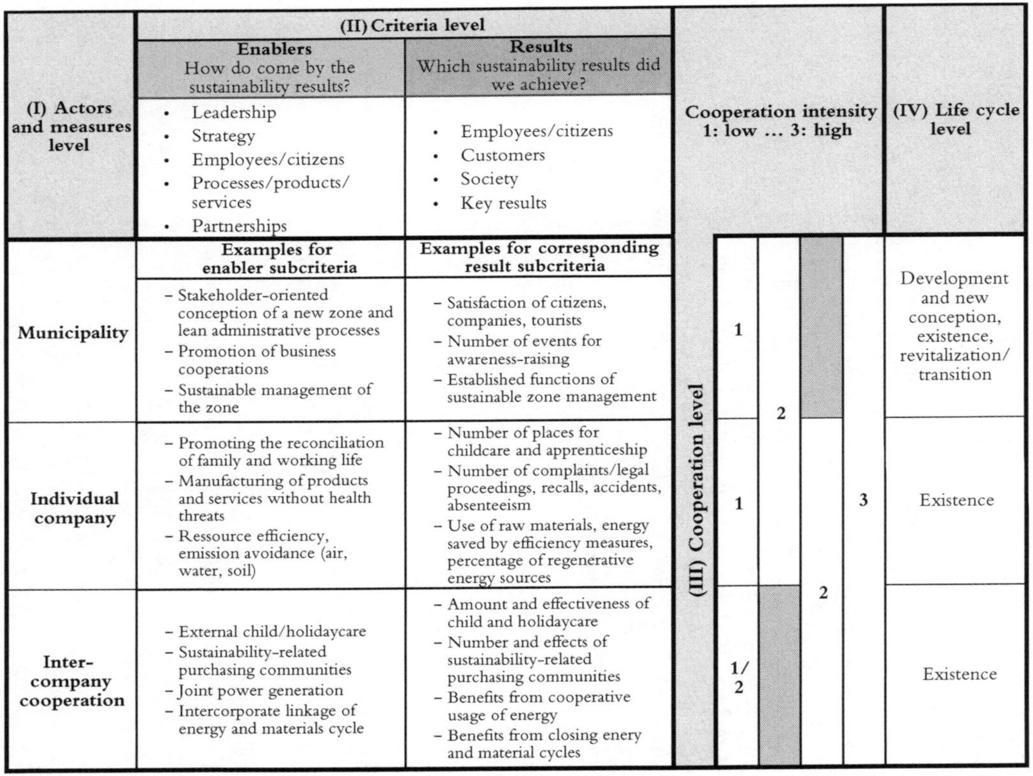

(I) Actors and measures level	(II) Criteria level		(III) Cooperation level — Cooperation intensity (1: low … 3: high)			(IV) Life cycle level
	Enablers How do come by the sustainability results? • Leadership • Strategy • Employees/citizens • Processes/products/services • Partnerships	**Results** Which sustainability results did we achieve? • Employees/citizens • Customers • Society • Key results				
	Examples for enabler subcriteria	Examples for corresponding result subcriteria	1	2	3	
Municipality	– Stakeholder-oriented conception of a new zone and lean administrative processes – Promotion of business cooperations – Sustainable management of the zone	– Satisfaction of citizens, companies, tourists – Number of events for awareness-raising – Established functions of sustainable zone management	1	2		Development and new conception, existence, revitalization/transition
Individual company	– Promoting the reconciliation of family and working life – Manufacturing of products and services without health threats – Ressource efficiency, emission avoidance (air, water, soil)	– Number of places for childcare and apprenticeship – Number of complaints/legal proceedings, recalls, accidents, absenteeism – Use of raw materials, energy saved by efficiency measures, percentage of regenerative energy sources	1		3	Existence
Inter-company cooperation	– External child/holidaycare – Sustainability-related purchasing communities – Joint power generation – Intercorporate linkage of energy and materials cycle	– Amount and effectiveness of child and holidaycare – Number and effects of sustainability-related purchasing communities – Benefits from cooperative usage of energy – Benefits from closing energy and material cycles	1/2	2		Existence

Figure 11.1 Elements of a certification scheme for sustainable industrial/commercial zones

Source: Fischer et al. 2015

industrial zone to improvement of the enterprises' access to high-speed internet. On the level of individual companies, as well as regarding inter-company cooperation, there are measures such as joint procurement, the common design of attractive workplace surroundings and recreation areas, closed energy and materials cycles between the enterprises and common investments in human resources development, whereby sustainable development can be significantly advanced in an industrial zone. Insofar, potential fields of action and measures must be identified and realized at all three levels of actors as well as between them.

Criteria level

In the EFQM model, the criteria descriptions allow for the identification of "excellent practices" on the one hand and for the analysis of the interrelations between enablers and the results of an organization on the other hand. Regarding the proposed certification system for industrial/commercial areas, the chosen criteria need to cover relevant enablers for a more sustainable development of the area as well as concrete "sustainability outcomes", accordingly, which can be measured through adequate indicators. Depending on the different actor levels (see above), the criteria categories of the model need to be adapted: for example "leadership" and "strategy" are only relevant for the inter-company level in case of a common management of the cooperation as it exists within a working district or through a sustainability manager in the area. Further adaption was necessary in regard to the "employees" criterion. The latter does not apply to the municipality level; "citizens" is the more adequate target group here.

The structure of the certification system proposes individual criteria for each actor level. This allows certifying separate measures on each actor level, for example sustainability concepts for a new area coming from the municipality or specific efforts from single companies in an existing zone. However, a comprehensive sustainability assessment requires looking at the cooperation and overall organizational ability of the area, as it is done with the following level.

Cooperation level

An important aspect of the certification approach is to promote and give prominence to the cooperation between private and public actors, but also with civil society, supporting sustainability of industrial and commercial zones. Often, the zones do not have structures and processes providing a common organizational ability that would allow managing problems jointly. Consequently, even basic but essential organizational prerequisites – such as regular meetings between company representatives, the municipality and further relevant actors – are often not yet installed. However, a high degree of organizational capability can be achieved when coordinated and cooperative measures of sustainable development are realized throughout the whole zone and on a long-term basis.

In the certification system presented, "cooperation intensity" is used as an indicator for the degree of organizational ability and thus the potential for common problem solving due to jointly implemented sustainability measures ("readiness for sustainability"). As shown in Figure 11.1, the cooperation intensity can be ranked on a scale from 1 (low), if only single actors initiate sustainability measures on their own, up to 3, if sustainability is jointly operationalized on all levels. In this context, particular emphasis should be attached to those aspects of sustainability which demonstrate an integrated approach, i.e. a high potential for change with regard to the operational and economic practice of enterprises.

Life cycle level

Finally, the certification approach offers the opportunity of being introduced within an industrial zone's various life phases. Based on the differentiation of actors (municipality, single company, cooperation), this allows for example the pre-certification of a municipality for its sustainability efforts in the conception phase. Such pre-certification can for example support a sustainability-oriented marketing strategy for a planned industrial zone or can help to apply for support programmes and sustainability project grants. In addition to the life cycle phases "development" and "new conception", it can also be applied in the existence phase for all actors alone as well as for their cooperation.

In sum, as already mentioned at the beginning of this section, comprehensive approaches for sustainability certifications for industrial zones are still in their infancy. The approach presented highlights the aspects of management and cooperation as access points, linked by the objective of improving organizational capability and the integration of sustainability measures in industrial zones. The EFQM-based certification system selected thereby distinguishes between different relevant actors and enables their individual assessment. Nevertheless, it brings the actors together into a cooperation model which offers the basis for determining the degree of readiness with regard to the ability to jointly coordinate and implement sustainability measures. Furthermore, introducing the certification system in various life cycle phases of an industrial zone is also possible.

Methods and instruments for developing sustainable industrial/commercial zones

In this chapter, some methods and instruments supporting sustainability efforts in industrial and commercial zones are presented. They were developed and tested in the course of two research projects conducted by the University of Kaiserslautern, Germany, in cooperation with several other research partners. Although sustainability requirements differ in some points between industrialized and industrially emerging countries (for example regarding demographic development trends and customer or employee needs), these examples are valid in both contexts: they do not propose to be the "only real deal" for achieving more sustainable zones, but rather show how specific concepts can be developed for each industrial/commercial area.

Here we show how sustainability criteria and fields of action can be systematically developed, building a basis for individual and zone-specific sustainability concepts. To illustrate, the so-called integrated sustainability triangle is introduced; it can be used as a heuristic to deduce sustainability requirements, indicators and measures from existent standard-setting sustainability documents such as the ISO 26000:2010 Guidance on Social Responsibility, the Global Reporting Initiative (GRI) Guidelines or sustainability indicator systems on national, federal, state and community levels. We also present some workshop concepts designed to help initiate a discourse between relevant on-site actors about common objectives and possible joint activities geared towards a more sustainable, future-oriented design of their industrial/business location. We also present a case example for a sustainability concept of an industrial park in Germany.

The integrated sustainability triangle as a heuristic for deducing sustainability requirements and concepts

The integrated sustainability triangle (von Hauff & Kleine 2005) not only covers all three dimensions of sustainability (see above) as "traditional" triangle models do, but also allows representing the manifold interrelations between them. For that reason, it pictures a continuum between the three dimensions in its inside. The first step when creating the model is to label the corners of the triangle with the three dimensions ecological, economic and social. Then the areas within the triangle are divided into different sections that correspond to the three dimensions, as shown in Figure 11.2. This results, for example, in some sections being located exactly between two of the dimensions.

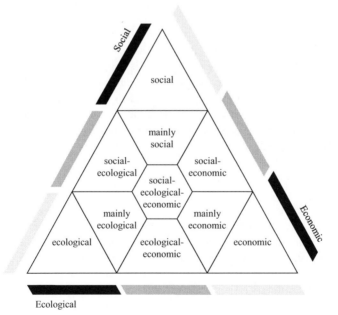

Figure 11.2 The integrated sustainability triangle and its sections

Source: Based on von Hauff and Kleine 2005, p. 14

If you consider the area between the ecological and the economic dimensions, for example, it is shown as ecological-economic. The term "eco-efficiency" is often used when referring to this context. An activity in this section may have a positive effect on both the environment and the economy: if energy consumption is reduced, the emissions caused by energy production are also reduced. A possible second benefit of the reduced demand for energy could also be a decrease in energy expenses.

In the research project, Sustainable Development in Industrial and Commercial Zones in Rhineland-Palatinate, the integrated sustainability triangle was used to systematically deduce sustainability requirements and areas for action for industrial/commercial zones. Existent sustainability standards and guidelines as well as indicator sets focus on the level of organizations (as ISO 26000:2010, UN Global Compact Principles or GRI Guidelines and indicators), the level of municipalities (as municipal sustainability goals and indicator sets developed in the context of local agenda 21 strategies) or the level of national and federal states (for example as focused on in this project, the sustainability strategy and indicators of Germany and the state Rhineland-Palatinate). Although sustainability in industrial and commercial zones addresses all of these levels and allows creating and using synergies between them to achieve respective sustainability goals on each, no stringent set of sustainability requirements and areas for action for the zone level existed. Thus, the question "What does sustainability of industrial/commercial zones mean exactly and which main areas for action are relevant?" needed to be answered. Therefore, the contents of the already existing and often well-accepted sustainability documents were used as a basis to answer this question in order to be adaptable to the "state of the art" of the sustainability discourse. Where indicated, these contents were re-specified for the zone level.

However, looking at the different kinds of sustainability documents mentioned above shows that while they often address similar and interwoven sustainability aspects, they are based on different systematics and have a rather incompatible structure. Here, the integrated sustainability triangle proved very useful to merge these documents, to identify and consolidate their contents and thereby come to sustainability requirements and main areas for action for industrial and commercial zones that are based on existent "sustainability knowledge" from different levels (organizational/municipal/national and federal state):

- First, the contents of the different documents (in form of sustainability criteria, action fields, dimensions etc.) were allocated to the ten sections of the triangle model.
- Second, this first allocation was reviewed and common aspects placed in different sections were consolidated and brought together.
- In the last step, the contents of the sections were used to formulate sustainability requirements and to deduce areas for action from an industrial/commercial zone's perspective.

The final results of this approach were 25 diverse areas for action (for example reaching from respect for human rights and international labour standards,

sustainable land use to common innovations for sustainability) and a set of 90 indicators for measuring the stage of a zone's development (see Fischer et al. 2015).
Together with municipal and zone representatives participating in the project, these
areas for action were "filled" with examples of about 80 measures for concrete activities. Of course, these aspects are not all relevant to the same extent for each
industrial/commercial zone. They rather represent a "vision" of sustainability based
on internationally and nationally/locally accepted sustainability goals and principles.

Besides painting a rather conceptual picture of sustainability in
industrial/commercial zones as shown above, the integrated sustainability triangle
can also be used to directly depict fields of activity for sustainability in industrial
and commercial zones. In Table 11.1 examples for distinct fields of activity are
shown for each section of the integrated sustainability triangle and specified with

Table 11.1 Exemplary fields of activity related to the sections of the integrated
sustainability triangle

Section of the triangle	Field of activity	Exemplary indicators
Ecological	• Environmentally friendly design of the zone	• Number of parks (trees, flower beds, water attractions)
Mainly ecological	• Competition/proposals for an environmentally friendly industrial park	• Number and quality of suggested improvements
Ecological-economic	• Resource efficiency • Waste management • Water management • Energy efficiency	• Reduction in waste volume • Reduction in water volume • Reduced energy consumption
Economic	• Profitability/competitiveness	• Economic benefits (increasing profits)
Mainly economic	• Joint logistic concept • Joint purchasing	• Number/weight of joint transport • Volume of joint purchases
Social-economic	• Joint training concept • Flexible work times • Internship job fairs • Open house day for students	• Number of joint training programs • Number of interns • Number of participants
Social	• Shared cafeteria • Childcare	• Number of visitors • Number of children enrolled
Mainly social	• Fitness center • Cultural events	• Number of employees enrolled in fitness programmes • Number of participants
Social-ecological	• Car pooling • Energy concept • Local transportation connections	• Reduced use of individual cars (reduction of CO_2) • In-house energy production units • Cycle times
Social-ecological-economic	• Sustainability management for commercial zone • Corporate design	• Number of meetings • Number of projects • Level of participation

appropriate indicators. The fields of activities used here are for illustration purposes as the size and organization of each industrial zone may be different. In practice, it is not recommended to aim for all fields of activities simultaneously: they cannot all be accomplished at once.

It makes more sense to first take an inventory of the zone and determine which fields of activity are already being targeted to some extent or identify those that have not yet been targeted at all. It is then up to the management or the responsible team at the zone to decide which fields of activities are particularly relevant. Subsequently, it is best to select three or four fields of activity in the industrial zone that can be measured by indicators, which will show how much progress has been made concerning the implementation of the activity. In this process, it is important to define specific targets to be achieved for each field of activity within a defined time period.

The result of this process can build the basis for a sustainability concept and strategy for an industrial zone. However, it is evident that a successful sustainability concept requires the participation and cooperation of all relevant actors on site, for example the companies in the industrial zone and responsible persons from the municipality. In this respect, it is important that all actors – particularly companies – recognize their benefit from the cooperation. At least in the beginning, this requires a regular, intensive and moderated exchange of possible cooperation options.

Workshop format

However, as already mentioned in Chapter 2, it cannot be taken for granted that relevant actors come together and have an exchange about common, current or mid-/long-term challenges and opportunities for collective action. With the objective of sensitizing the actors for joint sustainability needs and challenges, different exchange formats were developed in one of the above mentioned research projects and moderated by the respective project team. The formats of these events shall be briefly outlined below (see Fischer et al. 2015):

Round table "Sustainability in commercial and industrial zones"

The round table "Sustainability in commercial and industrial zones" was held approximately ten times and was open to all interested municipalities and industrial/commercial zones in the Rhineland-Palatinate. Its aim was to facilitate an exchange about specific sustainability challenges, for example regarding the handling of large industrial wastelands in small municipalities, managing the energy transition towards renewables and the problem of skills shortage due to the demographic change. The events took place in different locations and municipalities throughout the federal state, combined with site and company visits and a so-called "host hour", were specific challenges as well as approaches to solving problems were presented and discussed. Thus, all round tables addressed specific topics depending on the host municipality. Furthermore, external experts and referees were invited to the events and could directly contribute with their expertise.

Workshop "Developing a common vision and targets"

This workshop format aims to help municipalities and further relevant actors (for example planning offices, business developers, local authorities) during the conception phase of an industrial or commercial zone in order to systematically integrate sustainability concerns into their particular zone planning. Here, it is important to consider that "sustainability" needs to be specifically filled with life by the actors themselves: they need to develop their common vision for the zone as well as the targets to line it. The workshop is held in small groups, each finding ideas and requirements from the perspective of different stakeholders (municipality, companies, employees, citizen). These ideas are presented to and clustered by all participants. After that, the cluster headlines are used as a basis for formulating concrete objectives and are then underpinned in the discussion by adequate measures. After the workshop, a strategy paper can be developed using the results, allowing to guide the future zone development and to present the concept and joint idea behind the zone.

Workshop series "Creating value together for our site"

While the workshop above is designed for the conception phase, the workshops "Creating value together for our site" address zones which already exist. This is not a one-time event, but rather requires a series of moderated workshops, involving the companies on site. The series aims at developing a sense of community within the zone and gaining awareness for collective problems as well as common strategies and potentials for solving them.

Prior to the first workshop, it can be helpful to conduct a short survey among the companies on site, gaining information about the current status in the zone as well as about possibly joint concerns. The results of such a survey can deliver a good basis for the first meeting and for initiating a discussion about common interests and objectives. In subsequent workshops, small project teams can be set up to work on relevant topics (as for example on the improvement of the quality of free spaces, common activities for health management or buying and recycling cooperation). These project teams are working further after the event and can report on their success and experiences at the next workshop of the series.

Of course, such a workshop series requires adequate resources for organization, moderation and review. Thus, the installation of a common "zone manager" or "working area improvement district manager" can be helpful, especially when the companies cannot apply sufficient time to manage this process on their own.

Example: Development of a sustainable commercial park

The further development of an existing industrial area is being implemented in the context of a pioneering project under the framework of a sustainability strategy in the State of North Rhine-Westphalia (NRW). The so-called "Green Commercial District" project began as an initiative of the state's ministry of the environment in 2002, in support of the government's Agenda 21 strategy.

The project mainly relates to the establishment of a new commercial district in the community of Kürten, in accordance with ecological, economic and social criteria. The development concept is also being expanded to older locations in the state. The eight industrial areas in NRW participating in the model project were awarded the title "Eco-Industrial Park" on 11 April 2006. The development project was sponsored by the communities and the enterprises within the industrial zones. The Ministry of the Environment defined the implementation criteria to which the communities pledged their compliance in the form of a "Mayors' Declaration" (Wolf 2004, p. 255).

One of these locations is the industrial park Am Kruppwald an der Knippenburg in Bottrop, NRW. The industrial zone comprising an area of 120 hectares has existed since the 1960s and is fully occupied by approximately 25 large companies and numerous small- and medium-sized ones. All corporations have introduced an environmental management system and/or participate in the NRW "eco-profit" (*Ökoprofit*) system. Despite the already high level of integrated environmental standards, the companies are committed to pursuing the further challenge of transitioning their industrial zone into a "sustainable industrial zone". Supported by community participation, an interest group consisting of the 25 largest and some medium-sized companies meets regularly in Bottrop to discuss and develop the sustainability strategy.

To assume responsibility for the future is the guiding principal deliberately adopted by the companies. Surprisingly, for the most part this involves companies long established at the location with a great deal of business experience and successful management. It was clear from the start of the project that many decisions would have to be made which, at first impression, appeared to be "inefficient" and contrary to their former way of doing business. Such actions demand strong partners, frankness and openness, awareness of interrelationships, persuasive talents and personal integrity. It also requires the development of individual sustainability management and a functioning network.

Table 11.2 presents an overview of the goals set by the companies in their effort to achieve sustainable development (von Hauff & Wolf 2008, p. 202).

Particularly remarkable about the contents presented is the fact that they represent a comprehensive and equally weighted view of ecological, economic and social aspects, which in terms of an entire industrial zone is being described here for the first time. Contrary to the "eco-industrial parks" whose concepts mainly take the traditional ecological contents into consideration (for example energy and material efficiency, waste and water management, material flow management and life cycle management), here also those areas of the industrial zone planning and development that have previously been marginalized are being considered and enhanced.

Regarding ecological measures, these are for example rain water management, green roofs, use of renewable energies, conversion to alternative fuels, ecological building design, fewer paved areas; regarding social measures, these are for example, flexible work hours, increased job satisfaction, childcare, training programmes, healthcare services and restoration as important parameters for a sustainable industrial/commercial area.

Table 11.2 Examples of sustainability goals and measures of German industrial parks

Overarching goal	Goals and measures
1. Development of a sustainable area management	**Goal:** To review all decisions in terms of sustainability **Measures:** Establish an interest group, develop typical areas of joint decision making in commercial districts (security, purchasing group, waste disposal, common use of railway connections, etc.), develop operational synergies as well as horizontal or vertical networks, for example companies share same or different production steps for a product, use of non-product output, use of process water and waste heat from neighbouring operations, shared use of car pools, warehouses, logistics, etc.
2. Development of sustainable water management	**Goals:** To reduce consumption of water, protect ground water quality, limit waste water pollutants **Measures:** Reduce total amount of water consumption, increase use of process water, avoidance and purification of waste water, ecological disposal of waste water, production-integrated environmental protection measures, rain water management (seepage, remove soil sealing, controlled discharge, roof greening; used to save costs and to regulate hydrologic balance)
3. Development of sustainable waste management	**Goals:** To decrease the amount of waste by emphasizing waste avoidance prior to reutilization and prior to environmentally safe disposal **Measures:** Decrease disposal costs through the use of synergies, create a waste balance sheet and waste management concepts, quantitative waste avoidance by reducing the amount of bulk needed, increase service life, reduce use of resources, qualitative waste avoidance by avoiding the use of toxic substances, avoiding composite substances, waste separation/recycling in place of disposal
4. Development of an energy strategy	**Goal:** To reduce energy consumption and carbon dioxide emissions **Measures:** Introduce energy management systems, energy efficient management and production (rational energy conversion, avoid transmission losses, use of more efficient and economical building technology), decrease power requirements, decrease heat energy needs (energy savings measures for existing buildings, use of exhaust heat), reduce fuel use, conversion to alternative fuels, use of renewable energy sources (biogas, geothermal and solar energy)
5. Development of sustainable urban development structures	**Goal:** To improve quality and appreciation of urban development **Measures:** Corporate design for the entire zone, create a quality environment, design attractive road networks, a sustainable concept for conversions, expansions and new buildings, building density, use of ecological building materials

Table 11.2 continued

Overarching goal	Goals and measures
6. Development of sustainable transport services	**Goal**: To reduce traffic volume and associated traffic irritations **Measures**: Direct connections to the autobahn (reduces traffic), combined shipping and receiving in the zone (reduces traffic), reduce traffic circulation areas, use of rail terminals, schedule public transportation access for peak work hours, access to bike trails, reduce fuel use, conversion to alternative fuels
7. Development of social planning	**Goal**: To increase flexible work hours, training programmes, job satisfaction **Measures**: Individual childcare (24-hour services for ages 0–14, health clinics, homework tutors), joint training programmes, organization of training internships, in-factory training, exchange of trainees, programmes with schools, healthcare services, company sports, lunch meals served at factory cafeteria

It is important to note that a series of measures will hold a major economic relevance and/or simultaneously also a social and ecological relevance. For example, increasing material and energy efficiency, consideration of product and service life cycles, energetic renovation of existing buildings, promoting collaboration and synergies, improving the quality of urban planning for the zone, creating high-quality surroundings, building consolidation within the zone, ecologic (and therefore economic) area development, use of efficient building services, preventing waste water pollutants, cooperative training programmes, establishing a cross-company catering facility, etc.

Looking further into the details, it quickly becomes clear that all of these aspects of sustainable development have a substantial impact on climate protection and the quality of our environment: not only the traditional measures implemented to provide higher resource and energy efficiency decrease carbon dioxide emissions, but also constructing bike trails, using environmentally safe materials, reducing the volume of waste water, on-site childcare, realizing local facilities and utilities as doctors' offices or a common cafeteria (so workers do not have to drive to go for lunch) as well as systematic connections to the public transport system that also cover all of the work shifts.

Summary and conclusions

The subject of sustainable industrial/commercial zones is still breaking new ground, not only in Germany, but internationally too. However, the level of industrial and commercial zones offers a lot of potential for implementing sustainability measures that have positive effects for the companies involved, but also for the municipality on site and the whole business region. In this chapter, we described the rationale as well as the specification and the practical implementation of the concept of a sustainable industrial zone.

Initially, we therefore introduced the theoretical basis for this concept, lying in the global mission of sustainable development as it was formulated by the World Commission on Environment and Development in 1987 and underpinned through the Agenda 21, but also more recently in the new UN sustainable development goals. According to this, we developed a principal classification of industrial zones into the three dimensions of sustainable development followed by the inference of different access paths to the sustainable industrial zones approach. Whereas the partial approach only strives for and implements individually selected measures, the distinguishing features of the integrated approach are the large number of selected, coordinated and ultimately implemented measures. Consequently, only the integrated approach adheres to a comprehensive understanding of sustainable development.

However, an objective demarcation of the two approaches is not possible until a certification system for the sustainable industrial zone approach has been developed. Here we are still moving in uncharted territory allowing only for exemplary criteria to be developed, which require further differentiation and must yet be formulated into a consistent certification system. We presented a first delineation of such a certification system (Fischer et al. 2015) which focuses on managerial aspects and highlights the necessity of cooperation between companies and local authorities as well as their responsible persons for business development. This scheme allows certifying sustainability measures in different stages of a zone's life cycle as well as on different levels of implementation and actors involved.

The subsequent discussion has presented findings from research projects carried out at the University of Kaiserslautern in Germany, involving various industrial and commercial zones and thus demonstrating a specific relevance for practice. This involved in particular the methodical approach of the integrated sustainability triangle. The advantage of this method lies in the fact that the relevant fields of action and the indicators inferred from them can be classified systematically and can also be deduced from existing relevant sustainability documents dealing at the level of (federal) states, municipalities and companies or organizations in general. This enables the development of an intrinsically consistent approach to a sustainable industrial zone that is directly corresponding to the "state of the art" of the recent sustainability discourse and the principles, fields of action, indicators etc. they comprise. In the context of this approach it has been possible to demonstrate that the implementation of the ecological, economic and social fields of action can produce numerous benefits for the enterprises participating in the industrial zone, both in terms of a reinforcement of competitive capacity and long-term stability.

In conclusion, it must be emphasized that the approach of a sustainable industrial zone will have to be adapted to the relevant framework conditions of the existing or planned industrial zone. For that reason, the participation of all relevant actors on site is necessary in order to gain a common vision for the zone and to define goals and measures for their further development. Such a process can be supported by adequate concepts for a moderated exchange, as it was presented above. However, coming closer to cooperate and thinking about recent and future issues which could be managed together also requires some investment from the actors involved that cannot be presumed as a matter of course. Nevertheless, the experiences of the research projects mentioned above show that many industrial and commercial zones recognize the great potential of this approach and show a great deal of interest in it, even when the implementation of concrete measures sometimes is rather a long time coming. Correspondingly, it is reasonable to expect this concept to experience heightened reach in the future.

Notes

1 Both terms, industrial and commercial zone, are used synonymously in this text. Nevertheless, potential sustainability activities depend on the type of companies located in a zone (industrial manufacturing companies versus service, trading and distribution companies).
2 In 2007–2009 an initial comprehensive research project on the subject, From the Zero Emission Park to the Sustainable Industrial Zone, was carried out in Germany (under the scientific leadership of Prof. Dr. Michael von Hauff, University of Kaiserslautern). Subsequently, the project Sustainable Development in Industrial and Commercial Zones was carried out in the state of Rhineland-Palatinate from 2011–2015 under the same scientific leadership. This project addressed seven exemplary industrial/commercial areas in different stages of their life cycle (conception, transition, existence).

References

Cobb, C.W. (1989): The Index of Sustainable Economic Welfare, in: Daly, H.E., Cobb, J.B. (eds): *For the Common Good – redirecting the economy toward community, the environment, and a sustainable future*, Boston, pp. 401–457.
DGNB (2013): Das DGNB System für Stadt- und Gewerbequartiere sowie Industriestandorte. Online: www.dgnb.de/fileadmin/de/dgnb_ev/Veranstaltungen/DGNB_auf_Messen/expo/Standprogramm_2013/13.00_Bewertungnachhaltiger Quartiere.pdf.
EFQM (2012): *EFQM-Excellence Modell 2013*. European Foundation for Quality Management, Brussels.
Feser, H.-D. (2008): Nachhaltiger Wohlfahrtsstaat?, in: v. Hauff, M., Lingnau, V., Zink, K.J. (Hrsg.): *Nachhaltiges Wirtschaften*, Baden-Baden, pp. 1–22.
Fischer, K.; Baudach, T.; von Hauff, M. (2015): Nachhaltige Gewerbe- und Industriegebiete – Theoretische Begründung und konzeptionelle Ausgestaltung, *Volkswirtschaftliche Diskussionsbeiträge der Technischen Universität Kaiserslautern*, No. 39-15.
Haug, S. (1997): *Soziales Kapital. Ein kritischer Rückblick über den aktuellen Forschungsstand, Arbeitspapiere des Arbeitsbereiches II, 15*. Mannheimer Zentrum für Europäische Sozialforschung, Mannheim.
von Hauff, M. (2012): Anforderungen an nachhaltige Gewerbegebiete, in: von Hauff, M., Isenmann, R., Müller-Christ, G. (eds): *Industrial Ecology Management*, Wiesbaden, pp. 101–107.
von Hauff, M. (2014): *Nachhaltige Entwicklung – Grundlagen und Umsetzung*, 2nd ed. Munich.
von Hauff, M.; Kleine, A. (2005): Methodischer Ansatz zur Systematisierung von Handlungsfeldern und Indikatoren einer Nachhaltigkeitsstrategie – Das Integrierende

Nachhaltigkeits-Dreieck. *Volkswirtschaftliche Diskussionsbeiträge an der Universität Kaiserslautern*, Nr. 19-05.

von Hauff, M.; Wolf, V. (2008): Vom Zero Emission Park zum Nachhaltigen Industrie-/ Gewerbegebiet, in: von Hauff, M., Tarkan, B. (eds): *Nachhaltige kommunale Finanzpolitik für eine intergenerationelle Gerechtigkeit*, Baden-Baden, pp. 193–211.

WCED (1987): *Report of the World Commission on Environment and Development*. A/42/427. Online: www.un.org/en/ga/search/view_doc.asp?symbol=A/42/427.

Wilderer, M.Z. (2002): *Economic Growth, Environment and Development*, Delhi.

Wolf, V. (2004): *"Nachhaltige Gewerbeflächenentwicklung" Ein Modellprojekt in NRW, Ministerium für Umwelt und Naturschutz, Landwirtschaft und Verbraucherschutz des Landes Nordrhein-Westfalen*, Düsseldorf. Online: www.munlv.nrw.de.

Part III

Resource problems

12 Sustainable resources

Managing markets, increasing efficiency and establishing partnerships

Raimund Bleischwitz and Florian Flachenecker

Introduction

The contemporary debate offers two perspectives on natural resources, especially regarding minerals and metals: one perspective looks at environmental pressures and scarcities; it often contrasts environmental constraints with extraction figures that have been on the rise since decades. The other perspective looks at development opportunities for resource-rich countries and analyses the governance conditions that may help to turn natural endowments into prosperity for the people. Indeed, both perspectives are justified and resemble the broader debate on the environmental and socio-economic dimensions of sustainable development. Not surprisingly, there are a number of trade-offs and synergies between both angles that need to be considered. The aim of our contribution is to analyse key trends of international resource consumption and evaluate sustainability perspectives for resources focusing on material resources. We seek to demonstrate that the broader picture is not gloomy (*limits to* growth or *resource curse*) but nor should one become overly optimistic about transitions to market-based and equitable democracies based on commodities. Underlining the importance of natural resources, we argue that the notions of a green economy and green growth require incorporating the topic of sustainable resource management. A particular objective of our chapter is to highlight resource efficiency as an opportunity, which is in line with both perspectives. Evidence, however, shows that resource efficiency occurs insufficiently and under what we call a *web of constraints*, i.e. interconnected barriers to resource efficiency improvements. Such barriers obstruct efficiency gains at different levels and should be removed by more ambitious, better-coordinated and more internationally oriented strategies by multiple actors, including policy makers. Finally, we will draw several conclusions about the future role of resources in development cooperation.

International commodity markets – a rollercoaster

Material resources are vital for an economy. Societies need construction minerals and other materials for housing and urban development; they need steel and copper and other metals for mobility; and fuels plus a number of materials for energy systems, not to mention biomass and food for nutrition and human survival. Typically, the more economic activity takes place, the more materials are being consumed. The following analysis outlines global trends in material consumption and the impact of a rising material consumption exemplified by volatile commodity prices, followed by a brief outlook on commodity markets.

Global trends in material consumption

Global consumption of material resources has almost doubled in absolute terms between 1980 and 2009. Global gross domestic product (GDP) measured in constant 2005 US dollars has been growing faster compared to global material consumption, whereas population growth has decoupled from material consumption since the turn of the century, i.e. material consumption per capita has increased (Figure 12.1).

But what has caused the increase in material consumption over time? The academic literature has identified numerous drivers of material consumption (e.g. Bringezu et al. 2004; Moll et al. 2005; Steinberger et al. 2010; Weinzettel & Kovanda 2011). Besides a country's economic structure, technological change and

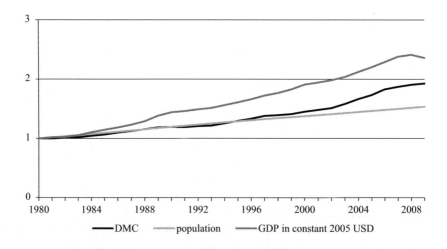

Figure 12.1 On the rise: domestic material consumption, GPD and population, 1980–2009

Notes: Data based on domestic material consumption (DMC), GDP in constant 2005 US$ and
population from 1980 to 2009. The base year is 1980, which = 1. DMC is a variable
commonly used by the OECD, EU and UN, among others, in material flow accounting.
DMC measures the mass (weight) of the materials that are physically used in the consumption
activities of the domestic economic system (i.e. the direct apparent consumption of materials,
excluding indirect flows). In economy-wide material flow accounting, DMC equals DMI
(domestic material input) minus exports, i.e. domestic extraction plus imports minus exports
(see Bringezu & Bleischwitz 2009).

Source: Calculations based on SERI, World Bank and UN data

resource policies, economic growth is considered a key driver of material consumption.

As visible in Figure 12.1, the growing consumption of materials is certainly correlated with economic growth – without inferring any causal relationship. The industrialized world, in Figure 12.2, represented by the USA and the UK, decreased its absolute domestic material consumption compared to the global trend, which is shown as the horizontal axis. Industrialized countries typically have stayed below the world's average of almost doubling material consumption between 1980 and 2009 (e.g. Canada, Finland, France, Germany, Australia, Japan). Thus, emerging economies have been driving the growth in material consumption (e.g. Brazil, Chile, Indonesia, Turkey – except South Africa and Russia since 1992) by increasing their material consumption above the global average, in line with average income growth.

Breaking down the group of emerging economies, especially China, India and Chile show a substantial increase in material consumption. China has exponentially increased its consumption by a factor of 7.5 since 1980, whereas India *only* tripled and Chile *only* approximately quadrupled its consumption. China's growth particularly started to pick up in the early 2000s, coinciding with its membership in the World Trade Organization (WTO). In the case of India and Chile, this increase can somewhat be explained by an increase in population (70 per cent between 1980 and 2009 for India and 52 per cent for Chile). Given China's relatively lower

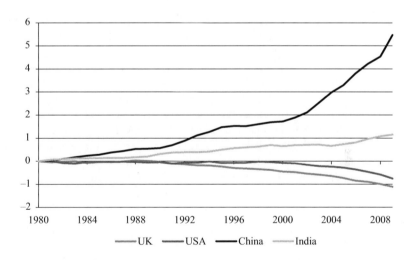

Figure 12.2 Emerging economies drive the increase in global domestic material consumption, 1980–2009

Note: Global average is represented by the horizontal axis. The base year is 1980. All positive values indicate a faster increase in material consumption compared to the world's average.

Source: Calculations based on SERI data

increase of around 30 per cent (partly due to policies restricting population growth) and without going into details, one should consider the industrialization in China and its increasing exports as the main driver for such a trend (Economy & Levi 2014).

Generally, the higher growth rates in material consumption could indicate a conventional catch-up scenario: once economic activity of emerging economies catches-up to industrialized countries, they also catch-up in terms of material consumption. Therefore, one has to keep in mind that the average *per capita consumption* in the industrialized world is still higher compared to the emerging economies. In 2009, the USA consumed 21 tonnes of materials per person compared to 4 tonnes in India, almost 16 tonnes in China and 12 tonnes in Russia (Lutter et al. 2014). The majority of EU countries consumed more than 16 tonnes per capita (EC 2013a). Resource-rich economies such as Chile, with 43 tonnes per capita, are rather an exception to this rule.

Occasionally, urbanization is considered a further driver of material consumption. Cities consume a lot of materials in absolute terms and also because most economic activity takes place there (McKinsey Global Institute 2011). However, urban areas may profit from economies of scale and density. Thus, material consumption per capita might actually be lower compared to rural areas. Hence, urbanization does not appear to be a key driver of material consumption, at least in per capita terms.

The impact of rising material consumption

We showed that there has been a substantial increase in material consumption, predominantly driven by economic expansion in emerging economies. This increase has several implications, both for the environment and the economy.

Environmental pressures can arise in each stage of material consumption, for example by emitting particulates during material production, erosions from mining and leakages of chemicals into the environment during the separation process of metals (UNEP IRP 2010). Environmental impacts are also related to negative externalities resulting from material waste. For instance, the greenhouse gas methane is emitted from landfills and thus not only negatively impacting the environment locally, but also globally by contributing to climate change (IPCC 2007). Such environmental costs associated with material consumption (including those interlinked with energy use) can also negatively impact economic activity directly and indirectly (UNEP 2014), such as negatively impacting human health and thereby reducing labour productivity.

There are also economic implications from an increase in material consumption. We will restrict our focus to material prices here. The rise in material consumption and thus demand for materials can be considered a key driver of the structural price increase of commodities since the year 2000 (Valiante & Egenhofer 2013). While demand pressures play an important role in forming commodity prices, other factors can likewise impact on price levels as well as price volatility (Ecorys 2012; Cavalcanti et al. 2011; Cuddington & Nülle 2014; Ma 2013;). Not surprisingly, there

Table 12.1 Main drivers of the price level and price volatility of materials

	Drivers
Price level	• Materials characteristics and properties • Economic growth perspectives (especially in key producer/consumer economies) • Investments in supply capacity (i.e. infrastructure, transportation) • Exploitation of market power (vertically and horizontally) • Input costs (i.e. labour costs, labour supply shortages, infrastructure) • Environmental regulation • Long-term energy costs • Storage capacities • Ore grades and related costs for energy and water (especially for metals) • Product development
Price volatility	• Financialization (for most commodities since the early 2000s) • Short-term costs fluctuations of connected resources (i.e. energy), i.e. resource nexus • Shocks to the business cycle • Close connection between futures and spot markets (i.e. high-frequency trading) • Short-term production interruptions (i.e. strikes, natural disasters, water and electricity shortages, political changes)

Source: Based on Valiante & Egenhofer 2013

is some overlap between the determinants of price level and price volatility (see Table 12.1). Nevertheless, price levels are predominantly associated with long-term developments and price volatility with short-term developments.

Figure 12.3 shows trends of commodity price indices. Starting during the early 2000s, prices have increased significantly followed by a recent downward trend. The structural shift in price levels goes hand in hand with the substantial increase of material consumption by emerging economies. Supply seems to lag behind, for instance due to low investments in the 1990s, decreasing ore grades and stricter environmental legislation. Therefore, nominal prices for example for copper more than tripled between the beginning of 2004 and mid-2006. The same amount of increase within those 2.5 years occurred during the 44 years before 2004. Iron ore follows a comparable pattern. The prices quadrupled between 1960 and 2004 – since then they even quintupled. For a limited amount of time (approximately 2004–2006), prices even increased exponentially.

Once the 2008 financial crisis in the industrialized world turned into a macro-economic crisis, demand for and trade of materials decreased sharply, also in emerging economies. This economic downturn resulted in a short-run oversupply and lowered expectations, initiating a downward spiral of material prices. However, prices did not remain on these lower levels, but increased rapidly again. Currently (2015), prices may seem to be less volatile again, but they remain at higher levels compared to the pre-2000s. What becomes apparent is that material price volatility

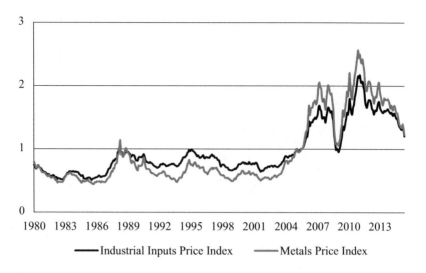

Figure 12.3 Volatility has become the new normal, 1980–2015

Note: Prices are non-seasonally adjusted nominal US$ and range from 1980 to 2015. The base year
    for both indices is 2005. The Monthly Industrial Input Price Index includes agricultural raw
    materials and metals price indices (based on copper, aluminium, iron ore, tin, nickel, zinc, lead
    and uranium price indices).

Source: Data extracted from IMF

(Figure 12.3 shows inter-month volatility) has become the new normal, in line
with energy prices (World Energy Council 2015).

Outlook of the commodity markets

What is the outlook for the years to come? The commodity price fluctuations of
recent years have lead to market uncertainties about return on investments and the
future of the mining industry (Humphreys 2015). Accordingly, exploration budgets have been cut. At a more disaggregated level, one may expect energy prices to
stay slightly lower compared to metals and agricultural commodities, which is
mainly due to new energy supply coming on stream (offshore oil, unconventional
fuels, expansion plans of major suppliers and the likely return of Iran and others,
plus an increase in renewable energies); such expansion is unlikely to be mirrored
by supply increases in the latter two areas. A key factor is the future development
in China and other emerging economies. China's steel demand, for instance, seems
to face a short-term recession, partly due to weak property markets. In the long-
run, it will be essential to see whether countries such as China will continue to
catch-up their currently low levels of steel stocks per capita, or to what extent any
saturation effects helps to level off demand for materials (Müller et al. 2011).

Generally, changes in material price levels and price volatility are unlikely to disappear in the future. The resulting uncertainties may impose substantial costs on companies and entire economies, thus the need to address these developments become essentially for firms and policy makers. Resource efficiency could serve as one strategy to lower the negative impacts of high and volatile material prices for both companies as well as entire economies, while addressing environmental challenges and causing multiple additional benefits (Flachenecker & Rentschler 2015).

The resource efficiency revolution – and the web of constraints

Resource efficiency can be seen as a core strategy to decouple the use of material resources from GDP and to innovate along the material value chains. Given the considerable rise in material consumption shown above, this seems fundamental. We also propose to see resource efficiency as a strategy to make supply chains more resilient against volatility and other uncertainties. Driven by price increases since the year 2000, efforts by industry and other factors, enhancements of resource efficiency have been labelled as a "revolution" (McKinsey Global Institute 2011). Renewable energies have been pioneering a more general upswing of clean technologies: global wind energy installations have soared about 25 per cent per year since 2006, solar PV even 57 per cent annually; the more recent market consolidation does not break those trends. But there is more to it. New smart products and materials emerge, be it in liquid wood, software-driven reshuffling of metal blankets or in e-mobility. Eco-innovation clusters emerge around buildings, IT applications, agriculture and food, recycling and industrial symbiosis, water treatment, grid analytics, bio-based materials, etc. New business models are widespread: leasing models bring down upfront costs for new treatment facilities and help maintain high-quality machineries, smart sharing services start to replace ownerships especially in urban markets, benefit sharing agreements between companies open the windows for better value chains.

Figure 12.4 shows the wide range of areas for what is called here *CleanTech* covering the traditional environmental technologies, energy, mobility and resources: in a wider understanding of resources indeed all areas could be named resource efficiency.

Following for example the European Union's (EU) Eco-Innovation Observatory, probably the biggest short-term gains are achievable in process innovation, as many companies have not yet fully grasped the opportunities of managing resources more efficiently (Eco-Innovation Observatory 2011, 2012). Piping construction, a key element for infrastructure development, increases resource efficiency by some 20 per cent by using reused offcuts. Given that more than half of European companies are paying at least 30 per cent of their total costs for their material inputs (higher than some believe!) and analyses validate cost savings in the range from 5–20 per cent, there are bills left on the sidewalk that can also be utilized to unleash investments in long-term resource efficiency strategies (EC 2011a, 2012, 2013b). Generally, investments in resource efficiency tend to yield positive net benefits, both from an economic and environmental perspective (Flachenecker & Rentschler 2015).

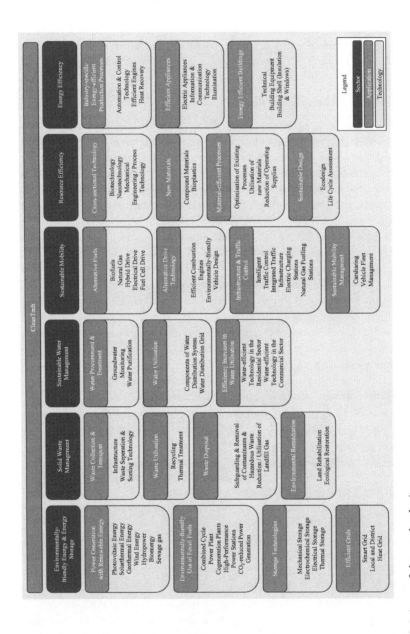

Figure 12.4 Areas of clean technologies

Source: DCTI et al. 2013 based on data from Roland Berger Strategy Consultants 2012

The question then arises: why are not all manufacturing companies and economies around the globe using resources more efficiently? Research findings indicate a *web of constraints* – internal barriers within firms and external barriers resulting from both market failures and policy failures (Flachenecker & Rentschler 2015; Jordan et al. 2014; POLFREE 2014a). A key reason is that resources are so diverse and their market applications too. It is thus not easy to understand the world of materials from mining onto production and consumption, recycling and waste, with so many heterogeneous infrastructures, products and services involved, plus the behaviour of end users that ultimately drive market expectations. This leads to acknowledge a second main reason: human decision making usually is not fully rational; it is driven by a bundle of rules, expectations, preferences and motivations. It is thus too easy to imagine one main barrier, or a few main barriers, that ought to be removed by smart market actors and/or policy makers. Rather, research suggests that usually barriers resemble more a complex *web of constraints* that include individual and institutional behavioural patterns, inertia and direct and indirect interconnections between the institutional, social and individual levels (POLFREE 2014b).

Figure 12.5 summarizes a number of such barriers as well as drivers at the firm level and illustrates the increasing importance of "external" factors at the level of markets and institutional frameworks rather than within business itself. It is, however, also important to recognize the multiplier effect stemming from volatile commodity markets and uncertain market expectations in the future: research and development (R&D) and investments into new resource-efficient products and "systemic eco-innovations"[1] are more likely to be postponed or stuck at niche markets, as the mass market roll out is much more risky than experimenting in a niche, which translates into reluctance from financial investors and policy makers alike to support financing and a more stable market demand. Thinking about how such *web of constraints* can be overcome and how promising good examples can be scaled up towards mass markets at an international scale is probably a key issue for development cooperation in the years ahead. In a wider sense, the notion of a *web of constraints* underlines the necessity more collaborative action, possibly at an international scale, and oriented towards long-term common goals.

The search for strategies to unleash resource efficiency thus should address a multitude of actors and incentives, possibly along a timeline with innovative niches to be created and processes of a broader transformation towards mass markets being pursued step-by-step.

Cross-country gaps in resource efficiency

The implications of a *web of constraints* undermining and obstructing efforts to increase resource efficiency implies differences across industries and countries, depending on the severity and interlinkages between such constraints. We aim to present an indication for such heterogeneity using a comparative empirical analysis on the macroeconomic level.

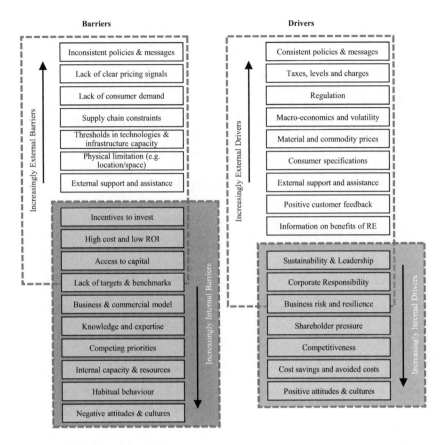

Figure 12.5 Why have resources been used inefficiently? Barriers and drivers

Source: adapted from POLFREE 2014c

Table 12.2 reveals significant gaps in resource efficiency performances across a number of countries. Between 1992 and 2009, the UK for instance more than doubled its resource efficiency whereas countries such as Egypt, FYR Macedonia and Morocco remained at their 1992 levels. In terms of efficiency increase, Bosnia and Herzegovina, Armenia and the Russian Federation among others outperformed the USA, Germany and Finland. Generally, the Europe and Central Asia and Middle East and Northern Africa regions performed better in terms of material efficiency improvements relative to Latin America and the Caribbean (West & Schandl 2013).

However, considering absolute material efficiency, the picture turns. The first column in Table 12.2 provides an insight into absolute material efficiency (GDP/DMC). Comparing the efficiency measures for the UK, Germany and the USA with most other countries in Table 12.2 reveals a substantial efficiency gap.

Table 12.2 Cross-country gaps in resource efficiency and the role of key sectors

	Resource efficiency (US$ thousand/tonne)	1992–2009 % resource efficiency change	Industry % of GDP	Natural resources % of GDP
United Kingdom	3.92	106	21	1.2
Germany	2.30	50	30	0.2
USA	2.04	52	20	1.3
Croatia	1.27	14	26	1.6
Slovakia	1.06	44	31	0.7
Finland	1.05	49	25	1.4
Hungary	1.04	55	28	0.9
Slovenia	0.94	23	29	0.4
Lithuania	0.87	75	28	1.0
Latvia	0.78	31	26	2.6
Turkey	0.75	30	27	0.7
Poland	0.58	65	33	1.9
Romania	0.52	39	37	2.8
Russian Federation	0.51	77	38	18.7
Tunisia	0.45	29	30	7.4
Georgia	0.41	20	22	0.9
Estonia	0.40	23	30	2.6
Albania	0.36	11	15	5.5
Bosnia and Herzegovina	0.34	88	26	2.3
Belarus	0.34	75	46	2.5
Azerbaijan	0.33	39	63	39.8
Armenia	0.32	80	37	5.2
Serbia (and Montenegro)	0.32	75	32	4.3
Jordan	0.32	40	30	2.8
Morocco	0.32	6	32	5.0
Turkmenistan	0.29	36	24	34.4
Bulgaria	0.27	26	30	2.8
Ukraine	0.25	44	30	4.6
FYR Macedonia	0.25	7	28	3.9
India	0.22	57	17	5.6
Moldova	0.21	31	20	0.5
Egypt	0.19	7	38	11.9
Kazakhstan	0.18	72	38	32.1
China	0.16	50	45	5.8
Kyrgyz Republic	0.11	36	34	15.0
Mongolia	0.04	52	33	28.7

Notes: Absolute resource efficiency (RE) in 2009, the increase in resource efficiency in 2009 compared to 1992 in percentage, the contribution of the industrial sector to total GDP in percentage for 2013 and the percentage of rents from natural resources (oil, gas, coal, minerals and forest rents) as part of a country's GDP in 2012. The industrial sector includes mining, manufacturing, energy production and construction. Material efficiency is measured as the ratio between GDP (in US$ thousand 2005 constant) and DMC (in tonnes).

Source: calculations based on World Bank and SERI data

The first non-EU country, Turkey, is less than one-fifth as efficient as the UK. The USA is more efficient than China by a factor of about 13. However, any such gaps should not be interpreted as definite and exact measures but as a general benchmark as the underlying data come with uncertainties.

Four aspects can explain part of the story behind these substantial differences across countries. First, a material-intensive economic structure correlates with low resource efficiency performance. This may partly be explained by statistical issues, i.e. the primary sector driving GDP and DMC upwards simultaneously, whereas the tertiary sector may increase GDP more than DMC. Additionally, a strong mining sector may trigger *Dutch Disease* issues, i.e. the macroeconomics and political economy in those countries that have been focusing on the core business of "getting the stuff out of the ground" may be more exposed to such macroeconomic developments (Gylfason et al. 1999). Second, as industrialized countries tend to import resource-intensive goods there is a bias and a potential burden-shifting associated with the international division of labour. With other words: the success of some countries is complemented by more resource-intensive patterns in others (Wiedmann et al. 2013). Third, the resource efficiency agenda has been driven by environmental policy considerations for example in the EU (EC 2011b) and Germany (BMUB 2015), a factor that is less visible in a number of other countries. Fourth, one may question whether resource-intensive economies may ever be able to follow pathways towards a service economy, and why they should do so (World Bank 2014). The latter indeed is a broader debate, which we will continue below and is also subject of other chapters in this book.

Nevertheless, the point to make is that such significant gaps exist despite data uncertainties and thus development cooperation has a role to play in overcoming gaps and improving resource efficiency not only within individual countries, but taking into account all repercussions arising in a globalized world.

Towards a coherent policy framework for resource efficiency

From the analysis above and the lessons learned, resource efficiency needs a policy framework to overcome the *web of constraints* resulting from a double motivation: (1) addressing environmental constraints and (2) fostering value creation by facilitating innovation (Bleischwitz 2012). Key pillars of the approach are shown in Figure 12.6. Such a policy framework is best conceptualized as a collaborative effort in a most coherent perspective done at multiple scales and involving a number of actors, all supported by evidence-based research, rather than a heroic attempt to develop and implement any "optimal" solution.

One key element of the policy framework proposed is to establish a "market order" that sets the framework conditions for an efficient use of resources. This requires internalizations of externalities through a regulatory regime based on the *polluter pays principle* and at an international scale *precautionary principles*, and the definition of instruments that foster eco-design of products and producer responsibility throughout the whole life cycle of product and services. Other important framework conditions are for example the removal of environmentally harmful

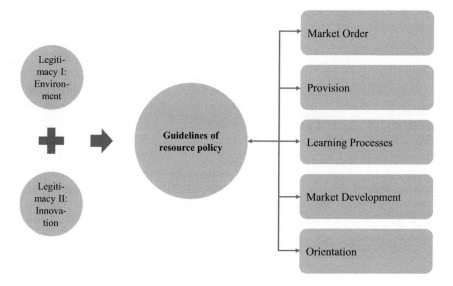

Figure 12.6 Key pillars of a resource efficiency policy agenda
Source: Bleischwitz 2012

subsidies and could include a transition to leasing models, in which producer maintain stewardship for the materials contained in products so that they can be reused, remanufactured or recycled at the end of their use; depreciation models; and accounting rules to create more even conditions for new business models based on performance rather than ownership. Setting such a "market order" right is crucial in the case of lower middle-income (LMI) countries with weak institutional set-ups and underdevelopment of environmental policy frameworks to correct prevailing market failures. In the case of resource-rich developing countries, extraction taxes together with international partnerships, greater transparency on the part of extractive industries (Bleischwitz 2014) and green sovereign wealth funds can apply resource efficiency to the primary sector while generating revenues that could foster education and health systems to increase the absorption capabilities of the country and overcome the institutional failures known as *resource curse*.

The second pillar of the framework proposed is "provision". This refers to the need to tackle information and knowledge deficits that prevent a more efficient use of resources and a better understanding of the resource interlinkages. This could take the shape of open access data sources such as a data hub on the *resource nexus* (Andrews-Speed et al. 2014) in collaboration with existing geological surveys and collaborate on defining coefficients for resource inputs across main interlinkages, benchmarks on resource productivity, main environmental pressure indicators and data at the sectoral, national and regional levels of material flows and opportunities for optimization. Indeed, existing providers such as the Green Growth Knowledge

Platform or the Natural Resource Governance Institute could be helpful with such endeavours.

Information and new data per se are insufficient unless they are accompanied by learning processes that increase the knowledge base on sustainable practices of resource use, facilitate knowledge transfer and capacity building at the local level and facilitate learning both through formalized processes such as improved education systems, but also through collaborative learning at the level of firms and industries through processes such as benchmarking, reporting guidelines, audit tools or business platforms. This is especially relevant for LMI countries where learning processes may not be well established and there is often a lack of institutional support for intercompany collaboration and learning.

Another key pillar of an eco-innovation strategy oriented towards resource efficiency is "market development" through policies that foster sustainable manufacturing and the uptake of new and radical innovations and foster transitions, where resources are used in cyclical loops that helps them to retain their highest value for as long as possible and remain in the productive systems through recycling and recovery processes. Using renewable energies as a striking example, Pegels (2014) identifies the drivers and success factors of a green industrial policy, which seeks to reconcile the synergies and trade-offs that exist between economic and environmental goals. At a future international level this could crystallize into international covenants for promoting sustainable patterns of resource management, including extraction and recycling. Recycling of metals and other valuable resources contained in e-waste should in principle provide win–win opportunities. Another waste stream of potential interest would be used cars. Currently, in terms of e-waste, used cars tend to be exported as second-hand goods from developed to less developed countries, where end-of-life treatment is poor and not well managed. Wilts and Bleischwitz (2012) propose the creation of a metal covenant based on a private law contract between manufacturers, recyclers and relevant authorities in destination countries. This could bring benefits at both ends of the supply chain and create incentives for eco-design of products as the *producer responsibility principle*, which is in place in Europe and other developed countries, would not be undermined by exports.

In the long term, though, Bleischwitz (2012) also proposes the creation of an international convention for sustainable resource management that would provide legal support at the international level for a better and more transparent management of natural resources and the creation of national and regional raw material funds, with a focus on resource-rich countries, to ensure that yields from extractive industries contribute to national/regional development and activities are based on a sustainable management of resources and introduction of resource efficient production patterns. This could be supported by the design of "roadmaps for sustainable resource management" as bilateral or multilateral agreements between developed nations and the BRICs (Brazil, Russia, India and China) (Bleischwitz 2012).

Finally, "orientation" refers to the need to establish long-term visions of sustainable development and resource efficiency at the global and regional level that provide guidance for policy design and target setting to move towards more circular, resource efficient and low carbon systems by collaborating towards certainty and guidance. Looking at international policy trends, such orientation is also needed to align the manifold mining visions with the circular economy and the wider aims of coping with the planetary boundaries. The World Business Council for Sustainable Development (WBCSD) Vision 2050 was a useful step in such direction, and it might now be time to establish an international process along with the Sustainable Development Goals (SDGs) that could align the various resource futures around the globe (WBCSD 2010).

Last but not least, as one would not expect one single policy instrument to be successful, *policy mixes* at a multitude of levels are needed in managing the global transition from current unsustainable consumption and production patterns towards green growth and poverty eradication. For sure, to manage such a global transition policies are well advised to establish social contracts with their people and major stakeholders that are able to overcome barriers and unleash the potential of systemic eco-innovations. Given the variety of systems around the world, the interplay between actors and institutions at different levels will likely lead to quite different resource futures (see Figure 12.7; see also Lee et al. 2012).

What's next? The SDGs, an emerging international alliance and the resource nexus

Following our empirical analysis, up to now resource efficiency has mainly been an issue for some manufacturing industries in industrialized countries, especially those concerned with commodity prices and oriented towards consumers with environmental awareness. Those companies have improved their production processes and started to offer smarter products to their customers, which translates into a "better" performance compared to other countries. Accordingly, the attempts to decouple resource use from GDP and create a green growth have not yet been successful at an international scale.

However, those active companies move ahead and have started to improve resource efficiency along their supply chains and collaborate with others for market development. The 2015 newly established G7 Alliance on Resource Efficiency aims to promote an exchange of concepts on how to address the challenges of resource efficiency, to share best practices and experience, and to create information networks (G7 2015a, 2015b). It plans a series of workshops and has invited the United Nations Environment Programme (UNEP) International Resource Panel to prepare a synthesis report highlighting the most promising potentials and solutions for resource efficiency in industrialized countries, emerging market economies and developing countries. The Organization for Economic Co-operation and Development (OECD) will also support this process. In line with these efforts, the 2014 Manifesto of the European Resource Efficiency Platform calls for at least a doubling of resource efficiency compared to pre-crisis trend and develops policy pillars to unleash such dynamics (European Resource Efficiency Platform 2014). Such proposals are mirrored by national resource efficiency strategies. The Global Reporting Initiative, amongst others, calls for more stringent policies.

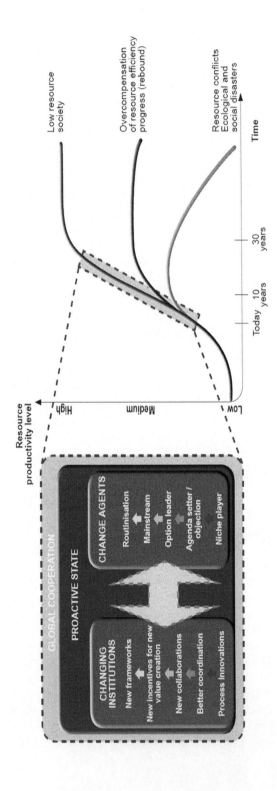

Figure 12.7 The role of institutions and actors in shaping resource efficiency

Source: Eco-Innovation Observatory 2012, p. 34, adapted from WBGU 2011

One may conclude that resource efficiency seem to arrive at the international level. It will be interesting to compare the recent launch of the new sustainable development goals with such efforts. In our view, the new SDGs (as approved in September 2015) are likely to have major implications for future resource markets. However, those implications are mixed. On the one hand, many of the new SDGs will lead to an increase in demand for a number of materials:

- Goal 2: "End hunger, achieve food security and improved nutrition and promote sustainable agriculture" implies increasing demand for land, mineral fertilizers, water, biomass and food.
- Goal 6: "Ensure access to water and sanitation for all" implies investments in water supply and a water distribution infrastructure, i.e. increasing demand for materials.
- Goal 7: "Ensure access to affordable, reliable, sustainable and modern energy for all" is likely to imply increasing demand for bio-energy and renewable energy, plus more traditional energy sources, which again implies more demand for land, biomass, water and materials.
- Goal 9: "Build resilient infrastructure, promote inclusive and sustainable indus-trialization and foster innovation" will require more construction materials, metals and other materials.

Adding the promotion of economic growth to it, as well as efforts to eradicate hunger and enhance health, the signals for future demand stemming from the SDGs for materials are clearly upwards. At least for key metals (aluminium, iron ore, copper and nickel, which altogether make up for more than 80 per cent of world production of metals), for construction minerals and for biomass, the SDGs are very likely leading to new and additional demand compared to business as usual forecasts. The situation for energy fuels is less straightforward as climate policy will probably lead to restrictions for using fossil fuels, if political efforts succeed, although major suppliers may not join any future international agreement and have announced plans to expand production; if prices for fossil fuels stay low, efforts to curb demand will be difficult to achieve.

On the other hand, the SDGs also endorse the sustainable production and consumption agenda, and call for global increases in resource efficiency as well as for aims to achieve sustainable and resource-efficient infrastructures by 2030 (Goal 9) and sustainable management and efficient use of all resources by 2030 (Goal 12). Moreover, they aim to "improve progressively, through 2030, global resource effi-ciency in consumption and production and endeavour to decouple economic growth from environmental degradation" (Goal 8).

The balance between such expected demand increases and other goals however is not entirely clear, in particular as key terms (such as sustainable management and efficient use of all resources) are insufficiently defined and will leave space for quite different implementation pathways. More research will thus be required to develop principles for a sustainable management of resources and to understand future dynamics on commodity markets.

The well-established principles of shifting the resource base from using non-renewable resources onto renewable resources (Daly 1990; Pearce & Turner 1990) are often quoted in the public debate and may drive a number of policies, yet they have been critically re-examined. Environmental research reveals very limited capacities of eco-systems to provide additional renewable resources at a large scale (Rockström et al. 2009; Steffen et al. 2015). The seven principles developed by Bringezu and Bleischwitz (2009, p. 8) instead focus on increasing resource efficiency and assume that non-renewable resources will maintain to have a share in providing materials (albeit possibly a smaller one compared to today). They are as follows:

1   Secure adequate supply and efficient use of materials, energy and land resources as reliable biophysical basis for creation of wealth and well-being in societies and for future generations.
2   Maintain life-supporting functions and services of ecosystems.
3   Provide for the basic institutions of societies and their co-existence with nature.
4   Minimize risks for security and economic turmoil due to dependence on resources.
5   Contribute to a globally fair distribution of resource use and an adequate burden sharing.
6   Minimize problem shifting between environmental media, types of resources, economic sectors, regions and generations.
7   Drive resource productivity (total material productivity) at a rate higher than GDP growth.

An interesting discussion therefore is related to the *saturation effect* in societies, i.e. a stage in development when a capital stock (housing, infrastructures, manufacturing industry etc.) will have been build up and countries will be able to increase GDP without further major increase in resource use. As most minerals and metals can potentially be subject to advanced recycling processes, societies may be able to provide more and more materials from secondary sources and, accordingly, establish a circular economy based on a low material input and throughput.

A more recent discussion is related to resource interlinkages, often referred to as the *resource nexus* (Hoff 2011; Andrews-Speed et al. 2012, 2014). The *resource nexus* is a set of interactions between two or more natural resources used as inputs into socio-economic systems. Those interactions are manifold, as one resource input requires others and one system can impact one or many other systems, accordingly there can be tensions, trade-offs as well as synergies. The nexus approach is an understanding of such interactions and interdependencies across natural resource inputs for socio-economic systems in order to be able to increase the efficiency of resource use and to ensure a sustainable and secure supply of natural resources. Although the scope of analysis may differ, a five-node nexus (water, energy carriers, biomass and food, land, minerals; see Figure 12.8) can be considered useful for general purposes. In our view, the nexus research can apply research findings on

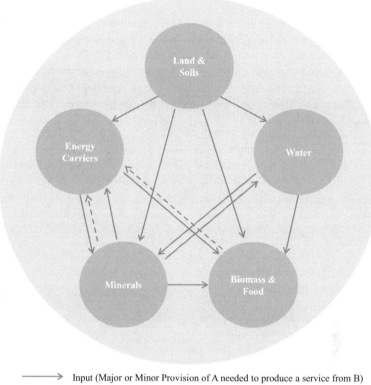

--------→   Input (Major or Minor Provision of A needed to produce a service from B)
- - - - ➤   Substitution (A may substitute B for a certain service)

Figure 12.8 The resource nexus

Source: Adapted from Andrews-Speed et al. 2012

constraints at the output side ("limited absorptive capacities of ecosystems") to analyse and assess implications on the use of resources; and originate new knowledge on constraints at the input side (e.g. due to increasing energy- and water-intensity of extraction) and conclude on implications for the supply and use of resources.

Going forward, the nexus research may be able to close the gaps between the three different research streams on ecosystem services and natural capital, research on commodities, material flows and various footprints tracked through economies, and research on security issues.

The resource nexus approach can be well applied to local conditions and by "actors on the ground"; it is thus gaining momentum and probably a useful tool in improving development cooperation in the area of sustainable management of resources.

Outlook

Despite commodity prices being lower than a few years ago (but still higher compared to previous decades), it is quite clear that any development cooperation agenda needs a strong angle on natural resources. Both the socio-economic importance and the environmental dimension underline the need to enhance resource efficiency efforts, especially given the raise in material consumption that is likely to prevail in the future. Those efforts may start at the level of manufacturing industries their processing innovation in order to save costs, but they may well go beyond and address resource interlinkages along supply chains and should try to develop new sustainable products and services. Yet, ongoing efforts are visible but will need more backing through development cooperation in order to bring actors together and address institutional issues. It is also clear that the new SDGs will lead to trade-offs with aims of sustainable resource management, if no such reconciliation takes place. Thus, we expect vital debates about the resource dimension of sustainable development in the years to come.

Note

1   Defined as "a series of connected changes improving or creating novel functional systems that reduce use of natural resources and decreases the release of harmful substances across the whole life cycle" (EC 2015, p. 11). This report provides a systemic perspective on eco-innovation.

References

Andrews-Speed, P.; Bleischwitz R.; Boersma T.; Johnson C.; Kemp G.; VanDeveer S. D. (2012): *The Global Resource Nexus: The Struggles for Land, Energy, Food, Water, and Minerals.* Washington, DC: Transatlantic Academy.

Andrews-Speed, P.; Bleischwitz R.; Boersma T.; Johnson C.; Kemp G.; VanDeveer S. D. (2014): *Want, Waste Or War?: The Global Resource Nexus and the Struggle for Land, Energy, Food, Water and Minerals.* London, UK: Routledge.

Bleischwitz, R. (2012): Towards a Resource Policy – Unleashing Productivity Dynamics and Balancing International Distortions. *Mineral Economics 24, 2–3,* pp. 135–144, http://dx.doi.org/10.1007/s13563-011-0014-5.

Bleischwitz, R. (2014): Transparency in the Extractive Industries: Time to ask for more. *Global Environmental Politics 14, 4,* doi:10.1162/GLEP_e_00254.

BMUB (Bundesministerium für Umwelt und Bauen) (2015): *Deutsches Ressourceneffizienzprogramm (ProgRess) II: Fortschrittsbericht 2012–2015.* Berlin: BMUB.

Bringezu, S.; Bleischwitz R. (2009): *Sustainable Resource Management – Global Trends, Visions and Policies.* Sheffield: Greenleaf Publisher.

Bringezu, S.; Schütz H.; Steger S.; Baudisch J. (2004): International Comparison of Resource Use and Its Relation to Economic Growth. *Ecological Economics 51, 1–2,* pp. 97–124, doi:10.1016/j.ecolecon.2004.04.010.

Cavalcanti, T. V De V, Mohaddes K.; Raissi M. (2011): Commodity Price Volatility and the Sources of Growth. *Journal of Applied Econometrics 30,* pp. 857–873.

Cuddington, J. T.; Nülle G. (2014): Variable Long-Term Trends in Mineral Prices: The Ongoing Tug-of-War between Exploration, Depletion, and Technological Change.

Journal of International Money and Finance 42, pp. 224–252, doi:10.1016/j.jimon-fin.2013.08.013.

Daly, H. E. (1990): Toward Some Operational Principles of Sustainable Development. *Ecological Economics 2, 1*, pp. 1–6, doi:10.1016/0921-8009(90)90010-R.

DCTI, EuPD Research, and KPMG (2013): *Cleantech-Standortgutachten 2013*. Berlin: DCTI, EuPD Research, and KPMG.

EC (European Commission) (2011a): *Attitudes of European Entrepreneurs towards Eco-Innovation*. Brussels: EC.

EC (2011b): *Roadmap to a Resource Efficient Europe*. Brussels: EC.

EC (2012): *SMEs, Resource Efficiency and Green Markets*. Brussels: EC.

EC (2013a): *Material Flow Accounts*. Vol. 2009. Brussels: EC.

EC (2013b): *SMEs, Resource Efficiency and Green Markets*. Brussels: EC.

EC (2015): *From Niche to Norm – Suggestions by the Group of Experts on a "Systemic Approach to Eco-Innovation to Achieve a Low-Carbon, Circular Economy"*. Brussels: EC.

Eco-Innovation Observatory (2011): *The Eco-Innovation Challenge – Pathways to a Resource-Efficient Europe*. Brussels: Eco-Innovation Observatory.

Eco-Innovation Observatory (2012): *Europe in Transition: Paving the Way to a Green Economy through Eco-Innovation*. Brussels: Eco-Innovation Observatory.

Economy, E.; Levi M. (2014): *By All Means Necessary: How China's Resource Quest Is Changing the World*. New York: Oxford University Press.

Ecorys (2012): *Mapping Resource Prices: The Past and the Future Final Report*. Rotterdam: Ecorys.

European Resource Efficiency Platform (2014): *Manifesto & Policy Recommendations*. Brussels: European Resource Efficiency Platform.

Flachenecker, F.; Rentschler J. E. (2015): Investments in Resource Efficiency – Costs and Benefits, Investment Barriers, Intervention Measures. London: UCL.

G7 (2015a): *Leaders Declaration G7 Summit 7–8 June 2015*. Schloss Elmau.

G7 (2015b): *Annex to the Leaders Declaration G7 Summit 7–8 June 2015*. Schloss Elmau.

Gylfason, T.; Herbertsson T. T.; Zoega G. (1999): A Mixed Blessing – Natural Resources and Economic Growth. *Macroeconomic Dynamics 3*, pp. 204–225.

Hoff, H. (2011): Understanding the Nexus. Background Paper for the Bonn 2011 Nexus Conference. Stockholm Environment Institute (November), pp. 1–52.

Humphreys, D. (2015): *The Remaking of the Mining Industry*. London: Palgrave Macmillan.

IMF 2015. "Primary Commodity Prices", www.imf.org/external/np/res/commod/index.aspx.

IPCC (2007): *Contribution of Working Group III to the Fourth Assessment Report of the Intergovernmental Panel on Climate Change Summary: Summary for Policymakers*. Washington, DC: IPCC.

Jordan, N. D.; Lemken T.; Liedtke C. (2014): Barriers to Resource Efficiency Innovations and Opportunities for Smart Regulations – the Case of Germany. *Environmental Policy and Governance* (March 4), doi:10.1002/eet.1632.

Lee, B.; Preston, F.; Kooroshy, J.; Bailey, R.; Lahn, G. (2012): *Resources Futures*. A Chatham House report. London: Royal Institute of International Affairs.

Lutter, S.; Giljum S.; Lieber M. (2014): *Global Material Flow Database Technical Report*. Sustainable Europe Research Institute and Vienna University of Economics and Business. Vienna, Austria.

Ma, Y. (2013): Iron Ore Spot Price Volatility and Change in Forward Pricing Mechanism. *Resources Policy 38, 4* (December), pp. 621–627, doi:10.1016/j.resourpol.2013.10.002.

McKinsey Global Institute (2011): *Resource Revolution: Meeting the World's Energy, Materials, Food, and Water Needs*. New York: McKinsey Global Institute.

Moll, S.; Bringezu, S.; Schütz, H. (2005): Resource Use in European Countries – An Estimate of Materials and Waste Streams in the Community, Including Imports and Exports Using the Instrument of Material Flow Analysis. Wuppertal Report No. 1. Wuppertal, Germany.

Müller, D. B.; Wang T.; Duval B. (2011): Patterns of Iron Use in Societal Evolution. *Environmental Science and Technology 45, 1*, pp. 182–188, doi:10.1021/es102273t.

Pearce, D. W.; Turner K. R. (1990): *Economics of Natural Resources and the Environment.* Baltimore: JHU Press.

Pegels, A. (2014): *Green Industrial Policy in Emerging Countries.* London: Routledge.

POLFREE (2014a): *D1.7 Synthesis Report and Conclusions about Drivers and Barriers.* Lead authors: Rene Kemp, Mark Dijk, Teresa Domenech, www.polfree.eu/publications/publications-2014/1.7.

POLFREE (2014b): *D1.6 Individual Behavioural Barriers to Resource-Efficiency.* Lead author: Moritz Kammerlaender, www.polfree.eu/publications/publications-2014/individual-behavioural-barriers-to-resource-efficiency.

POLFREE (2014c): *D1.5 Business Barriers to the Uptake of Resource Efficiency Measures.* Authors: Ton Bastein et al., www.polfree.eu/publications/publications-2014/Report_1.5_Business_Barriers_final_new_disclaimer.pdf.

Rockström, J.; Steffen W.; Noone K.; Persson Å.; Chapin S.; Lambin E. F.; Lenton T. M. et al. (2009): A Safe Operating Space for Humanity. *Nature 461* (September), doi:10.1038/461472a.

SERI (2015): Global Material Flow Database, www.materialflows.net.

Steffen, W.; Richardson K.; Rockström J.; Cornell S.; Fetzer I.; Bennett E.; Biggs R. et al. (2015): Planetary Boundaries: Guiding Human Development on a Changing Planet. *Science 347, 6223*, doi:10.1126/science.1259855.

Steinberger, J. K.; Krausmann F.; Eisenmenger, N. (2010): Global Patterns of Materials Use: A Socioeconomic and Geophysical Analysis. *Ecological Economics 69, 5* (March), pp. 1148–1158, doi:10.1016/j.ecolecon.2009.12.009.

UN (2015): *World Population Prospects.* Department of Economic and Social Affairs. Population Devision. New York: UN, https://esa.un.org.

UNEP (2014): *Sustainable Consumption and Production – Targets and Indicators.* New York: UNEP.

UNEP IRP (2010): *Assessing the Environmental Impacts of Consumption and Production – Priority Products and Materials.* New York: UNEP IRP.

Valiante, D.; Egenhofer, C. (2013): Price Formation in Commodities Markets: Financialisation and Beyond. Report of an ECMI/CEPS Task Force. Centre for European Policy Studies. Brussels, Belgium.

WBCSD (2010): "Vision 2050 – the New Agenda for Business. Geneva: WBCSD, doi:10.1111/j.1530-9290.2009.00117.x.

WBGU (2011): *World in Transition – A Social Contract for Sustainability. German Advisory Council on Global Change (WBGU).* Berlin: WBGU, www.wbgu.de/fileadmin/templates/dateien/veroeffentlichungen/hauptgutachten/jg2011/wbgu_jg2011_en.pdf.

Weinzettel, J.; Kovanda, J. (2011): Structural Decomposition Analysis of Raw Material Consumption. *Journal of Industrial Ecology 15, 6* (December 7), pp. 893–907, doi:10.1111/j.1530-9290.2011.00378.x.

West, J.; Schandl, H. (2013): Material Use and Material Efficiency in Latin America and the Caribbean. *Ecological Economics 94* (October), pp. 19–27, doi:10.1016/j.ecolecon.2013.06.015.

Wiedmann, T. O.; Schandl H.; Lenzen M.; Moran D.; Suh S.; West J.; Kanemoto K. (2013):

The Material Footprint of Nations. *Proceedings of the National Academy of Sciences of the United States of America* (September 3), Washington, DC: *National Academy of Sciences of the United States of America,* doi:10.1073/pnas.1220362110.

Wilts, H.; Bleischwitz R. (2012): Combating Material Leakage: A Proposal for an International Metal Covenant. *Sapiens 4, 2,* pp. 1–9.

World Bank (2014): *Diversified Development – Making the Most of Natural Resources in Eurasia.* Washington, DC: World Bank.

World Bank (2015): *World Development Indicators.* Washington, DC: World Bank, http://data.worldbank.org.

World Energy Council (2015): *2015 World Energy Issues Monitor – Energy Price Volatility: The New Normal.* London: WEC.

13 Sustainable energy

Stefan Thomas, Lukas Hermwille and Kilian Topp

Introduction: Energy and development in modern societies

The energy system plays a central role in the global economic and social system. Energy in general and electricity in particular are essential for human coexistence and every modern form of economic activity. In regions where no adequate supply can be ensured, modern life and business are not possible.

Most industrialized countries have achieved their level of development by means of exploiting fossil fuel resources – coal, oil and gas. Global energy systems are deeply locked into unsustainable practices (Unruh 2000). However, energy efficiency in end uses of energy – particularly buildings, appliances, production and transportation – and energy supply offer enormous potential for sustainable development and mitigating climate change (IPCC 2014). In addition, "the stabilization of greenhouse gas concentrations at low levels requires a fundamental transformation of the energy supply system, including the long term phase out of unabated fossil fuel conversion technologies and their substitution by low GHG alternatives" (IPCC 2014, p. 46). This involves large upfront investment and may entail certain risks, but also offers tremendous opportunities for our societies. It means a transformation of the energy system from a few central and large fossil- or nuclear-fuelled power plants, to a variety of mostly smaller, decentralized power plants based on renewable energies.

However, the transformation of the energy system cannot be achieved without taking the potentials of energy efficiency into full account. Supply and demand are (equally important) two sides of the same coin. The energy services modern societies ask for can be provided with much less input of primary energy and end energy use. In fact energy efficiency is on its way from "the 'hidden fuel' ... to an increasing recognition of its role as the 'first fuel'" (IEA 2014a, p. 18). There is a sizable potential to reduce the energy demand across the sectors of private households, transport, industry and the commercial and public service sectors. For instance, global industry energy efficiency today is only 30 per cent, meaning 70 per cent is wasted (GEA 2012, p. 516). Technology and good management available today can save between 10 and 30 per cent in industry sectors (GEA 2012, p. 516) and up to 80 per cent in buildings, appliances and lighting (GEA 2012, p. 653). A wide range of measures and technologies are cost-effective and energy efficiency therefore is a growing market. The International Energy Agency (IEA) estimates in its *Energy Efficiency Market Report* 2014 that the value of energy efficiency investment ranges between US$310 and 360 billion in 2012 (IEA 2014b). Lifetime energy cost savings created by this investment will be up to ten times higher.

The challenge of establishing markets of energy efficiency and also with regard to the governance of the energy system is that the "hidden fuel" is indeed invisible. Saved kilowatt hours are not a tangible product to be exchanged between seller and buyer. Energy efficiency is embedded in often more complex technological systems that often entail higher upfront costs. Nevertheless, in order to quickly and comprehensively move on up the pathway to sustainable, decarbonized societies, the diffusion of appropriate solutions is a critical success factor for sustainable development cooperation.

Such a radical transformation presents both the energy systems as well as entire economies and societies with great challenges. These challenges differ around the world. They result from the different prerequisites of the countries, such as the existing (energy) infrastructure, the level of economic development and economic structure, the topography, the potential for renewable energy, fossil fuel reserves and cultural preferences. In a nutshell, industrialized countries will have to find ways to develop sustainability in their – hitherto unsustainable – socio-economic systems, whereas developing countries will have to find ways to deviate from the beaten but unsustainable development pathways and achieve their development sustainably from the beginning.

Secure access to energy is essential to modern economies and thus for social prosperity as we know it today. Empirical studies estimate, for example, that income in rural Bangladesh rose from 9 to 30 per cent through electrification, depending on the security of supply. This income growth can be traced back to things as simple as the ability to use the evenings for economic activities. In addition to the income effects, the access to electricity considerably changes living conditions: health care is improved because more favourable treatment conditions exist and drugs can be reliably cooled; and the education level rises because the evenings can be used for studying (IPCC 2012, p. 721 et seq.; Khandker et al. 2009). The correlations between energy on the one hand, and the different dimensions of development – human development, social development and economic development on the other hand – are presented schematically in Figure 13.1.

Renewable energy and improved energy efficiency can and must make an important contribution here. However, this is by no means a matter of course. In developing countries the necessary transformation towards a sustainable energy sector will only succeed if the development of renewable energies and energy efficiency is integrated with the most pressing development problems; an energy transformation as a part of economic development is possible and useful.

In the following parts of the chapter we will address first the question of what sustainable energy is by locating it in the conceptual framework of the energy system rather than by providing singular definitions. Then we turn to an overview of relevant technologies and instruments before we zoom in on the situation of developing countries in the context of the world energy system. Finally we zoom

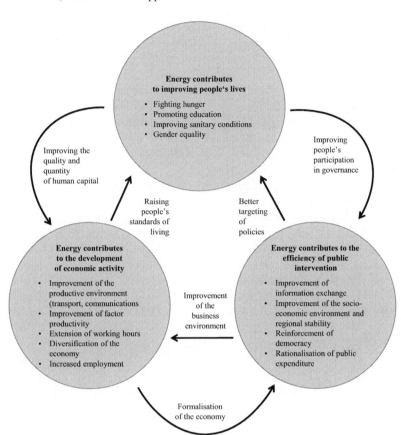

Figure 13.1 Correlations between energy (used in an energy-efficient way) and human, social and economic development

Source: Kaygusuz 2012, p. 1119

out again in order to look precisely at this world energy system and its future trends. At the end of this chapter we provide a collection of databases, organizations etc. for further reading and practical information.

What is sustainable energy?

Sustainability is a widely used but context-dependent term that has produced manifold definitions. Indeed, it can be labelled an "umbrella term" that needs to be filled or articulated (van Lente & van Til 2008). Sustainable development can also be seen as a "process or journey towards a destination, which is sustainability" (Hammond & Jones 2011, p. 21). This would in turn raise the question of whether sustainability is a state of equilibrium, a destination that can be reached and if actors can agree on the destination of choice. Certainly there are different ways and opinions on how to get there. Therefore, we will focus on the framing conditions, the guide rail of the energy system.

The global energy policy debate is based on the energy trilemma that defines the energy sector's triangle of objectives (Meyers et al. 2012, S. 29). The three target dimensions of this scheme mirror to some extent the three dimensions of sustainability: (1) fostering economic development, (2) protecting the environment and sustainable use of resources; and (3) enhancing social development and justice. In addition:

- **Security of supply** is about the securing of a functioning energy system. This includes both the technical network stability within the country, as well as an international component when it comes to access to (fossil) resources and dependence on suppliers.
- **Environmental compatibility** represents a major challenge in times of climate change. This includes the direct noise and pollution from power plants, boilers and vehicles, as well as the consequences of climate change, the consequences of the nuclear disasters at Chernobyl and Fukushima, and the impacts of the industrial extraction of raw materials.
- **Energy justice** includes not only the cost of energy supply – with its important aspects of the competitiveness of companies and the affordability of the costs for consumers – but also another component: access to modern energy. In view of more than 1.2 billion people without access to electricity worldwide, this aspect is currently central for developing countries.

The term "energy trilemma" implies that the three sides of the triangle involve three basic challenges, which together may be perceived as difficult or even impossible to overcome simultaneously. Energy policy, the concept suggests, may have to counterbalance the three dimensions in a compromise against each other. However, as most energy efficiency options and increasingly also renewable energies are cost effective compared to expansions of energy supply systems based on fossil or nuclear fuels, this suggestion becomes a misleading one. *In fact, cost-effective energy efficiency and renewable energies will meet all three objectives of the energy policy triangle at the same time.*

In view of climate change, it is becoming increasingly clear that the environmental compatibility dimension has thus far been too one-sided and as a result not sufficiently taken into account in this trade-off. The focus has been too much on short-term effects, for example, in relation to the short-term effect of conventional air pollutants. The current global energy system is extremely unsustainable – i.e., it is on the way to breaching the planet's environmental boundaries. The planet's long-term resilience is not only exceeded in terms of climate change, but according to expert opinion, also in the areas of biodiversity and the nitrogen cycle. Only within these boundaries can the welfare of humanity be secured in the long term. If the limits are exceeded, the danger exists of sudden and catastrophic environmental changes that also threaten the continued existence of human society as we know it today (Rockström et al. 2009; Steffen et al. 2015).

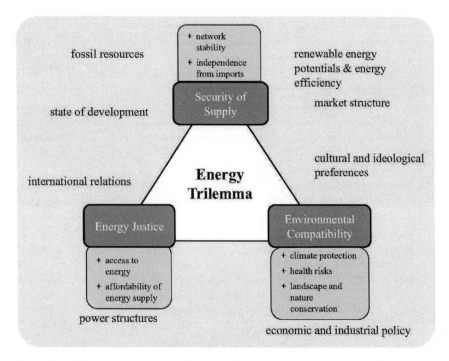

Figure 13.2 The energy trilemma and external factors

A possible explanation for this apparent failure is that the concept lacks a temporal dimension. A static, short-term optimization of the energy system designed on the basis of the energy trilemma can therefore easily lead to suboptimal long-term results. For that reason, the long-term consequences of our energy production – in particular the consequences of climate change – were for the most part not adequately considered in the past. The same applies to the future costs of the energy system. Investments in energy infrastructure are highly durable in general, but also need a long preparatory phase. Precisely in these two aspects are renewable energy sources superior to conventional fossil fuels; they are more climate friendly and quicker to build. However, they play out their cost advantages only in the long run.

Similarly, the energy trilemma is biased towards the supply side. Energy system optimization based under the interpretive frame of the energy trilemma therefore often blinds out energy efficiency and other demand-side measures. But to plan an adequate energy *supply system* in the long run, reliable assumptions about future scenarios of *energy demand* are required. Tapping the full potential of efficient appliances, buildings, processing technologies etc. will affect the need of power generation and transmission capacity. Technologies for renewables are often related to decentralized solutions and due to their lower investment costs compared to large-scale power plants open to different patterns of ownership. In other words: hopes of a "democratization" of the energy sector are attached to the energy transition. Whereas efficient technologies are often more expensive to purchase, the lower energy costs over the lifecycle make them cost effective and reduce the total costs of ownership.

To overcome barriers for market penetration, a set of policy instruments has been developed. Mandatory Minimum Energy Performance Standards (MEPS) and energy labels are the most important policies to increase the energy efficiency of appliances. MEPS prevent the marketing of energy-wasting products. Energy labels promote progress towards the best available technologies, along with further policies needed to help tackle the substantial information deficits and financing barriers. These include financial incentives and financing, as well as education and training programmes and information campaigns. If policies for an integrated energy system are to be effective and unintended consequences avoided, a coordinated policy package is needed. In the next section an overview of technologies and instruments is presented.

Technologies and instruments

In this chapter, we present more detail on the two technical pillars of sustainable energy – energy efficiency in energy end use and supply, and renewable energies. The objective for development cooperation on sustainable energy is then to support partner countries with using the energy-efficient and renewable energy technologies and solutions as well as with implementing the corresponding policies needed for market breakthrough of these technologies.

According to the REN21 (2014) *Renewables 2014 Global Status Report* "modern" renewables had a share of 19 per cent of the global final energy consumption (9 per cent of this coming from traditional biomass) in 2013. At least 144 countries had renewable energy targets and 138 countries had renewable energy support policies in place at the beginning of 2014. The number of countries is constantly increasing with developing and emerging economies spearheading the expansion in recent years and (95 countries with support policies, up from 15 in 2005) (REN21 2014).

Renewable energies are used in different ways and cannot only be classified regarding the specific sources but also according to different technologies and types of use. Table 13.1 gives a clustered overview. Solar energy, wind energy, hydro power and biomass make directly or indirectly use of solar radiation. Geothermal energy uses the internal heat of the Earth that is reducible to the radioactive decay in the Earth's interior.

Another primary energy source is the tidal energy determined by the gravity between Earth and Moon. Renewable energy can provide heat as well as electricity and fuel.

When we speak of the potential of renewable energy, the technical, the economic and the "sustainable" potentials need to be discerned. Still, even if restrictions for sustainable potential (no competition of biomass and land use with

Table 13.1 Usage of renewable energy sources

Primary energy source	Appearance	Natural energy conversion	Technical energy conversion	Secondary energy
Solar	Biomass	Production of biomas	Heating plant, conversion plant	Heat, electricity, fuel
	Hydro power	evaporation, condensation, melting	Hydroelectric power plant	Electricity
	Wind power	Atmospheric motion	Wind turbine	Electricity
		Tidal movement	Wave power plant	Electricity
	Solar radiation	Sea current	Tidal energy plant	Electricity
		Heating of earth surface and atmosphere	Heat pumps	Heat
			Sea temperature gradient power station	Electricity
		Solar radiation	Photolysis	Fuel
			Solar cell, Photovoltaic plant	Electricity
			Solar panel, solar thermal power unit	Heat
Moon	Gravity	Tides	Tidal power plant	Electricity
Earth	Isotope decay	Geothermics	Geothermic power and/or heating plant	Heat, electricity

Source: Adapted from Hennicke & Bodach 2010

food production, questions of biodiversity and noise emissions) are taken into account, the potential is huge and exceeds by far the global primary energy consumption (Hoffmann 2014).

In the following we focus and give a brief overview on the most important sources for renewable energy which provide the biggest share to energy generation and are applicable to developing countries.[1]

Photovoltaics

Photovoltaics (PV) offer a wide range of power spectrum from milli to mega-watt (mW-MW) and consequently of applications. PV installations range from small off-grid to the biggest share of rooftop systems on private buildings, to large installations on industrial buildings and ground-mounted PV parks. Whereas the market for PV has been dominated by Europe, the US and Japan in the past, the balance is currently shifting to Asian markets and especially China. China was the top market with 11.8 GW installted capacity in 2013, whereas the momentum in Europe declined due to changed regulatory regimes with reduced incentives for new PV installations (EPIA 2014).

In developing countries PV is used predominantly for electrification in rural areas. As large infrastructures are often not available, not reliable or too costly, PV systems are used for minigrids or off-grid installations. As alternatives for diesel engines, solar home or village systems constitute a sustainable and cost-effective choice to provide access to energy. Solar lanterns for example are now much cheaper than battery or kerosene lighting systems, based on life-cycle costs.

PV has a large potential to change the energy mix and substitute carbon-intensive fossil fuels. Although the market is growing rapidly, this potential is largely untapped in countries of the Global South, where solar radiaton is particularly effective. Power generation from PV is as cheap as 6 to 9 US cents per kWh today in many countries.

Solar thermal heating

Different to the PV installation which turns solar radiation into electricity, solar thermal installations convert it into heating of a carrier medium. By doing so solar collectors can ultimately provide space heating, warm water and with special technical applications also cooling. Solar collectors are largely free of emissons.

Different technical solutions are available for solar thermal installations. By the end of 2013, an installed capacity of 374.7 GWth, corresponding to a total of 535 million square metres of collector area was in operation worldwide contributing about 1.2 per cent to the overall domestic hot water and space heating demand in buildings (IEA-SHC 2015). Solar installations have a large potential to reduce the use of fossil fuels and reduce fuel costs at the same time. Solar heating systems are technically mature and well established, and often cost effective. Further developments for solar cooling can be expected and will offer more cost-effective potentials. However, for both heating and cooling, it should be kept in mind that an integrated, holistic approach for designing and constructing buildings is required in order to reduce the energy demand to a minimum from the outset.

Wind power

A record of new installed capacity was reached in 2014: 51,473 MW of new wind generating capacity was added in 2014 according to the global wind market statistics by the Global Wind Energy Council. In total, 369,597 MW were available at the the end of 2014 (GWEC 2014). Again China takes the lead with a share of 45 per cent, followed by Germany. The technology for wind turbines has also made substantial progress leading to larger technical productivity and increasing cost effectiveness. Wind turbines with up to 6 MW generator output can produce enough electricity to supply approxamitely 5000 average households.

Also off-shore windpower is on the rise. In 2014 1,713 MW of new offshore capacity was added, bringing the total to 8,759 MW according to the GWEC. So far, off-shore wind energy is by far concentrated along the European coastal lines in the Baltic, the North Sea and the Atlantic Ocean. But also in China and other Asian industrializing countries projects are in the pipeline as off-shore wind power is especially useful for the number of growing cities that are often located at the coasts. Due to the challenging conditions at sea and the more complex grid connection the costs are higher, but are also likely to fall following the economy of scale. Depending on location and capacity, on-shore wind power stations can generate the energy needed for its production and installation within four to seven months.

Wind power can also be used in developing countries – it is often competitive to unsubsidized coal- or gas-fired power plants despite its higher investment cost – and can be combined with other generators to hybrid power plants.

Hydropower

Hydropower is the oldest and one of the most cost-efficient sources for renewable energy. The kinetic energy of the water flow powers turbines and finally generators produce electricity.

The use of hydro power constitutes the biggest share of renewable energy sources so far: 15 per cent of the global electricity generation is provided by hydro power. The economic potential is exploited to roughly a third. There are considerable differences with regard to countries and regions. Especially developing and emerging economies in Africa, Asia and South America can still make use of hydro power. Large hydro power plants require high investments for construction and installation. However, they have a long life cycle and produce low maintenance costs. Therefore they belong the most cost-effective power plants. Pumped storage hydro power stations provide the benefit of being able to store electricity.

However, especially large hydro power installations can induce negative environmental effects. Dammed lakes constitute losses of land and affect ecosystems. The social effects also have to be carefully measured looking at relocation of local populations, ways of participation and the distribution of economic benefits and ecologic disadvantages. The use of small hydro power plants suited to local conditions can avoid some of the adverse environmental effects and represents a viable option for developing countries.

Sustainable biomass energy

Biomass is a very versatile resource for renewable energy. It can take different forms, such as sustainably grown or residual wood, remains of agriculture, forestry and industry, as well as the product of systematic cultivation of energy plants on unused land not needed for food production. In different processes, biomass can be converted into solid, fluid or gaseous energy resources. Biomass can therefore be used to provide electricity, heat and fuel. Biomass is suited to be applied for combined heat and power generation. If there is no option to use the waste heat as a consequence of decentralized sites for biomass production, purified biogas can also be fed into gas pipelines if available.

So-called "traditional" biomass is one of the major energy sources in developing countries and is predominantly used for cooking and heating. This is usually a very inefficient use of resources. Additionately, it creates serious health issues due to poor air quality. However, improved cookstoves are much cleaner and can save between 40 and 80 per cent of biomass (see www.bigee.net/en/appliances/guide/residential/group/2/).

Biomass can also be used for the production of fuel for the transport sector. Here especially, questions of sustainability related to conflicting land use arise. As agricultural areas are restricted, the production of biomass for energy generation should not supplant food production.

Energy efficiency

Energy efficiency technologies and management solutions are highly sector specific and much more diverse than renewable energy supply technologies. It would need too much space to present even an overview of the many dozens or even hundreds of types of technologies. We therefore take a somewhat closer look at buildings and include a set of useful references for the other sectors.

New ultra-low-energy buildings needing 60 to 90 per cent less final energy for heating and cooling than conventional new buildings can be constructed cost effectively in most parts of the world. Retrofitting existing buildings can bring similar improvements. Extensive energy-efficient renovation measures ("deep renovation") can achieve final energy savings of 50 to 90 per cent. These can be profitable investments, too, if done as part of typical refurbishment cycles and if the energy costs savings during the life cycle are considered (GEA 2012).

The Aqaba house located in Amman (Jordan), for example, provides energy savings of over 84 per cent against a reference building, achieved through optimal (passive) building design and insulation alone. The total energy consumption of the Aqaba house is 3205 kWh per year. Moreover, the reduction in water use compared to a conventional building is 51 per cent. The overall costs amounted to EU€ 154,000. Compared to a newly built conventional building in Jordan, the additional investment cost is approximately € 47,000. The building was estimated to have a payback time of 3.3 years, just for the design and construction, and 8.6 years with a solar cooling system.

Most recent scenarios (GEA 2012) (see Figure 13.4) show that state-of-the-art energy-efficient renovation and new build could result in worldwide overall energy savings of 46 per cent in 2050 compared to 2005 or 60 per cent of the energy consumption expected in 2050 for the suboptimal scenario, expressed in final energy demand for heating and cooling. Despite growth in the building stock, this translates into an absolute decrease in energy consumption from 15.7 PWh (15,700 TWh) in 2005, down to 8.5 PWh (8,500 TWh) in 2050. GEA (2012) estimates that the approximately $57 trillion of cumulative energy cost savings until 2050 in avoided heating and cooling energy costs alone substantially exceeds the estimated $15 trillion investments that are needed to realize this pathway. Such a transition will only be achieved with early, comprehensive and systematic

Figure 13.3 Picture of the Aqaba house
Source: www.bigee.net

implementation of state-of-the art energy efficiency measures in design, construction and technology in both new and existing buildings.

These measures are urgently needed because policy that only encourages suboptimal improvements, for example energy savings of only 35 per cent will lead to considerable "lock-in" effects. Once renovated or built, it will not be cost effective to further upgrade the energy efficiency of these buildings for several decades. In other words, inadequate action now means losing cost-effective opportunities for long-term investments, energy and carbon emission reductions. This scenario could lead to energy consumption for heating and cooling of 20.8 PWh in 2050 (i.e., an increase of 33 per cent). Both paths are visualized in Figure 13.4, the state-of-the art scenario in dark blue (with "deep renovation" in existing buildings and ultra-low new energy buildings) vs. the suboptimal development path in light blue. The overall difference in 2050 adds up to an implementation gap of 79 per cent of the 2005 energy use or more than 12 PWh/year (12,000 TWh/year).

Policy for energy efficiency in buildings

Looking at the potential energy savings in new buildings and the many benefits they bring the goal for policy-makers should be to make ultra-low-energy

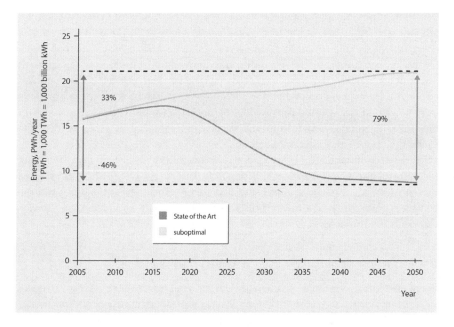

Figure 13.4 World space heating and cooling final energy use, 2005–2050, suboptimal and state-of-the-art energy efficiency scenario

Source: www.bigee.net based on GEA 2012

buildings the mainstream standard. For renovation and operation of existing buildings, the goal is two-fold: pave the way for high energy savings in each retrofit and in operation, and for increased rates of energy-efficient retrofit. To achieve these goals, all actors in the complex building value chain with their specific barriers and incentives need to be reached through policy. This requires a well-combined set of policies and measures reflecting the national circumstances.

Value chains in the building sector are long and complex. Actors as diverse as property developers, financiers, contractors, building designers and architects, component suppliers, investors, owners and users/tenants all have inherent incentives to improve the energy efficiency of buildings. But they also face strong barriers to take steps for efficient buildings themselves. It is important for governments in each country to analyse the building sector value chains and specific barriers and incentives inherent to each actor before designing and implementing policies for energy-efficient buildings. As described above, these policies are needed to correct market distortions and reduce transaction costs for actors to access the information about available technologies and solutions for energy efficiency. A governance framework is required to provide an overarching structure to coordinate and implement energy efficiency policies and measures and manage their interrelationships.

Different policies addressing the demand- and supply-side of markets should be properly combined according to national circumstances. This does not mean that governments seeking to improve the energy efficiency have to implement all possible policies in order to be successful, but they should combine a selection of instruments tackling the most important market barriers. As successful countries have demonstrated, a comprehensive and coherent policy package for energy efficiency in buildings will usually provide a sound balance between clear mandatory measures, incentives, information and capacity building or in other words, "the sticks, the carrots, and the tambourines".

In the recommended policy package developed in the bigEE project (Bridging the Information Gap on Energy Efficiency in Buildings), we distinguish between the set of specific policies and measures for energy efficiency in buildings and the common governance framework policies needed to guide and enable the former, shown in Figure 13.5.

Interaction between building-specific elements of policy package

To achieve the goal of making ultra-low-energy buildings the mainstream standard in new buildings we need to combine a variety of policy instruments and implement them as a package.

In this section we present the policy instruments we recommend to combine in a package for achieving this aim:

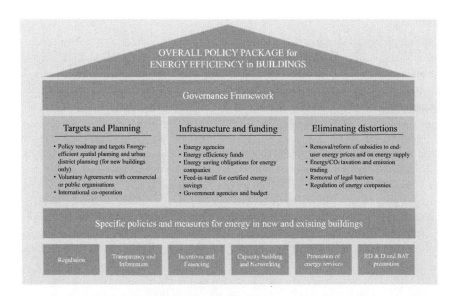

Figure 13.5 The bigEE recommended policy package

Source: www.bigee.net

- Mandatory *minimum energy performance standards* (MEPS) for all new buildings (and building components where useful) are the most important policy for energy efficiency in new buildings. They should be created by law and then strengthened step by step every three to five years, to finally require energy efficiency levels equivalent to ultra-low-energy buildings. MEPS reduce transaction costs as well as the landlord-tenant and developer-buyer dilemma by removing the least energy-efficient building practices and concepts from the market.
- They should, however, always be at least as stringent as the energy performance level leading to least life-cycle costs. In order to be effective, compliance with MEPS must be controlled at the local level in both the design stage and after construction. In a transition period before a law can make MEPS mandatory, a voluntary standard may help. Especially in developing countries, it may be useful to combine such voluntary or even the introduction of mandatory MEPS with financial incentives or financing for meeting the MEPS requirements, at least for poorer households (Iwaro & Mwasha 2010). Preferably, *other statutory requirements* such as individual metering, energy management for larger buildings and building portfolios, or regular inspections of heating, ventilation and air conditioning systems would complement the legal framework.
- *Education and training* of building professionals (architects, planners, developers, builders, building and installation contractors, financiers and other relevant market actors) is essential to prepare introduction and further strengthening of MEPS regulation up to ultra-low-energy buildings. Easy-to-use tools for energy-efficient building design and for life-cycle cost calculation are important for the training. Certification of successful participation to the training can make it more attractive for both the qualified market actors and their customers.
- The markets should, furthermore, be prepared for the next step(s) of MEPS regulation towards ultra-low-energy buildings through *policies tackling the substantial information deficits and financing barriers*. These include *building energy performance certificates* (and energy labels for components where useful), showcasing of demonstrated good practice buildings, *advice and financing support for investors, and financial incentives* – such as grants and tax incentives – for broad market introduction of ultra-low-energy buildings. It is mainly for such information and financial programmes that energy-efficiency funds or energy companies must contribute.
- Once a certain market share of (ultra)-low-energy buildings of a specific energy performance level is reached, the professionals are trained and used to the required practices, and the cost effectiveness of this energy performance level step is proven, this level can then be mandated by the regulation to become the new MEPS level. This would be one step of MEPS regulation towards ultra-low-energy buildings in new build.
- Future steps of MEPS regulation towards ultra-low-energy buildings should be prepared by innovation support through research and development (R&D) funding, demonstration (including in public buildings), award competitions, and maybe also already by financial incentives for broad market introduction. The public sector should lead by example through energy-efficient public procurement and ambitious targets for its own buildings, thereby paving the way for the other sectors to follow.

The *existing building stock* already provides larger potential for cost-effective energy savings than new construction in developed countries, and will gain in importance in emerging and developing economies. It is also the bigger challenge to retrofit the walls, roofs, windows and heating and cooling systems of existing buildings to highest energy performance levels in an integrated way.

Every year, many existing buildings undergo renovation for maintenance or beautification anyway. These opportunities should be harnessed to improve energy efficiency by adding thermal insulation or shading and using more energy-efficient windows, heating and cooling systems, instead of just replacing paint, tiles or windows as they were before. The reason for this recommendation is that it is very often cost effective to add the incremental energy efficiency investment at the time of renovation but not cost effective to repay the full renovation cost from energy savings. Renovation without improving energy efficiency therefore means a lost opportunity and will likely lock in high-energy consumption until the next renovation.

The operational goal for energy efficiency in existing buildings thus has two dimensions: achieving very energy-efficient and comprehensive, "deep" retrofits whenever a building is renovated, and increasing the rate at which buildings undergo such "deep" energetic renovations. Figure 13.6 presents the recommended

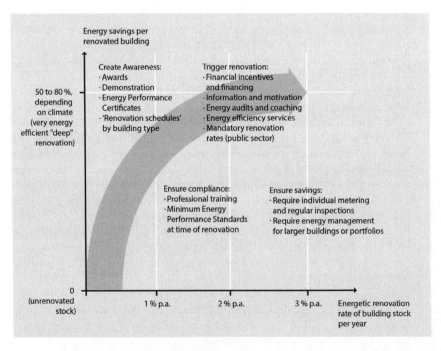

Figure 13.6 The interactions of policy instruments for energy efficiency in building renovation and operation

Source: www.bigee.net

combination of policy instruments for achieving this two-dimensional goal. More detail on how the policies need to interact and good practice examples can be found at www.bigee.net/en/policy/guide/buildings/recommended/and particularly at www.bigee.net/media/filer_public/2013/11/28/bigee_txt_0006_pg_ how_policies_need_to_interact_2.pdf.

Regarding energy efficiency and the related policies for appliances, we recommend the following online resources:

- UNEP/SE4ALL Efficient Appliances and Equipment Global Partnership Programme: www.unep.org/energy/eae/index.html
- bigEE Appliances and Policy Guides: www.bigee.net/en/appliances/guide/ and www.bigee.net/en/policy/guide/appliances/recommended/
- Super-Efficient Equipment and Appliances Deployment Initiative (SEAD): Superefficient.org

For further reading on energy efficiency in the industry and transport sector, the GEA (2012) provides detailed information.

Situation of developing countries

Sustainable energy use and supply is an enormous challenge but also opportunity in the rapidly urbanizing centres of many developing countries, with their quick development of buildings, transport infrastructures and vehicles, industries and appliance ownership. This rapid development offers chances of leapfrogging the fossil fuel system and inefficient infrastructures that are a legacy of the past for many industrialized countries.

However, according to the report *World Energy Outlook* from the International Energy Agency, 1.265 billion people worldwide in developing countries still have no access to electricity (IEA 2012). Most of these people live in rural areas in Africa and South and Southeast Asia. The biggest challenge for these people is not to redesign energy infrastructures in a sustainable way, but rather it is to establish an energy infrastructure in the first place. Social sustainability, the dimension of energy justice as specified in the energy trilemma, clearly is at the centre of attention. However, environmental sustainability should be integrated with it to the utmost extent possible.

Leapfrogging fossil fuels

Sustainable energy services can help to leapfrog unsustainable models of development. The expansion of energy efficiency, decentralized and renewable structures, isolated systems and mini-grids – especially in rural and sparsely populated areas – despite the higher costs for electricity generation, can on the whole be more cost effective, if as a consequence investments in the expansion of central power grids are renounced. The triumph of mobile technology in developing countries makes it clear that development does not necessarily have to follow the prescribed development paths of industrialized countries. Communication technology could only spread so quickly there because new opportunities made the costly expansion of a wired network unnecessary (Deichmann et al. 2011). Various economic analyses suggest that there is also high potential for renewable energy-based decentralized energy supply systems (Deichmann et al. 2011; Szabó et al. 2011; Thiam 2010).

Basically, the conditions for renewable energy in almost all developing countries are extremely good. Africa, for example, as a continent with the largest proportion of the population without access to electricity offers excellent physical conditions for the use of renewable energy. Even the most unfavourable locations in Africa still feature a very favourable potential for electricity from solar plants (Chineke & Ezike 2010). There is large wind energy potential, for example, in northern West Africa and the Horn of Africa. The Great African Rift Valley offers good opportunities for the use of geothermal energy. For the exploitation of hydropower, including small hydroelectric power plants, there are also suitable conditions in many parts of Africa, including in Ethiopia, Kenya and Uganda (IPCC 2012).

Even where there is already a connection to the power grid, (distributed) renewable energy can still provide an added value. The central power supply in many developing countries is very unreliable. The power supply frequently collapses for hours or even days. This often leads to high economic losses and makes it impossible for companies to optimize their business activities. While in industrialized countries the irregular availability of renewable energy is cited as an argument against an energy transformation, the decentralized renewable supply systems in many developing countries could even increase the security of supply because the supply of wind and solar power is indeed irregular, but in contrast to power outages, to some extent predictable, enabling businesses to plan their production better.

The financing challenge

However, there are also unresolved issues that stand in the way of the expansion of energy efficiency and renewable energies in developing countries. The problem of up-front financing must be emphasized. Even where renewable energy is in the long term more cost effective than fossil fuels, it is questionable whether a financing of the renewable energy infrastructure is possible. The reason is that the cost structure of renewable energy and energy efficiency differs greatly from that of fossil fuels. While the total costs incurred in energy efficiency and renewable energy – such as wind, solar, hydro and geothermal energy – are almost entirely in the form of investment costs at the beginning of a plant's operating life, the initial investment costs in many conventional power generators, such as diesel generators or gas turbines, is relatively low; instead, high fuel costs accrue over the plant's operating life. If the available investment funds are limited, it may thus seem useful from the perspective of political stakeholders, despite the higher total cost, to invest in fossil fuels to close short-term gaps in coverage. In the case of an acute supply crisis, political stakeholders could thus be tempted to achieve the greatest effect in the short term and capture political capital. Similarly, there usually is an incremental upfront cost of energy-efficient buildings, equipment or transport systems, while energy cost savings will only accrue over the 10, 20 or more years of their operation. The negative consequences of foregoing energy efficiency – higher overall costs over the life of the plant – probably do not carry much political weight.

The cost structure of renewable energies and energy efficiency is particularly disadvantageous in developing countries with a generally unfavourable investment climate. Capital markets typically demand a hefty risk premium for investments in countries that may suffer from ineffective governance structures, corruption and other security issues. Since the capital cost makes up for the lion's share of the total cost of renewable energies and energy efficiency, the general business environment has a profound impact on the viability of such projects. International development cooperation can make an important contribution here. Donor countries could shift the interests through guarantees and thus reduce the capital costs for renewable energy and energy efficiency projects in developing countries, and in this manner shift the cost structure in favour of renewable energy and energy efficiency.

Furthermore, most banks, including dedicated development banks, traditionally are set up to finance individual, large infrastructure projects. Energy efficiency and distributed renewable energy projects, however, typically have a much smaller scope than investments in coal, gas or even nuclear power plants. In comparison, smaller projects usually have disproportionately higher transaction costs, because the expenditure for feasibility studies is not significantly different from that for large infrastructure projects. Moreover, investors – even if the net return of renewable energy is competitive – favour investment in fossil plants due to a higher gross return (IPCC 2012, p. 882). For the financing of small, decentralized PV systems or run-of-the-river power plants, it may be necessary to mobilize private investors with the assistance of appropriate financing instruments, like small and micro loans. Such tools already exist, but they are far from widely disseminated (Brew-Hammond 2010; Mainali & Silveira 2011; Rao et al. 2009).

Outlook: The governance of (world) energy systems and sustainable development cooperation

The world energy system is fragmented and lacks an overarching architecture. There is no institution comparable to the World Trade Organization or the World Health Organization for this fundamental issue. Of course a variety of interlinked organizations (e.g. the IEA and the International Renewable Energy Agency) and initiatives (such as the UN's Sustainable Energy for All) (see also the list of further information and reading below) exists, but it can be ascertained that "as it stands, the global energy architecture is weak, fragmented, incomplete, and obviously ill-adapted to the scale and scope of energy problems at hand" (van de Graaf 2013, p. 4).

Following the categorization of the growing field of transition studies, we can distinguish the landscape, the regime and the niche level in a multilevel system (Grin et al. 2010). Surely the climate regime of the UN's Framework Convention on Climate Change, dealing with the externalities of the (fossil) energy system, influences the national policies and interactions. How the interplay evolves exactly is an interesting field of further research though. The UN has also singled out energy as a central issue of the 21st century in its Sustainable Energy for All initiative started in 2011. The three main objectives (aiming at the year 2030) are providing universal access to modern energy service, doubling the global rate of improvement in energy efficiency and doubling the share of renewable energy in the global energy mix.

Although the transformation from a fossil fuel-based, carbon-intensive energy system towards a more sustainable one is under way in various sectors and countries, van de Graaf (2013) argues that the global energy architecture still has a bias towards the North and business/market interests, and is not sufficiently addressing the pressing issue of energy poverty in developing countries.

Policies for sustainable development should avoid lock-in, should address co-benefits and harvest the full potential by taking an integrative approach reducing frictions. The challenge for sustainable development cooperation is to navigate through the diversity of initiatives and information resources, to identify the dissimilar interests of different actors and get access to reliable information.

The bigEE project, coordinated by the Wuppertal Institute, for example aims at providing a comprehensive knowledge platform for policies and technologies for efficient buildings. It is also a showcase example for the fact that information on (global) standards and best-available technologies is needed on the one hand, but that of course on the other hand these need to be adapted to national and local circumstances – therefore the global information is paired with a deeper analysis of important emerging economies, starting with China, South Africa and India.

For the use of renewable energy, countries have different resources, different sets of appliances dominate national markets and buildings need to be adapted to the climatic conditions. In general, for identifying the appropriate technology the encompassing principle should be taken into account that socio-economic factors crucially determine the successful implementation of innovative solutions. Culture and values are often overlooked as determinants of behaviour in comparison with the enthusiasm for technology or the focus on modelling rationality (see World Bank 2015). In order to move forward towards low-carbon, sustainable societies what the best suitable solutions are should be questioned case by case – for example passive options in the building sector facilitate large energy savings from the outset whereas the construction of glazed office blocks requires a lot of electricity consumption even with the most efficient air conditioners. Furthermore, for renewable energy projects that combine PV with biomass to secure a 24/7 supply, as well for buildings or appliances, it holds true that user behaviour and acceptance is decisive to make use of the technical potential. The technical potential for a transition to more sustainable pathways is undoubtedly there. Securing financing in times of volatile oil markets, reducing the averse effects of subsidies for fossil fuels, designing reliable and holistic policies, raising awareness for the multiple benefits of renewable energies as well as energy efficiency and building capacity will benefit the environment, people and create sustainable growth. All of these are good areas for successful development cooperation on sustainable energy.

Note

1 This part is based on and adapted from Hennicke & Bodach 2010.

References

Brew-Hammond, A. (2010): Energy access in Africa: Challenges ahead. *Energy Policy*, *38*(5), pp. 2291–2301. http://doi.org/10.1016/j.enpol.2009.12.016.

Chineke, T. C.; Ezike, F. M. (2010): Political will and collaboration for electric power reform through renewable energy in Africa. *Energy Policy*, *38*(1), pp. 678–684. http://doi.org/10.1016/j.enpol.2009.10.004.

Deichmann, U.; Meisner, C.; Murray, S.; Wheeler, D. (2011): The economics of renewable energy expansion in rural Sub-Saharan Africa. *Energy Policy*, *39*(1), pp. 215–227. http://doi.org/10.1016/j.enpol.2010.09.034.

EPIA (2014): *Global Market Outlook for Photovoltaics 2014–2018*. Brussels: EPIA.

GEA (2012): *Global Energy Assessment – Toward a Sustainable Future*. Cambridge and New York: Cambridge University Press, and Laxenburg: International Institute for Applied Systems Analysis.

Grin, J.; Rotmans, J.; Schot, J. (2010): *Transitions to Sustainable Development. New Directions in the Study of Long term transformative change*. New York/London: Routledge.

GWEC (2014): *Global Wind Report 2014 – Annual market update*. Brussels: GWEC.

Hammond, G. P.; Jones, C. I. (2011): Sustainability criteria for energy resources and technologies. In Galarraga, I., Gonzalez-Eguino, M., Markandya, A., *Handbook of Sustainable Energy*. Cheltenham.

Hennicke, P.; Bodach, S. (2010): *Energie Revolution. Effizienzsteigerung und erneuerbare Energien als neue globale Herausforderung*. München: oekom verlag.

Hoffmann, W. (2014): *The Economic Competitiveness of Renewable Energy. Pathways to 100% Global Coverage*. Beverly.

IEA (2012): *World Energy Outlook 2012*. Paris: OECD/IEA.

IEA (2014a): *Capturing the Multiple Benefits of Energy Efficiency*. Paris: IEA.

IEA (2014b): *Energy Efficiency Market Report 2014*. Paris: IEA.

IEA-SHC (2015): *Solar Heat Worldwide. Markets and Contribution to the Energy Supply 2013*. Paris: IEA-SHC.

IPCC (2012): *Special Report: Renewable Energy Sources and Climate Change Mitigation (Bd. 49)*. Cambridge: IPCC. www.cro3.org/cgi/doi/10.5860/CHOICE.49-6309.

IPCC (2014): Technical Summary. In *Climate Change 2014: Mitigation of Climate Change. Contribution of Working Group III to the Fifth Assessment Report of the Intergovernmental Panel on Climate Change*. Cambridge: Cambridge University Press.

Iwaro, J.; Mwasha, A. (2010): A review of building energy regulation and policy for energy conservation in developing countries. *Energy Policy*, *38*(12), pp. 7744–7755. http://doi.10.1016/j.enpol.2010.08.027.

Kaygusuz, K. (2012): Energy for sustainable development: A case of developing countries. *Renewable and Sustainable Energy Reviews*, *16*(2), pp. 1116–1126. http://doi.org/10.1016/j.rser.2011.11.013.

Khandker, S. R.; Barnes, D. F.; Samad, H. A. (2009): *Welfare Impacts of Rural Electrification A Case Study from Bangladesh*. Washington, DC: World Bank.

Mainali, B.; Silveira, S. (2011): Financing off-grid rural electrification: Country case Nepal. *Energy*, *36*(4), pp. 2194–2201. http://doi.org/10.1016/j.energy.2010.07.004.

Meyers, K.; Kim, J.; Ward, G.; Statham, B.; Frei, C. (2012): *Time to Get Real – The case for sustainable energy policy*. London: World Energy Council.

Rao, P. S. C.; Miller, J. B.; Wang, Y. D.; Byrne, J. B. (2009): Energy-microfinance intervention for below poverty line households in India. *Energy Policy, 37*(5), pp. 1694–1712. http://doi.org/10.1016/j.enpol.2008.12.039.

REN21 (2013): *Renewables 2013 – Global Status Report. Paris: REN21 – Renewable Energy Policy Network for the 21st Century*. Paris: REN21.

REN21 (2014): *Renewables 2014 – Global Status Report*. Paris: REN21.

Rockström, J.; Steffen, W.; Noone, K.; Persson, Å.; Chappin, S., III; Lambin, E.; Foley, J. (2009): A safe operating space for humanity. *Nature, 461*(September), pp. 472–475.

Steffen, W.; Richardson, K.; Rockstrom, et al. (2015): Planetary boundaries: Guiding human development on a changing planet. *Science, 347*(6223), pp. 1259855–1259855. http://doi.org/10.1126/science.1259855.

Szabó, S.; Bódis, K.; Huld, T.; Moner-Girona, M. (2011): Energy solutions in rural Africa: mapping electrification costs of distributed solar and diesel generation versus grid extension. *Environmental Research Letters, 6*(3), 034002. http://doi.org/10.1088/1748-9326/6/3/034002.

Thiam, D.-R. (2010): Renewable decentralized in developing countries: Appraisal from microgrids project in Senegal. *Renewable Energy, 35*(8), pp. 1615–1623. http://doi.org/10.1016/j.renene.2010.01.015.

Unruh, G. C. (2000): Understanding carbon lock-in. *Energy Policy, 28*(12), pp. 817–830.

van de Graaf, T. (2013): *The Politics and Institutions of Global Energy Governance*. Basingstoke: Palgrave Macmillan.

van Lente, H.; van Til, J. I. (2008): Articulation of sustainability in the emerging field of nanocoatings. *Journal of Cleaner Production 16*, pp. 967–976.

World Bank (2015): *World Development Report 2015: Mind, Society, and Behavior*. Washington, DC: World Bank. doi: 10.1596/978-1-4648-0342-0.

Further information and reading

bigEE (Bridging the Information Gap on Energy Efficiency in Buildings): bigee.net
Climate Technology Centre Network: ctc-n.org
Clean Energy Solutions Centre: cleanenergysolutions.org
Clasp Global Standards & Labeling (S&L) Database: clasponline.org
Energypedia: energypedia.info
International Partnership for Energy Efficiency Cooperation: ipeec.org
Renewable Energy and Efficiency Partnership: reeep.org
Renewable Policy Network for the 21st century: ren21.net
Sustainable Energy for All: se4all.org

14 Sustainable water supply and sanitation

Backbone of civilization

Peter A. Wilderer

Introduction

"Water is the essence of life". Presumably, everybody on Earth agrees. The more it is astonishing how poorly water is valued. Polluting water and over-extracting ground water are common practices around the globe. More than this, by deforestation humankind is thoughtlessly weakening one of the driving forces of the atmospheric water transport from sea to inland.

In this chapter the currently available information is compiled concerning the origin of water and the reasons why water has remained on Earth over billions of years. Subsequently, the mechanisms are summarized which drive the global and the terrestrial water cycle. We will discover the role forest ecosystems play in keeping the terrestrial water cycle revolving. Understanding such fundamentals are considered important for making proper decisions and efficient action in favour of the preservation of life on Earth in general, and for the sustainable development of modern civilization in particular.

Furthermore, we will discuss the role of system's stability and resilience as the basis of sustainable development. In this context we will learn about the adaptive cycle as an instrument to keep a system in the state of resilience irrespective of changing ambient conditions. Of concern are the rapid growth of the human population on Earth, the corresponding growth of the demands for water, food and other commodities, increasing pollution of soil, water and atmosphere, over-abstraction of resources and last but not least globalization of the lifestyle prevailing in the industrialized countries. Monitoring of and responding to such developments is important to decide which actions are to be taken. In the last part of this chapter some ideas are presented around sustainable water supply and sanitation in urban areas as a contribution to the preservation of the ecosystem functions, the functioning of the economy and the well-being of people alike.

How come that we have water on Earth?

Water is abundant in the universe. But as far as we know water is present in the galaxies and in the solar system only in its solid state of aggregation, namely as ice. Europa, one of the moons of Jupiter, is an example of such an ice-covered celestial body.

Recent findings suggest that Ganymede, the largest moon of Jupiter, harbours an ocean 330 km below the surface of the moon. According to calculations by Saur et al. (2015), the ocean contains more liquid water than all the oceans on Earth together. Does this mean that there might be life on Ganymede – life as we know it on Earth? The answer is a clear NO since the surface temperature on Ganymede during daytime is as low as -397 °F which equals -560 °C. At such a low temperature water transformation in a liquid-like phase requires extremely high pressure. Neither temperature nor pressure resemble conditions required to support life.

It is remarkable that in contrast to any other objects of our solar system the planet Earth hosts an enormous quantity of liquid water. Moreover the mean surface temperature has varied around +15 °C for more than 2.4 billions of years.

Where the water came from is a matter of discussion in astrophysics. Mainly two theories are taken into account: outgassing of water during the accretion period of our planet and heavy bombardment of icy objects caused by the inward-then-outward migration of Jupiter and Saturn. The latter occurred about 4 billion years ago. At that time, Jupiter and Saturn fell into a 2:1 orbital resonance creating a gravitational push against Neptune, which was driven past Uranus and plough into the dense planetesimal belt. The planets scattered the majority of the small icy objects inwards, while themselves moving outwards (http://en.wikipedia.org/wiki/Planetary_migration).

Whichever theory explains best the origin of water on Earth it should also explain recent findings according to which liquid water was present on Mars. Pictures taken by the Mars Rover *Curiosity* suggest that millions of years ago rivers flowed on Mars, leaving sediments behind which look almost identically to gravel sediments on Earth.

Obviously, liquid water disappeared on Mars but it remained on Earth. What went "wrong" on Mars? Recent findings made by the ESA VEX-mission (Venus-express) might give an answer. It was observed that under conditions of strong solar winds, parts of the ionosphere of Venus is blown far into the space. This effect is generated because the magnetic field of Venus is extremely weak compared to the strong magnetic field which protects the Earth from the loss of particles such as water molecules.

The magnetic field of Mars is a bit stronger when compared to Venus but still very weak compared to Earth. Thus it is likely that over the millions of years the water on Mars was gradually "blown" away. In the case of Mars, the NASA probe *Maven* was used to explore the loss of volatile compounds such as CO_2, N_2 and H_2O from the Martian atmosphere to space. Understanding atmospheric loss gave scientists insight into the history of Mars' atmosphere and climate (MAVAN 2014).

Obviously, humankind was not interfering with all such mechanisms outlined above. It appears that liquid water was retained on Earth because of the strong magnetic field which shields the Earth from solar winds. However, there is another theory which needs to be considered, namely the so-called Gaia theory proposed by James Lovelock (1979, 1988, 2000) and the theory of biotic regulation (Gorshkov et al. 2000). And here comes *homo sapience* into play. But before we can get into these theories we should discuss two important issues, namely: the quantitative dimension of water on Earth and the global hydrological cycle which the delivery of fresh water on continents and islands depends on, including terrestrial life.

How much water do we have on Earth?

About 71 per cent of the Earth's surface is covered with liquid water. This sounds a lot. More important than the surface coverage is the quantity of water available for life, transportation and industrial processes, however. According to Shiklomanov (1993) the total amount of water on Earth is estimated to be 1,386 million km^3. This number includes water in the form of ice (24 million km^3) and water vapour (12,900 km^3). The total volume of fresh water (groundwater, lakes, rivers, swamps) amounts to only 10.6 million km^3.

All these numbers appear very large. Are they really large? The US Geological Service calculated the size of a bubble containing the total volume of water on Earth. Such a bubble would have a diameter of only 1,386 km, which equals the distance between Hamburg (Germany) and Rome (Italy) or between Chicago and Denver (USA). The diameter of a bubble containing all the fresh water would be only 273 km. Figure 14.1 illustrates such a scenario. The small bubble in Figure 14.1 represents the total amount of fresh water on Earth. The picture makes us

Figure 14.1 The total amount of water on Earth (large bubble), and the total amount of fresh water (small bubble), accumulated in a bubble – a fiction presented by the US Geological Service

Source: https://water.usgs.gov/edu/gallery/global-water-volume.html 2014 aware of the limited nature of water on Earth. Better we avoid measures which might lead to any loss of water on our planet.

Lessons to be learnt
- Although a significant fraction of the Earth's surface is covered with water, the mass of water on Earth is rather small.
- Therefore, it is the obligation of mankind to deal wisely with water.

Hydrological cycle: A means to provide freshwater on land

With respect to the evolution of terrestrial life, the plate tectonic and the hydrological cycle are other peculiarities of the planet Earth. Movement and collision of plates lead to the formation of continents and islands which receive water by means of the hydrological cycle, depicted in Figure 14.2. Water is transported from sea to land and thus provides the precondition for the evolution of terrestrial life.

Processes such as evaporation, transpiration, condensation, formation of cloud and fog droplets, atmospheric water vapour transportation, precipitation, interceptions by plants, uptake of bacteria, plants animals and human beings, infiltration

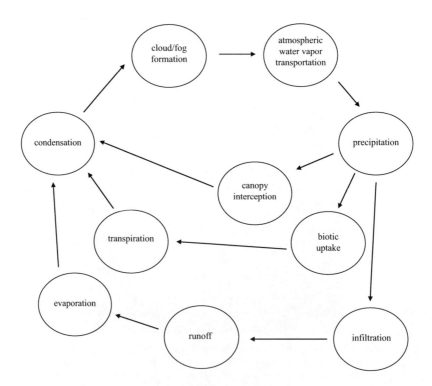

Figure 14.2 Graphical representation of the hydrological cycle

towards the ground water bodies, as well as surface and subsurface flow (runoff) are the components of which the hydrological cycle consists.

Water evaporates at the surface of oceans or lakes. Moreover, water gets transpired at the surface of plants and the skins of animals (evapotranspiration), forming water vapour which is released into the atmosphere. In the course of evaporation and evapotranspiration the water is purified. Dissolved substances such as salts are left behind.

In the course of condensation, the water vapour is transformed into the liquid phase of water termed fresh water. Droplets develop on the surface of micro-particles (aerosols) contained in the atmosphere forming clouds or fog. Under proper meteorological conditions those droplets decent to land in the form of rain or snow (precipitation).

On the first glance the hydrological cycle appears to be a natural phenomenon which humankind has no influence on. However humankind has long interfered with the hydrological cycle. By doing so, the persistence of life on Earth is taken at risk.

Lessons to be learnt
- Most of the water on Earth is salty and can sustain only marine life.
- Terrestrial life including humankind developed only because of the formation of land due to plate tectonics and the solar-driven transport of condensed water (i.e. fresh water) to land.

The importance of forest ecosystems for the functioning of the terrestrial hydrological cycle

In the 1950s and 1960s NASA asked James Lovelock, a chemist by training, to study the astrophysical information available at that time and answer the question "why we do have water on Earth but not on Mars?". Eventually, Lovelock came to the conclusion that the major difference between the two planets is that in contrast to Mars, life developed on Earth over the past 4 billions of years. Subsequently he proposed that life interacts with its abiotic environment on Earth to form a self-regulating, complex system that controls the conditions required to maintain the existence of water and thus the habitability of our planet. He coined this self-regulating Earth system "Gaia". His hypothesis has been heavily discussed in academic circles ever since. In a series of books (1974, 1988, 2000) Lovelock pointed out that interference of humankind with the self-regulation of life, of ecosystems in particular, by extensive emission of greenhouse gases, for instance, is likely to eventually lead to a dramatic catastrophe.

Based on thermodynamic principles, Gorshkov et al. (2000) came to the conclusion that ecosystems generate a meta-stable situation (Figure 14.3) which prevents the Earth system from shifting towards a geophysical stable state, comparable to the state of either Mars or Venus. This meta-stable state is mainly characterized by a mean surface temperature which from historical evidence oscillated over the past 4 billions of years by no more than +/- 10 °C around 15 °C,

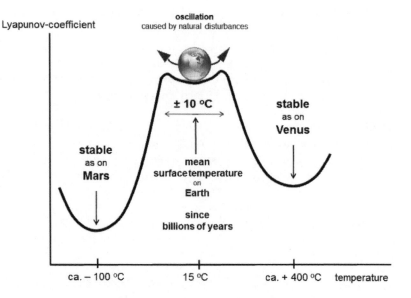

Figure 14.3 Graphical representation of the stability of Earth, Mars and Venus with respect to the global mean surface temperature, calculated using the Lyapunov potential function

Source: Adapted from Gorshkov et al. 2000

despite significant changes of solar radiation, hits of asteroids and outbreak from volcanoes. According to the calculations based on the energy balance equation of Lyapunov, elimination of major ecosystems on Earth would reduce the "height" of the "bumps" to the right or left of the point of meta-stability and drive the Earth system to destruction.

In continuation of this discussion, Makarieva et al. (2006) studied the role of forest ecosystems in supporting the hydrological cycle. They found that forest ecosystems transport humidity over thousands of kilometres into the hinterland. Clear-cutting of coastal forests disturbs the atmospheric humidity transport. Drying up of the hinterland is the consequence. This observation is supported by Nazareno and Laurance (2015), who argue that the current droughts in central Brazil are caused by the loss of forest ecosystems at the Atlantic coast and in the Amazon basin.

Makarieva et al. (2013) explored the physical and biological reasons of the biotic impact on the hydrological cycle. Their findings suggest a consecutive process of evapotranspiration, transport of moisture beyond the forest's canopy, condensation causing a drop in the atmospheric pressure through mass removal of water from the gas phase, followed by a horizontal transport of air, including water droplets which eventually leads to precipitation. Figure 14.4 illustrates this vertical/horizontal sequence of the sequence of processes.

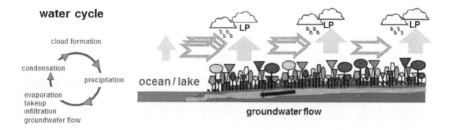

Figure 14.4 Graphical representation of the effect of forests on the horizontal transport of water vapor

Note: The sequence of pressure drop (LP: low pressure) and rainfall keeps the inland drying up

Source: Adapted from Makarieva et al. 2013

In summary, humankind is definitely responsible for changes of the hydrological cycle and its consequences. Clear-cutting of forests has obviously detrimental effects on climate, ecosystem services, rain-fed agriculture and on the supply of industry and people with fresh water and food. Afforestation is necessary to re-establish water cycle functions. However, abdication of clear-cutting is presumably a better option than afforestation.

Lessons to be learnt
- The global and the local water cycles provide fresh water to land-based biota and civilization.
- There are good reasons to assume that terrestrial ecosystems support the water cycle and the transport processes from oceans and large lakes to land.
- Preservation of the function of ecosystems is the key task of sustainable water management. It is the prerequisite of the preservation of the habitability of our planet.
- Stopping the clear-cutting of forests should be given priority over afforestation.

Ancient efforts to engineer flow and distribution of water as the cradle of civilization

Human intervention in the Earth system, be it technical or organizational, shows mostly if not always positive as well as negative effects. This is also the case for water management, the organization of assignments and processes, developed at times when humankind transformed from hunting and gathering to farming communities. The land required for faming had to be stripped from trees and bushes. Wetlands had to be drained. Fresh water had to be brought to agricultural fields.

It is certainly not a surprise that farming was first practiced along large rivers such as the Nile, Euphrates and Tigris, or the Yellow River in China. Those rivers provided water, but they also threatened farming communities during flooding events. Embankments had to be built to safeguard farming operations and villages. At the same time irrigation canals had to be built to transport water to and distribute it within the farmland. To guarantee equitable support, institutions became necessary to control water distribution systems and their operation.

To get all this accomplished a knowledgeable administration had to be initially established. According to Wittfogel (1957) an administration had to be established capable of recruiting and supplying a huge workforce to build dikes and canals, and owning the power to control the operation of water distribution and the subsequent commerce. This was the very basis for farming and the evolution of civilization. It was also the reason for major impacts on the water cycle.

With the growth of the human population and with the growth of cities, urban demand for water, food and commodities of all kinds increased. This made it necessary to transport water into cities as well as to distant farming field. During the Roman Empire, Roman engineers became masters of building and operating such water transportation systems.

The concept of transporting water over long distances – at the expense of the ecological balance of the locations where the water is abstracted – still remains in place. In California water is transported in huge canals over hundreds of miles from the north of the country to the farmland in the Central Valley and further south to Los Angeles and San Diego. In China, the North-East Water Transfer Project is currently (in the year 2015) close to completion. It aims to transport about 44.8 billion cubic metres of fresh water annually from the Yangtze River in southern China to the more arid and industrialized north, including Beijing and Tianjin. During the Soviet Empire the two rivers, Amu and Syr Darya, were almost entirely used for irrigating cotton fields with effect that the former largest inland lake, the Aral Sea, almost entirely dried out. Obviously, the administrations in charge of such water projects violated their obligation to care for the long-term well-being of both civilization and nature.

Lessons to be learnt
- Sustainable water management requires an administration knowledgeable in water technology, law and economics.
- Such administrations are equally responsible for the durable functioning of the ecosystems, and for the functioning of the water cycle in the region of concern.

Systems considerations

To achieve the most effective results of water management it is necessary to understand the dynamics of the system to be managed. Watersheds as well as urban areas are systems characterized by a wide variety of components and interrelated processes. Either of these components and processes is subjected to permanent alterations driven by changing ambient conditions. Political and economic conditions are changing but also technical opportunities, climate, educational status and the perceptions of people are changing – just to name a few. As long as the system is able to absorb such changes without losing its identity and integrity it is considered "resilient" (Dawson et al. 1994; Walker and Salt 2006).

Sustainable development resembles the process of absorbance which drives and secures the system in the state of resilience. The term "sustain-able" describes the ability to sustain. This term can be interpreted as the ability to function, despite ambient changes. In this case the system is saved from collapse.

The stable state of a hydrological system, also called "point of attraction", is defined by the value of factors (state variables) constituting the system, for instance the function of the local watershed, the municipal demand for water, access to and public acceptance of innovation concerning water treatment technology and water management, cross-economic conditions, societal preferences etc. A temporary disturbance (e.g., drought or heavy rainfall event) drives the system away from the point of attraction. Oscillation of state variables does not necessarily constitute a disturbance. It only causes the point of attraction to move. Since the state variables are likely to change all the time and since the point of attraction changes position, accordingly a water management system must cope with such dynamics to stay resilient.

In ecosystems, adjustment to changing state variables is driven mainly by self-regulation processes (Odum & Barrett 2004). Concerning anthropogenic systems, responses to such changes are governed by cognitive processes, by experience and by emotion, respectively. Required is knowledge derived from scholarly studies, education and training.

A rather dramatic situation develops when the impact of a major disturbance forces the system to move "out of focus". In this case, the system changes identity. It finds itself in an environment governed by a different regime. The evolution of life on Earth was driven by such regime shifts. Species who were not able to cope with the "new" environmental situation became extinct, but life as such persisted. Regime shifts were also common in the history of civilization. As in nature, civilization as such persisted nevertheless.

In this context it is worth knowing which forces drive ecosystems and manmade systems towards the point of attraction? Resilience theory suggests that the continuous revolving of the so-called "adaptive cycle" is the measure of keeping systems in the state of resilience (Walker and Salt, 2006). In Figure 14.5 the four major phases of a distinct adaptive cycle are presented: (1) growth following the start-up phase; (2) consolidation; (3) reorientation; and (4) and recommencement as a result of decision making and enforcement of decisions. The readiness to continuously consider reorientation and starting up again appears to be the most important step in keeping anthropogenic systems in the state of sustainable development.

Figure 14.6 depicts a situation which might evolve when actors are not ready to accept the need for reorientation and innovation but stick to methods which in the past proved to be successful. The consequences are often fatal. For instance, collapse of enterprises is a typical result of such a behaviour, equivalent to non-sustainability as explained previously.

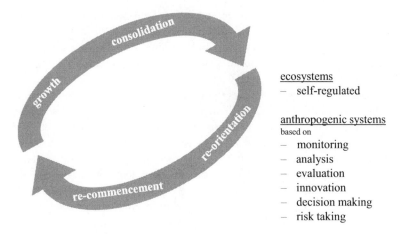

ecosystems
– self-regulated

anthropogenic systems
based on
– monitoring
– analysis
– evaluation
– innovation
– decision making
– risk taking

Figure 14.5 The four phases of an adaptive cycle and the measures driving the cycle in anthropogenic systems as compared to nature

Source: Adapted from Walker & Salt 2006

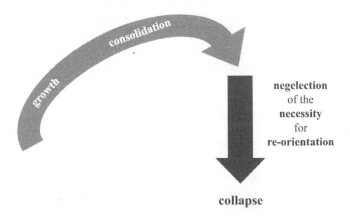

negelection
of the
necessity
for
re-orientation

collapse

Figure 14.6 Graphical representation of the consequences of resistance against change

Lessons to be learnt
- Sustainable development needs resilience thinking on the first place.
- Collapse prevention is the essence of sustainable systems management including sustainable water management.
- Continuous realization of ambient changes and readiness to respond proactively to such changes is the most promising approach to sustainable water management.
- It is dangerous to consider "eternal" validity of decisions which worked satisfactorily in the past.

The eco-social triad of urban water management

It has already been stated above that water management encompasses the organization and coordination of both natural environments as well as environments dominated by humankind. Human society and its economy form in concert with the aquatic and terrestrial ecosystems a super system which can be coined the "eco-social triad" (EST). Translated to the world of water management, the Venn diagram presented in Figure 14.7 visualizes the tight entanglement of the water specific subsystems of an EST, namely aquatic ecosystems, consumers and prosumers of useable water, water authorities and operators of water works and waste water treatment plants.

In Figure 14.7 aquatic and terrestrial systems are placed on top to remind everybody that water is essential for the biota as well as for the civilization (Bloesch et al. 2015). Subsequently, water must be treated as a global common, not as a tradable good. Moreover, it needs to be understood that over-abstraction and pollution of water to the disadvantage of aquatic and terrestrial biota is inacceptable because it puts the habitability of our planet at risk.

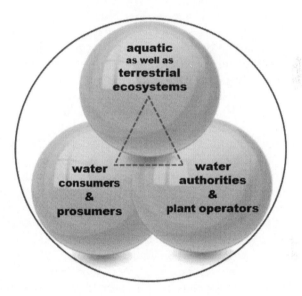

Figure 14.7 Entanglement of the three components of the eco-social triad, the aquatic ecosystems, the social system consisting of consumers and prosumers, and the governance system composed of water authorities and operators of water works (fresh water and used water)

Lessons to be learnt
- Water is a global common, not a tradable good.
- Preservation of groundwater bodies and avoidance of emission of pollutants are essential to preserve the habitability of our planet.

Evolution of water technology and water management: A brief historical review

To cover the growing water demand in ancient Roman cities canals and aqueducts were built to transport water over large distances towards the cities. Simultaneously, Roman engineers built sewer systems to transport rainwater as well human excrement (sewage) and used water from manufacturers and households for discharge in the closest river (Angelakis & Rose 2014). This concept is considered the "blueprint" of urban water management even today.

After the fall of the Roman Empire and until the advent of the Industrial Revolution in the 19th century recognition of the importance of water management was lost. The repeated outbreak of major diseases such as cholera, typhus and the black death were the consequences. Early advances in microbiology eventually triggered the rediscovery of the importance of urban water technology and management. Realization that the outbreak of epidemics was the result of the contact of people with human excreta led to the installation of sewers, first in London then in Germany and finally worldwide. Technologies for water purification (water works) and water distribution systems were installed to support citizens and businesses with hygienically safe drinking water.

As in Roman times the collected sewage was discharged into rivers without any purification. Accumulation of stinking sediments in rivers and extensive fish kill were the incentives for the installation of gravity sedimentation tanks prior to discharge. Still river waters deteriorated in quality, causing severe health problems for people in contact with pollutants, including pathogenic microorganisms. Experiments with various kinds of filters to remove such pollutants were only partly successful. A breakthrough was achieved through the work of researchers such as Fouler and Ardern and Lockett (1914). They invented the so-called "activated sludge treatment process" consisting of two components: reactors in which bacteria convert organic pollutants into biomass and gravity sedimentation units to separate the biomass from the waste water. However, the water quality in rivers, lakes and in the oceans deteriorated still further, caused by plant fertilizers contained in the biologically (pre)treated water. Subsequently, additional units were added to the portfolio of waste water treatment plants. Nitrification, denitrification and phosphorous removal systems completed the sequence of treatment processes. Among the substances which are currently of concern are micro-pollutants (e.g., pharmaceuticals, xenobiotics and micro-plastics), remaining in the effluents despite extensive physical, chemical and biological treatment. Additional treatment steps appear to be inevitable.

This course of development of waste water treatment systems can be described as a consecutive process to safeguard public health and economic growth, and to prevent deterioration of aquatic ecosystems. This concept corresponds with the intention to keep the adaptive cycle (Figure 14.5) revolving.

Does this stepwise process qualify as "sustainable development"? The answer is yes and no. The positive aspect is that waste water is considered a waste that needs to be treated. Discharging the treated water into rivers, lakes and coastal waters is the weak point of this concept, however. Only recently has the value of waste water as a source of valuable goods (e.g., water, fertilizers, heat) received attention. Moreover, a variety of novel tools for water purification is currently available, promoting a fundamental change to urban water management.

> *Lessons to be learnt*
> - The technologies currently applied to serve urban areas indisputably have their merits.
> - However, recent innovations, both on the technology and the management side, give rise to confidence that urban water management is approaching a new and elevated level of effectiveness in servicing people, economies and ecology.

Measures to develop sustainable water systems: Examples ready for development cooperation

Based on the information given above, some suggestions are presented here which might be helpful in the attempt to overcome water stress situations in low-income countries. The primary goal is to develop the local ecology, economy and society towards a state of sustainability.

Installation of knowledgeable water administrations

The solution of the rapidly growing water stress situation requires guidance and control by institutions acting independently of commercial interests. Staff members are expected to have up-to-date scientific knowledge encompassing technology, ecology, economy and law. To be able to act as caretaker of water as a common good, these administrations must be armed with a robust mandate.

> Task: Execution of water stewardship.
> Aim: Taking care of ecology, society and economy and their well-being.
> Method: Enforcement of scientifically sound decisions.

Decentralization of water management

Urban water management is a complex issue. The larger the system grows, the more complex it becomes and the more difficult it is to respond to slowly developing changes. Making the wrong decisions cannot be ruled out. It appears advisable, therefore, to adopt the so-called "subsidiarity principle" (Drost & Grambow 2015), meaning delegation of responsibilities and decision making to districts within the city where local concerns and changing conditions are comparably easy to recognize, and where system modification is relatively easy to accomplish.

This concept requires decentralization not only of administrative measures but also of infrastructural elements such as water supply and waste water collection, as well as water and waste water treatment facilities. Nevertheless, control by centralized institutions will be still necessary to keep the overall system on track. Modern cyber physical systems, also called the "Internet of Things", can be used to handle the flow of detailed information from the districts for holistic and effective decision making and control (Mainzer 2015).

Task:	Keeping water management and treatment efficient and affordable.
Aim:	Adopting innovation on the city and neighbourhood level.
Method:	Consider waste water as a source and reuse this resource progressively.

Enhancement of freshwater availability by enforcement of fair trade

Fair trade aims to help producers in low-income countries achieve better living conditions and to promote sustainability, preventing the collapse of the domestic ecological, social and economic systems. In the context of water management, the goal is to use the locally available freshwater preferentially for local purposes (growth and processing of food crops, supply enterprises and providing people with water). In particular, this requires ownership of agricultural land by local farmers, and cultivation of crops serving the needs of the local community. It also requires fair priced seeds and fertilizers as well as innovative methods for cultivating, fertilizing and irrigating farmland.

Task:	Optimizing the use of fresh water for local communities.
Aim:	Growing agricultural products in response to local demands.
Method:	Stopping the use of land in low-income countries for foreign markets and for the consumption of "virtual water".

Atmospheric humidity transport inland

The historic approach to artificially supplement local water resources (transport of water across long distances using pipes and canals) needs to be revisited. Using natural atmospheric water transport supported by terrestrial ecosystems (forests in particular) appears to be the more sustainable option.

Task:	Natural replenishment of local water resources, specifically ground water recharge.
Aim:	Safeguard inland regions from threats of droughts.
Method:	Stopping of clear-cutting of forests and draining wetlands.
Remarks:	When the land is already deforested, afforestation should be considered. However, several decades are needed until forest ecosystems reach their full capacity. Therefore, the stopping of clear-cutting is the better option. Afforestation in the form of tree plantations does not constitute a forest ecosystem.

Rainwater harvesting to overcome drought situations

Traditionally runoff from roofs and roads is collected by means of buried pipes or open canals, carrying the collected rainwater water either directly to the closest receiving water station or to a waste water treatment plant located prior to the discharge point. In either case, the water gets lost. For areas short of water this approach needs to be revisited. Where ever the geological conditions are appropriate, direct infiltration of the collected water for recharging the local ground water reservoir is worthy of consideration. The water could be collected in so-called "infiltration dams" and effectively used for ground water recharge (Haimerl et al. 2002).

Task:	Ground water recharge by direct infiltration of roof and road runoff.
Aim:	Safeguarding water supply during drought seasons.
Method:	Collection of rainwater followed by filtration and seepage into the aquifer.
References:	Athanasiadis (2005); Athanasiadis & Helmreich (2005); Athanasiadis et al. (2006); Matsui et al. (2001).

Acquisition of fresh water by fog collection

Where fog frequently occurs in a region, collection of fog droplets should be considered. Three-dimensional nets made of hydrophobic/hydrophilic plastic material exposed to the moving fog have proved to be effective in collecting and accumulating such droplets (Schemenauer & Cereceda 1994; Schiermeier 2014). Such an installation is shown in Figure 14.8. The German-based Water Foundation in cooperation with the Munich RE Foundation has successfully installed fog collecting nets at various places in Africa, the Middle East and Latin America (see www.munichre-foundation.org/home/Water/Fognets.html).

Figure 14.8 Water droplets of fog can be harvested by passing the fog through a net of plastic strips

Source: WasserStiftung (Water Foundation), Germany

Task:	Using fog as a supplementary source of fresh water.
Aim:	Installation of modern fog collecting nets.
Method:	Capturing fog droplets and storage of the collected water in sunlight-protected containers.

Abstraction of atmospheric humidity

To gain access to gaseous water, condensation processes must be initiated. This process begins as soon as a surface is provided at which the temperature falls below the dew point. In the sky, dust particles serve as primary condensation nuclei. On land, condensation surfaces are naturally provided in the form of leaves and blades of grass and shrubs.

Technically, condensation can be initiated by cooling surfaces exposed to humid air, for instance by pumping cool water through a bundle of pipes from the depth of a lake or from the ocean.

Task:	Use of condensation technology to capture humidity from air.
Aim:	Supplement fresh water resources by atmospheric humidity.
Method:	Expose cooled surfaces to humid air flow.

Replacement of gravity sedimentation by micro-screening and ultrafiltration

In water works and waste water treatment plants, particulate matter is commonly removed from water by means of gravity sedimentation. Noticeably, sedimentation tanks require most of the land area that a treatment plant covers. Currently there are several alternative separation methods (e.g. fine sieves, membranes). Most of them are relatively easy to operate and incur reasonable costs.

For instance, primary sedimentation tanks can be replaced by self-cleaning rotating screens. Such a devise is shown in Figure 14.9. The device could achieve more

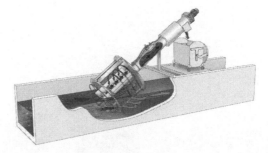

Figure 14.9 Graphical representation of a self-cleaning, rotating fine sieve for waste water treatment

Note: Such an installation could be used as an alternative to gravity sedimentation tanks. The size of waste water treatment plants could shrink significantly.

Source: Courtesy of Huber SE, Germany

than just removal of organic particulates, however. By dosing precipitants or floc-culants into the influent of the screen, dissolved chemical oxygen demand (COD) can be converted into particulate COD (Molahalli 2001), and COD removal efficiency can be increased to almost 80 per cent. This would make high-rate biological treatment systems obsolete.

Task:	Cleaning dirty water for further use.
Aim:	Replacement of space-consuming gravity sedimentation.
Method:	Application of self-cleaning sieves or membrane separation units.

Water reuse reduces the magnitude of water to be abstracted from natural resources

Using the traditional concept of abstracting water from natural resources and discharging the used water into rivers, lakes and eventually in the ocean needs to be critically scrutinized.

It is obvious that the quality of water depends on the purpose the water is used for. For instance, drinking water quality is not required for flushing toilets. By treating waste water as a source, applying purification technology tailored to specific quality requirements and reusing the water (Figure 14.10), the amount of water to be abstracted from nature can be significantly reduced.

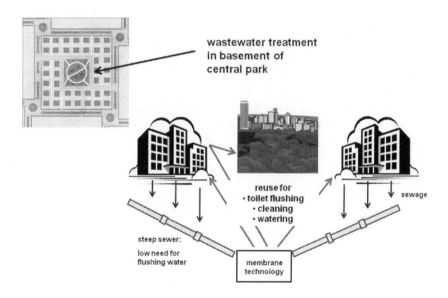

Figure 14.10 Cost-effective distribution of reusable water can be easily established in newly built settlements

Note: This option is commonly called semi-decentral water management

Task:	Substitution of fresh water with specifically purified waste water.
Aim:	Making use of waste water for non-potable purposes.
Method:	Collecting waste water in neighbourhoods, purifying it and using it for toilet flushing, cleaning or watering parks and gardens.

Summary and conclusions

It is good to know where the water on Earth came from. It strengthens our appreciation of a gift which is unique in our solar system. It is important to know why most of the water on Earth remained in the liquid phase over the past billions of years. Very likely large-scale ecosystems contributed to the preservation of the mean surface temperature on Earth at around 15 °C. Based on such assumptions it appears dangerous to sacrifice ecosystems in favour of land use for human purposes. Humanity as a partner of the global biota is permitted to make use of the Earth's resources. Pollution of resources such as ground water, rivers, lakes and coastal waters undermines the resilience of the Earth system, including social and economic subsystems, however. Pollution as well as over-abstraction of resources is unsustainable. Innovation and acceptance of innovation are necessary to solve the water problems of the 21st century. Acceptance of technical and management innovation keeps the adaptive cycle revolving and contributes to sustainable development.

References

Angelakis, A. N.; Rose, J. B. (2014): *Evolution of sanitation and wastewater technologies through the Centuries.* IWA Publishing.

Ardern, E.; Lockett, W. T. (1914): Experiments on the oxidation of sewage without the aid of filters. *J. Soc. Chem. Ind. 33*: 523.

Athanasiadis, K. (2005): On-site infiltration of roof runoff by using clinoptolite as an artificial barrier material. *Berichte aus Siedlungswasserwirtschaft Nr. 187*, Place: Siedlungswasserwirtschaft, TU Munich, Germany.

Athanasiadis, K.; Helmreich, B. (2005): Influence of chemical conditioning on the ion exchange capacity and on kinetic of zinc uptake by clinoptilolite. *Water Research 39*: 1527–1532.

Athanasiadis, K.; Helmreich, B.; Wilderer, P. A. (2006): Infiltration of a copper roof runoff trough artificial barriers. *Water Science and Technology 54*: 281–289.

Bloesch, J.; von Hauff, M.; Mainzer, K.; Venkata Mohan S.; Renn, O.; Risse, V.; Song, Y.; Takeuchi, K.; Wilderer, P. A. (2015): Sustainable development integrated in the concept of resilience (Zrównowa ony rozwój a koncepcja resilencji). *Problemy Ekorozwoju – Problems of Sustainable Development 10*, 1: 7–14.

Dawson, R.; Sharon, B.; Brooks, K.; McGuire, W. J. (1994): *Coping and adaptation: Theoretical and applied perspectives.* US National Technical Information Service.

Drost, U.; Grambow, M. (2015): *The principle of subsidiarity and internality as order principles of decentralized structures, illustrated by the example of water management.* Springer.

Gorshkov, V. G.; Gorshkov, V. V.; Makarieva, A. M. (2000): *Biotic regeneration of the environment: Key issue of global change.* Springer.

Haimerl, G.; Zunic, F.; Strobl, T. (2002): An infiltration test to evaluate the efficiency of groundwater recharge dams in arid countries. In: Singh, V.P.; Al-Rashed, M.; Sherif, M.M. (eds) *Surface water hydrology*. Kuwait, 23–27. March. Balkema AA Publisher.

Lovelock, J. (1979): *Gaia – A New Look at Life on Earth*. Oxford University Press.

Lovelock, J. (1988): *The Age of Gaia: A Biography of our Living Earth*. W. W. Norton.

Lovelock, J. (2000): *The Revenge of Gaia: Why the Earth is fighting back, and how we can still save humanity*. Penguin Books.

Mainzer, K. (2015): *Challenges of complexity in the age of globalization and big data*. Springer.

Makarieva, A. M.; Gorshkov, V. G. (2006): Biotic pump of atmospheric moisture as driver of the hydrological cycle on land. *Hydrology and Earth System Sciences Discussions 3* (4): 2621–2673.

Makarieva, A. M.; Gorshkov, V. G.; Sheil, D.; Nobre, A. D.; Li, B. L. (2013): Where do winds come from? A new theory on how water vapor condensation influences atmospheric pressure and dynamics. *Atmos. Chem. Phys. 13*: 1–18.

Matsui, S.; Kobayashi, S.; Kimura, S. (2001): Road surface waste water treatment device and tubular water treatment unit. U.S. Patent 7291262, 11 June.

MAVEN (2014): *Mars Atmospheric and Volatile Evolution Mission*. http://lasp.colorado.edu/home/maven/.

Molahalli, P. (2001): Chemical pre-precipitation of municipal wastewater using Mg^{2+}. Master thesis, RTH Industrial Ecology, Stockholm, Sweden.

Nazareno, A. G.; Laurance, W. F. (2015): Brazil s drought: Beware deforestation. *Science 347*: 1427.

Odum, E. P.; Barrett, G. W. (2004): *Fundamentals of ecology*. Cengage Learning, 5th ed.

Saur, J.; Duling, S.; Roth, L.; Jia, X.; Strobel, D. F.; Feldman, P. D.; Christensen, U. R.; Retherford, K. D.; MCGrath, M. A.; Musacchio, F.; Wennmacher, A.; Neubauer, F. M.; Simon, S.; Hartkorn, O. (2015): The search for a subsurface ocean in Ganymede with Hubble Space Telescope observations of its auroral ovals. *Geophysical Research: Space Physics*, DOI 10.1002/2014JA020778.

Schemenauer, R. S.; Cereceda P. (1994): Fog collection's role in water planning for developing countries. *Natural Resources Forum, 18*: 91–100.

Schiermeier, Q. (1914): Water on tap. *Nature 510*: 326–328.

Shiklomanov, I. (1993): World fresh water resources. In Gleick P. H. (ed.): *Water in crisis: A guide to the world's fresh water resources,* Oxford University Press.

Trenberth, K. E.; Smith, L.; Qian, T.; Dai, A.; Fasullo, J. (2007): Estimates of the global water budget and its annual cycle using observational and model data. *Journal of Hydrometeorology 8* (4): 758–769.

Walker, B.; Salt, D. (2006): *Resilience thinking: Sustaining ecosystems and people in a changing world*, Island Press.

Wittfogel, K. A. (1957): *Oriental despotism: A comparative study of total power*. Yale University Press.

15 Sustainable agriculture

Brigitte Kaufmann and Oliver Hensel

Introduction

Agriculture is considered the world's most important economic sector, since it is the most widespread land use form and it is the sector that contributes to income creation of the largest segment of the global population. Agriculture, together with forestry and fishing, is the sector which is most directly connected with nature and which is dependent on natural resources. Agricultural systems are therefore represented as complex social ecological systems (e.g. Woodhill & Röling 1998, Janssen et al. 2007, Kremen et al. 2012), in which humans strategically influence natural processes in ecosystems to produce goods (food, fibre, fuel) for which there is demand in society (Coughenour 1984).

Agricultural production has increased significantly during the past 50 years. In recent decades, however, the limitations in the availability of natural resources have became more obvious. On the one side, one realizes that further rise in agricultural yields that keeps up with the projected increase in the global population is not realistic, and on the other side, negative impacts of agriculture on the environment and society are getting more and more visible.

The development of agriculture in the industrialized countries was shaped in recent decades by far-reaching socio-economic changes and increasing globalization. This has led to a widespread specialization, mechanization and industrialization in the agricultural sector. Higher yields and increased productivity were the result, but also the reduction of the number of people employed in agriculture and a structural change towards larger farms in the countries of the Organization for Economic Co-operation and Development (OECD). The negative effects of this development are an increasing use of natural resources partly leading to resource degradation, for instance through pollution with pesticides in soil and water, loss of organic matter in soils, the increased emission of greenhouse gases and reduction of biodiversity.

Although this "industrialized" agriculture is often seen – also in the media – as the dominant and modern type of agriculture, it plays a minor role in feeding the world. Out of an estimated 570 million farms worldwide, 88 per cent are smallholder and family farms and 85 per cent have a size of less than 2 hectares, with 72 per cent less than 1 hectare. A wide variety of family farms worldwide results from the large differences in their respective contexts with for example different biophysical, ecological, social, economic and political conditions. When assessing the role of family farms and food-based micro-businesses in achieving sustainable food and nutritional security, there is hence the need to use a systems approach that can deal with this variety in systems and environments and the multitude of factors affecting functions and performances. Despite the fact that smallholder and family farms play an important role in food production, especially in countries of the Global South, the most nutritionally vulnerable people are those whose livelihoods are based on smallholder agriculture (FAO 2014). Therefore agricultural systems that work with low external inputs are, given their lower yields, often considered as not capable of ensuring food security worldwide.

Future developments must take into account the rising food demand of a growing population, coupled with a shortage in fossil fuels and the emerging competition for land for the production of biomass for energy generation. Additionally one needs to consider on-going trade liberalization (e.g. with the current TTIP and CETA negotiations[1]) and the concentration of agricultural suppliers (e.g. fertilizer, pesticides and seed companies) and food industry (multi-national companies in the processing and distribution).

How and to what extent a sustainable agriculture can be achieved have been studied since the 1990s in the agricultural sciences and related disciplines of ecology, economics and rural sociology, often using an interdisciplinary approach to consider ecological, economic and social factors that are closely interlinked in agriculture. The goal is that through sustainable agriculture, resource use should be reduced and resource degradation should be avoided or counteracted. Furthermore the economic and social needs of current and future generations should be met. Moreover, agriculture is seen to have the potential to provide ecosystem services, such as reducing the impact of climate change, contributing to the preservation of biodiversity and to the protection of watersheds. However, the extent of these potential ecosystem services depends on the production systems and the respective production conditions in the different regions of the world.

In the this chapter, we give more details and explain the issues mentioned in the introduction, starting with the importance of agriculture as land use system for the rural population and its contribution to food security. We then introduce the main characteristics of agricultural systems, categorize them and explain the functioning of low external input systems. The concept of sustainable agriculture is then introduced and the importance of sustainable use of the different agricultural capitals is explained. Aims and characteristics of sustainable agriculture are described and approaches on how to assess them through indicator systems are explained. Finally, as a possible pathway to sustainable agriculture we present the concept of agro-ecology and stress the importance of the involvement of farmers in the transformation process towards sustainablity.

Importance of agricultural production

Globally about 10 per cent of the world's terrestrial surface is currently used as arable land and 26 per cent as rangeland. Two-third of the world's arable land is situated in the tropics, mainly in semi-humid and humid regions. In these areas, farms can be either specialized in crop or in livestock production or combine crop and livestock production in mixed farms. Approximately 41 per cent of the terrestrial surface is classified as drylands, with about 90 per cent of them being situated in the low-income counties. Drylands house about one-third of the world's population and about 50 per cent of the world animal population, and are mainly used for pasture-based livestock production on the rangelands. Only about 25 per cent of drylands are used for crop production.

Global arable land has increased since 1961 from 12.6 million square kilometres to 15.6 million square kilometres in 2005. This corresponds to an average increase of about 70,000 square kilometres per year. At the same time, however, every year arable land amounting to 100,000 square kilometres is lost due to soil degradation. This means that in order to keep the size of crop land worldwide at a constant level, every year natural ecosystems need to be transformed and used for crop production. The conversion of natural ecosystems goes along with a reduction in biodiversity and especially in the case of deforestation large quantities of carbon dioxide are released.

For about 2.5 billion people that live in the rural areas, agriculture is the source of their livelihood. It offers employment opportunities for 1.3 billion smallholders and landless workers and is the foundation for viable rural communities (IBRD 2007).

In industrialized countries, the number of people employed in agriculture has decreased steadily since the time of the Industrial Revolution. Today, only about 4 per cent of the workforce of the OECD countries earns their living from agriculture. In these countries, the agricultural sector has undergone various structural changes that have led to a drastic reduction of small and medium-size farms. Exceptions are part-time farming, organic farming and farms specializing in labour-intensive production such as vegetable and fruit production. The majority of agricultural land in the industrialized countries is farmed by a relatively small number of large companies in a capital-intensive way. Due to mechanization, labour efficiency is high which means that labour demand is low. This specialized agriculture takes advantage of the economy of scales. Parallel to this development, however, the importance of upstream and downstream sectors in agriculture has increased (e.g. the production of farm inputs on the one hand and food processing on the other hand). In particular, the food industry is an important employer in industrialized countries, where the contribution of the food industry to gross domestic product (GDP) exceeds the contribution of agricultural production by far.

In the countries of the Global South, agriculture is often still a main economic activity, with on average 20 and 30 per cent of the population engaged in agriculture. Especially in rural areas the majority of households gain their income from agriculture and usually use the products also for their own food supplies. Livestock plays an important role for income generation, especially for the poor. It is estimated that of the world's 1.3 billion poor, 42 per cent gain a living from livestock keeping (Thornton et al. 2002). Usually in the course of the economic development of countries the role of agriculture in comparison to industry and services decreases. If in rural areas no alternative income possibilities arise, unemployment and migration to urban areas is a main consequence.

Agricultural production and food security

The debate on sustainable agriculture usually starts with questions about the need for further increases in agricultural production and yields. The world's population is, according to the UN estimations, to grow to 9.2 billion people in 2050, whereby the growth will mainly take place in the countries of the Global South. Theoretically current food production would be sufficient to achieve food security for the world's population, especially if the high amount of agricultural products and processed food currently lost as post-harvest losses or waste by consumers – amounting to about 1.3 billion tonnes per year – would be available for consumption. Also changing the eating habits in industrialized countries towards a higher share of vegetarian food would be beneficial to achieve global food security. However, the opposite trend is observed, particularly in emerging economies such as China, India and Brazil, where due to the growing prosperity and increasing urbanization, the proportion of animal-based food in the food basket is increasing. This means that crop production would have to rise because of the increased demand for animal feed and also because of the higher demand for biomass used for energy production as a substitute for the dwindling oil resources.

Increase in food production

During recent decades, agricultural production and yield increases have exceeded population growth, so the per capita food production, especially in the countries of the Global South, has steadily grown (Figure 15.1). Only in sub-Saharan Africa has the increase in food production stayed behind population growth. Thus, per capita production in 2004 was below that of 1970. Because of food imports and due to famine relief, the per capita food consumption has however also increased in this region.

High rates of increase in agricultural production over the last decade have especially been observed for high-value crops and energy crops; for instance for oil plants and vegetables and in the Global South additionally for animal products such as meat, milk and eggs. These products are mainly produced for the market.

The production of staple foods such as cereals and tubers has shown a lower increase in yields. The cereals wheat, maize and rice form the food base for the majority of the world's population. In general for crops, production is extremely inelastic, meaning that if the demand increases production cannot react accordingly. This is mainly due to the restrictions to further expand crop production. While the consumption of cereals for food and feed increased by 4 per cent and 7 per cent respectively, the use for industrial purposes, for example for fuel, have increased by more than 25 per cent since 2000; whereby the high rate is influenced by the much lower absolute value. More and more countries that previously were able to cover the domestic demand for agricultural products through their own agricultural

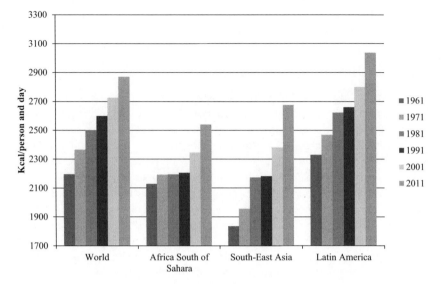

Figure 15.1 Per capita food energy consumption (in kcal per day) for different regions
Source: Based on data from FAOSTAT 2013

production, are becoming net importers of food. A main reason is that domestic agriculture is targeting export markets, while staple foods are imported because they are cheaply available on the world markets as a result of subsidies, especially in industrialized countries. Between 2009 and 2011, about 80 per cent of countries worldwide were net grain-importing countries. In many countries of the Global South, this development comes at the expense of the nutritional situation of the poorer part of population (von Braun 2008).

Food insecurity

Despite the increase in per capita production and consumption, the number of undernourished people has hardly declined worldwide since the 1990s. This indicates again that achieving food security for the world's population is not the same as producing enough food. Food shortages and malnutrition are rather in many cases a distribution problem or a problem of poverty. Using the World Bank poverty line of US$1.25 per person per day, in 2011, just over 1 billion people lived below that line. Overall, 2.2 billion people people live on less than $2 per day; many of them can be found among the rural population in the Global South. These are in particular small-scale farmers, pastoral livestock keepers and landless people who depend on agricultural production to gain their livelihoods. It is therefore important that precisely these population groups can generate enough income through agricultural production to overcome poverty and hence reach food security.

Apart from food supply or availability, the food security situation of a household depends on many more factors that can cause malnutrition (Figure 15.2).

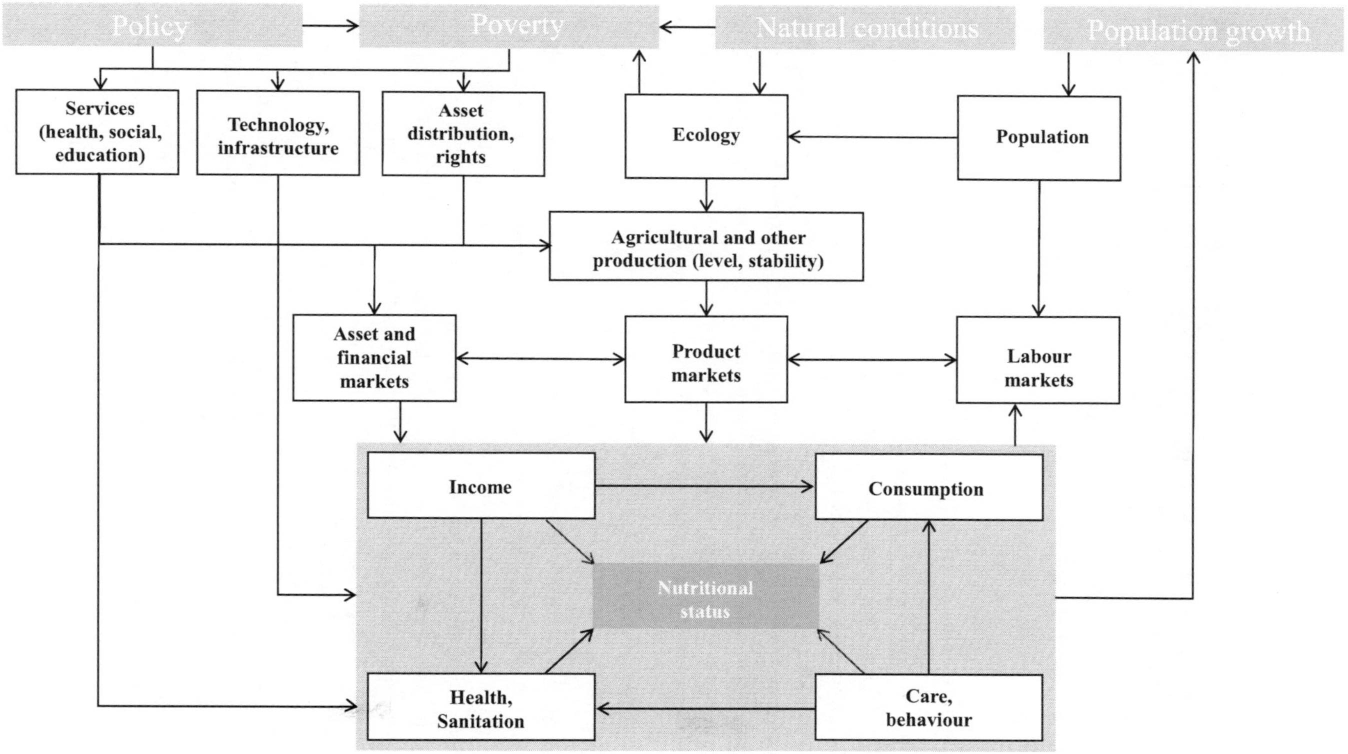

Figure 15.2 Causes and relationships of malnutrition

Source: Adapted from von Braun, 2002

In addition to households that suffer from chronic malnutrition, acute food shortages (famine) caused by for example droughts, floods or locust invasion can periodically affect many households that are otherwise food secure. Increasingly, manmade causes like armed conflict, forced displacement of entire populations or the disruption of social cohesion lead to food insecurity. In recent decades, sudden increases in the world market prices for the main food crops (wheat, maize and rice) caused by commodity speculations on the world market have had in some countries severe effects on the affordability of staple foods for the poorer parts of the population and compromised their food security. Often natural and manmade causes add-on to each other, which can lead to long-term crises. In 2015, 34 countries were affected by serious food shortages, 28 of them in Africa and 6 in Asia and the Middle East.

Main charactieristics of agricultural systems

Agricultural production systems are dynamic, thermodynamically open and purposeful systems. This means, they have been established by the farmer with the purpose of producing goods. They depend on the energy of the environment and their current state depends on their previous state as they change over time. With regard to energy transformation, agricultural production systems have the specific characteristics that farmers make use of biological systems (plants and animals) that directly (plants) or indirectly (animals) transform solar energy into chemical energy, protein (e.g. cereals or milk) or fibre for other human uses.

Context dependency of agricultural systems

Worldwide we find a very high variety of different agricultural production systems. Also within countries and regions within countries, different types are found. This can be explained by the respective differences in the production contexts that influence the suitability or feasibility or economic viability of a specific production system in the area. Figure 15.3 illustrates which factors generally have an impact on the type of agricultural production that can be found in a specific area.

These factors do not act in isolation but are also related to each other. One can say that in the first place agricultural production depends on natural conditions, i.e. the biophysical factors. These primarily include the climate and the topographic and edaphic characteristics. These determine whether and in what way the land is suitable for crop farming or whether it is suited to livestock keeping on rangeland.

The natural conditions have an impact on the socio-economic conditions in the regions concerned. In temperate areas we find the high-income countries, whereas most nations in the tropics are among lower-income countries, i.e. are among the states with low economic power, which in turn manifests itself in a lack of infrastructure, market access, industry and technology. Also at the country level, biophysical factors may have an impact on socio-economic factors. Areas where farming is possible are much more densely populated than for instance drylands, which are used by agro-pastoralists and pastoralists. Population density has a

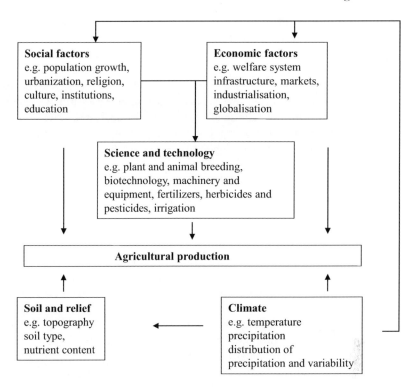

Figure 15.3 Biophysical and socio-economic factors influencing type of agricultural
production

Source: Adapted from Spedding 1996

significant impact on land availability and in humid areas population density can easily rise to 300–400 people/km2 as opposed to 2–20 people/km2 in drylands. This usually also affects economic factors, such as infrastructure facilities: the availability of tarmac roads, electrical grids, agricultural supply or markets, which are generally better developed in the more densely populated areas.

The main contextual factors influencing agricultural production are:

• Agro-ecological zone and water availability
• Population density and land availability
• Availability of inputs and technology
• Proximity to markets or cities, e.g. urban, peri-urban or rural locations
• Economic situation of the country, e.g. high-, medium- or low-income countries

As mentioned above, these different factors interact and form the production environment that is ultimately responsible for the kind of agricultural system found in a particular place. The different factors restrict the possibilities for production systems. This is explained in the following statement:

> The farmer manages a large number of related processes, transforming available resources into valuable products that s/he will either use directly or sell. The farmer's choice of plant and animal production processes and of methods and technologies are not only limited by biological and physical conditions, but also by economic and socio-political conditions, all of them contributing to the specific production environment in which the farmer operates. Within this environment, the farmer has discovered by trial and error appropriate techniques and the most suitable resource allocation with regard to the pursued aims.
>
> (Hildebrand & Waugh 1986)

This means that farmers with similar resource endowments and similar production environments also use ultimately similar plant and animal production processes. Hence, distinct knowledge on production conditions is a prerequisite for the development of measures to improve production. The production environment thus represents a restriction when it comes to changing agricultural production systems. In-depth knowledge on the production environment is necessary for the development of improvement measures, so that these will finally fit to the context.

However, if the production environment changes, or if one has found new ways to make use of resources by innovative technological possibilities that were formally not efficiently usable, then also the agricultural production may change. In particular, as the socio-economic conditions in some areas change relatively quickly, research and extension can support farmers to keep pace with these developments.

Categorization of agricultural systems

Agricultural systems are usually described at the farm level. A farm may consist of the subsystems crop production, livestock production and household. Within the crop production one can in turn look at the subsystem "field" and within the field the subsystem "plant".

Worldwide, there are a lot of different agricultural production systems. In order to describe these and to identify factors that affect their functioning, as well as to identify development opportunities for the agricultural systems, different classifications of agricultural systems have been developed (e.g. Ruthenberg 1980; Beets 1990; Dixon et al. 2001). The classification systems differ depending on which criteria were used to differentiate the categories.

When the criterion is the extent of the use of external inputs, intensive systems are differentiated from low external-input systems. In intensive agricultural systems, the production process depends on high amounts of support energy (mostly fossil fuels) for the production of fertilizer, the production and use of farm machinery and other farm infrastructure, such as for irrigation. All these are external inputs.

The production output of intensive systems per hectare of land or per animal is high, as the control of the production environement and the supply of plants and animals with the inputs they require for optimal production permits the use of high-yield plant varieties or high-performance animal breeds. These systems show high economic profitability when provided with functioning infrastructure and economic systems. The use of inputs permits the producer to influence the production environement.

In low external-input systems, the capital demand for the operation and the rate of the use of support energy is low. In these systems, yields are usually lower and the efficiency of production factors like land and labour is lower than in intensive systems. In most low external-input systems mainly farm-based resources are used in labour-intensive processes. Low external-input systems include the smallholder farms and pastoral livestock systems that are widespread in the tropics. In low external-input systems, the adjustment of production to the natural environment plays a major role. Since only limited external inputs are used, the production conditions can be controlled only to a small extent. In these systems varieties and breeds that are adapted to the respective existing production conditions (e.g. variability in climate, feed resources) are used. Their yield per hectare or per animal is significantly lower than that of high yielding varieties and breeds used in intensive systems. However in the former system costs of production are also much lower.

Intensification is usually accompanied by a specialization, so that the farmers can benefit from the economy of scales. Labour-intensive agriculture is transformed into a capital-intensive agriculture. The use of capital, such as machinery and equipment, reduces the required amount of work, thereby increasing labour productivity significantly. Inputs such as seeds, fertilizer and pesticides may be purchased at lower rates and for some crops, though contract farming, guaranteed prices are achieved.

The downside of specialization is environmental impacts that lead to costs that are usually externalized and are hence paid by society. For instance, intensive tillage can lead to reduced soil fertility and the use of synthetic fertilizers and pesticides can lead to restriction to a few high-yielding varieties, severely affecting biodiversity. In animal production, intensive systems (industrialized livestock production) raise increasingly severe animal welfare concerns in society. In the long term, monocultures, i.e. more uniform production, lead also to an increase in production risks from diseases and pests.

Whether intensive or low external-input systems prevail in the different regions of the world is affected by a variety of factors spanning from climatic to socio-economic reasons. Generally in temperate regions in the OECD countries intensive systems are prevailing. In most areas of the tropics and other areas with high climatic uncertainties low external-input systems are common. In recent decades, however, in both parts of the world the opposite development has been observed: reduced use of inputs in agro-ecological or organic farming in temperate latitudes and intensive farming at "favourable locations" in the tropics. Favourable locations in the tropics are for instance those at higher altitudes with temperate climates, and also those that are socio-economically favoured, for example, peri-urban areas, where nowadays industrial animal production units are established.

In the OECD countries, the extent to which the production environment can be controlled has drastically increased after the Second World War, and science and technology have played an important role in connection with the changes in the socio-economics in those countries. As explained above, the enhanced control of production conditions is based on the use of fossil fuels. The higher energy input serves to increase yields and production efficiency. This means that in intensive systems, the productivity of labour (and often but not always land) is much increased compared to that of low external-input systems. The energy efficiency must, however, be not increased in intensive systems. Usually even the opposite is the case and low external-input systems have significantly higher energy efficiency than intensive systems, especially when one looks at the energy used in production that is not solar but in form of labour, drought animals or (fossile) fuel (Figure 15.4). In systems in which manpower is used as the only support energy, energy efficiency is the highest, for instance 38 kcal of energy in production output are produced with the input of 1 kcal of support energy (i.e. manpower) in smallholder rice producing systems in Thailand.

At the other side of the spectrum we find pork production where only 1 kcal of energy in the production output is produced with the use of 10 kcal of support energy (mostly fossil fuel). The difference in the economic and energy efficiency results from the different economic costs of a unit of energy from various sources, such as manpower, draft power or fossil fuels and from the energy efficiency of the people or machines and technical processes employed.

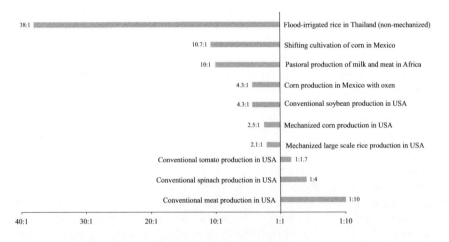

Figure 15.4 Energy efficiency in different agricultural systems (energy yield per support energy)

Source: Adapted from Gliessman 2007

Pathways towards sustainable agriculture

Sustainable agriculture is both a mission statement as well as a characteristic of the mode of production. For sustainable agriculture, there exist a variety of definitions. The various definitions can be subdivided into those that target the production principles, the philosophy behind them and are given in the form of principles, and those directly relating to certain aspects of production or even to individual farming practices. In the definitions, the ecological, economical and social dimensions of sustainability are considered. A representative of the first group is the definition used by the FAO (1995) which defines sustainable agriculture and rural development (SARD) as a process that meets the following criteria:

- Ensures that the basic nutritional requirements of present and future generations, qualitatively and quantitatively, are met while providing a number of other agricultural products.
- Provides durable employment, sufficient income, and decent living and working conditions for all those engaged in agricultural production.
- Maintains and, where possible, enhances the productive capacity of the natural resource base as a whole, and the regenerative capacity of renewable resources, without disrupting the functioning of basic ecological cycles and natural balances, destroying the socio-cultural attributes of rural communities, or causing contamination of the environment.
- Reduces the vulnerability of the agricultural sector to adverse natural and socio-economic factors and other risks, and strengthens self-reliance.

Definitions that fall under the second category, i.e. that explicitly list individual production aspects, are for example (Institute for Global Communications 1992):

- Sustainable agriculture conserves biodiversity, soil fertility and water quality, it maintains and improves the chemical, physical and biological soil quality, using natural resources in a close cycles and makes economic use of energy. Through sustainable agriculture high quality products are produced.
- Sustainable agriculture uses locally available renewable resources, appropriate and cost-effective technology and minimizes the consumption of external inputs, thereby improving the local independence and self-reliance of farmers and rural people and providing them with reliable livelihoods.

The first type of definitions relate to the overall vision and concept and the second to the production mode. With the first type, it is not made explicit how these principles can or should be attained and for the second type, not all production aspects mentioned are relevant for each system, hence it shows the need for situation-specific variation of the definition which is also dependent on the available knowledge and technology. Hence sustainable agriculture is a dynamic and not static concept. This means that actions that today are seen to provide a contribution to sustainability may no longer provide this under changing conditions.

Since most smallholder farmers in the Global South depend on their farm for the generation of livelihoods and have few alternative sources of income, it is of essential importance to them that their production system is sustainable. The ILEIA network (Centre for Information on Low External Input and Sustainable Agriculture, www.ileia.org), which has focused for almost four decades on research and extension of low external-input and sustainable agriculture mainly in the tropics, uses the following definition: "Agriculture is sustainable when it is ecologically sound, economically viable, socially acceptable, humane and adaptable". Reijntjes et al. (1992) summarize the terms used in the definition sustainable agriculture as:

- Ecologically sound: which means that the quality of the natural resources is maintained and the vitality of the entire agro-ecosystem is enhanced.
- Economically viable: which means that farmers can produce enough to obtain a living and gain sufficient returns to warrant the labour and costs involved.
- Socially just: which means that resources and power are distributed in such a way that the basic needs of all members of society are met and their rights to land use, adequate capital, technical assistance and market opportunities are assured.
- Humane: which means that all forms of life (plant, animal, human) are respected. The fundamental dignity of all human beings is recognised and the cultural and spiritual integrity of the society is preserved.
- Adaptable: which means that rural communities are capable of adjusting to the constantly changing conditions for farming.

Sustainable use of agricultural capital

Agriculture is a production sector that depends more than other sectors on natural, social and economic resources. These resources are referred to as agricultural capital. Agricultural systems depend on the services of the total capital stock. This capital stock includes five different types of capital, which are used in the agricultural production process (UNEP-UNCTAD CBTF 2007). These are:

- Natural capital: soil, water, air, animals, crops, natural vegetation. It is important as a source of food, wood, fibres and provides for example the following services: nutrient cycling, soil formation, biological pest control, climate regulation, wildlife habitat, flood control, pollination and carbon sequestration.
- Human capital refers to the totality of the capabilities of individuals resulting from their knowledge, skills, education and health and nutrition. It is increased by access to services that promote these capabilities (for example, schools, health services, adult education).
- Social capital refers to the relationship of the individuals within society; it consists of characteristics of social relationships, such as trust, which is necessary

for cooperation. It is based on rules and norms and sanctions of behaviour, reciprocity and exchange, as well as social institutions.

- Financial capital: money, liquidity, saving and credit facilities, markets for inputs and products. It refers to the stock and the flow of money and includes savings, access to credit, pensions, subsidies and grants.
- Physical capital includes the material resources that are manmade, such as production factors and machinery, as well as infrastructure such as roads, transportation facilities and factories.

In a sustainable agricultural production, one aims to use these five different types of capital in such a way that desirable outcomes are achieved, such as employment creation, prosperity, wellbeing and a clean environment. These outcomes contribute in turn to building and further strengthening capital. In production processes often trade-offs are made between the various types of capital, i.e. the gain in one capital can lead to loss in another. The aim of sustainable production is to increase agricultural capital and to keep it in balance.

UNEP-UNCTAD CBTF (2007) gives some examples on the interplay and possible trade-offs with regard of the use of and production of different types of capital in agriculture:

- An agricultural system in which the soil is eroded produces food at the expense of natural capital.
- A system in which carbon is fixed by increasing the organic matter in the soil helps to mitigate climate change
- A diversified agricultural system, which promotes beneficial organisms, increases biodiversity and thus natural capital.
- An agricultural system that expands the value chain, thereby promoting local economies and creates employment possibilities in rural areas increases human capital.

A major reason for widespread non-sustainable development in agriculture stems from the fact that natural and social capital are considered less important than financial capital. This is partly due to the difficulty of valuing these types of capital economically. While the value of buildings or machinery is easy to estimate, the determination of the value of a healthy forest and a functioning rural community or the humus content in the soil poses considerable difficulties. However, the determination of their value is a prerequisite when aiming at the preservation and increase of these types of capital. Another difficulty is that these goods are mainly public goods (and not under private ownership) and that they also for this reason do not have an established market value. This lack of valorization is also a reason why costs arising from damage for example of natural or social capital are externalized. As long as such costs can be handed over, it is for the individual producers reasonable from an economic point to continue with an unsustainable mode of production because they do not have to pay for the full cost of their production process but can make use of its full benefit. The determination of the available "agricultural capital" and its increase or decrease is a way to assess the sustainability of agriculture.

Objectives and characteristics of sustainable agriculture

We have seen above that the question how sustainable a certain kind of agricultural production is, is not easy to answer, especially because of the trade-offs made between the different pillars of sustainability. Nevertheless efforts are being made to operationalize the concept and to be able to compare the sustainability of different agricultural systems.

At farm level, objectives and characteristics of sustainable agriculture should be directed towards sustainability standards. However, a problem lies in the measurement of sustainability since it is a complex entity in which ecological, economic and social objectives are connected with each other. To deal with this challenge, indicator systems have been developed that relate to the various objectives. These indicators serve to operationalize the concept of sustainability. The aim is to determine the sustainability of certain production processes, but also to use the indicator system to improve the production processes, taking sustainability criteria into account.

For the individual sustainability goals, indicators are selected on the basis of which one can assess the extent to which goals are achieved. An indicator consists of one or more parameters; the parameters are calculated from data. In this way quantitative indicators can be determined.

Meaningful parameters are obtained if quantitative cause and effect relationships are known between the various production-related activities and the sustainability goals. These relationships have yet to be determined in many cases. Furthermore the choice of the indicators is also influenced by the environmental and social values of the society. These normative standards are necessary because economic and environmental objectives can not only be scientifically derived and justified, but values and ethical concepts play a crucial role as well (Wahmhoff 2000).

Sustainability indicators are used for fast and cost-effective evaluation of production processes. There are only a few examples of indicator systems that are suitable for use by farmers themselves for monitoring their production processes because very often the determination of required parameters is too time-consuming or requires specific measurement procedures. However, indicators based on parameters that are generally recorded during the production process could be used to give farmers a management tool that enables them to determine the sustainability of the agricultural production system and to identify its weak points. Thereby they could be used as learning tools, which in turn would be a prerequisite for implementing sustainable action into practice.

How sustainable or unsustainable certain production practices appear, however, also depends on the reference value for which the parameters are calculated. Some of the parameters that are underlying the indicators can either measure per area (e.g. hectare) or per yield (e.g. kilogramme). Usually, area is used as a reference unit since this creates comparability between different locations. Typical examples are yield/hectare, nutrient output/hectare, energy expenditure/hectare. If the yield is used a reference unit, usually more intensive production processes perform comparatively better in the assessment.

Another problem with the indicators is that the impact of certain production processes depends on the prevailing conditions. This also complicates the comparative assessment of different production processes in different locations. The influence of location is essential for the influence on the environmental impact of the production system or of individual production practices.

In addition, it should be noted that improvement options are also context dependent. They might only be useful for a particular group (for example, the producer or consumer), a certain period of time and on a certain level of production. Therefore, if indicators are used to assess the sustainability of production systems, one needs to work with an integrated set of indicators that reflect different perspectives of different actors and that are able to detect changes at the different levels and also in their chronological order (Giampietro & Pastore 2001).

If the indicators are to be used as a management tool by farmers, they should be based on the farm assessment procedures which are already used by them. It is essential that farmers are involved in the selection of indicators when it comes to being able to use the indicators systems as learning tools (Reed et al. 2006).

If a farm employs sustainable production practices it ultimately depends on the operational and technical production decisions of the farmer and the resulting practices. This means a system of indicators can only contribute to improving the sustainability of production if the results of the indicators are also taken into account by farmers and lead to an adjustment of the production process. It is therefore necessary to support them in shaping their farm-specific measures and not to propose "one size fits all" measures. Complex decisions of farmers require knowledge of functional interrelationships between certain production processes and sustainability outcomes and diverse (mostly time- and space-dependent) information about the components of their production system. This information could partly be provided by a system of indicators (Wahmhoff 2000). In order to help farmers to transform towards sustainable production, currently learning approaches are favoured that enable the farmer to identify improvement measures that are adapted to their prevailing production conditions.

Agro-ecological production principles

Sustainable agriculture is often based on agro-ecological production principles. Agro-ecology is concerned with the application of ecological concepts and principles in the development and management of agricultural systems. The idea is to improve the agricultural systems in a way that they are productive and simultaneously the use of local resources is enhanced, while negative impacts on the environment and society are minimized.

Agro-ecology is a system science, i.e. it focuses on the relationships between the components of the system (biophysical, technical and socio-economic) and does this by crossing disciplinary boundaries. Through an interdisciplinary approach complex dynamics can better be grasped. Agro-ecology aims to make use of natural processes and modes of operation that occur in ecosystems to make agricultural systems more productive, more resilient and equitable, i.e. ultimately sustainable.

This procedure is explained using an example: if agricultural processes are understood as chemical processes, pest management would be done with a chemical pesticide. If, on the contrary, one considers agricultural processes as biological or ecological processes, as is the case in integrated pest management, one makes use of ecological processes and in order to reduce problematic pests one introduces other beneficial insects (predators) and additionally applies practices to achieve an increase in the pest tolerance of crop plants. Hence in a mixed cropping system, cultivation can be established in such a way that beneficial organisms have a habitat and that the various plants support each other through allelopathic effects. These measures are intended to establish a balanced state in the agricultural ecosystem in which the different organisms keep each other in check. Problems are thus considered as signs of a disturbed system and the goal is to convert the system back into a balanced state. Therefore, agro-ecological production is not a matter of treating the symptoms but working on the causes of the disturbances (Altieri 1987).

The principles mentioned above can be implemented by various cultivation strategies and techniques. The individual strategies have different effects on productivity, stability and resilience of production systems, depending on the prevailing production conditions.

Cultivation strategies to increase diversity are, for example:

- expansion of crop rotation (for example, inclusion of nitrogen-fixing crops like legumes);
- mixed cropping and intercropping (growing different crops in a field that grow at different levels, such as maize and beans or sweet potatoes);
- inclusion of agroforestry in the system, such as in silvo-agro-pastoral systems (e.g. inclusion of trees, such as cork oaks in pasture or arable land in the south of Spain).

Meanwhile, there are a variety of resource-conserving and renewing technologies that can both improve the economic performance of the farm and at the same time lead to increased natural capital. Examples of these are measures in the area of soil fertility management, water and energy handling. These techniques have different origins; they can stem from traditional agriculture or from organic farming, but also from the relatively new field of "precision farming". They serve on the one hand to reduce the cost of production and, on the other hand to reduce negative environmental effects. Natural processes get priority over the use of external inputs. The use of byproducts or waste products that arise in other farm production processes should be favoured over the purchase of external inputs.

The disadvantages of agro-ecological production are that:

- labour and knowledge demands increase;
- preventive measures are given priority, which again are knowledge and labour intensive;

- no standard solutions are applied but instead farm-specific measures;
- the production process is less controllable since it makes use of adaptation to the production environment;
- revenues are lower compared to specialized production;
- practices and procedures are less standardized;
- labour efficiency is lower than in specialized production.

For these reasons agro-ecological practices are usually not applied on intensive farms, which need to make use of standardized processes and economies of scale to be profitable. However for smallholder farms that are often mixed farms with low land size, the use of agro-ecological principles has been shown to lead to increases in both economic and ecological benefits (Pretty 2005).

Involvement of farmers in the development of sustainable systems

An important goal of sustainable agriculture is the inclusion of farmers when it comes to changing production systems. This serves not only to take their priorities into consideration in the measures, but also to use their knowledge of the production system and the production environment. At the time of the Green Revolution, development projects were conducted following the transfer-of-technology (TOT) principle. In these projects Western knowledge and Western techniques were disseminated. Many of these projects failed, mostly because under the prevailing socio-economic and biophysical conditions this technology was either not applicable or did not bring the desired yield, and at the same time increased the production risk. It was recognized that it is important to consider the experience, knowledge and social structures of farmers when innovations are to be disseminated.

The involvement of farmers in an innovation process that aims to make their farms more sustainable enables the jointly developed innovations to better fit into the farming system and increases the likelihood that the measures are carried out after the duration of the project. If the inclusion is done in a partnership manner, then a strengthening of the self-reliance and self-confidence of the farmers or the community is also achieved. Therefore, TOT has now been replaced by projects that promote learning from and with farmers (Restrepo et al. 2014).

The involvement of farmers is particularly important when trying to increase the sustainability of agriculture by focusing on agro-ecological management or organic production. This is because agro-ecological production and organic farming put special demands on farmers' management (Röling & Jiggins 1998) because they have the following characteristics. They are:

- Observation intensive. That is, they require continuous observation of the state of the growing crops and the animals, but also of the whole operation, as this is the only way to detect the first signs of possible problems that may require action.
- Knowledge intensive. In order to manage a complex system which to a great extent is customized to the environment, in-depth knowledge and experience

i.e. experience on the relationships between the system and the enviroment are required. In intensively managed systems many standard procedures can be applied. In low external-input systems, knowledge of the spatial and temporal availability of e.g. certain fodder resources and their respective favourable combination is required in order to compile appropriate diets using few external means. The use of natural processes requires specific and location-specific knowledge (e.g. pest control by natural enemies requires knowledge of the beneficial organisms as well as the conditions under which they multiply, etc.).

- Technology intensive. Despite the low use of external production factors, agro-ecological production is dependent on sophisticated technologies that allow the economical use of the means of production.
- Complex. The whole farm has to be considered with its complex interactions between the various components and its synergies and trade-offs. Resource use goes along with resource conservation, so that long-term and short-term objectives need to be considered in parallel (e.g. improvement of soil fertility while producing from the soil).
- Situated. The success of production depends on whether and to what degree the farmer is able to use production processes that fit to the specific local situation and can make use of the given opportunities and deal with the given restrictions.
- Multi-layered. The diversity in the production system implies that the farmer must manage different and interlinked production processes.

By involving farmers in participatory research or development projects their knowledge and experience can be used. Their knowledge is then implicit in the result of participatory research, provided that farmers are involved in the project's actions and decisions and not only for the provision of information to the scientists. Once the knowledge of the local population is made explicit, one speaks of "local knowledge". Local knowledge is thus the knowledge of the farmers, which was visualized in any way, described or analysed. The term is used for all of the knowledge, abilities, skills and techniques of the local population which have emerged due to the direct interaction between humans and the environment (Altieri 1990). Since the farmers' knowledge motivates and guides their actions, learning about this knowledge improves the understanding of the situation and facilitates dialogue. This dialogue helps scientists to understand and farmers to learn about new options (de Jager et al. 2004).

There is an increasing consensus that development and sustainability goals are achieved when farmers are supported and put into a position to manage soils, water, biological resources, pests, disease vectors and genetic diversity in an innovative way. To achieve this, the knowledge of farmers should be combined with that of external actors, ideally through the formation of partnerships between farmers, scientists and other societal stakeholders that have an influence on agricultural production and value chains.

Collaborative learning to develop sustainable agricultural practices

When recognizing the role of the farmer as manager of the agricultural system, one understands that the production system will only be changed or improved if farmers change their actions in their production processes. Such a change in actions can be reached either by using "sticks and carrots" or by allowing farmers to gain new insights, this means to learn (Leeuwis & van den Ban 2004). Learning derives from a continuous loop between thinking and action: concrete actions result in certain experiences which are reflected upon and subsequently generate cognitive changes, from which new actions can result.

The aim of collaborative learning processes is for farmers to gain new insights through a process of dialogue, observation, diagnosis, experimentation and exposure to different types of knowledge resulting from analysis and experimental testing of management options (de Jager et al. 2004). There are several methodological packages available which can be used for such learning processes by farmers such as the soft system methodology (Checkland & Holwell 1998), participatory technology development (Veldhuizen et al. 1997) or farmers' experimentation (Hagmann & Chuma 2002).

When a learning approach is used, knowledge is created experientially, i.e. in the form of a transformation of personal experiences. Facilitated learning may also strengthen participants' capacity to initiate a continuous innovation process. This capacity seems to be particularly important in marginal areas where conditions are highly variable (Johnson et al. 2003). Participation is an essential component of any learning system since sustainable change can only be achieved with the involvement of relevant stakeholders and an adequate representation of their views and perspectives (Pretty 1995).

Collaborative learning, based on the assessment of the information processing underlying farmer management, changes the nature of the innovation process. Such a learning approach supports system changes from within while enabling the integration of relevant outside knowledge.

Improving monitoring increases the producer's capacity to deliberately affect the system. One reason for this is that data recording, storage and analysis can be used for feedback. Feedback plays an important role in shaping human practices. The basic reason for this is that feedback is crucial for human learning. In conceptual terms, feedback is information we receive about the outcomes, characteristics and consequences of our actions. By receiving feedback, a farmer can better assess whether or not his actions lead to the anticipated success. His learning can be enhanced by recording relevant quantitative information gained by monitoring. For example the livestock keeper will be in a position to compare his own operations and results with those of others and/or to compare operations and results in one season with those of other seasons or years.

Collaborative approaches to enhance innovation processes are of high importance in low external-input systems, with their higher diversity and their dynamic nature. In this situation, it is more efficient to enhance farmers' problem-solving capacity than to identify single solutions to location-specific problems. At the farm level, there are many factors that influence whether farmers engage in change and innovation. These are for instance their endowment with different agricultural capitals, especially those required for a successful introduction of an innovation but also their knowledge, capabilities, attitudes and values. Also the availability and access to information within the whole innovation system plays an important role. This means that potential innovations need to be checked for their demand on labour, skills, capital, information and potential risks and environmental effects in the respective production system and environment. A realistic assessment for these factors is only possible if the farmers who are interested in the innovation or who will apply it are included in the testing of the innovations. The efficiency of farmers' learning processes depends on the characteristics of the agricultural system and that of the innovation, the farmers' individual characteristics and access to agricultural capitals and on the effectiveness of the innovation system in which the farmers operate (Morriss et al. 2006).

Conclusions

The development of agricultural production in the OECD countries has been charaterized by far reaching socio-economic change and globalization. This has led in these countries to the domination of specialized and intensive agriculture that makes use of economies of scale. Results are increases in yields and labour productivity but also a drastic reduction in the number of people gaining their livelihoods from agriculture, resulting from a structural change that also effects living conditions and social life in many rural areas.

Globally, the large majority of agricultural systems are smallholder and family farms. Enhancing sustainability of their agricultural production requires the inclusion of farmers in the innovation processes that lead to more sustainable production. The reason is that the sustainability of their production systems results from a combination of many different production practices. Farmers need to be capable of assessing the outcome and side effects of their production practices and to be able to engage in innovation processes that are suited to bring about the envisaged sustainable outcomes.

Especially for the low external-input agriculture the adaptation to the respective production context is of major importance for efficient production. Improvement of these systems needs to take the strong relationship between the production system and the production context into account, so that they can be adjusted to the prevailing constraints but can also make use of the existing development opportunities. As the farmers are the managers of the systems, they know about the system–context interrelations, and their actions determine the state and development of their farms. Transformation towards sustainability can in this situation be achieved by supporting farmers in an innovation system approach to co-develop system- and location-specific innovations that enhance sustainability.

Note

1 The Transatlantic Trade and Investment Partnership (TTIP) is a proposed free trade agreement between the European Union and the United States. The Comprehensive Economic and Trade Agreement (CETA) is a free trade agreement which is currently being negotiated between Canada and the European Union.

References

Altieri, M. A. (1987): *Agroecology: The scientific basis of alternative agriculture.* Westview Press, Boulder.

Altieri, M. A. (1990): Why study traditional agriculture? In: Carrol, C. R., Vandermeer, J. H. and Rosset, P. M. (eds): *Agroecology.* McGraw Hill Publishing Company, New York, pp. 551–564.

Beets, W. C. (1990): *Raising and Sustaining Productivity of Smallholder Farming Systems,* AgBe Publishing. Alkmaar, The Netherlands.

Checkland, P.; Holwell S. (1998): *Information, Systems and Information Systems: Making sense of the field.* John Wiley and Sons, Chichester.

Coughenour, C. M. (1984): Social ecology and agriculture. *Rural Sociology 49:* pp. 1–22.

de Jager, A.; Onduru, D.; Walaga, C. (2004): Facilitated learning in soil fertility management: Assessing potentials of low-external-input technologies in east African farming systems. *Agricultural Systems 79:* pp. 205–223.

Dixon, J.; Gulliver, A.; Gibbon, D. (2001): *Farming Systems and Poverty. Improving farmers' livelihoods in a changing world.* FAO and World Bank, Washington D.C..

FAO (Food and Agriculture Organization of the United Nations) (1995): *Sustainability Issues in Agricultural and Rural Development Policies: Trainer's Kit Volume 1.* FAO, Rome.

FAO (2005): *Agricultural Trade and Poverty. Can trade work for the poor? The State Of Food and Agriculture (SOFA).* FAO, Rome, www.fao.org/sof/sofa.

FAO (2014): *The State of Food and Agriculture Innovation in Family Farming.* FAO, Rome, hwww.fao.org/3/a-i4040e.pdf.

FAOSTAT (2013): FAOSTAT, FAO, Rome, http://faostat.fao.org/default.aspx.

Giampietro, M.; Pastore, G. (2001): Operationalizing the concept of sustainability in agriculture: Characterizing agroecosystems on a multi-criteria, multiple scale performance space. In: Gliessman, S.R. (eds): *Agroecosystem Sustainability. Developing practical strategies series.* CRC Press, Boca Raton/London/New York/Washington, pp. 177–202.

Gliessman, S. R.; Agroecology (2007): *The Ecology of Sustainable Food System.* Zweite Auflage. CRC Press, Boca Raton.

Hagmann, J.; Chuma, E. (2002): Enhancing the adaptive capacity of the resource users in natural resource management. *Agricultural Systems 73:* pp. 23–39.

Hildebrand, P. E.; Waugh, R. K. (1986): Farming systems research and development. In: Hildebrand, P. E. (ed.): *Perspectives on Farming Systems Research and Extension.* Lynne Rienner, Boulder, pp. 12–16.

IBRD (International Bank for Reconstruction and Development) (2007): *World Development Report 2008. Agriculture for Development,* http://siteresources.worldbank.org/INTWDR2008/Resources/WDR_00_book.pdf.

Institute for Global Communications (1992): The NGO Alternative Treaties from the Global Forum at Rio de Janeiro, June 1–15 1992: Creative Common Licence, http://habitat.igc.org/treaties.

Janssen M. A.; Anderies J. M.; Ostrom E. (2007): Robustness of social-ecological systems to spatial and temporal variability. *Society & Natural Resources 20:* pp. 307–322.

Johnson, N. L.; Lilja, N.; Ashby J. A. (2003): Measuring the impact of user participation in agricultural and natural resource management research. *Agricultural Systems 78*: pp. 287–306.

Kremen, C.; Iles, A.; Bacon, C. (2012): Diversified farming systems: An agroecological, systems-based alternative to modern industrial agriculture. Guest editorial, part of a special feature on a social-ecological analysis of diversified farming systems: benefits, costs, obstacles, and enabling policy frameworks. *Ecology and Society 17* (4): 44.

Leeuwis, C.; van den Ban, A. W. (2004): *Communication for Rural Innovation: Rethinking agricultural extension*. Blackwell Science Ltd, Oxford.

Morriss, S.; Massey, C.; Flett, R.; Alpass, F.; Sligo, F. (2006): Mediating technological learning in agricultural innovation systems. *Agricultural Systems 89*: pp. 26–46.

Pretty, J. (1995): *Regenerating Agriculture: Policies and Practice for Sustainability and Self-Reliance*. Earthscan Publications, London.

Pretty, J. (2005): *The Earthscan Reader in Sustainable Agriculture*. Earthscan, London.

Reed, M. S.; Fraser, E. D. G.; Dougill, A. J. (2006): An adaptive learning process for developing and applying sustainability indicators with local communities. *Ecological economics 59* (4): pp. 406–418.

Reijntjes, C.; Haverkort, B.; Waters-Bayer A. (1992): *Farming for the Future*, London: MacMillan.

Restrepo, M. J.; Lelea, M. A.; Christinck, A., Hülsebusch, C.; Kaufmann B. A. (2014): Collaborative learning for fostering change in complex social-ecological systems: A transdisciplinary perspective on food and farming systems. *Knowledge Management for Development Journal 10* (3): pp. 38–59.

Röling, N. G.; Jiggins, J. (1998): The ecological knowledge system. In: Röling, N. G., Wagemakers, M. A. E. (eds): *Facilitating Sustainable Agriculture. Participatory learning and adaptive management in times of environmental uncertainty*. Cambridge University Press, Cambridge, pp. 283–311.

Ruthenberg, H. (1980): *Farming Systems in the Tropics*. Clarendon Press, Oxford.

Spedding, C. R. W. (1996): *Agriculture and the Citizen*. Chapman and Hall, London.

Thornton, P. K.; Kruska, R. L.; Henninger, N.; Kristjanson, P. M.; Reid, R. S.; Atieno, F.; Odero, A. N.; Ndegwa, T. (2002): *Mapping Poverty and Livestock in the Developing World*. ILRI (International Livestock Research Institute), Nairobi.

UNEP-UNCTAD CBTF (2007): *Capacity Building Task Force on Trade, Environment and Development. Organic Agriculture and Food Security in Africa*, www.unctad.org/trade_env/test1/publications/UNCTAD_DITC_TED_2007_15.pdf.

Veldhuizen, L. V.; Waters-Bayer A.; Zeeuw, H. D. (1997): *Developing Technology with Farmers. A trainer's guide for participatory learning*. Zed Books Ltd, London.

von Braun, J. (2002): Ernährungssicherung in Entwicklungsländern. In: *Deutscher Bundestag* (Ausschussdrucksache 14/113): Stellungnahme zur Anhörung des AWZ am 30.01.02. In: Deutscher Bundestag Drucksache 14/9200 Schlussbericht der Enquete-Kommission Globalisierung der Weltwirtschaft – Herausforderungen und Antworten. Berlin.

von Braun, J. (2008): Die Weltmärkte bewegen sich – Herausforderungen für die Produktion. In: *Deutsche Landwirtschaftsgesellschaft e. V.* (Hrsg.): Agrarpotenziale nutzen! Herausforderungen für Landwirte und Gesellschaft. Deutsche Landwirtschafts-Gesellschaft, Frankfurt am Main, pp. 13–36.

Wahmhoff, W. (2000): Nachhaltigkeit und deren Umsetzung als Forschungsaufgabe. In: Härdtlein, M., et al.: *Nachhaltigkeit in der Landwirtschaft. Landwirtschaft im Spannungsfeld zwischen Ökologie, Ökonomie und Sozialwissenschaften*. Erich Schmidt Verlag, Berlin: 2000.

Woodhill, J.; Röling, N. G. (1998): The second wing of the eagle: The human dimension in learning our way to more sustainable futures. In: Röling, N. G. & Wagemakers, M. A. E. (eds): *Facilitating Sustainable Agriculture*. Cambridge University Press, Cambridge, pp. 46–70.

Index

For Product Safety Concerns and Information please contact our
EU representative GPSR@taylorandfrancis.com Taylor & Francis
Verlag GmbH, Kaufingerstraße 24, 80331 München, Germany